Advance praise for *Our F*

"After World War II a remarkable set of Americans structured a generation of world prosperity. They forged economic and political institutions such as the Marshall Plan, the General Agreement on Tariffs and Trade and the Bretton Woods Monetary System. And instead of the depression many at the time predicted, both the industrial and developing worlds enjoyed more than two decades of the fastest growth of this century.

"Here Gregory Fossedal tells the little-understood story of Will Clayton, one of the key players in this drama. His story is not only fascinating history, but ought to be instructive reading in an era of economic pessimism, suffused with a feeling that we have lost much of what Will Clayton and his colleagues gave us."
— Robert L. Bartley,
Editor, *Wall Street Journal*

"This is a timely, well-told story of one man's extraordinarily successful effort to shape a global, peacefully competitive economic community."
— Senator Bill Bradley

"An important addition to our understanding of modern history and particularly of the early phases of the Cold War . . . insightful and revealing."
— Zbigniew Brzezinski

"Will Clayton was an unswerving champion of global democratic capitalism. Fossedal's study demonstrates democracy in action— that ideas rule the world, and that we are obliged in these revolutionary times to export the American idea to the whole world as Mr. Clayton sought to do."
— Jack Kemp

"Fascinating. . . . The historical vacuum surrounding Clayton has been filled at long last by Gregory Fossedal's account of his life in business and public affairs. Fossedal insists that Clayton was the architect and builder of U.S. economic foreign policy, partly during but mostly after World War II. The case is made with elaborate detail. . . . Fossedal's account of the development of the Marshall Plan in the spring of 1947 is riveting."

— Charles P. Kindleberger,
Professor of Economics Emeritus,
M.I.T.

"This is a fine book on the visionary Will Clayton, tough cotton-broker and diplomat who forged the historic GATT treaty to put world trade in order. Lovers of history, diplomacy and commerce will find much new and everything fascinating."

— Georgie Anne Geyer

"In an engaging and insightful style, Gregory Fossedal tells the story of Will Clayton, the unsung hero who helped build the global institutions of a new economic order after World War II. The book is so well written that the reader does not realize until completing it that he or she has learned all about the most complicated economic issues that continue to shape our world."

— Robert Pastor,
Carter Center,
Emory University

Comments about Will Clayton

"the principal architect of American postwar foreign policy."
— *Newsweek* magazine
October 27, 1947

"recognized by many as the idea man behind the Marshall Plan after World War II."
— *New York Times*
February 9, 1966

"up to now, Will Clayton is the Marshall Plan."
— *New York Times Magazine*
October 24, 1947

"Will Clayton was one of those rare public servants who was not only dedicated to the public's interest but had a world outlook in which he saw the position of the United States in relation and harmony to all nations. . . . History will inscribe his name in bold letters."
— Harry S. Truman
February 15, 1966

"Mr. Clayton had more to do than anyone else with shaping postwar economic policy for the rest of the world as well as for the United States. He was the driving force in a score of efforts to bring order out of chaos . . . a symbol of American constructive energy and faith in the future."
— Editorial, *New York Times*
October 16, 1947

"the first economist of the United States. . . .

"He was the first who took cognizance of the famous agreement of the sixteen Marshall Plan participants, and it was on his recommendations that the final version, now being studied in Washington before being sent to Congress, was drawn up. . . .

"It is, then, a little the 'Clayton Plan' that is found to be up for consideration."

> — Editorial, *L'Aurore*
> October 16, 1947

"[Clayton's] ideas and advice contributed richly to the development of new directions in international policy. Mobilization of our resources in two wars, planning on an international scale for emergency aid to the needy, and the marshaling of public support for the [Marshall Plan] owe much to his efforts."

> — John F. Kennedy,
> January 25, 1962

"I would call it the Clayton-Acheson-Truman plan."

> — Clark Clifford,
> 1989 interview for
> *Our Finest Hour*

"Clayton was my boss, and he was the only fellow I respected in government."

> — Ambassador Paul Nitze,
> 1958 interview

"Some others in the department, among them Acheson and Kennan, had arrived independently at approximately the same conclusion. But it was Clayton's disturbing report to the President and Secretary Marshall that lighted a match under this intellectual broth and set it bubbling."
— Cabell Phillips,
former *New York Times* reporter,
in *The Truman Presidency*

"Except for details, 106 bilateral agreements are ready for incorporation into the General Agreement on Tariffs and Trade.

"This vast project, which makes all previous international economic accords look puny, is the realization of Mr. Clayton's dream: that a group of like-minded democratic nations could deliberately reverse the historical trend toward the strangulation of world trade. . . .

"It is the big step that nobody but Mr. Clayton and a few of his colleagues thought would ever be taken."
— *New York Times*
October 15, 1947

"The man who's most responsible for the Marshall Plan was William Clayton."
— John W. Snyder,
secretary of the treasury, 1946–1953
Interview, March 15, 1980

Our Finest Hour

Our Finest Hour

WILL CLAYTON,
the Marshall Plan,
and the Triumph
of Democracy

Gregory A. Fossedal

HOOVER INSTITUTION PRESS
Stanford University
Stanford, California

Hoover Institution Press Publication No. 412

Copyright © 1993 by the Board of Trustees of the
  Leland Stanford Junior University

First printing, 1993
99 98 97 96 95 94 93   9 8 7 6 5 4 3 2 1
Simultaneous first paperback printing, 1993
99 98 97 96 95 94 93   9 8 7 6 5 4 3 2 1

Manufactured in the United States of America

The paper used in this publication meets the minimum requirements of
American National Standard for Information Sciences—Permanence of
Paper for Printed Library Materials, ANSI Z39.48–1984. ⊗

Library of Congress Cataloging-in-Publication Data
Fossedal, Gregory A.
  Our finest hour : Will Clayton, the Marshall Plan, and the triumph
of democracy / Gregory A. Fossedal.
        p.   cm. — (Hoover Institution Press publication ; 412)
  Includes bibliographical references and index.
  ISBN 0-8179-9201-4. — ISBN 0-8179-9202-2 (pbk.)
  1. Clayton, Will, 1880–1966. 2. Statesmen—United States—
Biography. 3. Marshall Plan. 4. United States—Foreign
relations—1945–1953. 5. Economic assistance, American—Europe—
History—20th century. I. Title. II. Series.
E748.C58F66   1993   92-33108
[B]   CIP

Contents

(Photograph section follows page 82.)

Foreword

ONE IS TEMPTED TO BEGIN ANY DISCUSSION OF WILL CLAYTON WITH a thorough review of his achievements. He rose, after all, from an eighth-grade education to build Anderson-Clayton, the largest cotton brokerage firm in the world, yet led the battle to save the cotton futures system from the speculative squeezes that so damaged farmers before Clayton's victory for "southern delivery." He was one of the handful of men who helped win the Second World War through their capable direction of many of the U.S. preclusive buying and procurement corporations set up under Jesse Jones. He also helped secure the stability of the postwar world through his critical involvement in the talks with Lord Keynes on the Bretton Woods agreement and the British Loan and by laying the groundwork for the Truman Doctrine through his advocacy of support for anticommunist forces in Greece and Turkey in the fall of 1946.

Most important, Will Clayton was both the architect and the chief negotiator of the General Agreement on Tariffs and Trade (GATT) signed in 1947 and, in my opinion and that of most knowledgeable observers at the time, the catalyst of the Marshall Plan.

But any portrait of Will Clayton must stress not just his formidable accomplishments but the remarkable man himself.

Will Clayton was my boss, and he was the only one among the many I have had for whom I had complete respect. He was without fault either in his personal or public life. He had a bright, clear mind and a strong character; he worked tremendously hard, and he knew how to organize people—how to delegate authority, how to supervise without interfering, and above all how to motivate those around him to perform to the peak of their abilities.

Thinking back over the last forty years, it is hard to name his parallel. General Marshall and, more recently, George Shultz come close. Clayton was special above all because of the *combination* of attributes—a combination that made him, in my experience, unique. Some men had Clayton's idealism, some his practical abilities, others his personal probity, others his leadership, and a rare few, some group of two or three of these.

When someone asked me recently how we could attract people of Clayton's character into government service, I answered, "I'm not sure there is anyone of his character . . . I'm not sure there was anyone else of his character back then, either."

My first extensive dealings with Clayton, which came through my own work in overseas procurement, provide a typical example of the man's nature. I was working with the Board for Economic Warfare (BEW), an agency under the direction of Henry Wallace. My original role had simply been to give policy advice with respect to procurement: the BEW, at least in its initial design, had been set up as more of an oversight or advisory institution than an executive one.

Then, as part of the complex fight for control over preclusive buying and procurement between Wallace and Jones, an executive order was issued giving the BEW the power to negotiate the procurement of materials abroad. I had little experience in such matters—the largest operation I had ever organized was a staff of three—and most of my colleagues at the BEW had even less. Suddenly I found I had responsibility for many of the areas of foreign procurement that had been handled, quite capably, by Clayton and his deputies. The BEW operation in Brazil alone grew to nearly a thousand people.

If Clayton had cared mainly about accumulating power for himself or fighting bureaucratic enemies, he and his staff might have let me and many others at the BEW flounder about. Instead, they helped me put together an organization, recommended good people, and warned me of my managerial defects. When I was forced to fire Bernard Baruch's brother, who by virtue of his connections was not without influence, Clayton's people backed me up. When I had trouble staffing the Brazil operation, I was able to get Clayton's son-in-law, Maurice McAshan, to head it up for me. McAshan, experienced in foreign procurement through his work for Anderson-Clayton, did an excellent job, despite the grumblings of some of my BEW colleagues that it was improper to accept the help of someone related to Clayton.

Throughout the feud over control, Clayton acted almost as an ambassador between two U.S. officials, Wallace and Jones, who for long periods would not even speak to one another. Back and forth between the two Clayton would shuttle, trying to keep the war effort on track despite the enmity of the two procurement principals. In taking on that thankless task, Clayton showed his selflessness. In thrusting it on him, Jones and Wallace showed the kind of personal trust Clayton inspired. Will Clayton had many enemies in Washington, in the sense that people knew where he stood and might oppose his policies. But even those opposed to him—among whom Wallace was certainly one—trusted and respected Clayton.

For this reason alone, Will Clayton is worthy of study and emulation. Gregory Fossedal's biography has brought this remarkable man to life in vivid detail. Reading it, those who knew Clayton will recall his human touches as a loving husband and father, a valuable friend, a daring businessman, and a tireless public servant. Those who know little of the man will find it a touching and uplifting story.

More than this, however, Clayton's story is an essential part of the historic initiatives that were launched or completed during his tenure as the State Department's chief economic policymaker. It would be impossible to understand how any of these bold acts of U.S. leadership—Bretton Woods, the Truman Doctrine, the Marshall Plan, the GATT, and the subsequent founding of the other great pillars of European unity—came about without reference to Clayton.

Yet in some recent histories and memoirs, Clayton's role is minimized or even omitted. Some of these accounts, no doubt, were self-serving, perhaps in pursuit of career or ideological goals. Most, I think, are simply incomplete, focusing on many of the other fine men who also contributed to U.S. policy but leaving out a central actor. It is perhaps understandable that Clayton would fade somewhat from view. He was singularly self-effacing and made no effort in the years that followed to promote the personal recognition he deserved. Nevertheless, this treatment of Clayton or, more precisely, nontreatment is something of a historical injustice.

Gregory Fossedal's biography should go far toward righting the record. It tells the story of the Marshall Plan and many other events accurately and with solid scholarship. Beyond reviving what was already known about Clayton, though, the book unearths important and original historical details. The meticulous account of Clayton's March 1947 memorandum on the Marshall Plan, for example, establishes clearly that the memo was briefed to more than a dozen U.S. and European officials, probably including Marshall and the president—thus placing Clayton's initial proposal for a European Recovery Plan not days or weeks but months before General Marshall's speech at Harvard. (Even many Clayton advocates have assumed that the memorandum was not used because it was evidently not typed out and circulated; Fossedal offers substantial evidence to the contrary.)

Yet while establishing Clayton's central role, Fossedal is fair-minded toward the many others who contributed to the Marshall Plan and the other daring endeavors of the time. Neither George Kennan nor Dean Acheson had, as Fossedal notes, "any pretense of economic expertise." But both had brilliant strategic minds:

Acheson's speech in April helped set the minds of the public and America's leaders to the need to craft an economic design, and Kennan's memorandum of late May, to which a number of Clayton's staff contributed ideas and economic data, reinforced the urgency of U.S. action, while providing a sophisticated understanding of the likely Soviet reaction. And then there was General Marshall himself—practical enough to bring men like Clayton and Acheson and Kennan together, visionary enough to launch their design, and crafty enough to sell it with usefully dramatic tactics.

"In a sense," as Fossedal writes, "it really was the Marshall Plan." Indeed, Will Clayton himself insisted as much: "If the plan had been a failure, Marshall would have taken the blame," Clayton noted in a typically self-minimizing remark. It is refreshing to see a history that, while telling Will Clayton's story, is objective and fair-minded toward the other fine men who served with him. The facts and this biography leave no room for doubt as to Clayton's central, animating function—a role that led *Newsweek* to refer to Clayton as "the principal architect of American postwar foreign economic policy."

—Paul Nitze

Acknowledgments

THIS BOOK IS DEDICATED TO JACK KEMP, BRUCE THOMPSON, AND Marty Peretz, leaders, respectively, of politics, commerce, and the Democratic party's battle of ideas—Will Clayton's three great secular loves. These men have shared, embodied, and extended the principles of freedom, democracy, and classic liberalism (rightly understood) that were Clayton's lodestar.

It is my privilege to call all three mentors and friends, models, and benefactors, in a word, heroes.

This effort would not have been possible without the help and support of a number of others. Naming them all would take yet another book. Among the most generous, however, have been Ray Geselbrach, Dennis Bilger, and the rest of the fine and friendly staff at the Truman Library; Clark Clifford, James Donovan, Paul Nitze, Thomas Curtis, Margaret Truman Daniel, Wilbur Mills, the late Claude Pepper, and two of Clayton's daughters, Mrs. Ellen (St. John) Garwood and Julia (Benjamin) Baker—all of whom shared their time to write or talk with memories of the era; the staffs at the Marshall Library in Virginia, the Yale University Library, the Columbia University Library's Oral History Project, Princeton's Mudd Library wherein the impressive papers of Harry Dexter White are kept, the State Department Archives, and the Library of Congress. Harlan Schenk and Paula Seals at the Houston Public Library were especially helpful, as was a nice woman at Princeton who sent an important bag, absentmindedly left there during a hurried follow-up visit, back to me by Federal Express.

As ever, the Hoover Institution, the think tank Glenn Campbell built, was an ideal place to conduct research and to write—thanks especially to Charles Palm, who oversaw the project and secured the deposit of Will Clayton's papers; Margaret Garvey, Kate Power, Diane Hicks, and Louise Doying, patient assistants to an impatient band of scholars; Wynona Goold; Frank Miele, Jim Christie, and Danielle Bujnak, who helped with research; and John Raisian, under whose direction Hoover has continued to be, quite simply, a great place to write books. Among the many colleagues who helped me with suggestions on the research were Melvyn Krauss, Annelise Anderson, Martin Anderson, Tom Henriksen, Bob Hessen, and Arnold Beichman.

My assistant Margaret Garvey provided singularly valuable help as a proofreader, administrative aide, and part-time library runner.

Mrs. Ellen Garwood, William Clayton's oldest daughter, gave generously of her time during my own research period to share recollections, information, sources, and occasionally, a lively disagreement or two. So did Mrs. Julia Baker, who provided insight into the personal side of Clayton.

Bridget Anne Fossedal came into this world during the work on this book and provided diversion and inspiration as they were needed. Thanks, Bridge.

Our Finest Hour

An Offer Declined

M<small>R</small>. P<small>RESIDENT</small>, I <small>CAN SEE WHERE YOU ARE HEADING</small>," W<small>ILL</small> C<small>LAY</small>-ton said, "but I just can't. My family. . . ." Uncharacteristically his voice trailed off. Harry Truman repeated that he was talking about the job of secretary of state. "I need the best man available," he said, and in his opinion that meant Clayton. Truman knew about Clayton's problems with his vociferous, strong-willed wife, Sue. Even before the end of World War II, she had wanted them to leave Washington, where she felt her husband was overworked and where she had become exhausted. But this was a matter of national interest.

No, Clayton insisted. He had promised his wife they would soon be going back home to Houston. Washington and the war had taken more than five years of their lives, and Clayton, age sixty-six, was not a young man.

"We shouldn't pursue this any further," Clayton told the president. Truman later told Senator Claude Pepper that Clayton "said it reluctantly and fast, like he was getting something out he had to say before he changed his mind."[1]

❑ ❑ ❑

We can't know what other words passed between Truman and Clayton, so it is difficult to say just how far matters would have gone if Clayton had responded differently to Truman's probe.* History records few examples of a presidential offer to serve as secretary of state being declined. It may be equally rare to find a case where the family considerations so often professed as a reason for refusing high office actually were the actor's prime motive.

But Clayton's family problems were real. His wife of more than forty years was suffering from arteriosclerosis, causing her an exasperating loss of memory. She desperately wanted to leave Washington and regain her husband's full attention. Within a few years, she would (briefly) divorce him.

On at least two recorded occasions, Truman confirmed the essence of this remarkable story.[6] As a Truman aide recorded on April 19, 1949, the day a story on Mrs. Clayton's divorce action ran in the *New York Times*,

> At our staff meeting the President mentioned the story and said that if it had not been for Mrs. Clayton, her husband would have been secretary of state. Clayton served the government for several years in several posts and, although wealthy and the head of one

---

*Truman had discussed Clayton as a possible secretary of state with a number of his intimates. James F. Byrnes evidently recommended Clayton as one of several possible successors when he went to discuss his resignation with Truman in April 1946.[2] Clark Clifford remembers Truman talking of Clayton as secretary of state and even suggests that the Marshall Plan—the American effort so important to the reconstruction of Western Europe—might appropriately be renamed "the Clayton-Acheson-Truman Plan."[3] It is possible that Truman and Clayton returned to the subject, perhaps several times. In the fall of both 1946 and 1948, press reports circulated naming Clayton as the next secretary of state.[4] Clayton's eldest daughter recalls that even as the family was packing up and preparing to return to Houston in mid-October 1947, a call came from Truman asking Clayton to come and see him "about the important matter we have discussed." But Clayton told him once again that he was bound for Houston and that this decision was final.[5]

of the largest cotton merchandising firms in the world, gave unstintingly of his time and energy.

The President said that he wanted to appoint Clayton secretary of state at the time Marshall was named and that it was due to Mrs. Clayton that the appointment was not made. I recall that about that time there was mention on one or two occasions of her efforts to have Clayton get out of the government and return to their home in Texas and it was my understanding that that was the principal reason for his refusal to take any other government post.[7]

Historians must devote their primary energies to what did happen, not to history's might-have-beens. Will Clayton did not become secretary of state. He did act as a participant, catalyst, and in some cases prime mover of such critical acts of statecraft as the Bretton Woods agreement on international monetary policy and trade cooperation, the Marshall Plan, and the Truman Doctrine to aid freedom fighters in Greece and Turkey when those countries were pressured by Soviet-backed rebels and Soviet military threats in the late 1940s.

In this instance, however, what Clayton did not do—sacrifice his wife's peace of mind to move up another rung on the political ladder—gives us a measure of the man. It suggests someone serious about the sanctity of marriage, which for too many leaders has been merely a pious platitude. Nor did he reject Truman's offer because he was slowing down with age; he was famous for his fourteen-hour days and his long, energetic strides through the State Department's corridors. Slender and tall (six feet, three-and-one-half inches), he was strikingly handsome, with an olive complexion, dark, partially gray hair, and alert hazel eyes. He felt he had contributed his talents to the nation's war effort and was content with his place in history.

In fact, he was one of the few men who served in Washington, D.C., in those critical years who did not write his memoirs or cultivate a biographer.[8] The deeds of Dean Acheson, Cordell Hull, Henry L. Stimson, Charles Bohlen, Jesse H. Jones, George C.

Marshall, George F. Kennan, James A. Forrestal, Paul H. Nitze, Edward R. Stettinius, David E. Lilienthal, Harold M. Ickes, Harry L. Hopkins, Henry Morgenthau, Bernard M. Baruch, James F. Byrnes, W. Averell Harriman, and Henry A. Wallace are deservedly collected and recorded. Clayton, by contrast, although certainly proud of his service, showed little anxiety about having his own historical niche preserved.

This book is meant to be Will Clayton's memoirs. The author is not a historian but an avid student of history, hoping to fill a gap left by historians. There is more at stake, however, than the recognition of Clayton's role in history. A full understanding of any event depends on a complete account of those who shaped it; what their aims, motives, and strategies were; and how they succeeded or were frustrated in their designs.

Consider the Truman Doctrine, which promised U.S. support for all countries struggling for democracy and offered a rationale for the program of U.S. aid to postwar Greece and Turkey. Historians, and even a few of the principals, have made two common assumptions about the Truman Doctrine's evolution. The first concerns the sheer chronology of events. It is widely assumed, perhaps chiefly because of Dean Acheson's dramatic and eloquent account, that the doctrine was a case of crisis management at its best, emerging in the aftermath of a stunning British decision to cut off aid to the Greek government—a decision announced so as to give the United States only a few weeks to act if it meant to fill the vacuum.[9]

This assumption lends credence to a second stream of thought about the doctrine as such—a stream that, being broad and contemporary in nature, may greatly undermine the cause of clear thinking about the principles of strategy. Its champion is one of the principals, George F. Kennan, a respected expert on Soviet affairs at the time the doctrine was enunciated, soon to be head of the new Policy Planning Staff at the State Department. Kennan argues that the Truman Doctrine was something of an afterthought, the creation of a few zealots trying to devise a broad rationale for opposing communism. "I believe," Truman told a joint session of Congress in March 1947, "it must be the policy of the United States to support free peoples who are resisting subjugation by armed minorities or by outside pressures." From this statement, and buttressed by the general consensus that the doctrine was indeed promulgated amid a crisis-management background, Kennan concludes that "all another country had to do, in order to qualify for American aid, was to demonstrate the existence of a Communist threat."[10]

To consider Clayton's contribution to the process, however, is to view the meaning of the Truman Doctrine in a revised light. He had taken action pointing toward the policy at least as early as August 1946. On August 23, he received a memorandum from the Joint Chiefs of Staff outlining the growing threat to Greece and Turkey from Soviet-backed forces and the weakening will of the British to intervene decisively.[11] He promptly put a pair of study teams on the problem, and soon a stream of reports flowed from Clayton and his assistants: "a succession of state papers and despatches," as the British historian Alan Bullock wrote, that served as "a preliminary sketch of the Truman Doctrine."[12]

Less than three weeks later, Clayton submitted a recommendation (with the agreement of the secretary of war and under secretary of the navy) for an immediate relaxation of U.S. restrictions on arms exports to the embattled countries. Byrnes approved.[13] Within weeks, Clayton had consulted with Greek and Turkish officials about expanding credits to them. On September 25, 1946, he met with the secretaries of war and navy to discuss integrating the supply of arms and emergency materials with a broad program of European recovery.

"Here was the concept," historian Walter Millis writes, "of giving political precision to our use of our economic and military resources; a concept that first took important shape in the 'Truman Doctrine' of the Greek-Turkish aid, and was to broaden very rapidly thereafter."[14] By October, Bullock concludes, Clayton and such key colleagues as Byrnes, Forrestal, and Loy W. Henderson had achieved "a reversal of earlier American policy and tacit acceptance of [the British] argument that the USA had as great an interest as Britain in seeing the buffer zone of the Northern Tier preserved intact."[15]

If the conventional understanding of an improvised policy is wrong, then Kennan's complaint—that U.S. foreign policy had become unconsciously or unduly messianic—may be overstated. It detracts nothing from Kennan's achievements, for example, to note that he had not been in the State Department at the time Clayton, as acting secretary, lay the groundwork for what became the doctrine or to note that Kennan was out of town the weekend the British surprised Acheson with their cable about rapidly withdrawing their support from Greece and Turkey. Kennan evidently did not know that Clayton had promoted something like Kennan's preferred, more limited doctrine in a memorandum to Byrnes the previous September 12:

> You will, of course, understand that it is not our idea that we should begin to sell military-type equipment immediately in large quantities to various countries subject to external pressure. We feel, however, that the new policy should enable us, with the discretion and restraint required by the circumstances, to supply military-type equipment to countries such as those in the Near and Middle East, the maintenance and integrity of which are considered to be of important interest to the United States.[16]

Having tried to rally support in the bureaucracy, the Congress, and the public, however, Clayton witnessed firsthand some of that doctrine's crippling limitations. For one thing, the discretion for maneuver opened up by such cautious and limited rhetoric was itself limited. American aid in such small amounts failed to turn the tide in either Greece or Turkey over the following six months. It also failed to generate the interest of the U.S. electorate.

By the spring of 1947, Europe was on the brink of collapse, and a policy of half-measures—aid and credits through competing agencies, arms sales to Greece and Turkey—had been tried and found insufficient. It was in this environment that Clayton joined those, including Truman, who felt U.S. policy ought to involve bold action and be articulated in the broadest possible terms. As Clayton wrote in a March 5, 1947, memorandum:

> The United States must take world leadership and quickly, to avert world disaster.
>
> But the United States will not take world leadership, effectively, unless the people of the United States are shocked into doing so.
>
> To shock them, it is only necessary for the President and the Secretary of State to tell them the truth and the whole truth.[17]

Thus where Kennan complained of the "congenital aversion of the Americans to taking specific decisions on specific problems," Clayton saw a government and a public able to act with alacrity if given a policy that might reasonably be expected to succeed.[18] Where Kennan saw the idea that we should assist those seeking to "work out their own destiny in their own way" as an open-ended commitment to total victory everywhere, Clayton distinguished sharply between levels of assistance. After all, the United States might support the aspirations of all people to be free but do so in very different ways as prudence governs. We might fight a war with some countries, as we just had in Europe. We might offer massive economic aid to other countries or in other circumstances, as we did repeatedly after the war, most notably through United Nations relief agencies in 1945 and 1946, in the Marshall Plan, and through such U.S. and international agencies as the Export-Import Bank, the International Monetary Fund, and the World Bank throughout the entire postwar era.

We might in other cases limit our assistance to mere rhetorical support or public diplomacy. Even as Truman spoke, a much smaller U.S. intervention, limited chiefly to diplomatic pressure and threatening troop and naval movements, had apparently succeeded in prompting the withdrawal of Soviet troops from Iran. Clayton's March 5 memorandum, picking up on a suggestion by Paul H. Nitze, proposed an effort to rebuild all of Europe on $5 billion a year—not a negligible figure but hardly unbearable, as Clayton noted, considering that "the war cost us over three hundred billion dollars."[19]

Besides, one can sometimes avoid large exertion later by means of a small effort now. "It will be said," Clayton wrote, that the broad strokes of a U.S. doctrine "will involve us in the affairs of foreign countries and lead us eventually to war. The answer to this is that if we do not actively interest ourselves in the affairs of foreign countries, we will find such affairs will become . . . hopeless."

Finally, Clayton drew a sharp distinction that Kennan failed to draw, even in his memoirs. Kennan wrote: "It [the Truman Doctrine] implied that what we had decided to do in the case of Greece was something we would be prepared to do in the case of another country, provided only that it was faced with the threat of 'subjugation by armed minorities or outside pressures.'"[20] But Truman had spoken of "free peoples" resisting subjugation, not merely any country that claims to be anticommunist.

Moreover, Kennan was not even in the State Department when Clayton, Nitze, Henderson, George McGhee, Emilio Collado, and others were busy collecting and crafting much of the material that later emerged as the Truman Doctrine. The tendency in many recent historical writings—to minimize or ignore the contributions of Clayton and his talented staff—is thus damaging to a clear understanding of the events and their significance.

Another example of this neglect can be seen in accounts of the Marshall Plan, possibly the finest hour of U.S. diplomacy. Clayton's memorandums of March 5 and May 27, 1947, each proposing a vast European recovery program, were two key documents leading to George C. Marshall's June 4 speech at Harvard and the successful negotiation with the Europeans that followed that summer and fall. The other key document was Kennan's May 23 draft, written a few weeks after he began studying Europe's economic crisis for Secretary Marshall as head of the Policy Planning Staff. In *The Fifteen Weeks*, Joseph Jones, then a speechwriter at the

State Department, wrote: "Acheson promptly sent the [Clayton] memorandum into the Secretary and arranged a meeting for that day. The memorandum and the conversation that ensued had a powerful effect both upon the content of Secretary Marshall's speech and probably upon his decision to make it. . . . In drafting the speech, [Marshall's aide Charles] Bohlen used primarily the Kennan and Clayton memoranda."[21]

Dean Acheson's memoirs note the potent impact both of Clayton's March 5 memo and of the May proposal that followed Clayton's tour of Europe. The second, he writes, "came to me on May 27 and went at once to the General. . . . When [Clayton, Acheson, Kennan, Marshall, and others] met on May 28, we had both papers before us." Of Marshall's speech, Acheson writes: "A little more than half . . . set forth the condition of Europe and the causes for it. This came straight from the two Clayton memoranda."[22] An even stronger assessment of Clayton's impact comes from veteran *New York Times* reporter Cabell Phillips: "Some others in the department, among them Acheson and Kennan, had arrived independently at approximately the same conclusion. But it was Clayton's disturbing report to the President and Secretary Marshall that lighted a match under this intellectual broth and set it bubbling."[23]

Suffice to say there is strong evidence that whether or not one liked Clayton's ideas for the Marshall Plan, they were a critical component in its construction.[24] Nevertheless, one encounters historians who write as if there were reason to doubt that Clayton had any impact. Thus, John Gimbel, in an account of the Marshall Plan's origins, writes,

> Clayton's memorandum of March 5 . . . was addressed to no one, and there appears to be no evidence that Clayton used it. Clayton's second memorandum surfaced in May. There is considerable confusion as to when. . . . A comparison of Clayton's memorandum and the [Kennan] report reveals fundamental differences. . . . Those differences, which were not resolved when Marshall spoke at Harvard, show conclusively that no agreed plan or policy existed in Washington on June 5, 1947.[25]

Now many State Department memorandums' precise dating, circulation, and impact are a matter to be debated only by those interested in bureaucratic history. In the case of the Marshall Plan, however, getting the facts right does make a difference.

To study Clayton's life and vision is to grasp the plan's tactical inventiveness fully. He had spent the better part of three years pleading, threatening, and cajoling the Europeans in an effort to win from them economic policies that, in effect, would be in their own interest: a reduction in trade barriers, easing of state intervention, and the linkage of their currencies to one another and to a specific unit of account, providing a stable world monetary system and manageable interest rates on a mountain of postwar debt. His tutorials met with indifference from the French, frustrated protestations of political impotence from the Germans and Austrians, and promises from the British that were not kept. All the while, the economies of vital democratic allies stagnated.

By the time of Clayton's trip in the spring of 1947, the continent was in chaos. "Europe is steadily deteriorating," he wrote. "Millions of people in the cities are slowly starving. . . . The modern system of division of labor has almost broken down. . . . Without further prompt and substantial aid from the United States, economic, social, and political disintegration will overwhelm Europe."

Thus a long, vexing effort to win cooperation convinced Clayton, a staunch disbeliever in bailouts, that he needed a carrot. The Marshall Plan, promising U.S. assistance if the Europeans could devise a scheme of free-market reform, provided the stimulus. Clayton returned to Europe two months later and, in the fall of 1947, won agreement on policy changes that had eluded him since 1944. It is obvious, as Flora Lewis wrote in the New York Times on the plan's fortieth anniversary, that these policy adjustments, not the money and credits provided by the United States per se, were the key. But U.S. aid in that sense proved to be the crucial catalyst, giving Europeans the psychological confidence to go ahead with a program of reform.

When Truman, Marshall, and the Congress heard a man of

Clayton's stature and business background (he had built a $75 million cotton merchandising company, so it was hard to dismiss him as a naive idealist) arguing for billions of dollars in assistance, they knew that it was urgent and required. Thus, to miss Clayton's part in the story is to miss a key principle in the Marshall Plan's success. And to miss the principle may promote a missed opportunity for economic statecraft in the future.

An equal and opposite error sees the Marshall Plan as a vast American conspiracy, conceived by Clayton and other economic imperialists, to isolate Moscow. Yet again, to study Clayton's life and his input into the Marshall Plan is to realize how sincere the U.S. offer of Soviet participation in the Marshall Plan was. Its purpose, Clayton wrote, was "to save Europe from starvation and chaos (not from the Russians)."

Clayton was anticommunist, not anti-Russian. He believed, forty years before other observers developed the notion further, that the fastest way to dismantle communism peacefully would be to apply our free-trade ideas even to the Soviet Union. The Soviets either would reform their economy to produce goods for exchange, opening up a wedge for Western ideas to accompany Western products and businesspeople, or would refuse, in which case their ability to trade with the West would do them little good.

Clayton's support for an offer to allow Russia to participate in the Marshall Plan, then, was no narrow, politically cynical concession. Others, of course, may have had different motives and outcomes in mind in accepting Clayton's argument that a Marshall Plan invitation ought to include the Kremlin (provided the Kremlin would reform some of its practices). That is all the more reason, however, to bear in mind that Clayton was a key participant, that the Marshall Plan was based heavily on his thinking.

"There might have been a Marshall Plan without Will Clayton," as Nitze put it. "But it would have been very different from the Marshall Plan that emerged, the plan that a small group of us had been thinking about since late 1946." Perhaps the best witness to that thinking was an editorial on Clayton's resignation in October 1947 written by one of his sharpest critics, the journalist I. F. Stone:

> In his last two press conferences, Clayton insisted again and again that East-West trade must be resumed, irrespective of political differences. . . . He, who was one of the architects of the Marshall Plan, seemed as much opposed to a dollar curtain as to an iron curtain. . . . One felt in Clayton that he was not afraid of bogeymen, that he was big enough to try to understand the differences in the world, and that he was . . . genuinely desirous of peace.[26]

Clayton's achievements are even more impressive in light of his origins. His family never had much money, and he began working as a boy. By 1936, he had been dubbed "King Cotton" on the cover of *Time* magazine and addressed a tercentennial gathering at Harvard University. Still, he kept his humility and his common touch. One of his secretaries at the State Department recalls showing up for work one morning to find Clayton down on the floor, fixing a scrap of carpet and some misplaced furnishings rather than ringing for a worker to come in and finish the job. The talented group who worked for him at the State Department remember him with fond respect. "Clayton was a very good boss," recalled Ambassador Winthrop Brown, one of his aides. "Very considerate, always worked harder than the men under him. . . . We felt awful when we were responsible for having advised him wrongly because when we did he always took the blame himself." Collado referred to Clayton as "almost a saintly character." Nitze said, simply, "Clayton was my boss and he was the only fellow I respected in government."[27]

Will Clayton, however, is more than an important or interesting figure of the past. His ideas speak forcefully to many of the issues facing the world today. For example, his argument for a League of Democracies, bringing together the growing roster of free and prosperous nations to promote and solidify the democratization of the world, is both forceful and contemporary. His ideas for achieving economic and political unity for Europe, seemingly quixotic to many of his contemporaries, proved to be far-sighted.

Most analysts if required to categorize Clayton today would tend to place him close to Ronald Reagan on the political spectrum. He opposed some of Franklin Roosevelt's policies, notably for agriculture, which led him to support, briefly, the Liberty Lobby, an anti-FDR group founded by the Du Pont family to oppose the New Deal. Yet he proved a loyal (and financially generous) supporter not only of Roosevelt but of a succession of Democratic party presidential nominees, including Woodrow Wilson, John W. Davis, Alfred E. Smith, Harry S. Truman, Adlai E. Stevenson, and John F. Kennedy. He had definite ideas about making and keeping the Democrats the party of growth and opportunity.

His foreign policy would commonly be described as that of a cold warrior. Yet Clayton was not an exponent of a narrowly defined, merely anticommunist "national interest." He saw no fundamental contradiction between strengthening the American idea—building up other countries into free, democratic economic competitors—and strengthening America. Rather, as Harry Truman wrote to one of Clayton's daughters on his death in 1966, he "had a world outlook in which he saw the position of the United States in relation and harmony to all nations." Hence, a Clayton foreign policy would not suddenly have run out of a sense of purpose with the announcement of *glasnost'* in the Soviet Union or the dismantling of the Berlin Wall. Indeed, for Clayton, these events would mean that the purpose of our foreign policy—building a world of freedom and democracy—had just begun to be realized, that the great prize was now within reach but not yet attained. For, as he wrote in 1955,

> The weakness of the foreign policies of the democracies lies in the fact that such policy is mostly negative—it is against something. The communist policy, on the other hand, is positive. They have a program to cure all the ills of all people everywhere. It is a false program, of course, but anyway it is something positive.[28]

Democrats and Republicans could hardly improve on Clayton's insistence that democracies must strive to focus on the positive, on the new tasks at hand, as the guiding maxim for U.S. foreign policy. Indeed, his critique is remarkably contemporary in an age when some proclaim "the end of history" and others wonder if U.S. diplomacy has any broad and liberal purposes at all in a postcommunist era.

From forth War's Bosom

2

WILLIAM LOCKHART CLAYTON WAS BORN ON FEBRUARY 7, 1880, TO parents as charged and determined as much of the postwar South seemed stagnant and defeated.[1] He spent his early years near Tupelo—a town in Mississippi that takes its name from the tupelo gum trees that line the marshes and the streams nearby. Surrounding the town is a region of forests and ambling hills, a land ceded to the United States by the Chickasaw Indians. The area was the site of intense fighting during the Civil War. Clayton's mother, born in a nearby village, told her son that, as a girl, she heard the guns at Shiloh pounding in the distance.

James Monroe Clayton, Will's father, was descended from a family of English settlers who arrived in Virginia in the 1600s. James Clayton began life as a schoolteacher. The job paid little, but it was a profession to which his intellectual passions suited him well. Shortly after he married, his parents died, leaving him, their only son, the deed to the family farm. It was not a providential change, as the farm suffered regular crop failures.

Clayton went deeper into debt to friends and relatives, growing depressed and resentful as the proceeds of each harvest failed to pay the previous year's bills. Mortgaging the farm to an uncle,

James Clayton struck out for opportunity elsewhere, but his business schemes fared no better than the farm. The family's fortunes hit bottom when Clayton contracted to build a section of railroad bed west of Jackson, Tennessee, where the family moved when they lost their Mississippi farm. The rains that had ruined so many cotton crops continued, making it nearly impossible to cut a needed pass through the shifting clay.

Clayton's resourceful wife, Martha Fletcher Burdine Clayton, devised a scheme that kept the family afloat, while cushioning James's pride as a provider. They had no money for rent, so she arranged with a widower who owned a large house that the Claytons would move in and, in return for room and board, she would cook the meals for the widower's family, her own, and enough boarders to pay for the food. Her hard work and ingenuity didn't make the Claytons prosperous but did keep the family intact.

❑ ❑ ❑

Will Clayton's younger brother, Ben, once commented that Will never really had any childhood. To an extent, that was true. The family's financial difficulties, though, did not prevent Will from developing a keen sense of adventure and curiosity. His father eventually found a job in a hardware store, and the family was able to move into their own small house. An expert fisherman and hunter, James took young Will and his friend Hu Harris on frequent trips.

Still, the family was chronically short of money. Although his scholastic abilities might easily have propelled him into college, Will, the oldest son, felt a strong duty to begin earning wages as soon as he could. Jackson was the county seat for Madison County and a thriving transportation center; the docket at the local courthouse was often overbooked by businesspeople filing documents, shippers applying for licenses, and litigants pressing cases. In 1893, Robert Hurt, the court clerk, asked the school to recommend a bright young man to help him. The school principal sent him Will

Clayton, who quickly saw many opportunities beyond the clerical. Businesspeople needed letters typed or cables sent, and attorneys needed depositions prepared. Out of his $10 a month pay, Will paid $4 a month for late-night shorthand and typing lessons. He attended his seventh-grade classes during the day, but he spent his evenings being tutored by the school principal, cramming for exams by the light of the only good lamp in the house, and running errands and odd jobs for the Model Laundry, his father's latest precarious venture.

Within a year, Will Clayton had a reputation as one of the fastest and most reliable clerks in the area. His services were in demand from many of the men who stopped in Jackson. Once he typed a speech for William Jennings Bryan, who made him retype it because the margins were too narrow. Bryan's address, attacking the high tariffs and tight money that were ravaging the South's agricultural economy, stirred and agitated the young typist. For days, he talked of little else.[2]

Another boyhood experience that left a deep impression on him took place in 1895, when a Civil War veteran invited him to attend a reunion of Confederate troops at Shiloh. A number of Union veterans were meeting there too, so the event became the first joint reunion of North and South. With the passage of thirty years, most bitterness had faded, and the meeting was so conciliatory in tone that Will wrote an account of it for the Jackson newspaper.

One businessman who used Will's services on his travels through Jackson was Jerome Hill, a cotton merchant from Saint Louis. Impressed with the fifteen-year-old typist and shorthand-taker, Hill offered him a job as his personal secretary in Saint Louis, at the rate of $65 a month. At that salary Will could contribute handsomely to the family finances, but his mother objected. Will pressed her for a yes, but her answer was the same: No. Finally, he threw himself face down on the floor, pulling at his hair and pounding the rug with his fists. "You mustn't hold me back, Mother!" he shouted. "Don't you see I can't turn it down?" She relented, hoping that in time one of James's business ventures would pay off and that Will could then return to school. In fact, when he left home for Saint Louis in 1895, Will Clayton, graduate of the eighth grade, had spent the last day of his life as a schoolboy. He remained a self-taught student until his death.[3]

In 1896, Will's mother reluctantly agreed to let him accompany Hill to New York City, where the American Cotton Company, the firm Hill represented, made its headquarters. Will kept his pledge to neither smoke nor drink, living a stoic life of long days at the office, reading and walking at night. Eventually, the overwork wore him down. One Saturday afternoon, he took a break from the office and went for a long walk along the docks. Striking up a friendship with some sailors, he asked if he could take a tour of the engine room of one of the ships in the harbor. For more than an hour, he stood in the steam heat, peppering the engineer with questions about the process. He walked home in the cold air soaked with perspiration. He showed up for work on Monday, but a secretary suggested the hospital might be a better destination. Will had pneumonia. He didn't write home to tell his family how ill he was until the worst of his bout was over and he was convalescing. Fletcher Clayton demanded that Will come home, and in the summer of 1897 he did.

❑ ❑ ❑

Will's future wife, sixteen-year-old Sue Vaughan, was five feet tall, with flashing blue eyes, blond hair, and wit. Her family lived in Clinton, Kentucky, where she excelled in her studies, as a high school debater and speaker, and in attracting suitors. One was the young Alben W. Barkley, who promised Sue that if she married him she would be marrying a future U.S. president.[4]

In the summer of 1897, Sue's older sister, Hattie, went to Jackson, Tennessee, to visit a school friend. But after a few days, Hattie came down with typhoid fever. Sue went to Jackson to nurse her. One day, a young man from the town came to inquire about

Hattie's health. Sue answered the door dressed in her older sister's clothes—in a long skirt for the first time in her life.

The young man asked, "Is this Miss Vaughan?"

"I'm Hattie's sister," Sue answered. She too was delighted with what she saw: a youth she later said was "tall, handsome, and serious as a knight of the Holy Grail."[5]

Will Clayton introduced himself and asked two questions. How was Hattie's health? And would Sue go rowing with him and a group of friends on the river that evening?

"I'll have to ask my sister, first, Mr. Clayton," she said.

"Miss Vaughan," he asked, "please don't call me Mr. Clayton."

"I think," Sue's eyes darted, "you'll have to be *Mr.* Clayton as long as I'm *Miss* Vaughan."

Will saw Sue as often as he could that summer. On some evenings, she would join the Claytons at their home for a family concert. Will's older sister, Burdine, would play Beethoven and Chopin on the piano, while their younger sister Leland accompanied on the violin. Sue's presence heightened Will's response to the music. When he returned to New York, he told himself, he would save a little money to buy cheap gallery seats at the opera. At other times, Sue and Will went for long walks and shared a mutual appreciation of Shakespeare and the classics.

Still there was a tension or reserve on Will's part that perplexed Sue. She later recalled that she found herself holding back, afraid to fall in love with the young man who told her defiantly that she was the first girl he had ever known who refused to let him kiss her.[6] One day they went on a hayride together, and Will acted as if she were his brother Ben's date. Did he not like her, or was he too shy to have it known she was his steady girl?

Will, already very much in love with Sue, could not bear the thought of failing to win her hand.[7] His family, his friends, and the people of Jackson would know that it meant something if they saw him out with Sue. If it meant something, it must mean that he had received a promotion and raise in New York and would soon be in a position to marry this effervescent girl. But he had not been offered more money, and he did not have nearly enough saved up to provide for a wife and family. The thought of failure, at both work and romance, haunted him.

If his pride drove him to act with a shyness and hesitancy that often confused his bride-to-be, it also spurred him on. For the next five years—they were married in August 1902—Will devoted himself to two goals: winning Sue and establishing himself in a financial position that would enable him to support her. In the summer of 1897, Will earned $2,000 working for Great-Uncle Lafayette Clayton, an attorney who had become involved in a famous and lucrative case that required a great deal of deposition work.

Eventually, the American Cotton Company wanted Clayton back in New York City—wiring to offer him $1,000 a year. He returned in the fall of 1897. His new boss, D.C. Ball, drove him so hard that he considered quitting. Ball would dictate to him all week late into the evening and then invite him to Sunday lunch at the the Waldorf Hotel, only to dictate to him again with frequent and capricious changes in his wording.

Keen to move into a different division and away from Mr. Ball, Clayton spent as much time as he could in the cotton-classing room, the large warehouse where the different samples of cotton would be graded before they were shipped to the mills. (The grade determines the cotton's price. This act of classing, then, is at core of the cotton merchant's business; he makes money by becoming a reliable consultant to the cotton buyer, who pays a percentage of the price to the merchant to gain his expertise.)

Throughout this period, Clayton wrote daily letters to Sue— sometimes more than daily.[8] His letters achieve a vitality of imagery and a sophistication of literary allusion not usually associated with an austere young man trying to make his fortune. Yet his way of expressing himself was direct. When Sue, attending Washington College in the District of Columbia, wrote to thank him for sending her a copy of *As You Like It*, he replied, "When I come down to Washington, I'll see if you're 'just as high as my heart.'"[9] A few books and thank-you notes later, he wrote, "When I send you a book or something, you send a letter of thanks that is worth a hundred books and more. Why, if I had the whole world I'd give it to you, just for the pleasure of having you thank me for it!"[10]

During his time in New York, he was an avid reader. He especially liked Sir Walter Scott's *Ivanhoe* and *Kenilworth*, which he recommended to Sue. Once he wrote, "I'm glad you liked *Janice Meredith*. Have you read *Richard Carvel*—another fine revolutionary story? I'm fond of those and of Civil War stories." On a different occasion he wrote, "It takes a lot of courage and grit to live up here . . . and work day and night, without a single pleasure in a whole month, or a single hour to read a book." Still, he was working with a goal in mind.

In 1899, Will visited Sue during his summer vacation and proposed. She was still not sure, though, about the young man who had pretended she was dating his brother. She told Will he would have to wait for an answer. He persisted, and his letters won Sue's confidence and wore down her resistance that fall. On Christmas Eve 1899, Will went to Washington to call on Sue and on Hattie, who was visiting her sister for the holidays. He later recalled how lovely Sue looked with her blond hair set off by a black coat and furs. That afternoon, while Hattie and a friend were out sightseeing, Will took Sue off to a secluded parlor on the mezzanine of the Riggs Hotel, where he proposed and she accepted. He called on her again on Christmas Day and then, typically, was back at work in New York on December 26.

Despite his grueling hours, Clayton took time to help secretaries, clerks, neighbors—almost anyone who needed a hand. One object of his benevolence was Ernest Jones, who, like Clayton, arrived in New York to work as a stenographer. Unlike Clayton, Jones, age fifteen, was both awkward personally and a bit shaky in his typing and shorthand. Clayton felt sorry for the young man and, without telling Jones, asked the boy's superior to give him a month's trial rather than fire him. Then he went to work on Jones's skills. As Jones later wrote:

He took charge of my typing and shorthand, dictating to me, in the evening, editorials from *The New York Times*, and making me type them without errors. . . . In one month's time I could take care of my job, and in three months' time Will let up a little, and I could actually see what New York looked like. Nobody else in the world would have given anything like this to a green boy to whom he had no obligations. Then and there began the hero worship I have never gotten over.

With my job secure, Will took my education in hand. He read *The New York Times* religiously, particularly the foreign news, the markets, and the editorials. He drilled into me that one must read a good paper (not Hearst's *New York American* which appealed to me with murders, the lost child, wife, etc.), and I remember his telling me again and again, "If you read and absorb every line on the editorial page of *The New York Times*, you will keep posted on all the worthwhile events at home and abroad." The next thing he drilled into me was that you cannot waste time. Time, to him, was something given you to prepare for the future.[11]

Jones's hero worship for Clayton matured into a deep friendship. The benefits were not one-sided. With Jones's encouragement, Clayton took a few dancing lessons and persevered with his evening study of French. French, the international language of commerce, gave Clayton access to cotton merchants throughout Europe after World War I. The dancing lessons took him out of himself a bit, broadening him beyond the sphere of work and blunting some of his intense competitiveness.

Clayton drove himself even at play. Jones (who went on to become president of Jones, Gardner & Beal, a thriving cotton firm in Rhode Island) recalled how, after the two became roommates, even the walk to work together to Manhattan sometimes became a daily contest:

We lived on the heights of Brooklyn, so that it was about a three mile walk over the Brooklyn Bridge to our office. After a while, a stroll across the bridge seemed very tame and slow until Will developed a racing technique.

He would pick out some young fellow stepping briskly along,

walk up alongside of him and perhaps half a yard ahead, and maintain his lead. Pretty soon the young man would get tired of this and speed it up a little, and the first thing you know a race would be on hand.

Well, old long-legged Will could not be beaten, but the result was that I had to dog-trot to keep up and when I arrived, I had plenty of exercise. In hundreds of races I never saw him beaten.[12]

Clayton won a small promotion in January 1900. It seemed jeopardized when he developed appendicitis. The illness brought him a benefit, however, when Lamar Fleming, a high official with the company, invited Clayton to his home to recuperate. Another official's illness created a vacancy for Clayton to become an assistant manager of the Cotton Sales Department. Soon Clayton was working directly for Fleming. His rise didn't come without new worries, though. Clayton, after all, passed over the heads of more senior men in the office, sparking jealousy. Furthermore, it came in the midst of a much larger fight for control of the company, pitting Fleming against a faction that he and Clayton believed was driving American Cotton toward bankruptcy.

Thus the years 1900–1902 were a difficult period of waiting and worrying. Sue remained far away, increasingly ill at ease as she read Will's frank letters about dances and other social engagements in New York, affairs populated by pretty and sophisticated women. American Cotton, meanwhile, seemed a questionable investment of Clayton's energies. The more he and Fleming did for the company, the more they aroused the fury of the mismanagers around them. At any moment all their efforts might earn them a pink slip. In October 1900, having lost $200,000 in just forty days, American Cotton managed to arrange a $2 million bailout loan, but without changes in the hierarchy, Clayton predicted that the money would only postpone the reckoning. American Cotton, he wrote to Sue, "will go to the wall as a grand example of greed, jealousy, and mismanagement. They will either break or be reorganized sometime in the spring." He was right. In May 1901, further in debt and about to fold, the firm reorganized, electing a new president and placing Fleming in a senior position.

With the company under sound management, Will and Sue were able, in the summer of 1901, to schedule their long-deferred marriage. Clayton quickly became Fleming's indispensable right hand. Within a year, Clayton was elected treasurer of the Texas Cotton Products Company, an American Cotton subsidiary doing a brisk, seven-figure business. At a salary of $2,400 a year, Clayton had built a career and a financial base. All the same, because he continued sending most of what he saved home to help his parents, he had to borrow $300 from Mr. Hurt of Jackson to pay for his wedding and honeymoon trip.

After a four-year engagement, Will and Sue were married on August 14, 1902, at Bellwood, Sue's home in Clinton, Kentucky. The couple set up house in East Orange, New Jersey, where Will would commute to New York City and where their first child, Ellen, was born in 1903. But they would spend less than two years in the New York area because Will Clayton had a new vision. That vision would soon catapult him to wealth and power and, in the process, help revolutionize the cotton industry, commodity trading generally, and the economic fortunes of the American Southwest.

3

To Dare Mighty Things

Cotton is the biggest cash field crop in U.S. agriculture. It is also the biggest single item in U.S. exports. At least 10,000,000 U.S. citizens, white and black, count on cotton for their livelihood. In the South, cotton is King, irrespective of price or politics.

To get $1,000,000,000 worth of U.S. cotton to market each year requires in infinite combination and permutation the use of gins, warehouses, compresses, ships, barges, railroads, trucks, spot markets, futures markets; the services of dealers, bankers, brokers, buyers, factors, graders, merchants.

The most important man in the chain is the merchant. The big cotton merchant can arrange every detail in the complex life of a bale of cotton from the platform of a gin in Georgia to the door of a spinner in Osaka. And the biggest cotton merchant in the world is William Lockhart Clayton, number one man of Anderson, Clayton, & Company of Houston, Texas.

Few [cotton men] have anything but respect for Will Clayton, number one private citizen of the nation's biggest state. He seldom fails to arouse in people he meets an admiration close to hero worship.

Time magazine, August 17, 1936[1]

IN THE SPRING OF 1904, WILL CLAYTON, FRANK ANDERSON, AND Monroe Anderson had little in the way of physical or financial capital. They carried their collateral around inside them, in the form of insight, experience, determination, and a willingness to take risks—what is today called *human capital*. By contrast, the American Cotton Company still had vast holdings and hundreds of employees, a far-flung empire with subsidiaries, managers, and facilities dotting the country and the globe. Yet within a few years, this firm would cease to exist, except insofar as some of its parts had been sold off to the rising young firms of the future. Chief among these upstarts was Anderson, Clayton, and Company, headquartered in Oklahoma City, Oklahoma.

The three men hatched their plans when Frank Anderson, who had married Will Clayton's older sister, came to visit New York. He came primarily in the hope of arranging a bank loan to expand his moderately successful operation as a cotton merchant in the growing fields of Texas and Oklahoma. The banks weren't interested.[2] But Will Clayton, chafing under the continuing mismanagement of the American Cotton Company, was. He could invest $3,000, thanks largely to Sue Clayton's inheritance of $2,500 on the death of her father. Frank Anderson put up $3,000, as did his brother Monroe Anderson, a cashier in the Peoples Savings Bank of Jackson with experience in commodity and farm trading. In the first year of operations, Will's brother Ben Clayton joined the firm to provide technical know-how about milling, ginning, and storing cotton. Thus on $9,000 capital, Anderson, Clayton, and Company, or ACCO, was formed in Oklahoma City on August 1, 1904. Arthur Baum of the *Saturday Evening Post* later called this $9,000 "the most potent investment in the world of cotton."[3]*

---

*It would be wrong to underestimate the contribution of Clayton's partners to the enterprise. But in the early twenties, Frank Anderson fell ill and, after recurring relapses, died in 1924. Ben Clayton became ill in the same period, retiring in 1929. Monroe Anderson contributed his banking experience for many years but knew

To understand how the firm became a colossus, let us look at the general structure of the cotton trade as it existed in 1904.[4] Now forty years after the Civil War ended, the South remained something of an underdeveloped area, with lower per capita investment and industry than in the North. The region contained a pool of workers, but many of them had few skills and little opportunity for education. Most worked at low wages in the cotton fields or as subsistence farmers. Less than one-third of the cotton growers owned their own land. Most were sharecroppers (35 percent in 1936) or tenant farmers (38 percent).[5] Neither the growers nor the merchants could amass the capital needed to transcend this primitive system.

Much of the value added to the cotton—ginning, spinning, weaving, grading, marketing—was done far away from the farms, in New York, New England, or near the great spinning centers of Havre, Bremen, and Liverpool. Some American merchants, such as the American Cotton Company, tried to improve these arrangements. Yet they generally tended to act merely as agents for one of the European firms.[6]

None of these arrangements was of optimal efficiency. They were bound to change as competition drove farmers and firms to find shorter lanes of transit to the cotton mills. The diversion of much of the cotton through New York, for example, served a certain function, providing a central marketplace in the same place that the large commodities futures markets operated. But it would cost less to ship the cotton directly from, say, Houston to the mill, either in Europe, the U.S. South, or the Far East. (This potential system, called "southern delivery," was one that Clayton fought to

---

little of the critical marketing and handling operations. Hence it is not an overstatement to refer to ACCO's steady growth being due first and foremost to Clayton's business genius. "Instead of a team effort," Ross Pritchard writes, "the main responsibility fell to Will Clayton." "To a man," the *Wall Street Journal* wrote, "ACCO executives attribute most of the company's growth to the foresight of W. L. Clayton."

achieve for many years after World War I.) Similarly, the continued growth of the United States, particularly in the South and the Southwest, was bound to produce new lines of finance, enabling well-positioned U.S. firms to move onto a more competitive footing with the established European houses. Clayton saw these trends— some of which matured quickly, others of which took decades— and decided to go into business convinced that the logic of efficiency that rules the market would, eventually, bring them to fruition.

In particular, Clayton noticed several flaws in the strategy and operation of the American Cotton Company that, even in the short run, might provide a niche for Anderson-Clayton. For instance, American Cotton engaged in a large degree of speculative buying on the futures market, and many of its large losses came from guessing wrong in that highly volatile exchange. Every merchant, of course, had to operate on the futures market to some extent. The price of cotton might rocket or plunge during the months the firm was delivering on a contract to one of the mills. When merchants buy futures contracts to prevent losses due to unpredictable, fluctuating prices, the process is called *hedging*, which is not designed either to make or to lose money in its own right. But American Cotton, moving well beyond hedging, sought to make large profits by speculating in the futures markets.[7] Speculation is not wrong, but it is risky and a diversion from the market function traditionally performed by the merchant—grading cotton and marketing it (just as it would divert a commodity investor to set up a cotton merchandizing operation). Merely doing a good job of the merchant's traditional role was difficult enough, as *Time* noted:

> Cotton is a complicated subject on a domestic basis. On a world scale it is staggering. Aside from the difficulties introduced by foreign exchange and local preferences, international cotton merchants have to think, deal, quote in terms of a thousand different kinds of cotton. In the U.S. alone official standards specify 37 different grades on quality, 20 grades on staple length, offering in combinations no less than 740 possibilities.[8]

In this central function, the American Cotton Company had failed to notice many emerging or potential efficiencies and had taken only halfhearted advantage of others. International marketing was becoming a reality. Yet the firm had not built its offices and contacts overseas rapidly enough to take advantage of the opportunity. Like most U.S. firms, it sold mainly to European merchants, meaning that the U.S. cotton farmer commonly had to go through two middlemen instead of one. Cotton merchants in the United States and Europe were laboring to pack all the services possible (at the lowest price) into the period of transit and storage. These efforts often encountered local and parochial resistance, however, and American Cotton had proved inept at overcoming (or at least smoothing over) that inertia.

The firm also had invested heavily in the new round-baling machine, which packed cotton into a much denser package for transport than the old square baler. The round bale didn't take up as much space in shipping and was preferred by the loading dock workers and millers for both its ease in handling and its uniformity. But many in the South resisted, especially those who owned square bale machines. The shipping industry had adjusted its rates to recognize the decrease in volume per bale, but the railroads continued to charge the old rate. Hence, American Cotton, as well as other firms, had overinvested in the round bale machine and had underinvested in hiring people on the scene who could help win acceptance for it and press for the full economic advantages it provided.[9]

The American Cotton Company was further weakened by its rigid, credentialist, centralized, hierarchical management system, which failed to reward effort, move fast, or provide flexibility to its people in the field. Clayton's rise was the exception rather than the rule and caused great friction. He felt that a more responsive system focused on people and incentives and that consensus would be a critical advantage to a cotton merchant.[10]

The flawed operations of the American Cotton Company created a potentially profitable opportunity for others who thought they could make better use of its vast assets. Clayton and the Anderson brothers foresaw that opening and other fortuitous trends as well. If finding credit was difficult, it was not impossible for firms with a solid reputation in Europe, and it would become easier with the growth of the United States. George H. McFadden, who became Clayton's largest competitor, had already amassed enough capital to transcend the pattern. This movement could be expanded by anyone who (like Clayton) commanded respect with some of the New York banks and would accelerate as the South and Southwest developed their own sophisticated financial institutions. George Champion, who dealt with Clayton in the 1930s and 1940s as a Chase Manhattan Bank officer, later observed, "Clayton's business was one where a great deal had to do with personal trust, and he had that trust from the bankers. Clayton could call in on the phone and arrange a loan quickly because everyone knew he was a solid businessman and a man of integrity."[11]

In the burgeoning cotton markets of Texas and Oklahoma, which opened for settlement with a twenty-thousand-person dash for land at the firing of a starter pistol on April 22, 1889, a man's rise in business depended more on what he could do than on who his parents were or how long he had served in a particular bureaucracy, public or private. The patriarchal and parochial society that was so characteristic of much of the Old South was not as evident in Oklahoma.

Clayton's eldest daughter later wrote:

The Oklahoma City of those days was a true melting pot of all kinds of people, often one-generation Americans of German, Bohemian, Danish, and Swedish stock, as well as descendants of the older families from the Eastern and Southern states, with a handful of Indians. This atmosphere of frenzied ferment and change was both crude and stimulating. It was exciting to see a town grow, under one's very eyes, from a string of stores and banks on Main Street to a city with churches, a capitol building, theatres, and even a country club. There was a magic electricity in the air, a quality which matched the sudden cyclones. In Oklahoma City, so breezily on the make, it was a question of sink or swim.

Yet, in spite of the rough element, the newness and hope created an air of optimism, of easy comradeship which—although deficient in culture—was doubtless a healthy atmosphere for a beginning business to grow up in.[12]

Anderson-Clayton moved quickly to establish itself in this atmosphere of prairie capitalism. Frank Anderson worked the fields, looking for the grades of cotton that were in greatest demand. Clayton kept abreast of the global market, probing for gaps, shortfalls, and new outlets. Within forty days of the firm's founding, one of Clayton's predictions came true: on September 7, 1904, the American Cotton Company folded. Anderson-Clayton quickly bought most of American Cotton's round bale machines in Oklahoma at garage sale prices.

In early 1905, Ben Clayton joined the firm, which began buying and establishing local refining facilities and plants for associated cotton products, such as cottonseed. When a mill in Elk City, Oklahoma, tottered, Anderson-Clayton bought it and set it up as the Elk City Cotton Oil Company, a wholly owned subsidiary.[13] Within its first year, the $9,000 firm had amassed assets valued at $140,000 and turned a $10,000 profit.[14] Clayton's theory for consolidation and improvement in services was simple and straightforward: whoever could improve "the economic line of transit" would thrive, and whoever failed to do so could not indefinitely remain in business.

Clayton's business interests were enlarging and so was his family. In 1907, when Clayton traveled to Europe, he took along his wife and two daughters, Ellen, who was four, and Susan, age two. While Sue and her girls stayed in Switzerland, Will visited England, France, Italy, Germany, Holland, and Belgium. He quickly found customers happy to deal with one less broker and thus pay a price for cotton that reflected one less middleman's markup. "Most American cotton merchants in those days," journalist Beverly Smith later wrote, "were content to sell their export cotton to foreign cotton merchants and let it go at that. Clayton's firm . . . was one of those which saw the advantages of setting up European offices and selling direct to mills in England, Russia, or Italy."[15]

One notable feature of this rapid growth was its logical consistency. Unlike some of the mindless conglomerates of the 1970s and 1980s, Anderson-Clayton remained specialized enough to provide concrete improvements in operation. The firm was "completing under its ownership a simple, basic, buying-ginning-milling function," Smith continued. This first stage of its rise was complete when World War I provided a major impetus for growth to the American cotton industry and the United States generally. "By 1914," Ross Pritchard writes, "ACCO had, modestly but firmly, consolidated its position among the American merchants."[16]

As pressure to build the business was at its peak, a personal tragedy struck the Clayton family. In 1909, Sue had given birth to Will, Jr., whose golden hair and sweet disposition made him the great love of Will Clayton's life second to Sue. He would show his son off to neighbors almost daily. When Will, Jr., was a year old, Sue offered to care for, along with her own three children, three of the four young sons of Will's sister Burdine ("Sid"), the wife of Will's partner, Frank Anderson. Sue made this offer so that Sid and her youngest boy could make a longed-for trip to Europe with her husband.

Sue soon found the load of caring for six children to be daunting. A few days after the Andersons left for Europe, the five older children came down with the measles. To this day, Clayton's daughter Ellen retains a vivid mental picture of her mother racing up and down the stairs to carry meals and medicine to the bedridden children, exhausting herself in the process. The five older children eventually recovered. But in the meantime, young Will came down with a serious stomach disorder and then developed a mastoid infection in his ears. Will, Jr., died at thirteen months. His death, a shattering experience for Sue, was equally so for Will. The birth of two more daughters, Burdine and Julia, did not completely fill the void left by the death of his namesake.

If the early growth of Anderson-Clayton sounds smooth and inexorable, it hardly was so. A financial panic hit the United States in 1907, squeezing even established firms. The banking system shut down for a week, a preview of the great collapse a generation later. Will Clayton told Sue several times that year that the firm might go under. She invariably responded, "If you work hard and fail, that's not your fault. The only thing that matters is that you never lose your integrity."[17]

Still, there was tension in a household that had been tranquil and loving. Their daughter Ellen recalls:

> For a long time, six o'clock meant for me entering the dark tunnel of my father's homecoming. When he came home at night he always wore a strained look, so much so that, even when I was very little, I was frightened lest he had taken on some task that was too much for him. The neighbors used to say they could tell when "Mr. Clayton" came home by hearing me cry after he had spanked me for some minor something. Looking back, I believe that one cause of my punishments was the tight rein my father kept on himself to smother impatience with irritating things at the office. His control had to break somewhere, and his temper flared out and spent itself on me.[18]

But as his company's survival and success became more assured, Will Clayton became an increasingly attentive father. As Ellen noted:

He always had lunch at home on Saturdays, and he took us to Sunday school and, during the first year in Houston, before he became even busier, he read to us from the Bible and occasionally from Dickens. Yet in none of this did he completely participate, with all of himself. He seemed to be communicating with us only through the surface layer of his mind, while, underneath, he was absorbed in something too complicated for us to reach, or for him to explain—like Poe, who composed poetry while working out problems in mathematics.[19]

Sue Clayton played an important role in Clayton's early success, not only supporting him but eliciting and developing the warmer, gentler, and nobler side of his nature. Her demands that Clayton be an attentive husband and father may have irked him sometimes, but they tempered his ambition and probably made him a better leader. His daughter later wrote:

The frictional meeting of his own far-seeing nature with the more usual, shortsighted outlook of others could have pushed him, at the beginning of his own business, either into unscrupulous acts of revolt and conquest, or into melancholy failure. Mother, with her natural ebullience, encouraged him out of the melancholy. And with her biting tongue and quick perception of the slightest breaking of his word to her . . . she sharpened the influence of his early code of honor. Whenever there was a question of being fair to some troublesome employee or business connection, she emphasized in her talks with my father a point of view which he shared—that one should be more than fair rather than not fair enough. It is a tribute to him, as well, that he should have chosen for his wife someone who would lash out at him with all her strength.[20]

Anderson-Clayton, which handled about 1 percent of the U.S. cotton crop in 1906 and 1907, established itself not in the absence of bumps and bruises but despite them. A good illustration is the fate of the round bale machine in which the firm invested so heavily. In 1912, ACCO bought the patent on a new, improved round bale machine, planning to reap still further gains on its initial capital purchases. But competitive behavior is not limited to one party, and the square balers responded by giving up their efforts to restrict the use of the round bale machine and focused instead on building a better alternative. Thus, the man who had invented the original square bale "Webb presses" created an improved square bale machine. The new machine had side doors, pressing the cotton in from four sides instead of two. This enabled packaged cotton to reach a new density of 32 to 34 pounds per cubic foot. (The old square bale machines compressed 12 to 24 pounds per cubic foot, whereas the round bale machine, which compressed 30 pounds to the cubic foot, was still less efficient than Webb's new design.) Most cotton was compressed twice, once near the gin point for inland transportation purposes and again at the port. Anderson-Clayton could have fought against the new efficiency, as the square balers originally had done; Clayton, however, recognized the superiority of the machine and preferred not to resist the tide of improvement. As the higher-density presses spread inland, he decided to cut the firm's losses and move on. So Anderson-Clayton wrote down its $1 million investment in the round baler and sold the machines for scrap metal.[21]

In the ten years from 1914 to 1924, Anderson-Clayton moved from being a solid domestic cotton firm, with good contacts abroad, to being the international giant of the industry. Several shifts in the international economy helped, and most of these would have taken place with or without World War I. But the war hastened the changes, as well as adding an intensified urgency to Europe's demand for U.S. products, especially cotton. Even as demand for cotton goods surged, the old supply lines and contracts were breaking down.

Indeed, the vagaries of war took some toll even on the generally far-sighted management of Anderson-Clayton. For example, the firm lost large shipments of cotton to Russia and Czechoslovakia during the war.[22] Still, it seems clear that the war was the decisive hinge in Anderson-Clayton's transition from modest success to international giant. It might seem a matter mainly of good luck. Yet many U.S. cotton men barely shared in that fortune. The guns that erupted in August 1914 frightened many normally cool heads into an unsound, short-term panic. If events aided Clayton's business, it was he who seized the opportunity they provided. As Ross Pritchard notes:

When the First World War broke out the mechanism of trade and exchange, upon which the movement of cotton depended, faltered. Cotton farmers, faced by the prospect of an immobilized crop, rapidly "unloaded" their cotton, forcing prices to unprecedented lows.

It was at this point that Will Clayton, confident in his belief that the world would sooner or later again demand cotton, made a bold move that was the turning point in the development of ACCO. With a carefully calculated risk ACCO bought cotton; unable to protect the vast amounts of cotton through the traditional hedging mechanism they built modern fireproof warehouses; and waited for the market channels to open. Anticipating a vast movement of cotton abroad to meet the war-time demands of Europe, ACCO transferred its main offices to the port of Houston, Texas. This move in itself was of considerable importance to the growth of the company for Houston was then at the threshold of an unparalleled expansion.

In order to be on hand with cotton on a moment's notice ACCO shipped vast consignments to foreign ports. (One ingenious method of shipment during these months [devised by Clayton] was the stacking of cotton bales in and around the stalls of Army mules being sent to Europe.) When trade resumed ACCO provided the first cotton. Exchanges gradually reopened, trade revived, and the calculated risk taken by Will Clayton paid off.[23]

In the consolidation phase, the firm benefited from Clayton's international outlook and his flexible approach to adding personnel. He correctly anticipated a backlash from Europe after the war. The European merchants would resent their replacement by upstart American firms whose friendly prewar relations and cultural ties to the spinners could not be ignored. Accordingly, Clayton spent the years 1914–1920 setting up a vast network of semiautonomous ACCO units in Europe. Wherever possible, he hired the ablest people from the old European firms.

By 1920, ACCO offices and affiliates were established in Bremen, Liverpool, the Havre, Japan, and China, with the Bremen office handling operations in Czechoslovakia, Yugoslavia, Poland, Hungary, and the Baltic states.[24] Lamar Fleming, Jr., son of Clayton's patron and friend at American Cotton, opened ACCO's first overseas office in Italy. For a time, financing for these offices could be arranged locally. As the firm grew, however, it became essential to have an office close to the New York banks and the New York Cotton Exchange for futures hedging. To handle such matters, in 1918, Anderson, Clayton, and Fleming, with Lamar Fleming, Sr., as a partner, was established.

One thing ACCO did not do, even after the war, was abandon or compromise its drive to improve services and shorten the line of transit between farmer and spinner. In 1917, ACCO built one of the first fireproof warehouses in Houston, featuring an advanced compression system that further improved baling for international transit purposes. In the 1920s, similar warehouses would spring up in New Orleans, at the docks in Houston, in San Pedro, California, and across the South. But during and after the war, the railroads still were reluctant to lower their rates to reflect the new efficiencies in cotton transportation, so ACCO expanded its motor trucking operations and carried cotton in barges on local rivers in Alabama, Mississippi, Arkansas, and Oklahoma. To make full use of the investment in shipping, the barges carried staples back upriver for sale to the farms.[25]

Clayton's aim was to abandon the less-efficient processes, no matter what capital and pride he may have had invested. As Arthur Baum wrote in the *Saturday Evening Post*:

Clayton the middleman eliminated middlemen. He bypassed the
steps that formerly existed . . . and cut across from farmer to
distant spinner in a direct course. Competitors claimed that ACCO,
by reducing the cost of cotton marketing, made everyone handle
cotton on smaller margins. The ability to reduce costs plus a
genius for minimizing trade risks was Clayton's contribution.[26]

The war, and his emergence as a cotton magnate, provided
Clayton with a brief opportunity to apply his ideas to the wider
problems of government and economic policy. He accepted an
invitation from Bernard M. Baruch to join the War Industries
Board in 1918, serving as a dollar-a-year man to expedite the distribution of cotton.

Clayton's growing profile attracted attention, while his afflu-
ence provided him with the opportunity and resources to make his
opinions heard. From 1920 on, he was in demand as a speaker,
fund-raiser, and adviser. He became active in Houston civic affairs
and, at the national level, in Democratic party politics and financing. He also attracted controversy, including a series of congressional investigations into his business. Not until 1940 did Clayton
take his first full-time post in government. Still, he was already
forming a philosophy of what constitutes a just and prosperous
economic order. It is worth reviewing the salient features of that
philosophy, as well as his activism on its behalf in the period 1920–
1940.

Almost all businesspeople will expatiate on the virtues of the un-
trammeled free-market system, but not all of them actually like to
compete in one. Clayton believed, however, that business leaders
had a moral and practical responsibility to participate in and nurture support for the market system, even if their narrow economic
self-interest might be harmed. It was a moral imperative because a
free market was, simply and empirically, more productive and more

progressive. On a practical level, if businesspeople did not accept
its outcomes, who would? The simple law of commerce was that if
any better product, or any better way of making it, could be found,
it would eventually win the day. Companies, unions, and whole
nations hostile to the idea might stomp down an entrepreneur's
vision for a time. Sooner or later, though, human ingenuity would
overturn the old order. Rather than resist the inevitable, the spirit
of enterprise was to accept the innovation that, once implemented,
becomes the established way of doing things and then becomes
vulnerable itself to still newer and better ideas. The Austrian economist Joseph A. Schumpeter called this churning process "creative
destruction." Embracing this outlook, Clayton wrote in 1932:

> All progress . . . is at somebody else's expense. Thus, progress is
> only justified if it is for the greatest good of the greatest number.
>   Out of this conflict and friction . . . there are bound to evolve
> new and better ways of doing things . . . which will effect substan-
> tial savings, will shorten the economic route from the farmer to
> the spinner, and will result in the greatest good to the greatest
> number. The unfortunate thing is that someone will have to
> suffer.[27]

A large element of justice exists in this process, Clayton argued.
Socialism, embodied in the Bolshevik experiment in Russia, far
from bringing dynamism and growth, seemed to him a thwarting
of "creative destruction," which takes wealth from those less capable of employing it efficiently and gives it to those better able to do
so. In another 1932 letter, Clayton wrote:

> I am merely an amateur economist but I am afraid that I can not
> agree with you regarding the capitalistic system and the necessity
> for a redistribution of wealth other than such redistribution as is
> constantly taking place through natural and normal processes.
> . . .
>   A man may display great daring and genius in the accumula-
> tion of wealth and still show woeful inability to take care of it. It

then automatically taketh wings to someone else who must in turn demonstrate his ability as a competent trustee. . . .

Look at the men who paraded their new wealth . . . three or four years ago. . . . Most of them are flat-broke and are going around in circles . . . dazed and wondering how it all happened. Out of it all will arise in due time after much hard work and useful planning a new group . . . who will be better trustees. . . .

In my opinion the ills of which you speak may not be laid to competition but to the many efforts . . . which have been made to thwart competition.[28]

At the same time, Clayton recognized that the dynamism of competition and progress creates frictions and casualties. The buggy maker is bound to resent the loss of sales to the automobile and is likely to try to restrict the advance of the automobile. Hence, a problem of politics and justice emerges. The imperative of fairness is to cushion the blow to those who will suffer from a given new product or method. Politically, the problem is how to win the cooperation of that same group or at least to avoid extreme and bitter factionalism. Clayton insisted, however, that the change itself not be blocked, or, he said, the benefits would be lost. Instead, government, besides acting as an impartial referee, was to be something of a trainer when one of the players was badly hurt. Paradoxically, this type of intervention might not thwart the free market's efficiencies at all. Instead, it could advance the market by reducing people's fears that if they wound up losing in a given shift, they would lose all.

This philosophy of limited and focused government was often parodied as one of no government, of a naked reliance on the brute force of business. Yet it was hardly that. For one thing, capitalists too might misbehave. Clayton told an audience in 1928:

I do not belong to the laissez-faire school, whose philosophy will not permit acceptance of any government regulation. I am sorry to say that business . . . has not always shown itself competent or willing to put its house in order.[29]

Yet he was hardly an ardent interventionist, writing in 1932:

> You ask me if it is possible to stabilize agriculture. Frankly I dislike
> the word. . . . If I understand the popular conception of "stabili-
> zation," it is a condition of fixity as opposed to one of fluidity—a
> fixed price, a fixed program of production, of employment. . . .
> Stabilization to my mind spells stagnation—a stop to progress. All
> history proves that nature abhors and in time destroys all such
> efforts.[30]

Today a man with this profile of beliefs would normally be
expected to be a Republican, a supply-sider. Yet Clayton remained
a Democrat all his life, despite his opposition to some of Franklin
D. Roosevelt's policies. As much as Clayton abhorred government
intervention, he thought the worst instance of it was the Republi-
can-sponsored tariff, which had suppressed growth in the agricultural South for years, driving up the cost of equipment and finished
goods.

Clayton's genuine populism instilled in him a loathing of statist
or authoritarian thinking. He expressed his views, sharply yet civ-
illy, in a 1936 letter to a friend who had sought his support for a
new political movement being formed by Lawrence Dennis, who
touted fascism as a cure for America's problems. Clayton wrote:

> I think that we already have the substance of fascism and the form
> is on its way. But it will be short-lived. . . . The philosophy of the
> NIRA, AAA and all the other anathemas is opposed to the philos-
> ophy of a free people. National economic planning and democ-
> racy are contradictory terms. If planning prevails, democracy
> dies. . . .
> The American people are not ready to write Finis above their
> door and quietly turn to a dictator. We will recover and march on
> to our obvious destiny—not in black shirts, however.[31]

Despite his occasional misgivings, Clayton was loyal to the
Democratic party as the party of growth and change. If its suscep-
tibility to faddish enthusiasms occasionally tugged it in the wrong

direction, at least the Democratic party was not the smug defender of static wealth and privileges for Eastern big business interests. As he explained in 1934:

> I was born on a cotton plantation in Mississippi and have always felt that I had three good reasons for being a Democrat: 1. Hered-ity, 2. Environment, and 3. Conviction. I would not change the first two if I could, but I am getting powerfully weak on the third.[32]

In 1936, Clayton wavered but ultimately backed FDR, in part on the basis of his hopes for Secretary of State Cordell Hull's Recip-rocal Trade Program.

Clayton presented his convictions about capitalism—and a so-phisticated statement on the relationship of political and economic freedom and justice—in an address to the Harvard Business School in September 1936. It remains one of the most balanced and fair-minded assessments of the free market's virtues and defects. The *New York Times* praised the address as a seminal defense of eco-nomic liberty yet one that, "unlike the usual defense of capitalism," conceded the flaws and dislocations that an intelligent model for advancing freedom must take into account.[33] A proper appreciation of the subtlety and complexity of Clayton's mind requires a lengthy excerpt:

> It is not sufficient for the preservation of private capitalism that it be merely the best system. Because of ignorance or abuse, or both, the best system may not be the one in which the majority of the people believe, and may have to give way to something else. Throughout the world, private capitalism is today undoubt-edly on the defensive.
>
> Looking for the causes of this development we shall probably find one of the prime reasons to be deep resentment of the swollen profits arising out of the war [World War I]. Even had the recipi-ents of such profits conserved and wisely invested them, abstain-ing from an undue amount of personal consumption, which, unfortunately, was not the case, society should and doubtless will

take measures to prevent profit from war. Capitalists will be wise to recognize and assist this movement.

It seems unquestionably indicated that a highly industrialized society, used to amortization of machinery and plant, must now make provision for human obsolescence and for recurring periods of unemployment. It does not seem too much to hope that when this responsibility has been placed jointly upon capital and labor some means will be found of lessening the frequency and shortening the duration of periods of unemployment.[34]

(Note Clayton's emphasis on cushioning the frantic change and dislocations caused by capitalism, not by subverting the process of growth but by smoothing it.)

He continued:

It is said that the wastes of competition condemn the system of private capitalism. Where an individual enjoys complete or almost complete liberty of choice, there will always be some obvious waste, but the material and spiritual waste hidden in the centralization of power and decision is infinitely greater. If man's course is to continue upward, he must retain his liberty of choice and its consequent burden of responsibility. To surrender these to an overlord is to halt human progress.

It is said that the power of large capital is used to improperly influence government. Too often this has been true. Tariff lobbies have written our tariff laws. Human nature remaining unchanged, they will probably continue to do so until the tariff is taken out of politics. When that is done, the way to peace, the world's most pressing problem, should appear less difficult.

Agreements between competitors to curtail production or to fix prices are to be condemned on economic grounds. What the world needs is more production at lower prices, bringing even higher standards of living. Faulty distribution due to clogged trade channels, arising from government tinkering throughout the world, and not over-production, is the thing that plagues us.

It is charged that the power of large capital is used to crush competition, and to exploit labor and the consumer. Unfortunately, at a former time, this charge had some basis, but if applied to the past quarter century, little substance can be found in it.

Today the larger the corporation, the more pitilessly does the searchlight of public opinion play upon it. There was a time when managers of large enterprises thought almost exclusively of the interests of stockholders, but modern business administration has a keen sense of responsibility toward competitors, labor, and the public. The possibilities of further improving the relations between capital and labor by stock ownership, profit sharing, decentralization of plant, closer contact, etc. are certain to be explored by enlightened capital.[35]

Despite his basic support for capitalism, Clayton appreciated the limits of the system as well, concluding:

Under private capitalism, the profits available for reinvestment are necessarily diminished to the extent of the personal expenditures of the capitalist. This, and not the profit itself, is the toll which society pays for administration of its productive and capital-gathering agencies. While in the aggregate this toll is perhaps not disproportionate to the service rendered, nevertheless, in many individual cases it is exorbitant. The wasteful vanity-inspired expenditures of some rich people constitute a grave indictment of our system. . . .

Under private capitalism, there is a decentralization of decisions, and keen competition in every department of life, the theory being that the competitive process fits men and capital into those places where they serve best. In practice the system by no means operates perfectly, but unless too much interfered with its failures are usually self-regulated before they have gone too far.

Liberty of person, of speech, and of press are possible only under a system of private capitalism. . . . When statutory equality comes through one door, liberty goes out the other.

The great majority of American people must be made to understand the system, and its abuses must be recognized and corrected. This accomplished, there is no doubt that our capitalism of the future will be of a nature to preserve and develop further that individual initiative, courage, and instinct for cultural and material progress which have made our country great.[36]

Clayton's political activism in the 1920s and 1930s was a consistent drive for the application of this credo to the U.S. economy.

Guiding his actions was his ability to see the long-range consequences of policies that might seem beneficial in the short run but
that ultimately would exact a toll, not merely in retaliatory tariff
walls or a worldwide depression but also in war. Free trade and free
markets not only provided access to customers and profits but were,
in his eyes, the road to peace as well.

By the time of the Harvard speech—indeed, by end of World War
I—Will Clayton's appearance had reached the remarkably even
plateau on which it would remain throughout his life.[37] From 1918
until his death in 1966, his face, body, and stamina changed remarkably little. His hair remained thick and partly blue-black most
of his life; he parted it down the middle when he was young,
sometimes on the left in later years. When his hair began to gray,
the result—in combination with his thick, dark eyebrows—was to
sharpen the intense, hawkish look of his face, as well as the expression in his eyes.

Clayton practiced physical fitness long before it became fash-
ionable. He was an early riser and would go up to the third floor of
the family's Houston home, where he maintained a small gym for
his personal use. Spartan by today's standards, this gym had only a
hoist bar and a set of weights. He worked out daily but harder if he
felt he had overindulged his sweet tooth the night before. As an
adult, Clayton's weight never varied by more than five pounds.

His two weaknesses were a pudding dessert that his wife made
for him, its distinctive taste coming from Kentucky bourbon, and
a divinity fudge that she spiked with sherry. Until late in life, when
a physician advised him to drink sherry daily, these were the only
exceptions to his teenage promise that he never would drink alco-
hol. He also never broke his promise about smoking, tempted neither by the cigars of his business colleagues nor by the pipes of his
State Department associates.

For most of his adult life, Clayton walked two to three miles a day to work, whether from his home to his offices in Oklahoma City or Houston or later from his home in Washington, D.C., to the old State Department Building next to the White House. He also had a passion for speed. He preferred airplanes because trains were too slow, and he drove his Pierce-Arrow as fast as the playful screams of his daughters would permit. (He loved driving so much that he once said that, in his second incarnation, he wished to be a bus driver so he could ride all over the United States.) He also was a proficient horseman, riding regularly until he reached age eighty-five, but he tended to gallop off ahead of his companions. He played tennis with his girls, though with more energy than skill.

As a concession to Sue, he agreed to learn to play bridge. She complained at first that he played mechanically, without passion or authentic interest; soon, however, his innate competitive nature kicked in, and he became a better player than she. Almost everything about Clayton suggests intensity, impatience, and stress. He advised his daughters to take a daily midday nap, even if only for fifteen minutes. It was the method he personally used, not only to recharge himself for the responsibilities and decisions he faced but to release some of the tensions he had built up.

❑ ❑ ❑

To an extent that few men of his stature and power have managed to achieve, Will Clayton kept his wife and children at the center of his life. He would drive his girls all over Houston to find the right dress or perfume, and he towed his family along on business trips to New York, Europe, South America, or Egypt, proud to be able to offer them opportunities for travel, adventure, and cherished memories that he, a poor boy from Mississippi, had never enjoyed.

Into the Arena | 4

AFTER RATIONALIZING THE OPERATIONS OF HIS OWN COMPANY, CLAYton turned his energies in the 1920s to battling an irrational feature in the existing system of cotton trading on the New York Cotton Exchange. In doing so, he declared war against powerful interests that a man of lesser energy, resources, and determination might never have challenged. The protracted battle—and his eventual victory—prepared him for conflict on a larger scale.

Before World War I there was some justification for requiring cotton on futures contracts to be routed through New York City, but when that rationale ceased to exist, the system did not change or reform itself automatically. A futures contract was simply a promise between two parties. One pledged to deliver cotton at a certain date in the future. The other promised to buy it on that date for a given price. Most of these contracts were bought and sold as hedging mechanisms, so usually there was no physical delivery of cotton, just people swapping bids and pieces of paper, while the cotton itself moved from the farmer to the mill. Occasionally, however, such a contract was "called"—the party who has promised to buy the cotton wanted it delivered.

Under the pre–World War I system, it was not an onerous burden that futures contracts specified that delivery take place in New York. New York was not only where the contracts were bought and sold, it also was a transit point between the southern growers and the New England textile mills, as well as between the South and Europe. But the world war, and the alterations in the cotton industry it accelerated, changed all this. More and more cotton moved directly from southern ports to the ultimate buyers in Europe and Asia. Increasingly, the services provided by cotton merchants were decentralized, packed in as early as possible in gins in Texas and Oklahoma; waiting for a ship in the ports of Houston, New Orleans, and Savannah; or during inland transit by barge, train, or truck. Forcing cotton to go through New York became an extra, costly step.

Cotton farmers and merchants found themselves paying an extra 1 to 3 percent to deliver cotton—a large expense for a commodity such as cotton, where profit margins tend to be slender. But one small group benefited from the increasingly obsolescent system and fought against reforming or revising it. This group included cotton merchants, mostly New York–based, who made their money not from marketing but from futures speculation, the firms and investors who owned large cotton warehouses and compressing facilities in New York and nearby industrial sites, and assorted accountants, attorneys, investors, and cotton men who made money by exploiting small differentials and fees involved when contracts were called.

In his fight for a new system of "southern delivery," Clayton sought to overturn the illogic of the old system, which imposed artificial costs on cotton for the benefit of a narrow elite. He was not the first person to take up this cause. A 1904 report to the New York Cotton Exchange had concluded:

> Experience for several years past proves that it is rarely profitable
> to bring cotton to New York in any quantity except to avert a

squeeze or corner. Who wants it here? Not the spinner nor the exporter. If this Exchange . . . certifies cotton in the South, we may prevent and drive away the manipulators and speculators whose chief desire is to find a market which they can squeeze or corner.

A similar report in 1907 asked:

Does it not seem absurd that . . . we should insist, that if a member wants to sell a bale of cotton, he must bring it here where nobody really wants it, where there is not a single mill to use it, and thereby add to its cost . . . a useless addition because it neither helps the spinner nor planter?[1]

Clayton's fight against mandatory New York delivery began immediately after the war ended. His crusade was met at first with a mixture of contempt and bemusement. One journalist reported that the New York interests thought it was "simply funny" for a maverick in Houston, Texas, to propose a great upheaval in their settled way of doing business.[2] Clayton found few allies during times of prosperity; from 1923 to 1925, however, when cotton prices fell sharply and profit margins were squeezed, he found renewed interest in his idea among growers and merchants alike. Senator Elliston D. ("Cotton Ed") Smith of South Carolina led those who demanded a federal inquiry into the marketing system.[3] At Smith's urging, the Federal Trade Commission launched an investigation, filing a review of the cotton seasons of 1923–1924 and 1924–1925 that unanimously recommended southern delivery.[4] Still, the New York interests were able to exert sufficient influence to keep the proposed changes tied up in congressional committees, and the reform drive stalled.

The economic turning point came in 1926.[5] It resulted from an audacious move by Clayton, one that took the war for southern delivery from the arena of theory and politics to the realm of practice and markets. In the process, Clayton not only reaped a vast profit for ACCO but, as he wrote to one friend in 1928, scalded the speculators, inflicting huge losses on the New York insiders by beating them at their own manipulative game.

Clayton's strategy was the flip side of his gamble of 1914–1915, when ACCO bought large stores of cotton in anticipation of a surge in demand. It came, this time, with an added twist.

In September 1925 heavy rains throughout the South reduced and delayed the cotton harvest and damaged the supply that did come to market. Cotton prices shot up so sharply that Anderson-Clayton and other firms could not fully protect themselves through their normal hedging operations in futures and spot markets. Anticipating a more normal market by early 1926, as the one-time shortage smoothed out, ACCO contracted to deliver a large amount of cotton in the spring and summer of 1926. In other words, the firm promised to deliver cotton at the high prices that had prevailed in late 1925. These sales were safeguarded by purchases of January, March, and May cotton futures. ACCO planned to buy some of the cotton it was contracted to supply not by its usual method, on the spot market, but by calling for delivery on a large volume of futures contracts.

The speculators who held those futures contracts were not expecting to deliver large amounts of cotton, which by the terms of the contract they would have to ship to New York, in 1926; they assumed that Anderson-Clayton was simply engaging in its usual hedging operations. This assumption provided the added twist. Seeing Anderson-Clayton holding all those delivery and futures contracts, they assumed the firm was planning to purchase large amounts of cotton by December 1925 for delivery starting in January. Accordingly, the speculators, hoping to profit from their inference, planned to minimize their own purchases of spot cotton in the months when ACCO would be bidding up the price.

The speculators got burned twice. They were left holding expensive inventories of cotton and promises to sell much later, when the market was high. In the spring of 1926, when cotton prices declined, Anderson-Clayton called for delivery on the futures contracts it was holding. Caught short, the New York operators had to deliver mountains of cotton to New York and bear the extra charges associated with bringing the cotton up north. (Clayton had quietly bought up warehouse facilities to accept delivery.)

The speculators had been scalded in a victory that was soon called "the killing of March New York," a reference to the carnage for holders of March contracts. In the process, though, many legitimate cotton merchants were hurt. Some, in fact, were ruined. The secretary of agriculture, W. M. Jardine, asked Clayton to explain his recent actions. As he would later for congressional investigators, Clayton pointed out that, with roughly 15 percent of the cotton trade, an all-time high for the firm, ACCO had nowhere near the market clout to manipulate the futures market. It was thus the greed of insiders, Clayton argued, that had created the panic that cost them so dearly. Clayton also used his exchange with Jardine to restate his case for southern delivery.[6]

Still there was bitterness and outrage among the cotton merchants. Clayton did not mind enraging New York interests, but the anger of his peers and friends troubled him. In the spring of 1926, hurt by the criticism of the legitimate merchants, Clayton changed his battle strategy from one of prodding government officials with facts and figures to a more public brand of diplomacy. Perhaps his most important act was to defend Anderson-Clayton's actions before a gathering of the American Cotton Shipper's Association in Atlanta.

In his speech, Clayton explained his firm's recent actions and pointed out that it was the New York speculators who had caused market havoc. The crisis, he stated, could have been averted by a system allowing certification on futures contracts at ports in the line of transit—southern delivery. "The ultimate solution of every commercial problem," Clayton concluded, "is dictated by sound economics, and so it will be with this problem. The war on waste and maladjustment in commerce is only settled permanently by the elimination of these things."[7] The speech was well received by Clayton's fellow cotton men. A correspondent from the *Memphis Commercial Appeal* recorded:

Sentiment appeared definitely antagonistic to the firm so . . .
Clayton was there. He had never made a speech before so large a
gathering. He was not an orator and had no ambition to become
one. Calmly, courageously, the tall figure of the new giant in the
cotton world arose. He explained the attitude of his firm. He
frankly invited any sort of investigation. . . .

[He] spoke for about five minutes. When he sat down, most of
the cotton men who had assembled in an unfriendly mood toward
Anderson, Clayton & Company felt like children who had been
justly but mildly reprimanded.[8]

If Clayton had restored his standing among his peers, however,
his adversaries in New York were all the more bitter. The political
shift in the southern delivery battle came when they tried to strike
back at Clayton by rousing their allies in the press and in Congress
to harass Clayton with spurious charges and investigations. Events
lent them a hand. The 1926–1927 cotton season brought a bumper
crop that sent prices plummeting. The decline was so serious that
Commerce Secretary Herbert Hoover authorized emergency loans
to farmers, enabling them to hold back on selling their crops in
such a depressed market.

At the same time, hoping to avoid a repeat of the outcry of the
previous year, Anderson-Clayton decided to buy and store a substantial amount of cotton in New York rather than rely on calling
in cotton from futures contracts. The need for extra storage facilities was intensified by the bumper crop. ACCO's decision irked the
New York speculators, who were often able to manipulate cotton
prices by threatening to call contracts for New York delivery. (They
knew cotton merchants wouldn't want to actually deliver the cotton
to New York and hence had a certain leverage. With the large
amounts already in storage, however, the speculators lost this clout.)
It also provided them with what they thought was a superb opportunity to blame the depressed prices of that year on ACCO, thereby
striking a blow against Clayton and his crusade for southern delivery.

Clayton's nemesis and the leader of the speculator faction was
Arthur R. Marsh, who had resigned as a professor of comparative

literature at Harvard University in 1899 to enter the cotton business, first as president of a small company in Texas, then as an independent cotton broker.

In 1928, Marsh, who recently had served as president of the New York Cotton Exchange, accused Clayton of "monopolistic manipulations." He identified the New York interests with those of the farmer, accusing ACCO of making its money on the exploitation of the humble workingman. He called for a federal probe of his charge that Anderson-Clayton had committed more than a dozen violations of the antitrust laws.[9]

Several members of Congress, eager to be in the forefront of defending the farmers in their home states, took up Marsh's call. Cotton Ed Smith proposed an inquiry by the Senate Agriculture Committee. Speaking in the House of Representatives, John E. Rankin of Mississippi singled out Anderson-Clayton as a prime target for such a probe. He even charged that Clayton had once called himself "the most powerful man in the world of cotton" and gone on to boast that no one in the world could trade a bale of cotton without knowing the Clayton position, a statement that was completely out of character for Clayton.[10]

Within a few days of the initial complaints, Clayton filed a complete report to the attorney general explaining ACCO's actions and denying any wrongdoing. The Justice Department soon released a statement indicating that it was not investigating Anderson-Clayton and that ACCO's report and Justice's own inquiries established that the company was not guilty of any monopolistic practices. Nevertheless, the congressional committees persisted and, by generating publicity, provided a forum in which Clayton could refute the charges against him and make his case for southern delivery.

The hearings, running from March 12 through May 8, pitted Marsh, Clayton, their attorneys, and the committee members against one another in day after day of grueling charges and counter-charges. On March 15, 1928, when Marsh began to testify, he added to his previous scattershot charges twenty specific antitrust violations by ACCO. He also accused Clayton of complicity in drafting the 1924 Federal Trade Commission report that favored southern delivery. The hearings featured a spirited exchange between Marsh and Clayton's lawyer, David Hunter Miller. Marsh claimed that Clayton's shipment of cotton to New York in 1927 was designed to corner the market. The cotton, he charged—1.5 million bales— was generally inferior, yet just a high enough grade that it could be used to meet delivery contracts. This mountain of cotton, Marsh said, was used to bludgeon reluctant operators into surrendering their contracts rather than be forced to take ACCO's low-grade, overstocked supply. Miller parried with Marsh:

> *Miller:* Is the charge of this cornering operation . . . based on the quantity of a million and a half bales?
>
> *Marsh:* . . . Primarily—yes.
>
> *Miller:* Would you still charge the operation if the amount were cut in two?
>
> *Marsh:* Yes.
>
> *Miller:* Suppose it were cut in three.
>
> *Marsh:* That would be more doubtful; but if it were cut in two there certainly would be a cornering operation.
>
> *Miller:* Suppose it were cut in four.
>
> *Marsh:* I should say then it would not be an illegal corner.
>
> *Miller:* If the actual figure were one quarter of what you have stated, then so far as a cornering operation in December, it would fall. Is that right?
>
> *Marsh:* In my own mind, yes.[11]

In fact, ACCO had shipped only 200,000 bales to New York, less than one-fifth the amount charged by Marsh. Miller submitted Clayton's sworn statement to that effect, backed with internal documents from the Anderson-Clayton files and verified by shipping and warehousing records. In his thorough and perceptive account of this incident, Ross Pritchard concluded that it was Miller's cross-examination of Marsh that settled the political struggle on southern delivery, turning a pack of congressional inquisitors initially hostile to Clayton into people "decisively against Marsh" and the New York interests.[12]

The rest of the hearings were an anticlimax. Clayton's attorneys, Miller and R. C. Fulbright, dispatched Marsh's charges one by one. The committee issued no formal statement exonerating Clayton, but from the tone of their questioning and their actions in the legislative sessions to come, its members made their verdict clear. At the conclusion of hearings, Representative Carl Vinson praised Clayton's actions, adding that he hoped Clayton would "contribute his constructive knowledge to Congress" to aid "in the curing of these evils."[13]

Clayton's vindication was so complete that, by the end of the process, he found himself arguing, on philosophic grounds, against legislation forcing southern delivery on the futures market. Six months later, as he may have anticipated, the New York traders announced their willingness to allow southern certification. "SINCE NEW YORK EXCHANGE HAS ADOPTED SOUTHERN DELIVERY," he cabled Carl Vinson in January 1929, "MAIN DEFECTS OF SYSTEM SUBSTANTIALLY REMOVED HENCE DO NOT SEE HOW I CAN CONSCIENTIOUSLY WORK FOR LEGISLATION WHICH APPEARS TO ME NOW UNNECESSARY."[14]

Clayton emerged from the hearings with a deep faith in the country's democratic institutions. "Even a Senate investigation has its uses," Clayton joked in a speech to a Houston civic group a few weeks later. "It has been the most interesting and instructive experience of my business life. I have learned more in six weeks . . . about politics as it is actually played than I would have in a lifetime. And it is still my unshaken belief that this is . . . the finest government in the world."[15]

To Clayton, the victory for southern delivery symbolized the potential of the U.S. economy to move to new levels of growth. If special interests could be defeated in that bruising battle, surely they would be defeated elsewhere as well. Just as Britain experienced another surge of growth in the 1840s and 1850s following the repeal of the Corn Laws, so the United States, and the South in particular—freed increasingly from the atavistic tariffs and financial manipulations not yet dismantled after the war—would leap to a new level of efficiency.

Thus in April of 1928, Clayton—understandably expansive—penned a letter to a friend in Memphis that contained what can only be called one of Clayton's worst predictions:

> I have a distinct feeling that we have about come to the end of another period or era . . . that we are going to have a new deal and that it will mean better and more normal times for every conservative interest in business. . . .
> In short, we are going to see better times for all of us.[16]

Within one year, though, nearly all of the assumptions on which that prediction rested had been capsized.

In 1928, the Republican party met in Philadelphia to nominate Herbert Hoover for the presidency. The party's platform reaffirmed "our belief in the protective tariff as a fundamental and essential principle of the economic life of this nation," pledging to extend the policy to "industries which cannot now successfully compete with foreign producers." The party promised to support "legislation creating a Federal Farm Board clothed with the necessary powers to promote the establishment of a farm marketing system." The platform also praised the cuts in income taxes of the Coolidge years but said only that further tax cuts would come "as the condition of the Treasury may from time to time permit." More disappointing to free traders, such as Clayton, was the Democratic party platform, which danced around the tariff issue with a gust of clichés and procedural cavils, proposing, for example, "abolition of log-rolling and restoration of the Wilson conception of a fact-finding tariff commission, quasi-judicial and free from the executive domination which has destroyed the usefulness of the present commission."[17]

Elected in November, Hoover immediately set out to fulfill his promise to continue the interventions in the agriculture markets he had initiated as secretary of commerce in 1927. As president-elect, he called for a special session of Congress to begin work on an agricultural marketing act, establishing a federal farm board with vast authority to buy and sell surplus crops in an effort to stabilize prices. Hearings in the Senate on proposals to increase U.S. tariffs across the board—the beginning of the dreaded Smoot-Hawley Tariff Act—were under way when Hoover took office on March 4, 1929.

Higher tariffs in Clayton's view were precisely what the United States did not need. He also feared they would needlessly cripple other countries. A decade earlier, he had written to a friend that the United States bears a special role in preserving the health of the world economy:

> Our unique position in the world clothed us with enormous responsibility. Enlightened selfishness dictated that we should mobilize our great influence and our vast resources to help the world rehabilitate itself. Instead we led the way to economic nationalism.[18]

During an extended trip to Europe in 1920, he had become acquainted with the critique of the Versailles settlement written by John Maynard Keynes and had observed firsthand the effects of the massive war debts on the continent. He shared Keynes's view that the postwar settlement had set the world on a course for disaster.[19] On his return from Europe in June 1920, Clayton wrote:

> How Germany will ever pay the colossal indemnity demanded of her is more than anyone can solve. I am afraid that Germany has already paid about all that she will. Meanwhile the indemnity will draw interest and double itself within 15 years. . . .
> The average German is very bitter against the Peace Treaty,

and is particularly bitter against France. There is a thirst for revenge.[20]

As a stimulus to economic growth, domestic and international, Clayton approved of two Coolidge-Hoover policies: the extension of loans abroad and reductions in personal income tax rates. He felt that if anything, U.S. terms on debt were still too stingy—imposing a burden on war-torn Europe and underdeveloped Latin America that might lead to default or depression. He thought economic conditions could be improved for everyone if the United States allowed a free flow of investment and growth abroad. That meant reasonable credit and trade policies and a dismantling of agricultural subsidies to domestic producers. Instead, the United States continued to squeeze debtors abroad for payment. Yet rising barriers to trade made it all the more difficult for foreign producers to sell goods to the United States. Seldom has a policy been more damaging to foreign and U.S. interests at the same time. As Cordell Hull, who was soon to become a close ally of Clayton's, fighting to undo the damage wrought by protective tariffs, said:

> American economic policy can no longer ignore the fact that since 1914 we have changed from a debtor and small surplus nation to the greatest creditor and, actual or potential, surplus-producing nation in the world.[21]

Throughout the 1920s, a Republican-controlled Congress tried to raise protective tariffs. The Emergency Tariff Act of 1921 (vetoed by Woodrow Wilson), and later the Fordney-McCumber Tariff Act of 1922, raised tariff levels to new highs—to an average ad valorem rate of more than 40 percent on dutiable imports from less than 30 percent under Woodrow Wilson.[22] A series of further tariff hikes passed the Congress from 1923 to 1928, but each time they were vetoed by President Coolidge. By 1929, the drift to higher rates was accelerating under the U.S. Tariff Commission, which had authority to shield particular industries that needed protection against foreign competitors. The panel raised the rate on twenty-eight out of thirty-three items considered. (President Hoover took no action to oppose these moves.)

Capping the whole campaign was the Smoot-Hawley Tariff Act, which Hoover signed in 1930 but whose impending passage may have caused the collapse of the stock market in October 1929. While the bill was being debated in Congress, Clayton wrote to his contacts, including Senator Morris Sheppard of Texas, appealing to them to vote against it. But it passed the Senate and House, with unexpected support from southern Democrats, who were bought off by the addition of agricultural items to the list of protected products. Clayton joined a number of prominent citizens who wrote to Hoover urging him to veto the bill but to no avail. The president signed the act, using six gold pens, sealing his own fate and the nation's. "All the evidences," Hoover said in 1930, "indicate that the worst effects of the crash upon unemployment will have been passed during the next sixty days."[23] He could hardly have made a worse prediction.

Considering what was at stake, Clayton's activity against the Smoot-Hawley Act and later his efforts to promote free trade as a core element in the Democratic economic program from 1930 to 1934 were limited and sporadic, hardly on the level of energy he had devoted to the fight for southern delivery. That he did not devote more energy and resources to the cause of antiprotectionism is puzzling. Clayton later admitted that he had made a great error: "I was so very wrong in that judgment" (that is, in failing to render greater assistance to Cordell Hull during the key years, 1929–1935).[24]

Perhaps the best explanation is that Clayton had a reading of the political situation that, though proven wrong by events, was plausible and widely shared. He told a friend that the Republicans were "not stupid enough" to listen to Hoover's "rot" and continue increasing the tariffs. Like many others, he found it hard to take seriously that Smoot-Hawley might actually become law; when the true situation became clear, it was too late.

Clayton had always viewed the Democratic party as the defender of free trade. Yet just as they seemed on the verge of power, the Democrats began backtracking. "I am disgusted," Clayton wrote to one friend, "with both Hoover and Smith [Alfred E. Smith, 1928 Democratic nominee for president]," on the tariff issue. By the time the Democrats did come to power, taking the Senate and nearly the House in the 1930 elections and the House and the White House in 1932, they had waffled on their historic free-trade stance.

When President Roosevelt appointed Clayton's now-close friend, Senator Cordell Hull, to be secretary of state, Clayton took it as a potentially great boost for trade liberalization. He began a campaign urging Chambers of Commerce throughout the South to pass resolutions calling for changes that would ease the burdensome international debt schedules, stabilize currencies, and promote free trade.

But Roosevelt also brought George Peek, a committed economic nationalist, into his administration, first to run the Agricultural Adjustment Administration, then (in 1934) to be his special adviser on trade. When Hull went to London to negotiate a sweeping reduction of trade barriers in 1933, Peek and other protectionists planted stories in the press that Hull's authority and influence with the president were limited. The Europeans began to doubt that FDR was committed to open and balanced international economic relations, and the conference failed.

The following year, Roosevelt won authority under the Reciprocal Trade Agreements Act to reduce trade barriers, but he already had that power under Smoot-Hawley and had not used it. In 1934 Clayton complained to Henry Wallace, "The Democratic Party, *except for a gesture*, has done nothing about the tariff." The Democrats, after being in power for eighteen months, had done almost nothing to support the principle of the "open door," as Hull called it. "The way to reduce the tariff," Clayton wrote impatiently to a fellow Democrat, "is to reduce it."[25]

By 1934, Clayton was convinced that Roosevelt's New Deal was embracing a nationalist, interventionist model, like Germany and Italy, and moving away from the classic liberal ideals of Jefferson, Bryan, and Wilson. Disgusted with both parties but especially bitter with a party he felt had "abandoned its principles," he wrote to a friend, "I am, like you, without a party. I could never vote for the old line Republicans, nor can I vote for the new line Democrats."[26]

❑ ❑ ❑

Clayton hardly was alone in finding himself a man without a party. Roosevelt's biographer, Arthur M. Schlesinger, Jr., writes:

> As conservatives lived on into 1934, they felt increasingly the need for an organization through which they could carry on their fight for American principles. The Republican party was too much identified with misrule and defeat. . . . [A] truly effective conservative organization required a broader base. It must as Dr. Henry Hatfield, Republican Senator from West Virginia, urged . . . "draw the friends of liberty and the Constitution from both parties."
>
> By the midsummer of 1934 their whispered discussions produced the decision to set up an organization to be called the American Liberty League. In essence, this was a group of conservative Democrats—Al Smith, Jouett Shouse, John J. Raskob, John W. Davis, Bainbridge Colby, the du Ponts—backed by a number of wealthy businessmen—Alfred P. Sloan and William S. Knudsen of General Motors, Ernest T. Weir, Will L. Clayton, the Texas cotton broker (though Clayton lasted only a few months), Edward F. Hutton and Colby M. Chester of General Foods, J. Howard Pew of Sun Oil, Sewell Avery of Montgomery Ward, and others.[27]

The Liberty League soon became a migraine to Roosevelt: Davis, Shouse, Hutton, and other leaders of the league roamed the country, generating headlines and enthusiasm from Roosevelt's critics, who by 1935 included Walter Lippmann, Dean Acheson, and H. L. Mencken. The *Washington Post*, the *Baltimore Sun*, and the

New York Times gave respectful news and editorial coverage to the league's initiatives, while demurring from some of its goals. The league's legal challenge to various New Deal programs helped produce a string of rulings from the Supreme Court declaring some of the programs unconstitutional.

In 1944, four years after the league had dissolved, Clayton explained to a congressional committee that his participation had lasted only a short time. His daughter later wrote that Clayton "joined the League because his old friend, John W. Davis, had asked him; he never attended a meeting. Later, because of certain League actions which he did not approve, he resigned."[28]

Clayton's involvement, however, lasted for at least two years, not "a few months," and was hardly casual. He kept thick files of materials from the league; clippings, letters, and telegrams covered by his marginal comments and notes fill several boxes. He was one of the first members to join the league's Executive Committee, replying within six days to a September 5, 1934, letter from Davis and explaining that he would have answered sooner but that he had been on vacation. He quickly contributed $5,000 and set about finding other donors. For several months, Clayton closed every letter he sent out of Anderson-Clayton with a postscript urging donations or enclosing a Liberty League pamphlet, sometimes both. In November 1934, when E. F. Hutton made a speaking tour through Arkansas, Texas, and the Southwest, Clayton convened the leading men of Houston to hear Hutton's pitch for the Liberty League's cause and coffers. Clayton also edited and helped draft papers for the league on the issue of international finance, at least into early 1936. His papers contain no resignation letter or any expression of strong disagreement with any of the league's published positions. When Sue Clayton announced in June 1936 that her husband had quit the league, the report made the front page of the *Houston Chronicle*, suggesting that this was fairly recent news.[29]

Clayton's involvement with the league was in large part an act of exasperation. "I am so disgusted with the present leadership of the Democratic Party," he wrote in 1935, "that I do not intend to have anything more to do with the Party until it returns to the Principles on which it was founded." But between 1934 and 1936, several important trends began to mature that ultimately softened Clayton toward the party and toward FDR personally.

Perhaps Clayton saw hopeful signs that the Democrats' principles were staging a comeback. In the spring of 1935, Cordell Hull negotiated a trade treaty with Belgium and Luxembourg reducing duties by 25 percent to 50 percent on dozens of U.S. imports from those countries. Admittedly, these were hardly America's largest trading partners, but the pact was a breakthrough and gave the free traders cause for hope.

Moreover, Clayton's views were changing or at least mellowing. He remained a firm opponent of government intervention in the marketplace. He recognized, though, that some people—like his father—do fail in the marketplace or have their jobs replaced by new technology. For these people, he felt, FDR's New Deal programs had been a blessing. Thus, in his 1936 Harvard speech, Clayton called for assistance to those displaced by the dynamics of growth.

Sue, a fervent New Dealer, influenced her husband's thinking and kept open his ties to the Roosevelt Democrats. Returning home from her trip to the 1936 Democratic Convention in Philadelphia, where she had been an alternate delegate for Roosevelt, she stopped off at the White House to pay her respects to the man the Liberty League was denouncing so vociferously. The papers reported that Sue Clayton was one of FDR's largest financial contributors; she made sure, she told the press, to give as much to Roosevelt as her husband had given to the Liberty League. A fellow Texan, Jesse H. Jones, involved Clayton as much as possible with FDR charities such as the March of Dimes, thereby bringing him closer to the gravitational pull of FDR's charm. If Clayton was less susceptible to FDR's blandishments than most men, he was not perfectly immune.

Another person who unwittingly helped mellow Clayton's views about Roosevelt and the New Deal was the 1936 Republican candidate, Alf Landon. The clincher for Clayton was Landon's September 26 speech in Minneapolis, where he blasted Cordell Hull's free-trade efforts and praised George Peek and the coterie of protectionists and economic interventionists. "I have been persuaded by the tenor of Governor Landon's recent speeches to vote for President Roosevelt," Clayton told the press on October 11. "The policy of the reciprocal trade agreements, inaugurated by the present administration, is at least a step forward. . . . Governor Landon condemns this policy and promises to scrap it. His position is an expression of such narrow, unenlightened . . . . provincialism that I am convinced that his leadership would not differ from that which his party inflicted on this country [in] 1920–32." A few days later, explaining his endorsement of Roosevelt's reelection to one of many troubled friends, Clayton used even stronger language, calling Smoot-Hawley "the greatest crime of the century" and noting that Hoover "could have prevented it. . . . The more I thought about it the less stomach I had for Landon and Hoover and their reactionary associates."[30]

By this indirect, lesser-of-two-evils process, Will Clayton reconnected himself to Franklin D. Roosevelt and qualified himself politically for appointment to an important government post in 1940.

5

Waging the Warehouse Wars

WELL BEFORE THE JAPANESE ATTACK OF DECEMBER 7, 1941, MOST informed observers knew that the United States would eventually enter the war on the side of Britain. Yet politicians, even the generally internationalist Wendell L. Willkie, waffled or flip-flopped when concrete aid was proposed. When the U.S. ambassador to Britain warned in the summer of 1940 that a victorious Hitler would turn his sights on the United States, a Republican senator called his remarks "little short of treason."[1] As many magazine editors urged aid to the embattled Finns (fighting against the Russians) as to Britain or France. Polls as late as November 1941 showed a sizable majority of voters favored keeping out of the war. In the end, it was an enlightened leadership that helped the American people realize that their own highest principles justified waging war against democracy's enemies.

Will Clayton and a group of prominent private citizens played a small but important part in the effort to shape policy and reshape public opinion. Like Roosevelt, they saw the logic and necessity of U.S. aid to Britain and the Allies. Indeed, the need to prepare the nation for war was one of the principal reasons Clayton supported FDR again in 1940.

In the early stages there was wide skepticism that the American public could ever be turned from its historically isolationist ways. Clayton did not share that skepticism, given his deep and abiding faith in democracy and in the American people. He saw them as being in general wise and generous in their collective judgments, if only they are "given the facts" by those they entrust to represent them.

That spring, as Hitler's armies poised to strike Sweden, Norway, Denmark, and France, Clayton joined a group of prominent Americans in New York to urge immediate U.S. aid to Britain. The group included investment magnate E. F. Hutton, writer Herbert Agar, James B. Conant of Harvard, Henry Luce, publisher of *Time*, Kansas newspaper editor William Allen White, and Dean Acheson, an attorney and former FDR aide. They issued a joint statement calling for the United States to lease destroyers and other military equipment to Britain. Then they began a campaign to persuade other leaders that aid to Britain was urgently needed. Clayton personally wrote to dozens of business leaders and raised thousands of dollars for the Red Cross, the Allied Relief Fund, the Friends of France, and other private relief efforts.[2]

This campaign was hardly the first such effort. Inside the administration, Harry Dexter White, Treasury Secretary Henry Morgenthau's right hand, had been an advocate of U.S. aid as early as 1938, vigorously so in 1939.[3] In speeches since the mid-1930s, Henry Luce had made repeated pleas for U.S. aid to usher in what he later called the "American Century."[4] Nonetheless, the efforts of Clayton and his associates in 1940 were vital in shaping public opinion.

By the summer of 1940, White's Committee to Defend America by Aiding the Allies boasted six hundred chapters and had attracted endorsements from newspaper editors across the country.[5] Petitions urging aid to England poured into the White House. Hoping to embolden President Roosevelt to act quickly, Acheson and three well-known lawyers sent a letter to the *New York Times* arguing that the president could legally sell, lease, or give material to Britain without prior congressional approval. Perhaps Clayton's biggest contribution was a visit he paid General John J. Pershing. The former commander of U.S. forces in World War I, Pershing was now old and infirm but venerated and influential. Clayton urged him to openly endorse aid to England, as did Herbert Agar on a second visit. When Pershing eventually agreed to break his silence, his plea for action became front-page news across the country, and historians regard it as a turning point in the battle to enlist public opinion on England's side.[6]

President Roosevelt, despite his sometimes coy, sometimes angry denials, was already inclined to do what those appeals requested. The outpouring of support from leading men of business, the military, and foreign affairs certainly helped broaden support for FDR's predisposition. As historian James MacGregor Burns observes, these prominent citizens had "stepped in at the critical moment," giving Roosevelt the confidence to assist Britain despite the lack of support in Congress. (After repeated efforts to convince leading Republicans to support an aid bill, Roosevelt secretly negotiated a deal with Churchill and announced it as an executive act, on legal authority that could be debated either way, but with a political and moral force deriving from the efforts of White, Acheson, Pershing, Clayton, and others.) "The idea of bypassing Congress on the matter was not new to Roosevelt," Burns writes, "but this kind of authoritative support could help immeasurably to prepare public opinion for a presidential act."[7]

The war brought Clayton to Washington, like many others, in a double sense. First, the specter in Europe converted him from a reluctant Roosevelt ally to an enthusiastic supporter.[8] The world as he saw it now faced a stark choice between democracy and Hitler's fascist imperialism. Although he certainly pinned primary blame for the war on Hitler's aggressions (aided by the short-lived Non-Aggression Pact with Stalin), Clayton reminded audiences that our own shortsighted squeeze of domestic and foreign debtors in the 1930s had helped create the economic conditions in which Hitler and the other despots took root.[9] "Instead of denouncing the dictators," he told one group, "we in this country might do better to examine carefully our own postwar [1918] policies to see if we ourselves may not have some responsibility for the resulting world disorder."[10]

Second, Roosevelt was seeking a controversial third term and was keen to begin U.S. aid to the Allies. To do this, he realized, he needed to broaden his political base. FDR also knew that if the United States entered the war, the key to mobilizing production would involve his ability to lure top business leaders and administrators to Washington. Will Clayton, who had served on the War Industries Board in 1918, was potentially one of those leaders.

One imperative that emerged in 1940 was to bring aid not only to the Europeans but also to Latin American countries suddenly cut off from their normal European markets. Roosevelt feared that the Latins, in desperation, might be tempted to sell critical supplies to Germany. In addition to sheer market pressure, an effective international Nazi propaganda machine was generating support in many Latin countries, especially Argentina and Brazil, for an economic alliance with Berlin. German radio broadcasts beamed at Central and South America heralded fascism as the new wave and buttressed the claims of Latin American strongmen that such a wave would reverse the continent's role as weak sister to the Yanqui North. Roosevelt's "good neighbor policy" had ameliorated some of Latin America's traditional hostility, but the memory of repeated U.S. military interventions was still fresh, as was that of Yankee bankers declaring Latin nations in default.

If the Western Hemisphere were not to be divided against itself, a vast U.S. initiative, involving economic aid and sophisticated diplomacy, would be essential.[11] The usual interagency feud arose about who should direct the effort, with the Commerce, Treasury, State, and Agriculture departments all staking a claim. Accordingly, in June 1940, Roosevelt asked his special assistant James Forrestal (a top executive at Dillon-Read recently brought into FDR's inner circle by Harry Hopkins) to arbitrate the dispute and come up with a plan of action.[12]

Forrestal met with FDR later that summer, proposing the creation of a new office, the coordinator of inter-American affairs, to work out of the State Department but in close cooperation with the others. His list of ten candidates who could handle the job included Ferdinand Eberstadt, a former investment banker, and Nelson A. Rockefeller, but his first choice was Will Clayton because he combined general business acumen with extensive dealings in Latin America.

Roosevelt liked the idea of naming a coordinator, but he frowned at choosing Clayton. "We can't have him," he said. "He contributed to the Republican campaign fund in 1940!" (Clayton was rumored to have given $25,000 to Wendell Willkie.)

After objecting to Eberstadt as well, Roosevelt warmed to Rockefeller's name. Forrestal responded somewhat implausibly that Rockefeller wouldn't be able to handle the job, but FDR held firm. Forrestal persisted, pressing FDR to at least name Clayton deputy, where he could in effect run the operation. Clayton, he said, was not the sort of man to stand on ceremony and ribbons: "He'll do the job even without the title." "All right," Roosevelt grinned, "Clayton can be deputy, because Mrs. Clayton contributed $10,000 to my campaign."[13]

Clayton had not actually contributed to Willkie's campaign. In 1940 he energetically supported Roosevelt. Even earlier, from 1936 to 1940, he sought to mend his ties with the Democratic party. His speeches blamed the "Republican tariff" and tight-money policies for depression and war. In 1939, Clayton joined Henry A. Wallace's agricultural advisory committee. Clayton's decision produced a flood of letters from friends distressed to see his increasing ties and cooperation with Roosevelt. Because Clayton had turned down similar offers from Democrats and Republicans over the years, he would not have accepted Wallace's offer lightly. His acceptance, therefore, reflected a degree of interest in enlisting himself on FDR's side.[14]

Similarly, in 1939 and 1940, Clayton served as state chairman for the President's Birthday Ball, an event held each January 30 to honor FDR and to raise money for the fight against infantile paralysis, the disease that had crippled him. The dinner was a favorite FDR charity; acting as one of its organizers would be a well-publicized political statement.

Texas was the home of many Democrats who, like Clayton, found many of Roosevelt's policies radical and imprudent. Unlike Clayton, many of them still opposed FDR and in 1944 would wage a serious fight to prevent his seeking a fourth term. These "Texas Regulars" were already at work in 1940, raising behind-the-scenes objections to the Birthday Ball as an unwholesome mixing of politics and charity. (This was a dubious claim in light of the fact that many leading Republicans, including national committeeman R. B. Creager, were cooperating wholeheartedly.) Clayton made the widespread complaints public two weeks before the event, but the report in the *Houston Chronicle* named no names—yet.[15]

The anti-Roosevelt Democrats got the message: stop grousing or the next story may embarrass you by name. The 1940 Birthday Ball was a bipartisan success, with Democrats and Republicans alike contributing generously. Clayton's handling of the rebel Democrats illustrates that, even before he took a post in Washington, he had developed solid political skills, including judicious use of the press.

Clayton's activism and acumen were not lost on FDR or his top advisers. Roosevelt was already anxious about the South and about Texas in particular, where a major defection could spoil his hopes for an historic third term. Moreover, the president recognized the need to build at least some support in the U.S. business community he had generally disparaged during his first seven years in office.

Hence, FDR's inaccurate assertion that Clayton had supported

Willkie is a bit of a mystery. Perhaps the president had received misinformation. More likely, he expressed misgivings about Clayton to see how Forrestal would react. Roosevelt later enjoyed telling intimates that Clayton won his position as deputy only because of Sue's hefty contribution to FDR's reelection.

Clayton, however, was not interested in serving as ghost coordinator for the long term, despite his cordial relationship with Rockefeller. So he offered to serve temporarily, until Rockefeller could get organized, find capable personnel, and draft initial policy papers. Brief though it was, from August to October 1940, Clayton's service was important. His recommendations for "hemispheric economic policy," which FDR requested in his June 15 memorandum, relied heavily on the benefits that would flow from unhampered free trade. "There must be no waving of the big stick," Clayton said in a speech at Waco, Texas, that preceded but anticipated his service in Washington. "We must play the commercial game fairly."

He recognized, moreover, that mere free trade would not be enough—a foreshadowing of his linkage of trade liberalization to monetary stability and U.S. aid for Europe after the war. Many Latin American countries were still technically in default from the heavy loans pushed on them during the 1920s, before the deflation of 1928–1938 and the Smoot-Hawley tariff ruined debtors around the globe. To restore themselves to solvency, they would need credits, assistance, and debt forgiveness. Accordingly, Clayton recommended extending direct aid to Latin America, suggested that a portion of U.S. transportation facilities be set aside for Latin American commerce, argued for using the Inter-American Development Commission to stimulate free trade and increased commerce within the region, and proposed tripling the Export-Import Bank's lending authority, to $700 million from $200 million.

Above all, to ensure that Latin America did not supply raw materials to the Nazis, he called for the creation of a preclusive buying program. This meant buying and stockpiling anything whose unavailability would create problems for Hitler's military machine. The proper instrument for operating this program, Clayton said, was the Reconstruction Finance Corporation, headed by Jesse H. Jones.

Clayton also realized that the United States would want to absorb all the raw materials for war production it could, even though it would hardly be in a position to export massive amounts of capital or consumer goods to Latin America until the war was over. Thus, the United States would run a large trade deficit with Latin America so that Latin Americans holding dollars or debt instruments could buy goods after the war.

Hence Clayton stressed the importance of returning, even during the war, to something resembling the normal arrangements for settling international accounts, that is, a system of currencies fixed against one another and against gold or some other anchor. This would ensure the Latin American nations that the dollars they held today would retain roughly the same value in the years to come.

At the very least, Clayton noted, some sort of settlement arrangements would have to be negotiated. Latin America had already been burned once in the century by a combination of broken promises from U.S. politicians and tight-fisted loan collection by U.S. bankers. Someone would have to rebuild the broken trust.[16] President Roosevelt endorsed most of Clayton's recommendations, which paralleled suggestions made by Leo Pasvolsky, Cordell Hull's chief adviser in the State Department on postwar economic policy.

❏ ❏ ❏

That Clayton did not consider his post under Rockefeller a long-term arrangement is clear from the fact that while he was serving as deputy coordinator, he did not resign as chairman of Anderson-Clayton Company. In early October, after seven weeks in Washington, he wrote appreciative good-bye notes to a number of friends and prepared to return to Houston.

Clayton barely had reached Houston when Jesse Jones phoned him from Washington, asking him to come back to work for the Reconstruction Finance Corporation (RFC). He declined, probably giving as one of his reasons that his wife, who was not in the best of health, did not wish to move again. Not to be denied the services of the man he needed, Jones prevailed on President Roosevelt to call Clayton directly, telling him that the president personally wanted him to run most of the raw material purchasing corporations within the RFC. Clayton declined again, but when he told his wife about the call, she told him, "If the president asks you to take a position to serve your country, you cannot refuse him." At this point, Sue may have phoned the president to announce Will's availability. In any event, FDR called again and Clayton agreed to serve, becoming deputy loan administrator of the RFC. Expecting that his new post would not be temporary, he resigned as chairman of ACCO, thus marking the end of his active business career.[17] (Six months later, happily engrossed in Washington, Clayton wrote to Lamar Fleming, Jr., ACCO's president, "I definitely do not want to contemplate going back to active direction of the business. The possibilities are that even when this war is over there will still be work which I feel I should continue to do.")

Jones and Clayton quickly consolidated their hold on the important business of preclusive buying. Price being no object, their goal was to purchase important minerals and raw materials before the Germans or Japanese could secure them. Clayton became the head of several new additions to the menagerie of RFC subsidiaries: president of the War Damage Corporation; chairman of the Defense Supplies Corporation, the Defense Metals Corporation, the Airlines Credit Corporation, the Rubber Development Corporation, and the U.S. Commercial Company; and vice president and trustee of the Export-Import Bank. These agencies focused mainly on foreign procurement both to meet U.S. needs and to block German and Japanese acquisitions, which meant that he was the de facto head of the critical war supply and economic sanctions program from 1941 until late 1943. Clayton thus became the chief operational commander of what might be called the "warehouse war," the supply counterpart to what Winston Churchill called the "wizard war," the critical Allied effort to gain superiority in high-tech communications and weaponry.

Today it seems obvious that the United States would eventually marshal its economic strength. Paul H. Nitze, however, who played a role in the warehouse war, recalls his outlook in the spring of 1940:

> On the morning of April 9, 1940, German troops crossed the Danish border and launched the lightning assault that in a matter of weeks crushed the resistance of the Low Countries, drove what remained of Britain's expeditionary army off the continent of Europe, and forced the surrender of France. France and Poland were gone, Stalin was Hitler's ally, and the British army was severely crippled. Thoroughly shaken by these developments, I did not see how Hitler could be defeated.
>
> While brooding over these developments, I walked into the office of my boss, Clarence Dillon, and asked him what hope he saw for the future. He said, "Paul, you are overly discouraged. The situation is extremely dangerous but not hopeless. Let us analyze it together. In this war, modern technology, as exemplified in the tank and the airplane, is of enormous importance. In the long run, Detroit can outproduce the Ruhr."[18]

But could it? In particular, would U.S. industry have access to the raw materials it needed to fulfill government defense contracts? That was the challenge Clayton faced in the warehouse war.

"Sanctions rarely work," writes historian Paul Johnson. Eugene V. Rostow, a veteran analyst of foreign affairs, calls sanctions "a fraud and a delusion . . . they didn't work against Napoleon. They didn't work against Hitler. They didn't work against the Kaiser."[19]

But U.S. economic warfare against Germany and Japan achieved important results. Its most ambitious purpose was to deny certain key supplies to the enemy. Shortages of particular metals and other commodities led to important enemy weapons shortages and to forced changes in weapons design that put them at a substantial disadvantage.

A related purpose, where outright denial could not be achieved, was to drive up the cost of procurement for the enemy. Rising costs cut both ways, but the United States was in a much better position to absorb such shocks: gross national product grew to $211 billion in 1944 from $90 billion in 1939, and military production surged even faster. Germany and Japan struggled just to maintain sagging production at constant levels after 1941. A shortage of almost any product, as Dean Acheson noted shrewdly, would tend to "run up the price *to the benefit of our larger purse.*"[20]

The United States also sought to ensure its access to commodities and goods needed for war production, not only oil, rubber, steel, and aluminum but special alloys and fuels. The effort also aimed at providing Latin America with a market that would serve as an alternative to what might otherwise have been a growing trade with Hitler-dominated Europe. Thus it would prevent U.S. economic isolation in our own hemisphere. Here, perhaps, Clayton and the warehouse warriors accomplished their most complete success, with the Allied armies achieving a smooth dependability of logistics and supply seldom paralleled in the history of warfare.

Finally, the warehouse war had an important political objective. It harassed the Germans and the Japanese into more overt acts against the United States while preparing the public and the business community for the idea of war.

The United States, for instance, was especially eager to keep wolfram out of German hands. This dark brown mineral with tungstic acid had the highest melting point of any metal at the time. No substitute was acceptable in making armor plating or for tungsten carbide and fire heads on armor-piercing projectiles. Clayton quickly set about buying up all known supplies, most of them in South America. By the time of Pearl Harbor, he had driven Germany almost totally out of the Latin American market for wolfram, tungsten, and other key minerals. "We are buying and will continue to buy," Jones reported to Roosevelt early in 1942, virtually "every exportable commodity in Latin America."[21]

That still left the much smaller Spanish and Portugese supplies, some of which trickled into Nazi hands in 1942. Between Clayton's joint purchases with the British, however, and Dean Acheson's mounting campaign to pressure the European neutrals into withholding supplies from Hitler, wolfram continued to dry up, with prices soaring from a few hundred dollars a ton in the 1930s to a peak of $35,000 a ton during the war. The United States and Britain stripped the Iberian Peninsula, paying approximately $175 million dollars for most of the remaining 10,000 tons of wolfram. The neutral Portugese insisted on honoring their contracts with the Germans, but U.S. officials paid them to engage in "disruptive delays" in delivery.

"Before the end of 1943," journalist Bascom Timmons records, "victory was in sight in the fight for wolfram."[22] One of the many consequences of the wolfram effort Clayton helped lead was that it enabled the army to follow through on plans to improve the design of U.S. tanks, many of which failed to stand up to even small German artillery in early battles in North Africa. By contrast, the much improved tanks in the campaigns for Italy and France were an important component of American victory.

Wolfram and the more than two hundred commodities Clayton bought at USCC were key components in many critical battles. The war was shortened, and lives saved, by a timely provision of gasoline to U.S. tank commanders and by choking off strategic minerals to the Germans and Japanese. From this perspective, the "battle of wolfram" emerges alongside Sicily, Omaha Beach, and the Ardennes offensive as a critical Allied victory.

The Germans and the Japanese were not Clayton's only enemies in the warehouse war. He often had to overcome internal resistance, even hostility. Powerful men of industry, and others inside

Roosevelt's administration, fought tireless bureaucratic wars because they thought Clayton's approach was wrong or because they wanted to run things themselves.

Early in the war, for example, Jones and Clayton established a subsidiary to stockpile rubber, a critical raw material. They anticipated that with the cutoff of sources in Asia, rubber would have to be obtained from South America. This would entail a vast increase in rubber farming, which had largely died out by the 1930s. Just as a hedge, though, they launched a crash effort to complete a series of U.S. plants to produce synthetic rubber. Thus the United States would have a backup source if rubber farming could not be expanded fast enough.

At Clayton's suggestion, Jesse Jones asked Bernard M. Baruch to prepare a special report on the potential for synthetic rubber production. Baruch's report—littered with gratuitous digs against Jones and Clayton (though not mentioning them by name)—ridiculed the synthetic rubber program, citing opinions of scientists and businessmen that it could not succeed, would be unreasonably expensive, and would take years before any benefits would show.

FDR too was skeptical, but Clayton and Jones continued the effort. Late in 1942, acknowledging some of Baruch's criticisms of the program's management, Clayton suggested appointing William Jeffers for what became an eleven-month stint as rubber director. Jeffers was one of the few railroad men Clayton had come to respect in his long battle for an economical line of transit for cotton, which had been impeded by the foot-dragging of many railroad executives over their government-protected rates. If anyone could make the program a success, Clayton argued, Jeffers could.

With Jeffers at the helm, and the subsequent work of the Rubber Reserve Corporation, the quest for synthetic rubber was a success. On June 11, 1943, Jones spoke at Institute, West Virginia, to celebrate the opening of the first plant. He was able to note, wryly, "The Rubber Survey Committee [headed by Baruch] stated in its report in September, 1942, that, normally, to develop an industry as large as this would require a dozen years, and to compress it in less than two years would be an almost super-human task. I am glad to say that the task has been accomplished in less than two years." By the end of the war, 87 percent of the rubber being consumed in the United States was synthetic, nearly all of it from the government's plants.[23] Most of the remaining supply came from national rubber drives, an early recycling effort that Clayton also organized.

Clayton's purchasing agents crisscrossed the country and the globe in search of raw materials. The key prerequisites for a job with Clayton's warehouse warriors were audacity, resourcefulness, audacity, competence, and audacity. His payroll included a ballet dancer who knew business leaders in a number of European and Latin American capitals, a former smelting plant worker from the Southwest, and an Eastern European refugee familiar with the forced-labor mines of Poland and Czechoslovakia.

There was, as far as Clayton was concerned, much of the romance and high drama one would find in such enterprises as Wild Bill Donovan's Office of Strategic Services. When a request for a mineral or commodity came in, out went agents from one of the mindnumbing list of agencies Clayton directed : USCC, the DSC, the DPC, the MRC, the RRC, and more than a dozen other RFC and Commerce subsidiaries.

"We need zinc," the Pentagon said, for the production of cartridge brass, so off to Australia, Argentina, Bolivia, Canada, and Mexico went Clayton's buyers. The supplies of zinc abroad, though, proved insufficient. So, loath though they were to adopt the concept in general, Clayton and Jones established a domestic subsidy program to stimulate U.S. production. The marketplace, they felt, would have come through eventually, but the country needed zinc now. Clayton ordered mines reopened and smelters refitted in Oklahoma, Kansas, and Missouri, and the military obtained its zinc.

Sometimes Clayton stockpiled items that the Pentagon did not want but might later. As early as the summer of 1940, for example, he voiced concern about the need for high-octane gasoline for airplanes. Dr. R. E. Wilson, a friend of his and president of the Pan American Petroleum and Export Company, wrote to him about the problem. Clayton told Jones that, according to Wilson, the maximum U.S. capacity for producing 100-octane gasoline was only 30,000 barrels a year. This meager amount wouldn't even cover the fuel needed for training pilots if the United States were serious about FDR's proposal to expand aviation production to fifty thousand planes a year.

The armed services, however, responded lukewarmly. Jones persevered, setting up the Defense Supplies Corporation in a few days, with Clayton as chairman, and subsidizing all the high-octane gas production one could reasonably finance. Within months, the military was back, practically begging Clayton for the fuel just beginning to flow out of the refineries. The Pentagon went on to buy more than 13 billion gallons during the war. The demand was so high that 100-octane fuel was never stockpiled during the war. Instead it went straight from the refineries to U.S. and British air bases and carriers.

Memos marked "urgent" poured over Clayton's desk daily. Requests for pig bristles, silk, scrap metal, burlap, manganese, Russian sheep casings, goatskins, shark livers, horsemane hair, 1.5 million ounces of quinine, and hundreds of other goods were almost always met. Many of the items sound exotic, but often they were part of an important manufacturing process or overseas swap that might alter the course of future battles, liberate countries, or save lives.

A 1944 request for a gasoline shipment to Spain, which looked commonplace enough, competed with requisitions from U.S. generals in Europe. But the background was that Generalissimo Francisco Franco, after years of cajoling, had finally relented to U.S. pressure to place a total embargo on key minerals to Hitler. Franco's tanks were sitting petrol-dry in the field, and the fuel was his price for cooperation. Clayton got the gas, and Dean Acheson used it to widen the wedge between Franco and Hitler.[24]

In most theaters of action, the warehouse warriors partially succeeded, sometimes stunningly. The scramble to win supplies and exclude the enemy was most effective in Latin America and was least effective with the European neutrals (Portugal, Spain, Sweden, and Switzerland), who were historically linked to the Germans as major trading partners and anxious to avoid a Nazi invasion and occupation. As the war went on, the neutrals grew increasingly inclined to throw their lot in with the Allies. Hence, to some degree, the political progress with the European neutrals, orchestrated primarily by Acheson at the State Department and Clayton in his various roles, was a consequence of victory as well as a partial cause.[25]

Of all their objectives, however, Clayton and the warehouse warriors succeeded most clearly in their role as gadflies, luring democracy's enemies into serious strategic errors and hastening U.S. entry into the war. Captured records of the Japanese war councils show that it was America's denial of oil and other key commodities—a reaction to Japanese aggression in the Pacific— that prompted Tokyo's desperate attack on Pearl Harbor. According to Clayton, this was a deliberate, premeditated aspect of U.S. policy. By August 1941, he recalled in a 1957 interview, "I was buying . . . all sorts of stuff from the Philippines, Malay Straits, Dutch East Indies, Australia, North Caledonia. . . . We were sure to find ourselves at war with Japan any time and we had to get all this material in before."[26]

W. N. Medlicott, author of the definitive history of the Allied economic blockade, connects the warehouse war with perhaps Hitler's greatest mistake. "The fear of the consequences of the blockade played a part in drawing Germany into the Russian adventure which ultimately proved so disastrous. . . . By the summer of 1944, the German economy was on the verge of decline both absolutely and relative to mounting Allied output. 'Economic warfare' measures fulfilled their purpose, if we take this to be the weakening of the enemy's production for war purposes."[27]

So much has been written about the infighting and backstabbing that accompanied the warehouse war—the "war within the war," as Jones's biographer, Bascom Timmons, called it—that the vast achievements of the people involved have sometimes been obscured. In Washington, *some* level of friction is inevitable; under FDR, a *high* level of friction was more than inevitable—it was a conscious method of statecraft. This fact magnifies, rather than diminishes, the glory of men like Clayton, Jones, Acheson, and Rockefeller. They not only produced but were able to do so amid the omnipresent Roosevelt web of competing agencies, overlapping responsibilities, and obscure lines of authority that were usually changing.

Jesse H. Jones and Vice President Henry A. Wallace, a competing tsar in the procurement process, despised each other. To the extent that the warehouse war achieved anything, much of the credit should go to Clayton and Acheson, whose politesse kept Jones and Wallace on speaking (or at least shouting) terms.

This bureaucratic war within the war was no trivial affair. By the end of World War II, the battle between Jones and Wallace had cost Jones his job in the cabinet in 1945 or, at least, was the proximate cause of his removal. Partly as a result of the same fallout, Wallace was not renominated for vice president in 1944. Hence he lost the presidency itself when FDR died in 1945.

The war within the war is even harder to understand when one considers the timing, the stakes, and the result. By the time Jones and Wallace degenerated into public name-calling and accusation late in 1943, each one trying to secure exclusive control of the stockpiling program, much of the economic battle had already been fought, and there were far more important questions. For example, there was the shape of the emerging Bretton Woods agreement and, with it, the whole postwar international economic order.

Precisely because many vital questions remained to be debated and decided, though, the clash of Jones and Wallace is an important story in its own right. Clayton—long a friend of both men and the man who normally met with Wallace because Jones did not want to be in the same room with him—was at the center.

When the Jones-Wallace battle was over in 1945, Clayton could give the same reply that Abbe Sieyes gave when asked what he had done during the French Reign of Terror: "I survived." One reason for Clayton's survival was that he gave priority to serving his country over any desire for personal power or future posts in the political hierarchy. His attitude was aptly expressed in a 1943 letter he wrote to a friend:

> No doubt the war will end someday, but the battle of Washington, never. As you know, I came without any political ambitions and having acquired none during my three years stay, I can look these fellows in the eye and tell them where to go.[28]

William Lockhart Clayton,
age twenty, 1900.
(*Courtesy Hoover Institution Archives*)

Martha Fletcher Burdine Clayton
and James Monroe Clayton,
Will Clayton's parents.
(*Courtesy Ellen Clayton Garwood*)

Will Clayton and daughter Ellen,
age two, Oklahoma City, 1905.
(*Courtesy Ellen Clayton Garwood*)

Third annual picnic of Anderson, Clayton, and Company, May 12, 1923. (*Courtesy Ellen Clayton Garwood*)

Arthur R. Marsh, former president of the New York Cotton Exchange (left), Senator Elliston D. ("Cotton Ed") Smith of South Carolina (center), and Will Clayton in the Senate Building, March 29, 1929. Marsh and Smith bitterly opposed Clayton's efforts to end the New York squeeze on cotton futures by allowing southern delivery. (*UPI/Bettmann*)

TIME
The Weekly Newsmagazine

Volume XXVIII

COTTON'S CLAYTON
"A harsh method, perhaps, but the only one...."
(See BUSINESS)

Number 7

Will Clayton (left) and Representative Marvin Jones of Texas, chairman of the House Agriculture Committee (right), took part in a conference called July 13, 1939, by Secretary of Agriculture Henry A. Wallace (center) to discuss means of increasing exports of American cotton. (*UPI/Bettmann*)

Supreme Court justice Stanley Reed (left) administers oaths of office to Under Secretary of State Joseph C. Grew (second from left) and four new assistant secretaries (beginning at Grew's left), Will Clayton, Archibald MacLeish, Nelson Rockefeller, and James Dunn, December 20, 1944. (*UPI/Bettmann*)

Will Clayton arrives for Potsdam Conference, July 24, 1945.
(*Courtesy Harry S. Truman Library*)

Will Clayton and his wife, Sue, on their way to Geneva, April 9, 1947.
(*Courtesy the National Archives*)

Will Clayton signing the International Trade Organization (ITO) Charter for the United States in Havana, 1948. Although the ITO was never ratified, most of its provisions were realized in the ongoing General Agreement on Tariffs and Trade process. (*Courtesy Harry S. Truman Library*)

Will Clayton (left) and John Foster Dulles appear before the Senate Foreign Relations Committee May 4, 1949, to urge ratification of the North Atlantic Treaty. (*UPI/Bettmann*)

Will Clayton receives farewells from reporters attending his final
news conference at the State Department. Clayton announced his
resignation with a strong plea for Congress and the American
people to help European recovery. October 18, 1947.
(*AP/Wide World Photos*)

esident John F. Kennedy (right) confers with former Secretary of State Christian Herter
nter) and Will Clayton in a series of conferences on foreign trade policy, December 1, 1961.
e Herter-Clayton report helped lay the foundation for the highly successful Kennedy
neral Agreement on Tariffs and Trade round of the 1960s. (*UPI/Bettmann*)

Former Secretary of State Dean Acheson (left) and Will Clayton appear before the House-Senate Joint Economic Subcommittee hearing on foreign trade policy. December 6, 1961. (*UPI/Bettmann*)

The War within the War

6

IN THE EARLY 1940S, WILL CLAYTON ACTED AS A COURIER, NEGOTI-
ator, and mediator between Jesse Jones and Henry Wallace, two of
Washington's most powerful men. They not only rank among Roosevelt's most remarkable intimates but are two of the least understood.

Even among his admirers, Henry Wallace is often viewed as a
Hamletlike figure, an impractical visionary, a quixote too pure for
political victory in a tainted world.[1] Yet Wallace was a successful
businessman whose idealism flowed from a conviction that certain
principles work, not an indifference to whether they work or not.

Born in Ames, Iowa, in 1888, Wallace by age sixteen was exper-
imenting on his own with plant and livestock genetics to improve
productivity. Through age forty, in fact, his energies were devoted
to studying farm problems. He published new data, highly useful
to farmers, for his family-owned newspaper, *Wallace's Farmer*, on
everything from the cost of breeding hogs to the tendency of ur-
banization to reduce family size. People in cities, he showed, have
fewer children, which led him to conclude that American farmers
must support a free-trade policy that would allow them to expand
into foreign markets. In 1926, Wallace founded a company to pro-

duce and sell hybrid corn. Four decades later, the higher yield from hybrid seed accounted for 25 percent of U.S. corn production.

Wallace's philosophy resembled Clayton's in many respects, especially in its passionate, almost spiritual faith in the progress possible in an open, democratic society. To Wallace, free people, armed with information and technology, could produce abundance and comfort for all. "Science," he wrote, "cannot be overproduced. It does not come under the law of diminishing utility."

But offsetting his undeniable intelligence and energy, Wallace was shy, abstruse, and introverted. "He has no small talk," as one intimate observed. These traits, plus his vague pantheism, made him seem eccentric to friends and downright odd to others.

Nonetheless, Roosevelt tapped Wallace for secretary of agriculture in 1933 (Wallace's father had held the same post from 1921 to 1924). Although he was associated with many of Roosevelt's most radical New Deal programs, which he carried out enthusiastically, Wallace expressed skepticism about their long-term practicality. The plowing under of surplus cotton and grain, he said, "were not acts of idealism in any sane society. They were emergency acts made necessary by the almost insane lack of world statesmanship from 1920 to 1932."

Wallace argued the onetime plowing under was the only way out of the emergency farmers faced in 1933. From then onward, he implemented policies that increasingly harmonized with his own ideas, and parts of them, such as the conservation and modernization provisions of the 1936 agriculture act, won approval from free enterprisers such as Clayton. "Wallace was an awkward figure in Washington," historian Arthur M. Schlesinger, Jr., wrote, "but talking agriculture, Wallace could be exceedingly crisp, hard-hitting, and impressive." Roosevelt recognized and respected Wallace's abilities. So, hoping to shore up support both regionally (in the Midwest) and ideologically (with his party's radical wing), he chose Wallace for his running mate in 1940 and won an unprecedented third term. When he became vice president in 1941, Wallace sought some field of policy he could call his own. It was unlikely that he would be given a major voice in the conduct of the war or foreign policy. But the economic aspects of the war—foreign procurement, supply management, the great arms buildup—differed. Here was a sphere limited and focused enough to be attainable, broad enough to excite his interest, and arguably well within his range of competence and experience. With this as his goal, it was inevitable that Wallace would clash with Jesse Jones, who already had staked a claim to leadership of the warehouse war.

Born in 1874 in Tennessee, Jesse Jones was the son of a moderately prosperous farmer.[2] When he was twenty-four, an uncle who had just hired him to help run his lumber empire in Houston died unexpectedly, naming Jones one of the heirs of his estate. Jones not only managed the business ably but, beginning in 1902, quickly parlayed his own assets—about $3,000—into one of the great fortunes of the Southwest. By the end of World War I, he owned or had built most of the Houston skyline, controlled major shares of many banks, was part owner of the *Houston Chronicle* (he later bought it and the *Houston Post*), and was a local and national political broker.

In 1924, Jones (after pleading unsuccessfully with Clayton to take the job) served as finance director for the campaign of John W. Davis, the Democratic presidential nominee. The campaign was doomed, but it brought Jones into contact with Clayton and another young Democrat whom Jones saw as a potential protege: Franklin D. Roosevelt. As the unhappy voting tabulations poured into Democratic headquarters on November 4, Roosevelt issued an apt prophecy: "On the basis of returns we have already received, I believe the party is defeated. But there are men in this room tonight who will live to see the Democratic party in power again."

Jones brashly convinced the Democratic National Committee to hold the party's 1928 convention in Houston. He sent his personal check for $200,000, along with a promise that Houston would build a huge arena; although he never had consulted the city about the plan, Jones was confident he could worry about that detail later.

In 1931, when two of Houston's largest banks were preparing to declare bankruptcy, he quickly convened the city's most successful businessmen—Will Clayton, Captain James A. Baker, S. M. McAshan, and Joseph Meyer—to buy and reorganize the banks. "After the all-night vigils, conferences, plans, counterplans, and objections," wrote attorney Frank Andrews, who participated in the meetings, "his plans were carried out without a single bank failure in this great city. . . . No depositor lost a cent or was denied his cash on demand."

Jones's success captured interest in Washington. In January 1932, President Herbert Hoover launched (with Democratic support in Congress) the Reconstruction Finance Corporation (RFC), which was to use its $500 million in capital and $3 billion in borrowing authority to shore up weak banks and businesses. Jones agreed to serve on the board. With his considerable energy, and as a leading Democrat in a period when a Republican president governed with a weak hand, Jones rapidly became the RFC's de facto chairman, doing on a national scale what he had done for Houston. By the end of 1932, banking failures, which had been running at $200 million a month in January, dropped to a rate of $10 million a month, thanks largely to the RFC. By November 1932, reopenings exceeded failures almost five months before FDR proclaimed a bank holiday in 1933.

"FDR closed the banks," went a popular saying that irked many New Dealers, "but Jesse Jones re-opened them." Roosevelt had originally planned to recraft the RFC, which as a joint creation of Congress and the executive enjoyed considerable independence. But the practical reasons for leaving the RFC intact were sizable and growing. Shortly after his inauguration in 1933, FDR named Jones what he already was in practice, chairman of the RFC, and Jones's twelve-year reign was under way. (Senator Robert A. Taft often referred to Jones as a "fourth branch of government.")

Every two years, when Jones's term as chairman expired, his political enemies—chiefly Wallace and Harold Ickes, the brilliant, cantankerous, and suspicious secretary of the interior—campaigned to have him replaced. Yet each time, FDR reappointed him, and after his own reelection in 1940, he named Jones to be secretary of commerce as well.[3] If Jones did not lust for power, he also did not give it up easily.

Although Clayton's official duties made him a close ally of Jones's, he was a personal friend of Wallace's too. At times he disagreed, sometimes heatedly, with both, infrequently with Jones, often with Wallace.

In a bitter dispute over whether Houston should buy a large tract of land for the expansion of its port facilities, Clayton did not side with Jones. Although several of Jones's friends never spoke to him again after this battle, Clayton and Jones agreed to disagree amicably. Conversely, after World War II, Jones led the fight against a U.S. loan to Great Britain, even though Clayton personally had negotiated it and regarded it as essential for European recovery. Jones's opposition could hardly have come at a more delicate time or have been more fervent. Yet Jones continued to promote Clayton for secretary of state, both in his public and private dealings with President Truman and in the inner circle of White House advisers.[4]

Clayton and Jones shared common friends and business contacts in Houston and were in fairly close agreement ideologically. Clayton and Wallace, by contrast, had less in common. Clayton nevertheless had a knack for putting Wallace at ease. He would start every meeting by urging Wallace to talk about his latest diet, his recent travels, or a favorite new book. James Stillwell, a Clayton aide who attended many of the sessions, remembered Clayton urging Wallace "to tell us his wheat bread story. Wallace had quit eating flour and was grinding his own. . . . We'd have to stop him

from talking, once he got wound up, in order to start the meeting."
If Clayton's approach sounds patronizing, it was not; he liked Wallace personally, commenting later, "Wallace was big: a crackpot in
some ways, but a generous fellow." Clayton never forgot the favor
Wallace had done him in 1936 when Clayton's old foe, Senator
Cotton Ed Smith, still bitter from the southern delivery battle,
proposed a bill that would severely limit hedging activities by merchants on the Cotton Exchange. Although nominally applicable to
all firms, its limits were designed to damage only one company:
Anderson-Clayton. "It would have put us out of business," Clayton
recalled. When the president seemed ready to support the bill,
Wallace told him that Smith had misled him about its implications
to advance a personal vendetta against Clayton. FDR withdrew his
support, and the bill languished in committee.[5]

Despite their mutual admiration, Wallace saw Clayton as a
quasi-reactionary. "In his Monday talk, the President indicated that
he meant his fourth term to be really progressive. He was going to
get rid of 'Jesus H.' Jones and Will Clayton," Wallace noted in his
diary on July 5, 1944.[6] Instead, a few weeks later, FDR dropped
Wallace from his reelection ticket and in December promoted Clayton to direct the U.S. postwar economic policy.

In 1939, not long after the Nazis invaded Poland, Roosevelt announced his intention to create a large cartel for dealing in Latin
America. Congressional critics, led by Senator William E. Borah,
balked. Clayton, worried about the scheme, helped Borah and
others work for its demise, even though he endorsed Roosevelt in
1940. The plan appeared stillborn, and FDR abandoned the project.[7]

At this point Jones called FDR's attention to the recommendation in the Pasvolsky and Clayton memorandums to triple the
lending capital of the Export-Import Bank. "Go ahead and see what
you can do," Roosevelt said, "but I think that in the present mood
of the Congress, you will fail." Jones took on the task, relishing the

opportunity to accomplish an objective in Congress that FDR had pronounced unachievable.

Borah attacked the Clayton proposal too, so Jones went to see him—armed with a list, prepared by Clayton's staff, of every recent Export-Import loan, not one of which was in default or delinquent. On the basis of that assurance, Borah supported the plan, which promptly passed both houses.

On June 28, 1940, Congress enacted another bill, this one consolidating Jones's domestic stockpiling power as head of the RFC. Within a year, Congress also approved an unusual resolution—opposed by the *New York Times*—allowing Jones to continue to serve as federal loan administrator while also becoming secretary of commerce. On June 25, 1941, FDR signed a bill giving Jones and Clayton nearly unlimited authority to buy, store, and supply strategic war commodities.

❏ ❏ ❏

Clayton's success on Capitol Hill in the 1940s was legendary and played an indirect role in the endgame of Wallace versus Jones. Allen Drury, United Press International's congressional correspondent at the time, observed in his diary that Clayton generally had both houses "eating out of his hand. . . . Will Clayton is a big, tall, well-built Texan in his 60s, with . . . a handsome, rather rugged face, and the smoothest manner imaginable," Drury noted.

Clayton's popularity was based in part on his reputation for giving straightforward answers. A member of Congress might not like what Clayton told him, but Clayton would not evade the issue with jargon. "Clayton, whatever his views may be, never hesitates to state them with complete frankness, and his replies seemed to suit [Senator Ed] Johnson even if the sentiments did not," Drury observed. Blessed with a remarkable memory, Clayton could call up statistics about foreign exchange rates or U.S. budget figures with astounding speed and accuracy. In addition, he knew shorthand and so took extensive notes on conversations and research findings. He could compress hundreds of facts and quotations onto a few dozen four-by-six notecards that he always carried and could maintain eye contact with a committee member while he searched for a verbatim quote from a memorandum or a recent meeting.

During testimony and private meetings, Clayton's calm, even voice sprinkled the air with words of deference and civility. He rarely grew angry; when he did, his voice grew lower, not louder.

Clayton seemed to take a professorial joy in explaining things. During his testimony on preclusive buying, the Bretton Woods agreement, and the Marshall Plan, members of Congress occasionally referred to him as "Dr. Clayton" or "Professor Clayton." Even during the often-heated debate over the disposition of surplus war property, Drury noted, Clayton "defended himself ably and very suavely, never lost his temper, and [yet] never really conceded an error." Clayton seldom wrote off or attacked a member even when he knew he was unlikely to win that member's vote. Clayton met with Senator Taft frequently in 1945, trying to win his support for the Bretton Woods agreement. Those meetings failed in their immediate object. The friendship and mutual trust that resulted proved vital, however, after the 1946 elections, when Taft became a member of the Republican majority in the Senate. Clayton and Acheson met with Taft, Arthur H. Vandenberg, and the other Republicans in December 1946 and were able to secure promises of swift action on trade and economic aid—pledges that proved vital to the success of the Truman Doctrine and the Marshall Plan in 1947.[8]

It is doubtful Congress would have entrusted any other members of Roosevelt's administration with such plenary powers as Jones and Clayton wielded during the warehouse war. "Just as Roosevelt had found the RFC an agency organized and ready to combat the Depression," Bascom Timmons observes, so in 1940 "it was the only one ready to build plants . . . to buy and sell equipment and material . . . and to pay subsidies where necessary to obtain the basic materials of war."[9] But these powers had to be exercised in the face of conflicting pressures from Henry Wallace, a powerful adversary.

FDR's reelection in 1940 at once strengthened his political hand and made him grateful to Wallace, his running mate, who immediately sought an important role in the war effort. The warehouse war was an interdepartmental affair and hence ripe for a claim of vice presidential oversight. Despite the comity between Jones, Hull, Acheson, and Clayton, the State Department in particular was resentful of Jones's and Clayton's new powers. So were the progressives, such as White and Morgenthau at Treasury, who, although willing to acquiesce in Clayton's management, would have preferred an ideological ally running the show. Coordinating cabinet departments and high officials could only be carried out by someone with the clout to obtain information, elicit opinions, act with dispatch, and, above all, secure the president's approval directly. These requirements argued for Wallace.

Even Clayton-Jones allies, such as Bernard Baruch, were complaining about problems in the vast supply train. If there were no major scandals, there were the inevitable miscues and overcharges that can be found in any hastily built, multibillion-dollar procurement operation.

Faced with the need for a clear-cut decision, FDR acted, as he often did in such situations, ambiguously. Whether out of guile, lassitude, or a prudent desire to stall one decision while others pressed more urgently, on July 30, 1941, Roosevelt issued an executive order creating the Economic Defense Board, soon rechristened the Board of Economic Warfare (BEW). Vice President Wallace became BEW chairman in December.[10]

Acheson later wrote, "At first sight, to seasoned bureaucratic infighters, it bore all the earmarks of futility and early demise . . . [a] paper tiger." Wallace, however, proving that he was no amateur in the power game, quickly turned his paper tiger into a real one. As deputy he chose Milo Perkins, whom Acheson described as "a fighter, imaginative, armed with funds so abundantly available to the war agencies." Within the year, the BEW had a staff of almost three thousand. Perkins peppered Clayton, Acheson, and others with memos, ideas, requests, and suggestions. "Some of them were good and we did them; most of them we didn't take too seriously because the BEW didn't have any real authority at first," Clayton later recalled. The growing staff, however, gave Wallace grounds to demand authority from FDR and generated a paper trail of BEW ideas that were ignored or turned down.[11]

Throughout the spring of 1942, Wallace criticized Jones and Clayton on the rubber question at BEW meetings, reporting to Roosevelt his worries that the program was stalled. In retrospect, Clayton and Jones were stockpiling as much natural rubber as could be found, and their plan for synthetic rubber was both plausible and eventually effective. At the time, though, a serious shortfall appeared possible.[12]

Hence on April 13, 1942, Roosevelt issued Executive Order 9128, withdrawing final oversight from Jones and Clayton and allowing Wallace to command whatever contracts and purchases the BEW wanted. Even this order failed to resolve the war within the war. For one thing, the BEW did not yet have its own purchasing authority from Congress. Statutory authority still resided with the RFC and its subsidiaries, which were now commanded to pay the BEW's bills. In addition to weakening Jones and Clayton, Roosevelt's order gave the BEW vast authority over such sacred State Department turf as "represent[ing] the United States Government in dealing with the economic warfare agencies" of Allied countries and in sending abroad "such technical, engineering, and economic representatives, responsible to the board, as the board may deem necessary."

But if the order (and the ensuing confusion) obligated Jones and Clayton to write checks for BEW projects, it did not take away their authority to write checks for themselves. Hence the phrase "preclusive buying" took on new meaning, with two agencies authorized to undertake nearly all the same activities. From April

1942 until the summer of 1943, the war within the war was at its
most intense pitch.

One frustrating and illustrative encounter came when Clayton
sent Douglas Allen, an experienced foreign trader, to South America to obtain natural rubber from the tropical jungles. At about the
same time, Wallace took an interest in the same mission. His diary
entry of June 3, 1942, reads:

> Caldwell King, president of Johnson and Johnson in Brazil, told
> the most fascinating story of a trip up the Amazon.
>
> It seems that the greatest supply of wild rubber trees is found
> in the state of Acre and the adjoining part of the state of Mato
> Grosso. . . . The health conditions in these areas are deplorable
> with about one third of the rubber workers dying within the year,
> another one third sick, and less than one third in sufficiently good
> health to work hard. The trouble comes from malaria, malnutri-
> tion, venereal disease, and bad water. . . . King thinks it will
> require about 40,000 workers or including the families about 200,000
> people to take out 20,000 tons of rubber annually. He says that at
> the present time there has been so much diversion of labor from
> customary farming occupations in the Amazon area that there is
> a great shortage of food.
>
> King . . . has been paying three times the going rate of wages
> and in addition furnishing a substantial noon meal. As a result,
> his workers have turned out five times as much per person as
> workers doing similar work elsewhere in Rio.[13]

Thus began one of dozens of Wallace brainstorms that created
a headache for Clayton. Wallace argued that a broad program to
provide for the health and dietary needs of the workers would give
the United States needed rubber supplies at or below the cost of
synthetic plants. The program would also open up and encourage
trade with Latin America, as well as offer an opportunity for social
improvement on an international scale. Wallace proposed that the
United States provide shipments of staple foodstuffs to improve the
region's diet, including vitamin-enriched flour; modest health and
education services might be provided as well. He also argued, as he

did with numerous other contracts, that the United States should insert a fair labor clause as a condition for contracting for the rubber, thus bringing the shield of U.S. labor protection laws to the Amazon Basin.[14]

To Clayton, introducing such conditions into the purchase of a small supply of rubber was quaintly do-goodish at best. At worst, it was uneconomical and a bureaucratic nightmare. Acheson agreed, adding that from the State Department's point of view, fair labor clauses, however well-intentioned, were an interference in the internal affairs of other nations. (Wallace supported the same idea in discussions about Bolivian tin, Chilean copper, and Nicaraguan and Guatemalan fruit.)

In the summer of 1942, Clayton met with Acheson, Wallace, and Perkins, hoping to dissuade Wallace. "He has the power to do it," warned Howard Klossner of the RFC board. Clayton and Acheson begged Wallace to understand that although it might be desirable to provide better nutrition and health care to the natives of South America, it was not a proper objective of war procurement policy.

Far from persuading Wallace, the meeting whetted his appetite for an even broader program.[15] "How many people are there in the Amazon Basin?" Wallace asked Douglas Allen. "No one has taken a census, but the best estimates I have are that there are probably 1,500,000," Allen said. "Don't they suffer from an inadequate and unbalanced diet?" Wallace asked. Allen said that this was probably true but, then, social conditions were also deplorable in some parts of the United States.

Wallace closed his eyes, drummed his fingers against his forehead, and announced that 350,000 tons of food would provide this population with a much more balanced diet. The food, he said, should be given free of charge. Allen and the others objected that this plan would be an affront to local customs, habits, and the sovereignty of the local governments. Clayton questioned whether such a large amount of food could actually be shipped and distributed. "That will be no problem at all," Wallace said, presumably pondering how he could exert the BEW's considerable autonomy to acquire the necessary docks, ships, and crews. Perkins ended the meeting on what Clayton and Acheson regarded as a hopeful note, "Henry, I guess we just can't give away food in the Amazon and still get rubber; maybe we had just better forget about it."[16]

Wallace's scheme momentarily forgotten, Clayton sent Allen back into Brazil. But in came a cable, issued directly by the BEW without Clayton's assent, instructing Allen to buy 350,000 tons of food and deliver it to the Amazon Basin without delay. The BEW, the cable added, was already arranging to send an 11,000-ton ship with a full cargo, including a large quantity of rice. Even as an exasperated Allen cabled Clayton, Wallace decided to delay the first shipment. The BEW was already busy, it seemed, considering how to integrate the dietary supplements with a much broader program of housing, hygiene, and social counseling. An organizational chart was drawn up for a vast, Tennessee Valley Authority–style project with a budget of some $400 million.[17]

Allen resigned, telling Clayton that Amazon Basin rubber was not worth $400 million. Clayton told Allen to delay his resignation and await developments. A few days later, Jones issued a directive expelling the BEW from the natural rubber program and setting up the Rubber Development Corporation with Clayton as chairman and Allen as president.

Although it involved months of dodging Wallace's furious cables and memorandums, Clayton won the battle on the Amazon front. By early 1943 it was clear that the synthetic rubber program would succeed. Domestic rubber drives and Latin rubber farming had fulfilled demand for 1942. "The $400 million was never spent," Timmons writes, although Wallace did send a BEW expert to the Amazon. The envoy "had patiently explained to 'leaders' of the Indians in the jungles how to grow spinach, lettuce, string beans, cauliflower, and some rare North American greens. But the natives, accustomed to a diet of acorn meal and frijoles, showed little interest."[18]

One could argue the wisdom of Wallace's idea for improving

production, but the same cannot be said for the economic merits of some of the other schemes worked out by the BEW. At times, BEW staff seemed unable to distinguish a legitimate firm from a fly-by-night outfit or a plausible visionary idea from a ridiculous one.

For example, in an effort to secure Mexican mahogany, the BEW signed a contract with the Export-Import Lumber Company of Buffalo for delivery of 2.5 million feet of wood—issuing the usual directive to the RFC to pay the bill. The mahogany, in turn, was to be produced by the Tehuantepec Lumber Company, which had stumpage rights in Mexico. Tehuantepec, in turn, was controlled by a third corporation, the Resources Corporation International of Chicago.

Before paying out any money, Clayton, Klossner, and others looked into the matter and found that the impressive sounding Export-Import Lumber Company was a father-son partnership and that neither man had any experience in the lumber business. Officials of Resources International were under indictment in connection with the company's stock offering. Tehuantepec Lumber had continued troubles with the Mexican government, which accused it of cutting timber on public lands.

Nonetheless, the arrangement surged ahead, with the United States advancing a first payment of $500,000 in 1942. In the end, only a fraction of the wood ordered and paid for ever arrived and at a price that exceeded the estimated cost by $100 per thousand board feet. "It is an interesting sidelight," a 1945 report from the comptroller general dryly observed, "that, for a six-month period during the course of this operation, the senior forestry specialist of BEW was an ex-official of Resources Corporation International, and at the time of his employment in BEW, was under indictment for fraud."[19]

☐ ☐ ☐

While Clayton and Jones tried to recapture control of the warehouse war's rubber supply program, Wallace broadened his attacks.[20] On January 20, 1943, the *Federal Register* published his Order Number 5, stripping the Clayton-headed RFC subsidiaries of all authority to buy, stockpile, and sell foreign materials. Roosevelt, who was away at the Casablanca conference, had no advance knowledge of the order. But Wallace was confident that Roosevelt would not countermand it on his return. Jones and Clayton, confident in their authority, carried on business as usual. At the same time, Clayton convinced Jones to seek an understanding with Wallace. The two men even dangled the possibility of moving the U.S. Commercial Corporation, the largest RFC subsidiary, under the control of Wallace and the BEW.

Months of meetings, letters, draft agreements, and redrafts ensued. Clayton represented Jones, who refused even to appear in the same room with Wallace except at cabinet meetings or under direct orders from Roosevelt. Meanwhile, Clayton operated as if the Wallace order did not exist.

The final act of the drama opened in June when Wallace realized that Jones and Clayton had effectively frozen the BEW out of the funding process in Congress and then occupied him in a dead-end negotiation. Wallace had never cultivated relationships on the Hill; he was, by most accounts, one of the least active and most disliked presiding officers of the Senate since Andrew Johnson. Thus Congress continued appropriating money directly to the RFC and Commerce Department subsidiaries. Although obligated to pay out whatever Wallace ordered, Clayton and his aides adeptly delayed and sometimes disrupted BEW operations.

To make matters worse for Wallace, Clayton's allies in Congress were mounting an open war on the BEW. Senator Harry F. Byrd of Virginia, who chaired a special committee on economy in government, threatened a massive investigation; Senator Kenneth McKellar of Tennessee proposed to abolish the BEW altogether.

Jones denied that he or Clayton had directly prompted these initiatives, but Wallace felt that they must have done so. As the war over the transfer of Clayton's RFC subsidiaries dragged on, Wallace and Jones wrote to Roosevelt on June 3, each blaming the other for unfairly interpreting the mass of executive orders already issued. Wallace wrote again on June 10, pleading that FDR intervene to settle the negotiations with Jones and Clayton. He also asked him to urge Congress for direct appropriations to the BEW.[21]

Lacking any assistance from Roosevelt, and needing desperately to reverse the hostile tide in Congress, Wallace acted on his own. He sent a long, plaintive letter to the Senate Appropriations Committee, chaired by Senator Carter Glass of Virginia. Released to the press on June 29, 1943, the twenty-eight-page document contained detailed charges of the RFC's foot-dragging and concluded that Jones was "hampering" the war effort. "It seems to me," Wallace wrote, "that we could end this wrangling and improve the administrative efficiency so essential to winning this war if program money were appropriated directly to the BEW for its purchase and development of all imported strategic material."

FDR, asked about the Wallace letter at his next press conference, declined to comment on its content but said its release surprised him. In private, he told his aide Jake Early that it was a flat violation of his order of August 21, 1942, instructing the cabinet and other agency heads to abstain from public controversy about one another's actions in the war effort. He also told James F. Byrnes, his "assistant president," to smooth the matter over.[22] But before Byrnes could talk to them, Clayton and his aides drafted, and Jones released, a tart rejoinder:

> The release given out by Mr. Wallace today is filled with malice and misstatements. He makes two serious charges:
>   1. That RFC has failed in the purchasing and stockpiling of strategic and critical materials. The facts are that not more than 10 percent of our purchases or commitments for these materials have been initiated by BEW. . . .
>   2. That RFC and I have obstructed and delayed programs of

development and procurement initiated by BEW. There has been no serious delay by us of any vital program.

I will answer that statement in detail, and be glad to have a committee of Congress investigate.[23]

Jones and Clayton of course had delayed a number of BEW initiatives, but they hardly considered them "vital." Their call for a congressional investigation testifies to their confidence about the propriety of their own actions and their position on Capitol Hill.

The president ordered Byrnes to bring Jones and Wallace together for an attempted reconciliation on June 30. Jones demanded an abject apology from Wallace, and the effort failed. A few hours after the meeting, Wallace issued the following statement: "I had no intention to reflect upon his [Jones's] patriotism or his interest in the war effort. I intended to assert that the delays in RFC in acting upon projects had delayed the war effort. I did not intend to create the impression that his personal motive was deliberately or intentionally to delay the war effort."[24] Moments later he restated the assault, retracting the retraction.

Sentiment in Congress continued to drift in favor of the RFC and Commerce. Even as James Byrnes's peace effort was failing, the Senate added an amendment to the War Agencies Appropriation Bill forbidding the use of any funds for salaries or other purposes in connection with foreign purchases by the BEW unless the "programs and policies" involved had been approved by the full BEW board and a written copy filed with the secretary of state.

Anticipating a full-scale congressional hearing, Clayton began preparing a point-by-point rebuttal to Wallace's charges. In a scene reminiscent of his preparations for his 1920s appearances before Congress, Clayton called in staffers, collated receipts, and drafted and redrafted careful answers to Wallace's accusations. The draft document was initially intended for private circulation to the Senate committee and the White House.

Clayton, who had tried before to negotiate a truce, now began to adopt Jones's fighting spirit. The thought of prolonging the status quo, he said later, "was just awful." Even fighting and losing would be preferable to a protracted internecine conflict. Hours after Wallace's somewhat conciliatory clarification was released, Jones openly called Wallace's charge "dastardly," accused him of overstating an agreement to hold further transfer-of-authority talks, and repeated his call for an independent inquiry. Clayton, Klossner, and their staffs worked over the Fourth of July weekend, finishing a detailed rebuttal to Wallace's letter to Senator Glass. "I think we've got him," a confident Jones told Clayton.[25]

The thirty-page Clayton-Klossner letter was masterful in content; its handling was anything but. Puffed up by Clayton's solid defense of RFC actions, Jones released the letter to the press on July 5 without consulting Roosevelt or Byrnes. Clayton never commented directly on how he might have advised Jones to handle the report, but lacking any evidence to the contrary, it seems likely that he agreed with its release. If so, he unwittingly assented to Jones's self-destruction. In the coming days, a controversy that the president had asked everyone to smother was instead reignited. Milo Perkins fired back on Wallace's behalf; the House Ways and Means Committee entertained a resolution to investigate the battles; and the fresh news provoked new rounds of Senate floor speeches, news reports, and editorial cartoons, all of which had subsided over the July 4 holiday.

If Jones had submitted the report privately, he could have been a smiling spectator as his friends in Congress continued to embarrass Wallace. At the same time he could have gone to Roosevelt as an innocent victim, arguing that it was Wallace who had made public charges against him, which, in the interests of harmony, he had not answered in public.[26]

Instead, Jones overplayed his hand. FDR had enough worries without the Jones-Wallace feud. The Allied invasion of Sicily was imminent, being ultimately launched on July 10. FDR was as furious at Jones as he was at Wallace. Speaking for the president, Byrnes chided both men:

> Public recriminations by the head of one war agency against another are bound to hurt the war effort and lessen the confidence of the people in their government. . . . I must urge that no further statements be made by either of you except in response to a congressional inquiry.[27]

On July 15, 1943, Roosevelt relieved Jones and Wallace from all purchasing authority in the foreign field. His executive order took U.S. Commercial, the Rubber Development Corporation, and the Export-Import operations away from Clayton's sphere, though the RFC did retain some subsidiaries dealing with domestic purchasing. Wallace's BEW was abolished outright; its function, along with those of the RFC subsidiaries, was transferred to the Office of Economic Warfare headed by Leo Crowley.[28]

The costs for Jones, Wallace, and Clayton were high. Wallace remained as vice president for the time being but served, as historian John Morton Blum puts it, "without portfolio." The episode epitomized Wallace's inability to get things done and to get along, even with fellow Democrats in the cabinet and the Congress.

At the Democratic nominating convention in 1944, Roosevelt gave Wallace only a lukewarm, perfunctory endorsement to be his running mate. When FDR let it become known that he was willing to run with either Senator Harry S. Truman or Supreme Court justice William O. Douglas, the delegates chose Truman, though not without a stiff fight from Wallace.

After the bitter battle with Wallace, Jones remained secretary of commerce and head of the RFC but not for long. Two months after his reelection in November 1944, Roosevelt yielded to Wallace's plea that he be named secretary of commerce. Jones, infuriated at this humiliation, resigned his RFC post and headed home for Texas to plot revenge and write his memoirs.

For Clayton, the fall of 1943 became a time of waiting. He still had nominal responsibilities as assistant secretary of commerce, but most of his responsibility for foreign procurement had been taken away, along with Jones's. The unexpected spare time turned out to be beneficial for Clayton and the country because it allowed him to devote more time to a special interdepartmental committee, formed by Hull and Morgenthau and chaired by Harry Dexter White, a committee of sufficient importance that it is dealt with in the next chapter. For the most part, Clayton did the sorts of things that, to experienced Washington hands, are a sign of waning power: he traveled, giving speeches and building public support for the war effort and for a free-trade postwar order.

It also was an opportunity for him to spend more time with his wife and daughters. Sue, who had taken over as chair of the National Women's Democratic Club, began giving more dinner parties to try to soothe the hurt feelings of both sides of the recent feud. A gifted hostess, she shone at the many luncheons, dinners, and bridge parties they gave at their Woodland Drive home in Washington's northwest quadrant. Their guests included John Maynard Keynes, the British economist; Jean Monnet, Charles de Gaulle's brilliant lend-lease negotiator; Arthur Krock and James Reston of the *New York Times*; plus the reigning and rising stars of Washington: Nelson Rockefeller, Bernard Baruch, Paul Nitze, David Lilienthal, Joseph Grew, James F. Byrnes, and W. Averell Harriman.

Sue Clayton's expanded social role left her with ambivalent feelings about her husband's career. Even as Will began to work more normal hours and use occasional weekdays for relaxation and pleasure, she longed to have him return full-time, rather than take another hectic assignment for the government. She pressed him for a promise to return home to Houston soon, and he obliged by tendering his resignation from all remaining posts in January 1944.[29]

Unfortunately for Sue Clayton, Bernard Baruch had other plans. He urged Roosevelt to create a Surplus War Properties Administration (SWPA) to handle the sale of the vast horde of commodities, capital equipment, factories, and other inventory amassed since 1939 following the end of the war. Baruch recommended that Clayton head SWPA, despite the outrage his appointment would provoke among the New Deal set, adding, "before he is finished, the Right Wingers will not like [Clayton] either."

Clayton seemed ideal for the post, having already established a popular following on Capitol Hill. If he proposed a program for handling surplus war property, it would sail through Congress, Baruch believed. Byrnes and FDR agreed, and so the president dispatched Byrnes, his "secretary of resignations," to inform Will Clayton of his new job.[30]

The trouble was that Clayton's resignation letter was sincere; he was not angling for a new job. Besides, he had given his word to Sue. It took a conference between Byrnes and Clayton to convince Roosevelt that Clayton meant to turn down the post. But FDR wanted Clayton for the job, so he called Clayton into the White House. Clayton reiterated that he wanted to leave Washington, had made a promise to his wife, and so would not be able to run SWPA. At this impasse, Roosevelt composed a letter:

January 20, 1944

Dear Mrs. Clayton:

Recently Will told me of his desire to leave Washington. I am sure that he was influenced by the very natural desire to comply with your wishes.

He has been doing a grand job and I want to draft him to remain here and take over some new duties. However, I know that so far as he is concerned, you are the real Commander-in-Chief, and I am writing to ask you to order him to remain here and undertake the task for which I am drafting him.

Please let me know when you have issued the orders.

Sincerely Yours,
Franklin D. Roosevelt

P.S.—Don't relinquish your authority over him![31]

Sue, unable to resist this personal plea from the president, released Will from his promise to leave Washington. He was now free to take up the challenge of running the biggest garage sale in history.

The privatization of surplus property involved an estimated $100 billion in commodities and capital goods, about half the total value of goods and services produced by the U. S. economy in its last peacetime year, 1940.

To Clayton and other business-oriented leaders, the liquidation of surplus property was an opportunity to put the nation back on the path to economic normalcy. But Harry Hopkins, one of FDR's closest advisers, and Henry Wallace wanted the government to retain control of many large plants, especially those that manufactured airplanes and trucks. Wallace also wanted the synthetic rubber plants to be destroyed after the war to revive trade with Latin American rubber exporters.

Clayton initially resisted requests from Representatives Hamilton Fish, a New York Republican, and Wright Patman, a Texas Democrat, that he draft the enabling legislation for his new agency. Having just endured the exhausting feud with Wallace and the BEW, Clayton was in no mood to deal with a complex board and overlapping executive authorities or with the congressional meddling he knew would accompany them. Besides, his notion of the best design for selling off the surplus property would seem—if he advanced it himself—like a power grab. A strong administrator, able to make decisions, seemed to Clayton the right design. Such an administrator would ultimately be accountable to Congress and his directors, but Clayton wanted the head of his agency—whether himself or someone else—to be able to act decisively. (The enabling legislation ultimately drawn up by Clayton's staff gave the director of SWPA the authority to make decisions involving amounts of less than $1 million, with decisions about larger amounts going before a committee. All properties that became available for bidding would be announced, listed, and advertised before they were sold.)

Clayton recognized that if his staff drafted such a structure, the resulting Clayton bill (as it undoubtedly would be called) might seem self-aggrandizing. After protracted discussions, Fish and others prevailed on Clayton to relieve their congressional staffs of the drafting burden; Clayton's staff drafted its own legislation. The surplus property bill came before Congress one day before the long summer recess; it was nearly Labor Day before the bill moved to the House floor.[32]

That delay provided valuable time for the usual array of interest groups and public-spirited skeptics to press for protective provisions, exceptions, set-asides, and guarantees. Along with the problem of surplus property, observed a *Washington Post* editorial supporting Clayton, the surplus property administrator now faced a glut of "surplus politicians." Western senators, for example, wanted public lands not to be sold en bloc to the highest bidders but broken up and dealt out to individuals and small businesses, even at some sacrifice of revenue to the government. Some proposed restraints came from Clayton's old foes within the administration. Harold Ickes—delighted to see a protégé of Jesse Jones's stumbling—proposed a series of amendments to weaken the SWPA administrator's authority and provide for numerous "special-case" procedures. James G. Patton, president of the National Farmers Union, attacked plans to dispose of farmlands as "written in the interests of swollen profits for private real-estate developers."

Opposition to the SWPA design, however, was not limited to a handful of New Dealers. The amendments that offended Clayton were supported by Bob Reynolds and other southern Democrats, his traditional allies. Publisher Henry Luce, attracted by the stimulus that small-business set-asides would create, weighed in against Clayton in a *Life* magazine editorial. "To foster this freedom of the market," Luce wrote, "the Government may seem to be playing favorites at times. Its favorites under the [Senate-amended version of the] Surplus Property Act are veterans, small farmers, and small businessmen. But without favoritism these groups would be at a positive disadvantage. . . . For big business and corporate farming enjoy trading advantages which threaten ultimately to close the door on individuals and newcomers if competition is not ceaselessly renewed."[33]

Clayton too felt strong ties to small business. He had begun his own business career as a newcomer. "If I thought I could strengthen the national economy as this bill suggests," he told Reynolds in one hearing, "I wouldn't hesitate one moment." To Clayton, it was a matter of efficiency. The simplest way to dispose of the government's surplus was to sell it to the highest bidder. If there were entrepreneurs who could make better use of the property, they would take possession of it soon enough or make an appropriate bid in the first place.

Clayton lobbied aggressively for passage of his preferred SWPA legislation. "Clayton," wrote Allen Drury of United Press International, "has the smoothest manner imaginable when it comes to handling recalcitrant committees." Even Clayton, however, could not overcome a coalition that included Harold Ickes, Henry Luce, Robert Reynolds, and Henry A. Wallace. After months of cajoling, the final bill created a weak administrator and dozens of exclusions and set-asides. "So much for the handsome Texan's hold on the Senate," Drury noted. Early in October 1944, after Roosevelt signed the surplus properties bill that Clayton had opposed as unworkable, Clayton submitted his resignation to James Byrnes. A year later, after repeated difficulties in getting the effort launched, Congress passed a new surplus property act similar to the one Clayton had originally proposed.[34]

Although he had no desire to head up the surplus property program as designed by Congress, Clayton wanted to remain in Washington. "There are some other matters, important economic matters," he wrote to a friend, "that I may care to be involved in after the war."

His resignation also had a domestic political component. FDR had already survived the effort of Texas Democrats to deny his bid for a fourth term. He was still seething at their revolt, which he connected to Clayton and Jesse Jones. There was reason for suspicion. A principal sponsor of the insurgents was Lamar Fleming, Jr., the head of Anderson-Clayton. Another was George Butler of Houston, who had married one of Jones's nieces. Jones and Clayton each met with FDR to discuss the affair, and each made an effort to demonstrate his support for Roosevelt and opposition to the Texas Regulars. But only Clayton's gesture succeeded. Jones complained that he could not control his nephew, and when he later issued a public statement opposing the Texas Regulars, he did not mention Roosevelt personally, instead arguing that "no political convention has the authority to deny any qualified [delegate] the right to vote for any candidate he wishes to support." (The Texas Regulars had proposed that unless their demands were met, the state's delegates to the electoral college should be instructed to vote against "any" candidates for a fourth term as president, that is, FDR.) By contrast, Clayton told FDR he would resign if it would spare the president any political embarrassment. For Roosevelt, this offer cleared Clayton of any suspicion of disloyalty. "He said he thought Will Clayton was absolutely pure on this score," Wallace confided to his diary.[35]

Clayton also helped himself with a ringing attack that autumn on Governor Thomas E. Dewey, Roosevelt's 1944 opponent. Clayton's assault, in a pair of well-publicized speeches, focused on Dewey's postwar economic designs, contrasting the Republican party's professed interest in free trade with its history of opposing Cordell Hull and the Democrats' reciprocal free-trade agreements. Clayton's attacks on the Republicans carried special weight among the free enterprisers who formed the backbone of FDR's opponents.

Building a new world economy was the chief issue that interested Clayton in the closing days of World War II. For him, the two spheres of freedom, economic and political, could not be neatly separated. Free trade would promote democracy, and democracies would allow the flow of people, ideas, and goods to remain free. In a speech just a few months before America's entry into the war, Clayton said:

> To understand what is happening in the world today, one must go back to the Industrial Revolution. . . .
>
> The Industrial Revolution established throughout the world the principle of the division of labor on an international scale; it brought about the interdependence of nations; it presented to mankind the inevitability of choice between economic liberalism and political absolutism. We are now witnessing, one may hope, the final struggle in that choice.
>
> The idea of democracy stirred in men's minds and hearts from early times. It is no mere coincidence that it commenced to take widespread form at about the same time as man's inventive genius enormously speeded up the production and distribution of goods. . . .
>
> It may be said that for over 20 years now, most of the world has been engaged in an effort to destroy the principle of the international division of labor on which our modern civilization depends. The machine continues to grind and grind but somehow much of its produce does not move . . . where needed. Nationalism, autarchies, isolationism . . . are all of the same breed; they grew out of man's stupid attempt to circumvent this [natural] law. [36]

"The world has now shrunk," Clayton said in a 1943 speech, "to a point where we can no longer sit in a small corner of it, hugging our insularity and our riches to ourselves. . . . America's stake in the world's trade means much more for us than a great expansion in peacetime production and employment. It represents a great new hope of peace for America and for the world." [37]

In November 1944, the great exponent of those lofty principles, Cordell Hull, long debilitated by illness, resigned as secretary of state. Roosevelt named Hull's deputy, Edward R. Stettinius, to succeed him. Recognizing that the department would now need a first-rate mind to work on the vast problems of postwar recovery, Roosevelt named Clayton to serve as assistant secretary "in charge of all economic affairs," as his cable to Clayton read. [38] Here was

Clayton's chance to concentrate all his energies on his and Hull's design for a worldwide free economy.

Even before Clayton took up his new post, an important step toward that design had been achieved. At Bretton Woods, New Hampshire, in the summer of 1944, the United States and most of the free nations of the world agreed to establish a system of stable, international money, which provided the critical foundation for trade liberalization and the economic growth that followed. Clayton played a major role in forging that agreement.

Economic Statecraft

Crafting Bretton Woods

> Keynes and White, Clayton and Dalton and most
> of the other protagonists are gone.
>
> But the subjects are still with us—the role
> of the dollar, of sterling and of gold, the ade-
> quacy of international liquidity, fixed versus flexible
> exchange rates, protectionism versus free trade,
> universalism versus regionalism, nondiscrimina-
> tion versus preferential arrangements.
>
> And behind these old subjects lie the same
> fundamental issues—how to reconcile liberal
> international trade policies with domestic stabil-
> ity and growth, and how to devise international
> arrangements benefiting not just the world com-
> munity as a whole but each of its parts.
>
> —Ambassador Richard N. Gardner,
> Sterling-Dollar Diplomacy (1969)[1]

FEW AGREEMENTS IN THE TWENTIETH CENTURY HAVE BEEN AS IMPORTANT as the forty-nation pact signed in July 1944 at Bretton Woods, New Hampshire. Yet few have received so little attention or understand-ing relative to their historical weight.

To many people, monetary policy calls to mind hopelessly ar-cane and complex concepts. It appears as a forbidding minefield in which a single misstep could land one on "the real prime interest rate" or "exchange rate volatility," not to mention the forbidding "quarter-to-quarter change in M-2, seasonally adjusted."

Will Clayton not only understood these intricate issues, he actually could explain the benefits of the Bretton Woods agreement to businesspeople and members of Congress, few of whom were versed in economic theory. To understand Clayton's role in the agreement, we need to understand that it promoted three critical and interlocking improvements.

First, the agreement facilitated the creation of an international money. This does not mean that people all over the world literally carry around a new, global currency in place of dollars, francs, pounds, or yen. Instead, under the Bretton Woods pact, every currency was linked to every other at a fixed rate of exchange. A yen and a dollar could be traded for one another, at a specified rate in the short run, and at generally stable rates in the long run. The dollar, at the center like the hub of a wheel, became the world's de facto money for most international transactions.

Second, Bretton Woods provided for stable money. All the various national currencies were to become connected to the dollar, like spokes to the hub of a wheel. The dollar, in turn, was tied to gold, with the United States promising to redeem dollars held abroad for gold at $35 an ounce. The usefulness of this arrangement did not derive from any superstitious belief that gold possessed magical qualities. Rather, tying the dollar to gold was a practical way to stabilize the value of money. The amount of gold mined every year is a small (and relatively constant) percentage of existing worldwide gold reserves, hence a currency tied to gold cannot be printed without limit because the underlying supply of gold cannot be increased to keep pace with the currency printing presses.

Third, and perhaps most important, the Bretton Woods pact established a mechanism—the International Monetary Fund (IMF)—for achieving the objective of worldwide cooperation on monetary policy. The framers of the pact were hardly so unrealistic as to imagine that there never would be any frictions or dislocations in the system. Some countries might have balance-of-payments problems, so they could apply to the IMF for a short-term loan to balance their books. Some countries might find it impossible to maintain the value of their currency at the agreed level, but they could adjust it in consultation with the IMF, rather than unilaterally. Still other countries might require long-term development assistance but not be able to attract sufficient private capital, so they could apply for loans and credits to another Bretton Woods creation, now called the World Bank.

The design created at Bretton Woods grew out of the lend-lease talks with Britain in May 1941. The chief British representative in those early negotiations, as he was again at Bretton Woods in 1944, was John Maynard Keynes, a brilliant, dapper, and highly persuasive advocate for His Majesty's causes. At the 1941 meetings, Keynes suddenly alarmed the U.S. representatives by warning that postwar Britain might be so strapped financially that it would have to return to the practice of imperial trade preferences, bilateral negotiations, and competitive currency manipulations that had worked such havoc in world markets during the 1920s and 1930s. Keynes's dour prediction may have been a tactical maneuver to improve lend-lease terms and to encourage the Americans thinking about alternative, internationalist postwar arrangements generally. If so, it worked.

Keynes's U.S. counterpart, Under Secretary of State Sumner Welles, began work on a statement in favor of postwar free trade and monetary cooperation that might be issued at the forthcoming meeting of Prime Minister Winston Churchill and President Franklin Roosevelt at Newfoundland in August 1941.

The economic sections of the so-called Atlantic Charter affirmed the principles of nondiscrimination between trading nations and extolled harmonious cooperation. The charter, though, created no mechanism for enforcement and so opened the door for evasions and exceptions. "The Atlantic declaration," Welles exclaimed, "means that every nation has a right to expect that its legitimate trade will not be diverted and throttled by towering tariffs, preferences, discriminations, or narrow bilateral practices." A noble goal but not one to which the British felt committed.[2]

What was wanted was an institutional mechanism to bring those lofty principles into practice, including a monetary foundation on which trade and lending agreements could be built. Late in 1941, the United States and the United Kingdom agreed that "at an early convenient date," talks would begin, "open to participation by all other countries of like mind . . . with a view to determining . . . the best means of achieving the above-stated objectives."

This effort to settle one of the most complex issues of postwar policy was an audacious undertaking in the midst of a war that was not yet going well. Monetary policy would encourage or retard trade, as well as profoundly affect the real cost of interest on the eventual war debt.

By early 1942, both White and Keynes had written substantial draft proposals for a postwar monetary and trade order. Also by that spring, both countries had in place a lineup of technical experts and department representatives that would, over the next two years, hammer out the Bretton Woods pact. Jones named Clayton as the Commerce Department's representative to the American Technical Committee, bringing to his vast knowledge of the international system—or nonsystem, as matters stood—an easy affability with the more active members of the U.S. team of analysts and negotiators.[3]

The groups were as diverse as they were impressive. Keynes towered above the British team, of course and, by some accounts, overshadowed the whole enterprise. (To read interviews with such American participants as Hawkins and Collado, however, is to hear an account of Clayton's brilliant and running refutation of Keynes on such points as cartelization of commodities.) Keynes's ideas about the global economy had, of course, a profound influence on White, Clayton, and the rest of the group, as they did on all post-

Depression economics. Accompanying his role as theorist laureate, however, were Keynes's easy social grace and a repartee that could be either biting or self-deprecating. Keynes could appreciate a well-aimed shaft in any direction, as at a 1945 embassy reception where he ran into Sue Clayton during the tedious talks over the British loan. "How are you, Lord Keynes, and when are you going home to England?" Mrs. Clayton asked. Keynes smiled. "As soon as I can get through with your stubborn husband," he said. "Oh, Lord Keynes," she replied, "I'm so glad you find him stubborn too!"

Perhaps most important, and often forgotten, was the fact that Keynes had built his own considerable fortune through shrewd investments between the wars. He was one of the few great economic modelers able to make money in practice; this experience not only gave him great practical knowledge but made it impossible to dismiss what Keynes said as merely the opinion of an obscure academician or bureaucrat.

The rest of the British team was hardly to be dismissed, either. Joining Keynes in many of the discussions in Washington were Lord Halifax, the British ambassador to the United States; Lionel Robbins, an academic economist serving temporarily in the government; and Sir David Waley. Halifax's relationship with FDR was such that on some occasions, Cordell Hull, Roosevelt's secretary of state, would press the British aristocrat to help secure support for a proposal from the American president. On the home front, Keynes reported chiefly to Sir John Anderson, chancellor of the Exchequer, though Churchill himself was an active force in the negotiations, penciling in a suggestion here, a change of phrase there. (By contrast, FDR showed little interest in the economic details of sterling-dollar diplomacy generally and even less in the monetary talks.)[4] The team shone with sufficient brilliance to prompt one anonymous British wag to compose the following verses:

In Washington Lord Halifax
Once whispered to Lord Keynes:

"It's true *they* have the moneybags,

But *we* have all the brains."[5]

But the Americans, while lacking any single actor of Keynes's international celebrity, were not without brains of their own. Harry Dexter White had neither Keynes's polish nor his "moneybags." Shy, diffident, he preferred the company of a good book or editorial page to cocktail banter. When White did try to loosen his tie and socialize, the results were sometimes unfelicitous: Clayton had to drag White home from a 1945 victory celebration when the Morgenthau aide passed out from too much liquor. Nevertheless, White was practically a one-man think tank at Treasury, his department's equivalent of the role to be played by the introverted but brilliant George F. Kennan at State. White came to a midlevel post at Treasury from a small university in the Midwest, but his beaverish work habits and broad, liberal sensibility quickly made him indispensable to Morgenthau. White's posthumous reputation acquired a spicy flavor—some would say sinister—when he was accused of spying for the Soviet Union. He died in 1948 before he could answer the charges, including a claim that he provided the Soviets with copies of the plates used to produce U.S. occupation currency so they could mint their own currency in any detail.[6]

To White's relentless, technocratic demeanor, Clayton added politesse, an instinctive feel for the reaction of southern Democrats on Capitol Hill, and critical, hard-headed business acumen. Leo Pasvolsky of the State Department, Hull's utility infielder, was an active and important voice and balanced White's emphasis on the monetary side with a fervor for trade liberalization to match that of Hull and Clayton. It was Pasvolsky, as the last chapter notes, who combined with Clayton to draft the key documents leading to FDR's successful courtship of Latin America during the war. In addition he had written, over the long fight for free trade since 1933, most of Hull's principal reports and speeches—"or rather," as Acheson put it, "one might say, he wrote Mr. Hull's principal speech; for, whatever the occasion or title, the speech was apt to turn into a dissertation on the benefits of unhampered international trade and the true road to it through agreements reducing tariffs." Emilio Collado, working on economic warfare and the Western Hemisphere for the State Department at the time, later an aide to Clayton, provided figures and studies on the stabilization of commodity prices—a major concern of Latin America then as it still is in the 1990s. Ben Cohen and Acheson, while adding little in the way of economic understanding, provided vital political guidance. The administration was concerned early on about building understanding and support for the agreements, and Acheson and Cohen were deft massagers of bruised congressional and diplomatic egos. They also enjoyed the most intimate relations with FDR of anyone on the American side and added a touch of Rooseveltian, Ivy League urbanity to the proceedings.[7]

The technical committee began to meet in the summer of 1942, by which time substantial background work had already been performed. Both the Keynes and the White drafts were circulated to key officials in government. Both plans envisioned a fixed-rate system linked to gold, though Keynes laid heavy emphasis on "obtaining the advantages, without the disadvantages, of an international gold currency." Keynes worried that a strict gold regime might have, as it had in the 1920s, a deflationary bias, driving down commodity prices, drying up liquidity, and squeezing debtors and countries in legitimate need of a currency adjustment. (Britain had unwisely attempted after World War I to restore gold at its prewar price and thus, given sterling's central role in the world's monetary system, helped bring on a decade of sagging prices and debtor agony.) Both papers called for an IMF-style institution—Keynes labeling his a "Clearing Union," White, his, a "Stabilization Fund"—to smooth over the dislocations inevitable when one is trying to maintain a generally stable, fixed-rate system. The British plan, reflecting concerns about liquidity, provided for more generous funding and less stringent lending guidelines for the international bank; the U.S. plan, less money and more focused objectives.

Already, then, the two main issues for negotiation had emerged: 1. How to achieve monetary and exchange rate stability, particularly in the face of dislocations, and 2. How to make sure that this "stability" did not become a synonym for tight money, debtor agony, and economic stagnation.[8]

At the same time, there was a remarkable consensus that monetary order was highly desirable, and a key to achieving such desirable things as freer trade and a liveable interest on debt.

One may nevertheless ask why Keynes and White focused on the seemingly indirect method of international monetary coordination to achieve such straightforward goals as tariff reduction, low interest rates, and a level of credit sufficient to spur economic growth? If trade barriers were high, one might simply reduce them. If interest rates were a problem, one could merely supply liquidity at lower rates. Burdensome debts could be written down or forgiven. So why enter into the thicket of trying to establish a new international monetary system?

Clayton, who had devoted considerable thought to these questions since the 1920s, understood why agreement on monetary policy was a sine qua non for achieving cooperation on free trade and high rates of economic growth after the war. In a 1937 speech, he declared:

> A good case could probably be made out for the assertion that no other single event in history has contributed more to the material progress of the world than the adoption of the gold standard, enabling men freely to make contracts across national frontiers and to project their activities far into the future. Today we find that practically all the nations of the earth have, strictly speaking,

left the gold standard. Nevertheless, gold remains the world's only international measure of value.[9]

A stable monetary system was the key to increased international trade, Clayton understood. He wanted to declare a truce in the perpetual war between debtors and creditors, between Republicans who favored tight money and Democrats who pushed for easy money. Neither inflation nor deflation, in his view, was in the true general interest.

The problem of the 1920s, Clayton appreciated, had not been the existence of the gold standard as such. Instead the problem was the effort to return to the prewar price of gold, which produced a drastic downward spike in prices in 1920 and 1921 and another round of deflation after 1926.

Clayton explained the connection between money and trade in a 1945 network radio speech in which he argued for Senate ratification of the Bretton Woods agreement:

> Let us suppose for the moment that each state in this country had its own currency. The United States would then have 48 different currencies with fluctuating and uncertain relations between them.
>
> A person in Massachusetts selling goods in Ohio would receive Ohio money which could not be spent outside of Ohio. If a merchant in Philadelphia desired to purchase goods in New York, he would first need to acquire some New York money with which to pay for the goods. The rate for New York money would be frequently changing. Let us assume, furthermore, that in order to purchase or sell the currency of another state a licence were required, and that applications for licences were frequently denied. A person who had sold goods in another state would thus be unable to bring home the proceeds to his state.
>
> It is clear that such conditions in the United States would be intolerable, and would reduce trade to a fraction of its present volume. Yet, these are the conditions which have existed for 10 to 12 years throughout much of the world. The purpose of the Bretton Woods proposal is to eliminate these conditions, and thereby quicken and expand the exchange of goods and services between countries.[10]

In the abstract, then, monetary cooperation was a lubricant to trade liberalization and economic growth. In the concrete circumstances of 1941–1942, it was essential. Unquestionably there would be large debts after the war. Under a stable monetary regime, those debts could be managed at rates of 2 or even 1 percent. With money linked to gold at a stable price, debtors would not face a collapse of prices, as in the 1920s, so they would not be tempted to default on loans, erect trade barriers, or engage in self-defeating currency manipulations to achieve short-term debt relief.

It was understood that there would be large imbalances in trade and capital flows in the postwar era. The United States, which had built vast productive facilities during the war, would need export markets. Europe, which was already devastated, could be rebuilt only if it were able to import U.S. capital in the short term, to be paid for eventually by goods and services exported to the United States in the long run. But if a mutually beneficial arrangement that would take ten or twenty years to fulfill could be worked out, both sides would want assurances of monetary stability. To drop their trade barriers, Britain and France would want mechanisms for adjustment, as envisioned for the IMF.

Clayton did not question Keynes's claim that to secure a free-trade, stable-money world, the United States would have to provide generous aid to debtor nations and dislocated industries. Indeed, he welcomed such policies as prudent and just. "If democracy and private enterprise are to survive in the world," he told his 1945 radio audience, "they can only do so by measures which will prevent a resumption of the type of international economic warfare which was indulged in by practically all nations between the two world wars."[11] Thus although the precise methods of helping others adjust might seem mere technical processes, they were a central issue for Clayton. Get them right and the design for stable international money would be solid and enduring. Fail and the whole enterprise may unravel.

❏ ❏ ❏

Clayton was pleased with the general thrust of the U.S. and British drafts, but he was troubled by two features of Keynes's plan and by the broad strains of thought they rested on. One Keynes proposal called for the creation of an international cartel to buy and sell agricultural produce and other commodities. In theory, the cartel would buy up particular goods when their prices were depressed and sell them during times of shortages to bring prices down. Its aim would be to smooth over the price swings for individual growers and processors and to exert a stabilizing impact on prices to consumers as well. Other cartels, Keynes realized, had been run by particular countries and companies and thus had contributed to the very forces of destructive nationalism that he wished to combat. But this stockpile would be global, he argued, and would be democratically accountable to the governments and people of the world.

In practice, Clayton feared, Keynes's proposal would magnify the absurdity of various national interventions in commodity markets to a global scale. Far from refining the market mechanism, Clayton believed, the cartel would thwart it. Under a market system, when the price of a product falls, some suppliers will produce less of it or even go out of business until the total supply reaches a new equilibrium. By contrast, if a "floor price" is established for such a good, producers are encouraged to produce more as long as the guaranteed selling price is higher than the cost of production. Clayton's scribbled notes on the margin of a set of minutes from the technical comittee provide a key to his thinking: "Two ways to stabilize—prices of dozens of goods through supply buffer—better and easier to stabilize currencies themselves—at the center . . . cannot have a gold standard and not have it."[12]

If the cartel plan were merely a boondoggle, Clayton still would have resisted the scheme, but he might have acquiesced reluctantly if he were confident of its eventual demise. There was, however, a broader danger. Such a cartel might corrupt the whole enterprise of promoting stable money and free trade. Some producers and countries might feel shortchanged by whatever decisions were made by the cartel. Their recourse would be not to the market but to the cartel, a political body. The cartel itself, operating under the World Bank or IMF, would create a powerful temptation for aggrieved nations to tinker with individual currencies or with the overall level of liquidity.

For an international AAA, there would be no foreign markets to dump into. The only recourse, as the unwanted stockpile of goods mounted, would be to liquidate the stock, accept a huge loss, and get out of the cartel business.

As Clayton had long argued, a system open to inflation or deflation will eventually produce both, as shifting coalitions tug the monetary authorities first in one direction, then another. Henry Wallace endorsed this analysis. "The immediate threat is inflation," he told an NBC radio interviewer. "But as Will Clayton points out, inflation [because of the political struggle for compensation] leads inevitably to deflation. The two can't be separated. . . . [If] we have a serious inflation, we're bound to have a corresponding deflation."[13]

These tendencies, Clayton feared, would be reinforced by a second feature of Keynes's plan. Ever concerned with inadequate liquidity, Keynes recommended a more powerful international bank, with much broader discretion than the U.S. proposal. Such a bank, instead of being largely limited to issuing guarantees on private loans, would be able to carry out its own investment program directly. (The U.S. design carried fairly stringent limits on such direct lending.) It would also have overdraft facilities amounting to an estimated $26 billion.

To keep the bank's own books in balance, Keynes proposed that the bank issue its own currency, the "banqor," which would be essentially unconnected to the price of gold—an internal accounting device providing, as Richard Gardner notes, "vast reserves of liquidity" whose creation was not directly limited by the monetary discipline imposed on member currencies. "Since no limits were set on the value of individual credit balances," Gardner writes, members would be able to "pursue policies of domestic expansion without fear of the consequences on their foreign balance" and without explicitly devaluing their own currency. Implicitly then this portion of Keynes's plan provided a way to circumvent the stability of money value that the other monetary provisions were designed to create.

The British, as Gardner observes, wanted to be free to pursue a monetary policy of "domestic expansion" without suffering immediate international consequences. One principle or the other—international monetary stability or unlimited national reserve creation—would have to give way.

To Clayton, the genius of Harry White's design for the IMF was precisely that it would aid countries in making a temporary monetary adjustment but no more. "It would give a country that was short of foreign currencies time in which to adjust its affairs without being compelled to alter its exchange rate or impose exchange restrictions," Clayton observed. "Access to this pool of resources," however, would be "carefully protected by provisions to prevent its abuse."

White's international bank would catalyze private lending and finance without the kind of liquidity that would make it a de facto agent of monetary expansion. "The Bank would not take the place of private lending institutions by guaranteeing such of their loans as had been approved by the Bank. Most of the capital of the Bank, in fact, 80%, would be available only for the purpose of such guarantees."[14]

Clayton's goal, insofar as he participated in the negotiations, was to draw the British (and some members of the U.S. team) as close as possible to the design crafted by White. Clayton favored direct persuasion: presenting evidence, explaining complexities, and analyzing the flaws in competing proposals. This method often proved effective. Still, he did not flinch from subtle maneuvers, bureaucratic infighting, and sheer economic and political force, if these proved essential.

Clayton's first contribution to the unfolding drama was, in fact, a gambit. His aim, shared by Hull and Acheson, was to derail or deflect Keynes's commodity cartel proposal, isolating the idea from the overall monetary plan where, Clayton believed, it would fall of its own weight. In early talks, the British had shown little willingness to abandon the scheme altogether. "The British listened, nodded politely, and brought the proposal up again in the next meeting or draft," Clayton recalled.

As the winter of 1943 approached, a new factor became increasingly important: the cooperation of Latin America. Early private talks on the monetary plan had been held between the United States and Britain, but as their talks moved forward, the attitude of other allies and neutrals would become relevant. For example, the idea of stockpiling and stabilizing commodities directly, as Keynes proposed, was likely to be very appealing to the Latins and other developing nations.

Most Latin American countries were heavily dependent on the export of a few commodities for most of their foreign exchange earnings and much of their gross national product. Hence a proposal to guarantee a fair price for coffee, oil, beef, wheat, sugar, or rubber might attract their support. In the United States and Britain, the pressure that might be exerted by a specific industry or sector was often neutralized by competing interests. But Latin America's resources and interest groups were less diverse and thus could more easily unite to exert political leverage.

"The Latin Americans," Clayton later observed, "had even a stronger recent history of protectionism than we did." He viewed their situation with empathy, seeing parallels to the condition of the American South in the 1890s and early 1900s. He also was confident that in a few years Latin America, like the American South, would come to realize that its interests lay in an expanding volume of world trade, not in trade barriers or commodity stockpile schemes. If the Latin Americans endorsed White's plan for Bretton

Woods, a growth in production and trade would be realized and the cartel idea eventually would be forgotten or rejected. The trick was to bridge the time gap.[15]

In early 1943, a device for doing just that presented itself. With encouragement from the British, several Latin American countries had already voiced interest in joining the discussions on agricultural stabilization. To strengthen the idea that the cartel and the fund were connected, and add participants who were interested in strengthening that connection, was the last thing Clayton and the free traders wanted to see, especially in the early stages of the talks. Yet some such role seemed inevitable.

Secretary of State Cordell Hull called Clayton to solicit his advice. Was there not some way to throw all this momentum into a different direction?[16] Clayton suggested a maneuver. If interest in talking about food and agriculture was so high, then why not hold a conference on the subject? In effect, the United States would undercut the position of Britain and many of the Latins by agreeing with them. Yes, agricultural stabilization was a vital idea— so vital that it ought to be considered at a conference of its own, not tangled up with "technical discussions" on postwar monetary policy. Clayton managed to divorce Keynes's cartel from White's international monetary plan, yet in such a benign way as to be almost beyond suspicion.

Clayton's proposed sidestep even had beneficial domestic side effects. Paul Appleby, under secretary of agriculture and an unabashed economic nationalist, had been, in Clayton's words, "laying out all sorts of hints that he wanted to be more involved on the international aspects of things." A conference on food and agriculture would be a neat and harmless way to occupy Appleby and others in the administration who thought like him.[17]

Hull added a subtle political maneuver of his own. Knowing that the president was likely to agree to any such noble enterprise as a conference on "food and agriculture," with its implicit suggestion of relief for starving masses and troubled farmers, Hull broached the idea to FDR in only bare terms. He realized that the less that was said, the better. "Yes, splendid," said Roosevelt, and within a few days, Acheson and Collado found themselves assigned to pull such a conference together. Only Hull had a clear idea what the conference was to accomplish, namely, nearly nothing.[18]

Acheson recalls in his memoirs, "I asked what the president wanted done about food and agriculture." Sumner Welles replied brusquely, "That, my dear Dean, is for you and Pete [Collado] to work out."* Undaunted, Acheson pressed again but found that "further questioning elicited only that the president regarded food and agriculture as perhaps man's most fundamental concern and a good place to begin postwar planning."

Accordingly, Acheson and Collado began planning the conference as best they could, naming as delegates Clayton, a federal appeals judge from Texas, the under secretary of agriculture, and a group of lesser-known officials. Years later, Acheson confessed he was still in the dark about the origins and purpose of this Potemkin-style food conference that he had been asked to organize at Hot Springs.[19]

Clayton's strategem to separate monetary reform and the agricultural cartel scheme may have eluded Acheson and Collado, who also were working on the Bretton Woods negotiations, but the British did not miss the significance of the U.S. proposal. The State Department's draft agenda, sent out on March 9, 1943, included "possibilities of international [agricultural] agreements, arrangements, and institutions designed to promote efficient production, and . . . the attainment of equitable prices," as well as a consideration of "trade, financial, and other arrangements necessary to enable countries to obtain the foodstuffs and other essential agricultural products which they need."[20]

Ten days later, Lord Halifax, Keynes's close confidant, sought

---

*A man of dignity and sophistication, Welles was often so grave and punctiliously formal as to appear morbid. Once, when a woman's remark at a party made Welles laugh, he quickly caught himself, straightened up, and said, "Pardon me. You amused me."

assurances from the Americans that "the Conference, while dealing in such detail as may be possible with matters . . . which involve economic and financial issues over a wide field, confine themselves to discussion of the most appropriate method by which these matters may be handled and brought to an agreed conclusion."[21] In other words, anything could be talked about, but if the subjects of cartels, monetary coordination, or trade barriers came up, the conference would not discuss their substantive merits but only the procedural question of what bodies ought ultimately to resolve them.

Keynes found even that door too wide to contain Cordell Hull and his band of free-trade advocates, so a few days later the British embassy sent the State Department a further suggestion: "His Majesty's Government wishes to avoid the appointment by the Food Conference itself of committees to deal with wider questions of economic and financial policy, or the issue of invitations by it to other bodies to report on such questions. . . . They think that the Food Conference should confine itself to pointing out the need for these wider questions to be dealt with by appropriate experts." Hull tactfully allowed these clarifications to pass unnoticed, with the result that other nations preparing for the conference generally appointed delegations suitable to a broad, wide-ranging set of talks, rather than the more closely drawn British proposal.

As the delegates assembled at Hot Springs, it was clear to Clayton and Lionel Robbins, the British representative, what the flurry of cables and memorandums had been about. Any advantages Hull had won, and there were probably some, had been achieved before the mock conference began. Yet the Hot Springs meeting provided the impetus for the formation of the U.N.'s Food and Agriculture Organization. Perhaps the most significant result was that two important negotiators in the dollar-sterling diplomacy, Robbins and Clayton, met and discussed (with mutual skepticism) Keynes's proposal for commodity buffers and left with a shared personal respect.

❑ ❑ ❑

In September 1943, Cordell Hull cabled the British that the U.S. team was ready to begin intensive talks. By this time, there had been several exchanges of drafts and at least some movement toward a common center. Still, the British continued to push Keynes's proposal for a commodity cartel and a relatively unrestricted international bank.[22]

One typical exchange took place on October 11, 1943, when the two sides met to discuss the design for the international bank. Keynes and Robbins represented the British; Harry White led the American delegation, with Clayton playing an active role. Clayton served as an important supplement to the U.S. team, adding to White's dogged grasp of the U.S. proposals the stature, investment experience, and personal bearing to parry with the great English economist.[23]

White began the meeting by tabling his latest plan for the international bank, stressing that it was only a draft. Keynes launched into his overriding obsession, the matter of liquidity. The minutes for the meeting record:

> Lord Keynes raised a question as to the formula according to which capital quotas should be determined, and the amount of gold a country would be called on to provide. He went on to express doubts as to whether the Bank would contribute much toward equilibrium in the balance of payments. He said, "if the United States, for example, had an export surplus of one billion dollars, how would the Bank help to adjust this situation?" The British contribution to the Bank would, he added, worsen their balance of payments. The plan, he said, did not give enough consideration to the debtor-creditor position of countries.[24]

Keynes's comments reveal that there was still widespread confusion in distinguishing "the fund" from "the bank." The fund, now the International Monetary Fund, was to help eliminate or smooth adjustments in exchange rates when a country ran into trouble maintaining the par value of its currency. This might be caused or abetted by a trade surplus or deficit, but the fund's role was in any case monetary. The bank, now the World Bank, was to be charged mainly with assisting private lending institutions by providing loan guarantees for badly needed projects. It was to focus on postwar rehabilitation, though at the low levels of funding the bank eventually received, it could hardly play a major role in postwar reconstruction. Back and forth the discussion went between Keynes, White, and Clayton, joined occasionally by Robbins.

When debates over economic policy bogged down, each side sought recourse to the classic threat that if a concession to its position were not granted, recalcitrant politicians at home might not approve the whole package. The minutes continue:

> Lord Keynes asked the extent to which proceeds from loans would be freely available to be spent anywhere the borrower chose. . . .
>
> Mr. White replied that for political reasons the capital contribution of the Bank would doubtless need to be restricted in regard to the place of its expenditure. He thought it possible that there might be more freedom regarding money borrowed from the market. . . .
>
> Lord Keynes replied that the main lines of the plan make it appear very restrictive of the use of funds, but that on closer analysis it seems this feature is mitigated by several jokers. The rigid structure, however, would not facilitate the task of explaining the Bank and dealing with criticisms of it at home.
>
> Mr. White said there were no jokers in the plan.
>
> Mr. White asked Mr. Clayton whether he felt it would be politically feasible to ask Congress for funds which were to be spent in other countries.
>
> Mr. Clayton said further that Section IV, I-c, seemed to cover the situation as to statutory freedom regarding the utilization of proceeds of loans. This provides as follows:
>
> "c. The Bank shall impose no condition upon a loan as to the particular member country in which the proceeds of the loan must be spent; provided, however, that the proceeds of a loan may not be spent in any country which is not a member country without the approval of the Bank."

Lord Keynes replied that it was this paragraph that bothered him.[25]

For Clayton, both the sticking points in the negotiations were symptoms of a similar fear. His response to each was to try to explain to both the British and any skeptical Americans that a sound monetary plan would meet their concerns. But attempts to ensure liquidity through unsound banking practices or international cartels were unnecessary and potentially dangerous. They were unnecessary because it was manifestly in the interests of the United States to provide sufficient dollar reserves and an adequate reduction in trade barriers after the war so that other countries could buy U.S. exports. They were dangerous because attempts to meddle with sound credit and commercial and monetary policies might undermine the monetary design itself.

Clayton felt that the United States should allow Keynes's proposals to remain open for discussion and adopt a flexible negotiating stance on any alternative suggestions that could address British concerns about liquidity and trade balances. This conciliatory approach was Clayton's style in all the conferences he attended. As his aide Pete Collado later said:

He could make compromises, for he was a reasonable man, and a man of the world; but, having made that compromise, he did not take off from that point on the next problem. Others, when they compromise, often leave behind the principle of their stand, but Clayton, never; on the next problem, he came back to his fundamental concept again.[26]

Collado also noted that Clayton "was superior to other economists in that inside his head he had a clear, simple notion of where he wanted to go. It was like a brightly lit up lane inside him."

At one 1943 meeting about the international bank, Keynes and White seemed on the verge of a bitter argument over the question of lending restrictions on the bank. Clayton broke the impasse by suggesting that the United States soften its stance. The minutes of that meeting read:

> Mr. White referred to the provision that a competent committee was to consider whether a loan would raise the productivity of the borrower, and whether the balance of payments of the borrowing country were favorable to the servicing of the loan.
> Lord Keynes remarked that an incompetent committee might come to more useful conclusions.
> Mr. White said that Lord Keynes assumed that a country could not adjust its balance of payments so as to repay loans. Mr. White disagreed with this position.
> Mr. Clayton remarked that he felt the plan as it now stood had too many conditions, and was too tight in certain respects. He suggested that the American group endeavor to prepare a draft which would be less rigid, and see if we could not meet some of the criticism of Lord Keynes.[27]

The "less rigid" proposal of the Americans was to increase funding for both the fund and the bank and to increase the commitment of U.S. funds. Clayton favored a large American commitment to postwar reconstruction anyway. The design of the fund made it his favored instrument. The U.S. voting share was not a majority but big enough to veto major proposals. And the mere fact that the United States was putting up a substantial portion of the funds would give it the decisive role.

Keynes would have preferred fewer restrictions on how the fund's money was used and, in particular, felt that members' rights to access for loans should have been more automatic, less a matter of discretion. But he was willing to settle for more money.

The agreement reached at Bretton Woods called for $8.8 billion in resources for the fund, with a U.S. contribution of $3.175 billion—considerably less than Keynes's initial ambitious appeal for overdraft facilities of $26 billion but well above the initial White plan.[28]

Both sides were nervous about the anomalous shape that the bank was beginning to take. The British felt that they would receive few of its reconstruction funds anyway and hence chafed under the bank's proposed role in settling the problem of sterling balances abroad. This, they argued, should be settled by the countries directly concerned. Clayton recognized that this issue was a place for prudent concession, particularly since the United States too was interested in circumscribing the bank's role.

Hence there was rapid movement toward the notion that the bank should serve mainly as a guarantor of private loans, not as a provider of substantial direct loans. The bank emerged with $10 billion in capital but could not lend more than that amount. Thus it was not to become a fractional reserve bank. Eighty percent of its capital would be earmarked for assisting with private loans.

However sound these limits were, they left the bank somewhat ill suited to carry out its mission of postwar reconstruction. Keynes's initial design saw the bank as able to make loans, which, if "uneconomical" and "uncollectible" in a narrow sense, would serve the interests of the global economy. If it could not do this, what need was there for such a bank? In 1946 and 1947, the bank's inability to do its job would become a major problem for Clayton.

By the same token, the IMF emerged as too strong for its role. If $10 billion were sufficient for postwar reconstruction, $8.8 billion was too much for the short-term bridge financing the IMF was to apportion to countries having problems with their exchange rate. This clout became a problem when the Bretton Woods design was scrapped in the early 1970s and politicians began looking to the IMF not as a small clearing union but as a solution to the world petrodollar crisis and then the world debt crisis.

The lack of balance between resources and responsibilities for both the World Bank and the IMF is in one sense a tribute to the flexibility of the negotiators, whose first concern was to set up a world currency system. Both sides were less worried about far-off institutional matters. Their design lasted for a quarter of a century, a long time indeed in a volatile international economy.

❏ ❏ ❏

By the spring of 1944, both sides were moving toward an agreement on the nature of the IMF and the World Bank. Keynes remained as patient and persistent in pushing his commodity cartel idea as Clayton and White were in resisting it. By this time, Clayton was not attending the meetings regularly; he was swamped with other issues, including the looming battle over surplus war property. Keynes's cartel proposal would surface periodically. Harry White, weary of talking about the same things over and over again, had a firm grasp of the issues but lacked Keynes's experience as a successful trader in international markets. So White would send a courier for Clayton, asking him to hurry over and deliver what one aide later called "the economics lesson to Lord Keynes."

Just who was tutoring whom depends on whose account of the sessions one is reading. Keynes's biographer, Sir Roy Harrod, describes his arguments for the commodities stockpiles as "brilliant," the same term he uses to describe most of Keynes's sallies. Ambassador Richard Gardner, a more objective observer, seems to agree that Keynes and White tended to dominate the meetings, with others contributing only occasionally.[29] Lionel Robbins, however, one of the key British participants, later told Collado that after hearing Clayton in the exchanges, he would "love to have a chance to live with Mr. Clayton for one year, just to observe and to see what it is that makes an entrepreneur tick." Leroy Stinebower, another U.S. negotiator, observed that "Keynes, Lionel Robbins, [and] Dennis Robertson sat spellbound" as Clayton held forth on the implausibility of an international board's improving on the market's pricing mechanism for commodities. "In fact," as another U.S. participant, Harry Hawkins, later claimed, "the Keynesian theory of public spending was refuted by Clayton."[30]

The warm friendship that developed between Clayton and Keynes dispels the notion that their differences represented a clash of egos or parochial partisanship. Clayton recalled learning a great deal from Keynes, for example, about the U.S. stock market. Keynes, for his part, was gracious and appreciative toward Clayton, recognizing him both as a worthy intellectual ally and as Britain's financial savior in 1945–1946.

In the great cartel debate, both sides felt that they were winning. A neat illustration of the confidence of both Keynes and Clayton emerges from their accounts of the same discussions. Clayton described the commodity cartel debate in a 1958 interview:

> Keynes had a crazy idea for an International [Commodities] Corporation. The idea was that when the market went down to a certain point this corporation would buy up supplies to stabilize prices . . . copper, lead, zinc, rubber; chiefly raw materials of agriculture. Every nation would put up capital, step in and store goods when the market went down. I talked against this until I was tired. . . .
>
> Then they had a big meeting and I wasn't there. Keynes was for this scheme and Keynes didn't always come, but this time he was there. . . . They sent a runner for me to come quick and answer Keynes.
>
> I said to Keynes, "I'm sorry, I can't agree with you. I don't think human beings acting for the government are smart enough to step in and save the world in this way. . . ."
>
> Then I gave him an example of cotton selling at 22 cents a pound in 1928. The government set up the Federal Farm Board with $500 million to stabilize the price of commodities. In 1929, in the depression, cotton started to go down and went down to 16 cents a pound. The Farm Board said to the cooperatives, "We will lend you 16 cents a pound; if cotton goes down further, we will take cotton; if it goes up you make a profit." The board put all its money into this cotton loan, and cotton went down to 5 cents, and the Farm Board went broke.
>
> "At which point, gentlemen," [I asked], "in this descent of prices, would you have the International Commodities Corporation start buying the cotton and storing it?"
>
> No one in the group could answer my question.
>
> Well, they dropped the idea [for a time.] Then came along an old gentleman, an Englishman—nice as could be, but not too bright—who was head of the FAO [the Food and Agriculture Organization set up after the Hot Springs conference], and who

had been head man at the University of Edinburgh: Sir John Orr.
By George, he was going to buy it all!
 I asked, "Sir John, who will put up the money?"
 Sir John said, "Oh, that's a detail we haven't gotten to yet."[31]

Keynes, with no less self-assurance, reported on his own successful efforts to promote his commodity plan. In his diary for
October 15, 1943, Henry Wallace noted how Keynes perceived the
same discussions:

> Lord Keynes told me some of the details of what he has been up
> to here in the United States. He has been working not only on
> postwar currency stabilization and an international investment
> bank but also on commodity agreements, buffer stocks, and in-
> ternational controls of cartels. He claimed himself to be enor-
> mously heartened at the progress made. . . .
>   Keynes apparently is willing to take the statesmanlike attitude
> that the best way out for England is to take steps to bring about
> worldwide prosperity. He feels that the steps taken in agreement
> with our officials on currency matters, commodity agreements,
> etc., are sufficient to lay the foundation for worldwide prosperity.
> . . .
>   Lord Keynes is very proud of himself for using the currency
> stabilization thing as a front to deceive the newspapers while he
> met with numerous public officials on all kinds of other matters
> of importance. . . .
>   In working on the problems of buffer stocks and commodity
> agreements, he said that there were two extremes of thought on
> the part of the Americans: one, represented by Will Clayton, who
> took the extreme laissez faire position, and the other represented
> by Paul Appleby and Les Wheeler, who took the extreme planning
> position. He said the British took the middle ground between the
> two positions.[32]

Keynes's commodity proposal survived all the way to the 1944
Bretton Woods conference. At that point, according to journalist
John Chamberlain, Harry White dealt with it in an ingenious man-
ner suggested by Clayton. One by one, various Latin American

countries would propose adding another product to be stabilized by the IMF or an associated cartel. A proposal for coffee won substantial support; wheat, beef, and oil were added to the list. Then a member of the U.S. delegation approached the Cubans: were they going to fail to suggest sugar? Up jumped the Cuban delegate with a ten-minute speech on the importance of sugar to international monetary stability.

"At that point," recalled Chamberlain, who was present at the conference, "White took Keynes aside, and Keynes knew he was licked. By the afternoon, there would have been another 50 or 100 items to stabilize. So they went back to gold for monetary stability and the others would have to be talked about sometime in the future."[33]

The matter of liquidity was finally solved by U.S. flexibility on the "key currency" proposal, which had first been broached in one of White's drafts but was later seized on by Keynes as a means of guarding against a dollar shortage after the war. The key currency proposal gave the fund the discretionary authority to limit or promote the use of a key currency in short supply. Realistically, this meant the dollar and possibly the pound sterling.[34]

Clayton did not want a tight rein on the supply of dollars abroad. "In order for the United States to take advantage of these potential markets," he told a 1945 CBS radio audience, "it is necessary to assist foreign buyers in acquiring dollars with which to pay us until they can restore their own productive capacity." To Clayton, the scarce currency clause at worst did no harm because it left the value of the dollar still linked firmly to gold and stability. At best, it might provide a further international political barrier to deflationary or inflationary monetary policies.[35]

Clayton played only a small and indirect role in the Bretton Woods conference itself, conferring with the State Department about the delicate matter of whom to include on the U.S. delegation. By the time the conference was concluded in July 1944, Clayton was nearly ready to assume his new post at the State Department. Congressional ratification of the Bretton Woods agreement and enabling statutes, concluded in July 1944, could hardly be assumed. By the time the agreement came up for serious debate, in 1945, the end of the war was in sight and the isolationist yearning to pull back to our own concerns was strong. Steering the Bretton Woods proposals through Congress would be one of Clayton's first tasks.

Clayton was put in charge of foreign economic policy at the State Department in December 1944. This involved Clayton in a substantial confirmation battle that is described in the next chapter. But the fight for Bretton Woods, and the free-trade world it hoped to promote, was precisely where he wanted to be. He was sworn in on December 21.

Shortly before the New Year, the new assistant secretary of state for economic affairs took his first official action, writing in his long, elegant strokes to his friend Cordell Hull, who was recuperating at Bethesda Naval Hospital:

> The first letter I sign on State Department stationery is to you. I want to thank you for your confidence and I want to assure you that your foreign policy is so thoroughly ingrained in my system that I shall always work and fight for it. I do hope your health will soon be completely restored and that I may have the opportunity of seeing you occasionally and benefiting from your wise counsel.[36]

Against this Hull vision—and many of its diplomatic and legislative manifestations in the years to come—stood a powerful and often persuasive figure in the U.S. Senate.

8

Between Taft and Keynes

Selling Bretton Woods

ROBERT A. TAFT, THE SENIOR REPUBLICAN SENATOR FROM OHIO, ranked as one of the Senate's most effective and feared members.[1] In addition to his political skills he was the eldest son of President William Howard Taft; he projected a sense of dynasty. Two barriers blocked Taft's path: his politics and his personality. At times it seemed as if no were his favorite word. Taft voted against the Reciprocal Trade Agreements, against the Truman Doctrine, against the Marshall Plan, against the British loan, against the North Atlantic Treaty Organization, against the Nuremburg war crimes trials. His personality could be overbearing as well; he would thump tables and shout to interrupt colleagues on the normally sedate Senate floor.

Still, it would be wrong to think of Taft as totally negative or even predictable. He urged tax rate cuts in the fiscally cautious Republican party. Like Democrat Will Clayton, he earned the wrath of budget-balancers by supporting some of the welfare, education, and health programs championed by President Truman.

Whatever views Taft held he held firmly and forcefully, and he did not hesitate to tell others if he disagreed with them. If he did not shrink from calling a senatorial colleague's idea "nonsense," so, in the Bretton Woods period, he did not refrain from calling the Keynes-White-Clayton blueprint "baloney."

To read Taft's detailed, informed rebuttals to Clayton's and Acheson's arguments for the Bretton Woods agreement is to admire his intellect. Taft always did his homework. He knew more about the nuts-and-bolts operations of the World Bank and the International Monetary Fund (IMF) than any of the administration's witnesses except White, and he possessed a better grasp of international trade than most other senators combined. Taft's blind spot was his failure to appreciate the vital positive good that international monetary cooperation would bring. ("Taft always got the details," Clayton later commented, "but he usually missed the big picture of what we were trying to accomplish.") If Taft's opposition did nothing else, it probably sharpened the arguments of Clayton, White, and others who supported Bretton Woods.[2]

To Taft, the U.S. contribution to the IMF was a matter of "pouring money down a rat hole." He and other critics took particular exception to the fact that the United States not only would "play Santa Claus" but would do so through an international organization in which it had only one-third of the votes. This concern was shared by important segments of the banking community and the press. The American Bankers Association pointed out, for example, that in a normal banking relationship, the lender determines creditworthiness. But in the case of the IMF, "we should be handing over to an international body the power to determine the destination, time, and use" of funds. Nor, the opponents of the Bretton Woods agreement feared, was there assurance that this money would secure the actions we expected from others: the end of trade discrimination, exchange rate manipulation, and other harmful practices.

As an argument against the Bretton Woods accord, Taft cited, as did many, the testimony of Lord Keynes, who in pitching the proposal to a skeptical British parliament stressed that the empire was not absolutely required by the fund agreement to give up, in the short run, "one exchange restriction, one trade restriction, or one sterling area." (Keynes favored dropping these after one to three years. The Bretton Woods agreement provided that countries that did not abolish exchange restrictions after three years could be censured and, after five years, could be denied access to the fund.)[3]

Taft demanded to know what specific provisions would prevent other countries from voting to distribute among themselves the $6 billion the United States would provide to the fund and the bank, taking no action to promote stable money and liberalized trade, and dashing off on a spending spree.

Moved by similar fears, the *New York Times* had already proposed a program of "moderate gold loans" on a bilateral basis in exchange for specific reforms. The loans, the *Times* said, should be made "so far as possible . . . by our private investors, who, through their representatives, would be in a much better position diplomatically to insist on sound policies within the borrowing nation than our Government would be." Several senators noted that U.S. loans after World War I had not been repaid. The amount, according to Taft's estimate, was more than $12 billion, but he ignored the argument that U.S. trade policy and world monetary policy had made those debts virtually unpayable by 1929. "I predict," said Senator Kenneth Wherry, "that we will again pour out untold billions of dollars."[4]

To a certain extent, those who voiced these arguments were simply misinformed about the bank's operational rules and about the fund's whole purpose and design. The bank was largely limited to coguaranteeing the very sorts of private loans that Taft and Wherry proposed as an alternative. The fund, meanwhile, was not a bank in any sense; Keynes's label, a "clearing union," was more accurate. Its purpose was to balance books, while countries with an out-of-line currency or trade imbalance either corrected the problem by means of their own choosing or repegged their money at a different exchange rate. The framers of the fund preferred the former solution. But in any case, monies provided to the IMF—in its original design—were not so much handed out as kept within a central pool.

The first task for Clayton and other administration spokespersons was to devise a strategy for answering these objections. Harry White, frustrated by what he saw as the high incidence of economic illiteracy in Congress and in the press, was initially of a mind to give no quarter. White's attitude, as Richard Gardner observes, was, "Let the critics complain that America could not 'control' the Fund's operations; he would admit the fact and take a firm stand on the Fund's international character." Clayton and Acheson, though, had already canvassed Congress and were alert to the potential threat that Taft and other opponents posed. The administration's response was not to shun those who were skeptical about the Bretton Woods accord but to acknowledge and then defuse the critics' protectionist and isolationist sensibilities by showing, in effect, that Taft and his allies were the ones who failed to understand the "national interest." White and his aides at the Treasury Department created an impressive flow of essays and articles explaining that Bretton Woods was not a harebrained scheme but a hardheaded design for specific, achievable objectives; Acheson worked on winning over individual members of Congress; Clayton barnstormed the country, persuading bankers and business leaders that ratification of Bretton Woods would produce solid, concrete economic benefits for American investors and workers alike.[5]

Other countries also would benefit from Bretton Woods of course; to Clayton, there was nothing softheaded about conceding that fact. "There is not one single element of the 'Santa Claus' philosophy in this policy," Clayton told the Economic Club of Detroit. "On the contrary, quite aside from the question of future peace, the United States will be one of its principal beneficiaries. . . .

To sum up: We have the goods for sale, and there are [foreign] buyers who must have these goods; the problem is to find the dollars with which to make payment. . . . In all probability our total investments abroad, Government and private, may easily reach 15 to 20 billions of dollars in the first few years after the war—assuming always that we are successful." Bretton Woods, Clayton argued, would provide the liquidity and the stable monetary system needed to realize the Treasury Department's estimate that Detroit could expect a foreign market of "more than a million cars a year."[6]

What did all this mean to "John Anderson" (the average American)? an interviewer asked Clayton on NBC radio. Clayton answered, "Today we are exporting over 14 billion dollars worth of goods a year. We simply can't afford after this war to let our trade drop off to the 2 or 3 billion figure it hit in 1932 during the depression. That would make another depression almost certain, and John Anderson wouldn't like that. . . . I think [implementation of Bretton Woods] would mean at least 3 to 5 million jobs in industry, and maybe another million more for farmers and people who handle farm products. Compare this with the number of men and women who'll return to civilian life from the armed forces and you'll see how important it is. It would supply about half of the jobs we need for veterans." But who could be sure that a system with "fair rules of the game" would leave the United States prosperous and competitive? Clayton answered, "The industries that depend on tariff protection have the lowest wage rates in the country." (A survey showed that thirty-four protected industries paid an average wage of $1,100, whereas thirty-four industries with little or no protection paid an average of $1,800.) Indeed, as Cordell Hull tirelessly argued, "Before the first World War, the country in Western Europe enjoying the highest standard of living had the lowest tariff and the country in Western Europe with the lowest standard of living had the highest tariff."[7]

In making many of these economic arguments, Clayton and other administration lobbyists were mixing issues a bit. Some of those five million new jobs would flow directly from the Bretton Woods provision of monetary stability. Other job-creation benefits would come only if the State Department and the IMF were successful in promoting tariff reduction and monetary reform both at home and abroad.

This gap between the certain and the merely possible provided an opportunity for Senator Taft and other critics to launch a second, more sophisticated attack on Bretton Woods. They did so by pointing out what seemed to be a fundamental inconsistency or contradiction in the administration's arguments.

Proponents of the Bretton Woods agreement repeatedly stressed that it meant not only that U.S. money was going out but that the United States would receive the economic benefit of seeing foreign antitrade policies reversed. "A country's right to assistance from the Fund," one of White's pamphlets explained, "is contingent upon its adoption of policies in harmony with the purpose of the Fund." The bank and the fund, Acheson promised, "would eliminate the use of some of the most flagrant devices for discriminating against the trade of the United States by other countries." An assistant secretary of the treasury went so far as to claim that if Bretton Woods were approved, *all* restrictions on current transactions would be "quickly removed in the countries which have not been devastated by the enemy."

Clayton was more cautious in predicting the outcome of these policy changes. "The success of the Bretton Woods agreement," he wrote to Bernard Baruch, "depends more on the eventual elimination of trade discriminations and the reduction of trade barriers than any other single thing. The evil practices which Bretton Woods is supposed to correct grew out of the existence of trade discriminations and excessive trade barriers, and these must be corrected; otherwise, any beneficial effect which Bretton Woods might have will be transitory and costly." Congress listened to Clayton's views on the general economic effects of Bretton Woods, but his testimony was not compelling on questions relating to the fund's mechanics. He had paid little attention to the technical, structural aspects of the negotiations; in fact, he told the House Banking and Currency Committee, he had not read over the final agreement before appearing on its behalf.[8]

In short, then, the general impression given by the Truman administration was one of a very powerful International Monetary

Fund—at least when it came to our trading partners. Clayton's testimony only somewhat muted this message.

The same witnesses, however, were adamant in denying that the Bretton Woods order would compel the United States to alter its domestic economic policies. "I do not see that we delegate any sovereignty to the [IMF] Board," Clayton told Representative Jesse Wolcott. "It has no authority that I know of over the tariff policy of the United States."

But as Clayton had just pointed out, a central pillar of Bretton Woods was that countries can injure one another's trade by exchange rate manipulations. The House minority leader, Joseph Martin, pressed Clayton, "If we turn the manipulating of values of currency or exchange over to an international board, would the international board control the exports and imports of all the countries on the same basis?"

"If they were set up for the purpose of manipulating," Clayton conceded, "they would have very great power." But what was to stop the fund from doing this? Only the fact that such manipulation was the exact opposite of what the fund was set up to do, which was to stabilize money and promote free trade. The implication was that if the fund did engage in exchange rate manipulation, the whole agreement was null and void, and the United States and other countries, having been cheated, would withdraw, leaving behind $3 billion.

These apparent contradictions were heightened by the case Keynes was making in Britain on behalf of the Bretton Woods agreement—stressing the strong obligations the pact would place on the United States to manage the dollar and debts responsibly, while downplaying the reciprocal accountability the fund placed on Britain and other debtor nations.[9]

Into this complex morass of "moral responsibility" and "reciprocal obligation," Senator Taft asked which version was true. That is, was the fund a strong, quasi-sovereign form of international monetary government or was it an economic equivalent of the

League of Nations of the 1920s and 1930s, a weak body empowered only to write reports and issue recommendations?

Either answer would spell trouble in Congress. A *strong* fund would strengthen the charge of critics that the United States was signing over dollars and sovereignty to an organization controlled by others. A *weak* fund diluted all the hoped-for benefits of U.S.-led trade liberalization.

In fact, *any* unequivocal answer would not only have been politically unwise but inaccurate. Politically, the fund had great powers of influence and persuasion, especially over the democracies, that is, the countries that dominate international trade. For example, its reports were a source of much consternation to the succession of British governments that failed to stabilize the pound in the 1940s and 1950s.

Yet, what power did the fund really possess? The fund's governing body could ultimately deny funds to a country that persisted in exchange rate manipulations and restrictions. This might be a powerful threat indeed—but only so long as the member-nations saw it in their interest to belong to an institution that promoted monetary stability and free trade. But if the fund ceased to play that part, what power could it exercise?

Despite his lack of familiarity with the final, specific Bretton Woods terms, Clayton delivered one of the more subtle assessments of the fund's powers. His views emerged in a congressional hearing, during a semantic dispute over the word *pressure*.

> Mr. Smith: . . . There is nothing in the Bretton Woods Fund agreement which would put foreign nations in a position where they could exercise a degree of pressure to force the United States to reduce or set aside its tariffs?
>
> Mr. Clayton: Well, that is not the question that was asked me. The answer I gave was that there was nothing in the agreement of which I was aware that would make it possible for foreign countries to *dictate* a change in our tariff policy. . . . There is a power to make recommendations to any country, with respect to their policy on international trade or currency or exchange. . . .

Mr. Smith: Mr. Clayton, you disagree then with Lord Keynes on this point, do you?

Mr. Clayton: I have disagreed with him about several things.
. . .

Mr. Smith: Mr. Clayton, you then emphatically state that the United States would not be placed in a position where pressure could be brought against us to alter our tariff schedules?

Mr. Clayton: No; I do not say that: It is possible that pressure might be brought on you. I do not think any country could have any undue pressure brought on it, though. . . . I do not mind friends bringing pressure to bear on me if they think I am not acting right in a certain situation, and I take it that the United States would not mind representations and recommendations.
. . .

Mr. Smith: Suppose at [some] point, the Fund said, "We are not interested in any more dollars," and our employment is hinging on the flow of these dollars; what situation would we be in?

Mr. Clayton: We do not have to furnish any more dollars to the fund!

Mr. Smith: That is true, but I am asking what will happen to this employment situation.

Mr. Clayton: Regardless of the Fund, Mr. Smith, if our situation in respect to international trade and our policies are wrong, what you visualize as possibly happening to the employment situation is going to happen anyway.[10]

In their quest for a yes-or-no answer, for mechanistic guarantees, the congressmen conjured up evermore alarming scenarios to press on Clayton, White, and the other supporting witnesses. What if one of the bank's loans wound up going to a foreign or U.S. political party? What if the IMF ministers ran off with all the gold? What if they ordered the United States to purchase Russian wheat?

Clayton was not limited to theoretical speculations to make his case. For one thing, the Bretton Woods agreement created incentives—stable money and guaranteed trade access for the members—for cooperating with the fund's recommendations, as well as objective criteria to determine whether monetary disequilibrium was occurring. How could the United States and other countries know whether it was U.S. monetary policy that needed to be eased, or whether other countries needed to tighten their own policies? Bretton Woods provided an objective measure of value—gold— that would supply the answer. If the United States (or any other country) were willing to trade its dollars to the clearing union in exchange for gold, it was a sign that the dollar had not moved out of line, so other currencies would need correction. But if the United States (or any other country) were gladly trading in gold to acquire dollars, then it would be a sign that dollars had indeed risen in value relative to gold, in which case U.S. policy should be eased.

As the debate advanced, Taft and the opposition conceded the benefits of reconstruction loans and stable currency but promoted alternative instruments to achieve those goals. Taft and others proposed, for example, that the U.S. Export-Import Bank could achieve all the direct trade benefits of the IMF and the World Bank without any risk of turning the power over to foreign finance ministers. In his testimony before a committee of the House of Representatives, Clayton (who had run several U.S. loan and credit programs like the Export-Import Bank) turned the tables on Taft and other critics, saying:

> I would just like to add that from my experience in international trade and international lending, I have a high regard for the respect that these foreign countries have for their obligations. The experience of the Export-Import Bank of this Government, in foreign lending, has been excellent up to now. It is now 11 years old. So far as I know, they have only one default, and that is a minor matter due entirely to the war. Take, as an example, Latin America. The bank in the last 11 years has made commitments of $800 million to Latin American countries. Only $263 of

those commitments were ever used; $13 million of that $263 million has been repaid. Every single loan has been serviced regarding interest and payment, on time, and not a single one is in default. . . .

It is conceivable that [the fund] may have one or two absolute defaults; somebody goes on the rocks and we never get the money back into the Fund. But that will be a relatively small matter and a relatively small loss to the Fund when you compare it with the advantages that are to be had from this plan.[11]

By the end of the debate, the opponents had conceded the general goals of Bretton Woods. Their practical objections about the order in which particular elements of that design were brought into being could hardly carry much force. One could argue, as Representative Jesse Wolcott did, that tariff reductions should have come first. No agreement on trade liberalization had been reached, however, during the war. Here was an agreement by forty-four nations to take the important step of creating a sound monetary foundation for world trade. Would the Senate decline someone's help in patching a hole in the roof because the house also needed plumbing repairs? Clayton, who was by no means unsympathetic to Wolcott's belief in the importance of a trade agreement, put the matter succinctly when he said, "You have to do something first."

Other critics argued, and Clayton conceded, that a reconstruction program of aids and grants was an essential part of the same final plan and that the bank and the fund, even in combination, were not wholly equipped for the task. Yet with agreement on the fund and the bank, talks could progress to issues of reconstruction and relief programs. These efforts, as Keynes explained, belonged to "another chapter of international cooperation, upon which we shall embark shortly if you do not discourage us unduly about this one."[12]

In effect, proponents like Clayton were asking that the United States invest some $3 billion dollars in the fund—a sum equal to a few weeks of war expenditures, as Clayton pointed out—on the better than fair chance that from this advance would flow years of economic benefit to the United States. Senator Taft wanted a large number of assurances up front, a reasonable enough position in most lending situations; Clayton wanted the United States, which was in the best position to be generous, to provide money and establish institutions for a war-ravaged world *first*. He was confident that concessions and reforms by other nations would follow.

If Clayton were wrong, the United States might lose a few billions. But if Taft were wrong, the loss would be of a far greater magnitude than mere money. The United States might lose the whole world of international borrowers and trading partners, indeed, an economically peaceful world itself. (The same balancing of risks was to play itself out again when Clayton lobbied for United Nations relief, the British loan, and the Marshall Plan.)

Perhaps the best symbol of the congressional deliberations came toward the end of the debate on one of Taft's amendments, which proposed that the fund could not commence operations until two-thirds of its members had approved a clause automatically excluding members that had not corrected restrictive currency practices. Senator Joseph Ball, sympathetic to the amendment's thrust but recognizing that a formal requirement could force a renegotiation of the whole treaty, proposed a friendly softening amendment. The measure, Ball said, could be stated in the form of an instruction to the U.S. delegate to argue for the change at the first meeting of the fund, and the period of required adjustment could provide that, "say, after 3 or 5 years there should be a limitation against the use of the Fund by members who at that time still retained restrictions." Senator Robert F. Wagner, rising to comment on Ball's proposal, simply read section 4, article XIV, of the Bretton Woods agreement, which provided for a fund report on such members after three years and allowed the fund to deny the same member access to the currency pool after five years. Except for a bit of residual discretion by the IMF, everything Ball asked for, White and Clayton had already won at the negotiating table.[13]

A few hours later, nearly all the Democrats, and most of Taft's fellow Republicans, voted in favor of the Bretton Woods Agreement

Act. The decisive factor for the undecided senators was, it seems, a sense that the United States was responsible for the postwar economic world and if it could not guarantee that it would be a world of economic liberalism, it must at least make an effort.

Senator Taft had certainly been right in one of his criticisms: U.S. approval of the Bretton Woods design did not produce immediate or automatic tariff reductions. Nor did U.S. approval bring immediate approval of Bretton Woods by Great Britain. The new Labour government, headed by Clement Attlee, was distracted by nationalization schemes, war debts, and obligations to pay for controlling the British sector of defeated Germany, so parliamentary action on the Bretton Woods agreement was delayed. By the end of 1946, England still had not acted on Bretton Woods but had, true to Senator Taft's prediction, asked Washington for a $6 billion, no-interest loan just to make ends meet.

Will Clayton's next challenge was to promote this loan so that England's costly victory in the war against Hitler would not be negated by collapse and bankruptcy in the postwar world. The threat of Nazi Germany was now past; the menace of Soviet Russia and the cold war lay ahead.

9

Year of Nondecisions

The Road to Hiroshima

On April 11, 1945, Will Clayton completed several days of testifying before congressional committees on the Bretton Woods proposals and on U.S. plans for trade liberalization and postwar relief and reconstruction. The next day promised to be less hectic, though hardly a holiday. Clayton's calendar included meetings with State Department staff and then British officials in the morning, lunch and a meeting with the French in the afternoon. Clayton was in his office in the old State Department when the news came in the late afternoon. Pete Collado was there too, along with members of the French economic team who were requesting U.S. aid. "This is a sad, sad day for Europe," Jean Monnet said. "It's a sad day for the world," Clayton said. Clayton, Monnet, and Collado looked out the window as the Marines lowered the flag at 5 P.M.

Franklin Roosevelt was dead. At 6:45, Harry Truman was sworn in as president. "Boys, if you ever pray, pray for me now," Truman said to the reporters in the Senate press gallery the next day. "I don't know whether you fellows ever had a load of hay fall on you, but when they told me yesterday what had happened, I felt like the moon, the stars, and all the planets had fallen on me."[1]

❑ ❑ ❑

Truman, ill-prepared by FDR for the job he had inherited, faced a cascade of choices and decisions during his first eighteen months in the White House. U.S. relations with the Soviet Union, already frayed at Yalta, were rapidly deteriorating. After Germany's surrender, Truman, less than a month after Roosevelt's death, had to decide what line the United States would take on German reparations and on the postwar status of Poland and other Soviet-occupied countries. What was to be done about ending wartime price controls, and how were the tide of GI's returning from Europe going to be integrated into the economy? How could the United States ensure full employment? What should be done about the coming international trade talks? There was the matter of deciding to use the atomic bomb to end the war against Japan—a project kept secret even from the vice president until FDR's death.

Truman entitled his memoir of the frenetic first eighteen months in office (from April 1945 through the crushing congressional elections of November 1946) *Year of Decisions.*[2] But he might as well have called it "the year of nondecisions."

Many individual actions, of course, were taken; dozens of crises and exigencies were dealt with. Yet Truman and his advisers met these challenges in an essentially ad hoc manner. Any decisions were largely tactical, not strategic. On the two fundamental issues—reviving Western Europe and dealing with Soviet domination of Central and Eastern Europe—the action was a kind of holding pattern. Although the United States passively resisted the emerging Iron Curtain, it took no forceful action against it. The United States granted no substantial loans to the Soviet Union, but neither did it form a design for bringing about a return to economic normalcy in the many countries it did loan to.

Even the momentous determination to use the atomic bomb against Japan left open many of the questions that would govern its significance in the emerging world order. Some saw the bomb as a nuclear pistol—the utility of which depended on U.S. maintenance of a near monopoly on technology—as opposed to the sharing of atomic know-how as envisioned in the wartime agreement between the United States, Russia, and Britain. The United States came to no decisions about these matters in 1945 or 1946.

The above is meant more as a description than as a criticism. Perhaps it was prudent to delay some decisions, even though it seemed clear, as Averell Harriman cabled in April 1945, that "the Soviet program is the establishment of totalitarianism, ending personal liberty and democracy as we know them."[3] As long as some hope remained for a peaceful reconciliation with Stalin, our recent wartime ally, Truman preferred not to destroy that hope through a confrontation.

On the economic front, Europe might need a bold and massive U.S. aid program to recover, but in the meantime, the International Monetary Fund, the World Bank, the Export-Import Bank, and the U.N. Relief and Rehabilitation Administration were already engaged in limited assistance programs. Perhaps the United Nations, like its ill-fated predecessor, the League of Nations, would prove ineffective, but there was certainly some justification for trying to settle disputes under U.N. auspices before the United States tried any unilateral actions.

Truman, who had been vice president less than three months before FDR died, made no pretense of expertise in such matters. Several months after he took office in April 1945, Truman called in Will Clayton to report on the operational status of the IMF and the forthcoming trade negotiations. Truman listened to Clayton's detailed report, jotting notes energetically. When Clayton was finished, Truman sighed and said, "I don't know anything about these things. I certainly don't know what I'm doing about them. I need help." Truman's humility ingratiated him with Clayton, while Clayton's clarity and directness struck a chord with Truman.

Truman may not have known much about the operations of the State Department. But he knew that he trusted Clayton and the other "businesslike" men there who could give him a straight answer to a question or carry out an order without delay.

The pace at which these issues pressed on Truman was accelerated by the unexpectedly swift victory of the Allied forces against Germany and Japan. Decisions on postwar affairs that planners had intended to make in 1946 were thrust forward by more than a year. Adding to the pressure on Western officials was a political climate of uncertainty and dubious executive authority. Truman faced a skeptical Congress that was expected to become Republican in the November 1946 elections. The internal political instability of the Allies was illustrated at Potsdam, when Prime Minister Winston Churchill and Foreign Secretary Anthony Eden went home for the British elections only to be replaced a few days later by Clement Attlee and Ernest Bevin, who were chosen by the new Labour majority.

After the cabinet meeting on April 25, 1945, Secretary of War Henry L. Stimson lingered to talk to Truman. He had asked the president for a chance to brief him privately on a sensitive matter. Once they were alone, Stimson handed him the so-called S-1 memorandum: "Within four months, we shall in all probability have completed the most terrible weapon ever known in human history."[4] It spelled out the genesis of the Manhattan project, its current status, and a forecast about the availability of an actual atomic weapon. Early in July, Los Alamos expected to be able to test a prototype weapon. Although any particular bomb might be flawed, the scientists working on the project had solved the basic conceptual problems and knew that such a bomb could be built and used.

Less than one month after the first test, they could have a bomb ready for use against Japan. "Japan had always been the target," write Richard G. Hewlett and Oscar E. Anderson, Jr., in their history of the Atomic Energy Commission. If it worked, the awful weapon might make unnecessary a manned invasion of Japan that was expected to last nine months or more.

But the bomb, Stimson noted, would have implications far beyond the hastening of VJ-day. Scientists working on the project were troubled by the possibility that America's leaders would not appreciate its awful significance. Stimson's memorandum, Hewlett and Anderson write, "faithfully reported their central thesis" that the United States could not retain its monopoly on the atomic weapon indefinitely. Russian production was only three to ten years away. In the future almost any nation, even a small one, might construct a bomb or even several bombs in secret. Any ruler who possessed such a bomb could wreak destruction on almost any country, including the United States. The only safeguard seemed to be an international regime that, Stimson wrote, "would involve such thorough-going rights of inspection and internal controls as we have never heretofore contemplated."

To weigh these large matters and suggest policy, including whether and how to use the bomb, Stimson recommended appointing a special panel to advise the president on nuclear policy. Truman agreed and, a few days later, named an interim committee that included Vannevar Bush, president of the Carnegie Institute and director of the Office of Scientific Research and Development; James B. Conant, president of Harvard University and chairman of the National Defense Research Committee; Karl T. Compton, president of the Massachusetts Institute of Technology; Ralph Bard, under secretary of the navy; George L. Harrison, president of New York Life Insurance Company and a special assistant to Stimson; and Will Clayton, the assistant secretary of state for economic affairs. At Stimson's urging, Truman also named his own personal representative, James F. Byrnes, soon to become secretary of state.

Subsequently the committee appointed a scientific advisory panel that included J. Robert Oppenheimer, the director of Los Alamos Scientific Laboratory where the bomb was being assembled; Arthur H. Compton and Ernest O. Lawrence, the directors of the atomic projects at the University of Chicago and the University of California at Berkeley; and Enrico Fermi, director of Chicago's Argonne National Laboratory.[5]

Before Franklin Roosevelt's death, Clayton had been scheduled to attend the United Nations conference in San Francisco, due to convene on April 25. The change of president, however, kept him in Washington, contributing to a section of one of Truman's first presidential statements, an affirmation of support for the Bretton Woods plan and of Truman's hope for its swift approval by Congress.

Clayton's selection to serve on the S-1 committee may have reflected a process of elimination. Someone had to represent State. Yet Edward R. Stettinius, Jr., Hull's successor, was due to be in San Francisco to attend the United Nations conference. Dean Acheson and Joe Grew had submitted their resignations effective that summer and were eager to remove themselves from department affairs.

Grew, who had recommended Clayton for the S-1 committee, was deeply interested in the surrender terms that would be offered to the Japanese. He pressed Truman several times that summer to consider modifying U.S. demands for Japan's unconditional surrender. Instead, Truman urged that the Japanese be allowed to retain their beloved emperor if they would lay down their arms, thereby avoiding the five hundred thousand to one million U.S. casualties that General George C. Marshall anticipated if an invasion of Japan were necessary.

Clayton's selection suggests that Grew felt, probably correctly, that Clayton shared this predilection for somewhat more generous terms. Grew may also have felt that Clayton, with his experience and connections in industry, and in wartime procurement and international trade in particular, would be a more effective representative of this generous view than Grew himself could be. Both the weapons and the commercial applications of atomic energy were closely bound up with the procurement of uranium and thorium; questions of international control focused on regulation of the same.

Clayton may have known about the atomic project before his appointment to the S-1 committee. He had after all directed the overseas procurement program and the surplus war property disposal effort. He was also involved in the negotiation, concluded in July 1945, of an agreement to purchase monazite sand from Brazil. Other related purchasing agreements may have crossed his desk at the Surplus War Property Administration and at the State Department before the S-1 committee was created. Another reason that Clayton was no novice to atomic affairs was that, in the fall of 1944, after his resignation from SWPA and before being asked to go to the State Department, Clayton had worked briefly as Byrnes's deputy at the White House. Byrnes was one of the few civilians in government who knew about the S-1 program, and so perhaps did Clayton.

Clayton attended the S-1 committee's meetings on May 9, 14, and 18 to receive general briefings and to agree on reports to be requested from the scientific advisers and from a pair of similar panels from industry and the military.[6] The critical recommendations on use of the bomb and the proper U.S. approach to the Soviets, the British, and other countries were drafted during day-long sessions held on May 31 and June 1.

The committee was interested in considering ways in which the psychological benefits of the bomb might be gained without its actual use on a military or civilian target. In practice, the distinction was bound to be blurred because the collateral effects of the bomb—heat, winds, and radiation—would be felt for a wide distance, causing the death of thousands of noncombatants who lived or worked near almost any useful military target.

At the meeting of May 31 and the ensuing luncheon, Clayton and George Harrison pressed the scientists to present a wide array of options. (Clayton, writes diplomatic historian Herbert Feis, "was quite vocative" at the meetings.) Clayton asked if one of the bombs could be dropped on some preannounced spot in the desert, or off the coast of Japan, to demonstrate its horrific effects.

The problem, the scientific experts replied, lay not so much in constructing such a demonstration in theory as with the immediate limitations on bomb production. The materials and refining facilities on hand would allow the production, in the immediate future, of only a handful of bombs. If a display test worked in the technological sense but failed to sway the stubborn Japanese leaders, the chance would be that much greater that the United States would not be able to bomb an actual target. By contrast, an actual bombing would be impossible for the Japanese to ignore.

Besides, a demonstration test might fail. The scientists were confident of the general design of the bomb and that at least one would work, but they could hardly be certain that a high percentage of the early bombs would work. If several targets were selected, only one or two early bombs needed to perform for the enterprise to succeed.[7]

Accordingly, the committee unanimously recommended that the bomb be used, without prior specific warning, on a military target with a surrounding civilian population, such as an armaments factory. "We can propose no technical demonstration," the scientific panel reported, "likely to bring an end to the war; we see no acceptable alternative to direct military use."[8]

The final draft of the report was not submitted until two weeks after the S-1 panel issued its recommendation to the president, leading some scholars to conclude that the decision to use the bomb was more or less foreordained and that the input of the scientists was just an afterthought. Elting E. Morison, author of a biography of Henry Stimson, makes such a claim.[9] The minutes of the meetings, however, show that the committee based its recommendation on the fact that the scientists had considered the possibilities of a demonstration and warning and found them too risky. Naturally, however, they preferred that the question be considered in a formal, written report.

Truman received their report in mid-June before leaving for Potsdam and well before finally issuing the order on July 24 that set in motion the bombing of Hiroshima and Nagasaki in August. He was prepared to rescind that order if the Japanese responded favorably to a joint ultimatum, hinting at the bomb, issued by the United States, Britain, and China on July 26, but the Japanese spurned the warning.[10]

There is much evidence, however, from the minutes that were declassified in 1984, that Morison and others were correct in speculating that the basic orientation of the committee—to use the bomb in some fashion—was decided from the moment of its creation. The question of *whether or not* to use the bomb is never mentioned in the minutes, better than 90 percent of which are devoted to questions of postwar international control of technology and the proper organization of a domestic industry for weapons and industrial research. Not until the afternoon meeting of May 31 did the committee take up the question of the bombing of Japan, and it was not a long or detailed debate. The minutes read:

> After much discussion concerning various types of targets and the effects to be produced, the Secretary [Stimson] expressed the conclusion, on which there was general agreement, that we could not give the Japanese any warning; that we could not concentrate on a civilian area; but that we should seek to make a profound psychological impression on as many of the inhabitants as possible.[11]

Indeed, Compton reports that May 31, which he describes as "the occasion for fullest consideration of whether and in what manner the bomb should be used," had a decided post factum quality. "[At] the morning's discussions it seemed to be a foregone conclusion that the bomb would be used."[12] The subject came up again on June 1 but in a brief section—"VI. Use of the Bomb"— suggesting a decision already made rather than any deep moral wrestling. The entire section reads:

> Mr. Byrnes recommended, and the Committee agreed, that the Secretary of War should be advised that, while recognizing that the *final selection of the target* was essentially a military decision, the *present view* of the Committee was that the bomb should be used against Japan as soon as possible; that it be used on a war plant surrounded by workers' homes; and that it be used without prior warning. It was the *understanding of the Committee* that the small bomb would be used in the test and that the large bomb

(gun mechanism) *would be used* in the first strike over Japan.[13] (emphasis added)

Earlier minutes of the committee strongly support such an inference. Stimson never urged the committee to grapple with the moral questions involved in any use of the bomb, for on May 18, when the core members of S-1 met in an executive session, one of the items for discussion was a seventeen-page draft statement for the president to issue after the bomb had been used against the Japanese.[14] The log of the meeting says:

> Bard, Byrnes, Clayton, Conant, and Harrison were the members present. Arthur Page and General Groves were present by invitation. Consideration was given to the draft statements of publicity, it being agreed that publicity concerning the test should be kept to a minimum, that following actual use the President should make only a short announcement to the effect that the weapon had been employed and the S/W should release a longer statement giving the general story of the project.[15]

Morison puts the role of S-1 in perspective on the question of using the bomb against Japan when he writes:

> Taking all things together it is reasonable to suppose that the Secretary of War was, in the first months of 1945, acting within a developing assumption that the bomb would be used. It is also reasonable to suppose that the men working with him were acting upon the same kind of assumption.
> In the months immediately preceding May 31, [at least] six of the eight men on the Interim Committee had lived with the knowledge of atomic energy for a long time; five of them had been directly at work on the development of the project.[16]

For the scientists, the question of using the bomb against the Japanese was important but paled against the issue of how this awesome source of power was to be handled in the future. Questions of technology, management, and diplomacy were intertwined. For example, the United States was more likely to win an international agreement to curtail the production of atomic weapons if it would agree to share atomic know-how and work to establish a control system.

If workable controls could not be agreed on, different options would need to be discussed, with the United States hoping to maintain sufficient leverage to ensure the peace. But how long would it take Russia or some other country to build atomic bombs? And what were the prospects that the United States could secure any advantage that would be meaningful in strategic and political terms? Clayton, looking toward the broad future of the global economy, and Byrnes, eager to maximize U.S. strategic leverage vis-à-vis the Soviets, showed a special interest in these questions.

Clayton was skeptical of international cooperation and unilateral advantage. The Soviets, he pointed out, had declined even to supply general statistical information when they applied for U.S. loans and credits. Were they going to be more forthcoming when the issue concerned a sensitive technology from whose development they might gain substantial benefits? The very notion of international control went counter to the totalitarian mentality, and mechanisms of verification lost much of their usefulness when applied to countries that lacked the checks and competing interests of a free political economy.

At the same time, Clayton tended to side with the industrialists and the scientists on the implausibility of hoarding scientific know-how. Technology was bound to become diffused. The Russians, moreover, had already seized some of the leading German scientists and would benefit from their knowledge if they were put to work for Moscow.

It was prudent for the United States to pursue this technology as fast as it could, Clayton argued. But there should be no illusions that any advantages gained thereby would be particularly enduring or even particularly usable.[17]

Not satisfied with either cooperation or unilateral control, the committee moved toward a policy that sought to preserve both options. The committee adopted A. H. Compton's recommendation of May 31:

> 1. Freedom of research be developed to the utmost consistent with national security and military necessity.
> 2. A combination of democratic powers be established for cooperation in this field.
> 3. A cooperative understanding be reached with Russia.[18]

Clayton did not object to point three, even though his other statements about the Soviets make it certain that he would have liked to. He believed that, in the long run, the failure of totalitarianism would force reforms; in the short run, rather than treating the admittedly slim possibility of Kremlin cooperation with contempt, the United States should go about its business, allowing the Soviets to opt out of cooperation if that was their choice. The final S-1 report recommended, at Bush's suggestion, a fourth item calling for a domestic program aiming at the fastest possible creation of atomic material and of facilities for industrial use and for refining and production of weapons.[19]

The committee recommended, and Truman accepted, that the United States inform the British and the Soviets only "minimally" about the bomb at the forthcoming Potsdam conference.

Clayton shared the doubts of many scientists that such a weapon could be used as a lever. "The problem," as he put it in a later conversation, "is that it's only good for destroying a whole civilization. Once the secret was out, and it was going to get out, then you can't really do anything with it."[20] But the committee had not suggested, nor had Truman determined, that the bomb could be so used. The scientists had not suggested that Truman foreclose the possibility of cooperation, though some of them would argue this was done by default.

Instead, the United States would tersely inform Stalin that the bomb was to be used, drop it on Japan, and then see what resulted. It was a fitting beginning to a year of nondecisions.

10

Potsdam and the Morgenthau Plan

IN ONE OF THE MORE REMARKABLE VAGARIES OF HISTORY," WRITES economist and diplomat John Kenneth Galbraith, "millions of words have been written about whether Roosevelt did well or badly at Yalta. Almost nothing has been written about how well or badly Truman—or Churchill, Attlee, and Stalin—did at Potsdam."[1]

The disparity is the more striking if we consider that Potsdam (which ran from July 11 to August 2, 1945) was the first conference, and in some ways the definitive one, endeavoring to deal with postwar realities as opposed to postwar planning. At Yalta, Stalin agreed to hold elections in Poland and in Central and Eastern Europe. By the time of the Potsdam meeting, Stalin's grip on much of the continent was secure, and there was a growing assertion of Soviet control in the occupied countries—an "iron fence," as Churchill called it, though he improved the phrase to "iron curtain" in his speech nine months later in Fulton, Missouri.

The Yalta participants could talk about the emerging United Nations organization. At Potsdam, the U.N. was a fact. Hence they would soon have to rule on the admission of governments from Bulgaria, Hungary, Czechoslovakia, and other Soviet satellites. In the Yalta talks, Stalin pressed for U.S. acceptance of a reparations scheme guaranteeing the Soviets 50 percent of an estimated $20 billion to be extracted from Germany, and FDR had blandly accepted the figure "for purposes of discussion."

Potsdam took place months after VE-day; the administration of Germany and the extraction of reparations had already begun. When the advance men from the State Department, who in June had helped prepare the site for the conference, returned to the scene in July, they found that many of the furnishings had been removed by the Soviets. In some cases even the toilet fixtures were gone. The incident set the tone for the conference to come: a mixture of hard-headed, unsympathetic bargaining, sometimes over the fate of millions of people, with a healthy dose of the comical, the mutually incomprehensible, and the macabre.

Clayton attended the Potsdam conference as chairman of the U.S. Economic Committee, with principal responsibility for the reparations question. Reparations to a large extent meant Germany, the principal aggressor in the war and the major economic power in continental Europe.

Besides being a potent emotional issue, reparations were the most urgent point on the agenda. Decisions about reparations were being made every day in the field, as the Soviets stripped assets from across Europe and British, French, and American field commanders wondered what to do about zones under their control. The timely reparations issue thus provided an early, concrete, undelayable test of the extent to which the Soviets—who at the time were pressing for U.S. economic aid—would be cooperative partners with the United States or outright adversaries.

Reparations are a sensitive and emotional question following any war but especially so in the aftermath of Hitler's Holocaust. Morgenthau, who had lost friends and relatives to Hitler's death camps, was intensely emotional about the subject. When Harry White questioned one of Morgenthau's ideas for the occupation, which proposed the virtual abolition of industry in the Ruhr heartland (instead of displacing some fifteen million to eighteen million persons, White proposed to keep the Ruhr producing but under international control), Morgenthau exploded:

> Just strip it. I don't care what happens to the population. . . . I would take every mine, every mill and factory, and wreck it. . . . Steel, coal, everything. Just close it down. I am for destroying it first and we will worry about the population second.[2]

Morgenthau was not the only one who held this view. Cordell Hull, who had spent much of his life bemoaning the punitive settlement imposed on Germany at Versailles in 1918, said at one point: "This Nazism is down in the German people a thousand miles deep and you have just got to uproot it, and you can't do it by just shooting a few people." Consequently, Hull favored denuding Germany after the war far in excess of legitimate concerns about removing Germany's capacity to produce armaments.

Among Roosevelt's top advisers in the fall of 1944, only Secretary of War Henry L. Stimson made a strong case against a harsh occupation regime, but Roosevelt's feelings were much closer to Morgenthau's. Of an early proposal of Stimson's, which while certainly calling for the dismantling of German weapons facilities envisioned a positive effort to rebuild the civilian economy, FDR complained:

> It gives me the impression that Germany is to be restored just as much as the Netherlands or Belgium. . . . There exists a school of thought both in London and here which would, in effect, do for Germany what this Government did for its own citizens in 1933 when they were flat on their backs. I see no reason. . . . The German people as a whole must have it driven home to them that the whole nation has been engaged in a lawless conspiracy against the decencies of modern civilization.[3]

Thus from its completion on September 4, 1944, and well into 1945, the Morgenthau plan for Germany represented the guiding spirit of the administration. If Morgenthau's scheme was hotly opposed by Stimson and debated in the press, it nevertheless seemed to reflect FDR's thinking. Morgenthau's plan ("Program to Prevent Germany from Starting a World War III") began by calling for "the complete demilitarization of Germany in the shortest possible time after surrender."

Large geographic chunks of the country were carved off and ceded to Poland, France, and the Soviet Union. The Ruhr would be virtually abolished as an industrial entity. "This area should not only be stripped of all . . . existing industries but so weakened and controlled that it cannot in the forseeable future become an industrial area." Within six months of the end of the war, "all industrial plants and equipment not destroyed by military action shall be completely dismantled and transported to the Allied nations." Even so, such economic activity as remained in the Ruhr would be run by an international authority.[4]

The rest of Germany would be divided into a northern and southern half, a pair of confederations featuring strong local control by the Republics of Bavaria, Baden, Prussia, Saxony, and smaller states. All German schools, universities, newspapers, and radio stations would be closed until Allied military control could be established.

The Morgenthau plan did not include, though its author had mused about it, breaking up German families to facilitate the reeducation of a generation of German youth who had been raised on Nazi propaganda. Morgenthau asked Stimson at one point:

> Don't you think the thing to do is to take a leaf from Hitler's book and completely remove these children from their parents and make them wards of the state, and have ex-U.S. Army officers, English officers, and Russian Army officers run these schools and have these children learn the true spirit of democracy?[5]

Clayton, like Stimson, agreed with Morgenthau on the strict control of war industries, a strong denazification program, and other political measures to make sure the war against fascism had not been fought in vain. Like White and Stimson, however, he was appalled by some of the plan's features. Prewar Germany had accounted for a substantial share of European trade, and the European economies generally depended on trade for 15 to 25 percent of their total output. Coal and other raw materials were in desperately short supply in Britain and France and were readily available from the Ruhr; it seemed folly to let these needed goods go to waste. Along these lines, Stimson had written a memorandum to FDR criticizing the Morgenthau plan:

> I can conceive of endeavoring to meet the misuse which Germany has recently made of this production by wise systems of control or trusteeship, or even transfers of ownership to other nations. But I cannot conceive of turning such a gift of nature into a dust heap . . . condemning the German people to a condition of servitude in which, no matter how hard or how effectively a man worked, he could not materially increase his economic conditions in the world.[6]

With Clayton serving in the State Department, Stimson acquired a new ally. Shortly after Yalta, Secretary of State Stettinius asked Clayton to prepare a State Department "interpretation" of the U.S.-Soviet understanding on reparations. Using the same high Allied reparations claims whose validity he would later minimize at Potsdam, Clayton drew up an alternative to the Morgenthau plan. It was clear, Clayton argued, that the Allies might never get the large amounts sought out of an economically stripped Germany. Accordingly, Clayton's "Draft Directive for Germany" did not call for the annihilation of German industry. Instead, he recommended that after weapons plants and related facilities had been dismantled, the goal of U.S. occupation policy would be, as Stimson had proposed, to restore "as quickly as possible" a healthy level of economic production under a central German administration. To ease the transition, Clayton recommended a strong central authority that could pick up where Germany's own strong central government had left off.* Zonal commanders would have some discretion, but they would not rule as quasi-independent heads of state, as envisioned by Morgenthau.[7]

Morgenthau was disappointed with both FDR and Clayton, writing in his diary, "Sooner or later the President just has to clean his house." He was furious at Stettinius, who heightened the interdepartmental squabble by sneaking Clayton's paper in for FDR's signature without showing it to the secretaries of war or treasury. Roosevelt tried to solve the problem by creating another committee—the Informal Policy Committee on Germany (IPCOG)—to write a plan that would be agreeable to all the departments.

Clayton chaired this new committee, which included John J. McCloy from war, Harry White of treasury, Ralph Bard from navy, and W. H. Fowler of the Foreign Economic Administration. The panel leaned strongly against Clayton. McCloy, who worked for Stimson but did not share his views, favored a punitive design like Morgenthau's. White was inclined toward Clayton's views but was intensely loyal to Morgenthau; he thus supported a harsh administration of Germany, though he believed it to be counterproductive.

Weary of intrigue, Clayton consented to a joint draft, written largely by McCloy, that papered over the differences. That memo, "Summary of U.S. Initial Post-Defeat Policy Relating to Germany," gave Morgenthau his way on administrative matters. Economi-

---

*The ensuing debates over the Clayton design for Germany often were about the issue of centralized versus decentralized control, with Clayton favoring a central administration and Morgenthau, a decentralized one. As a matter of general political philosophy, the positions normally would have been reversed. The issue under contention was not centralization per se but concern about how thoroughly Germany had to be weakened to preclude it again becoming a potential aggressor. Clayton favored the centralized scheme because his goal was the maximum German recovery that could be safe; central control would be both efficient, because it was what existed in Germany, and consistent with minimum security guarantees, because the Germans would need to be controlled more tightly politically if economic expansion were to be safe for the Allies. For Morgenthau, the whole goal of the occupation policy was to weaken the German economy to the lowest level consistent with human decency.

cally, it allowed for the Allied forces to "permit or establish control
of essential national public services such as railroads, communications, and power . . . finance and foreign affairs . . . and the
production and distribution of essential commodities." In contrast,
it specified:

> No action shall be taken, in execution of the reparations program
> or otherwise, which would tend to support basic living standards
> of Germany on a higher level than that existing in any one of the
> neighboring United Nations. . . . Recurrent reparations should
> not require the rehabilitation or development of German heavy
> industry and should not foster the dependence of other countries
> upon the German economy.

Byrnes regarded the paper as a clear-cut victory for Clayton: "It
said nothing about making Germany an agricultural and pastoral
state." But what the memo actually said depended on how one
interpreted words like "tend to support" or "heavy industry" or
"dependence." FDR approved the March 23 IPCOG directive signed
by Clayton, McCloy, and Morgenthau. At Clayton's request, McCloy
left for Europe (he and White were immersed in preparations for
the Bretton Woods debate) to see firsthand the difficulties of occupation and report back to IPCOG. There matters stood when Truman assumed office in April 1945.[8]

Clayton's decision to dispatch McCloy proved a deft stroke. In
Europe, McCloy saw the breakdown of an economic system long
intimately tied to German output. Complaints poured in to Mc-
Cloy from the Allied field commanders: no coal in Berlin or in
France, the Poles were taking it; no food coming from the Ukraine,
it was going to the Russians. People were starving. The burden of
locating and paying for supplies, for running a political economy
for millions of people, was inevitably falling on Stimson, McCloy,
and the War Department.

The goal of laying Germany to waste, McCloy discovered, was
redundant; it lay wasted along with the rest of Europe. Even Charles
de Gaulle said he preferred a controlled German recovery over a

scorched-earth policy. France and the rest of Europe needed growth, not vain sacrifices.

On April 26, McCloy reported to Clayton, who promptly forwarded the report to Truman. "There is complete economic, social, and political collapse going on in Central Europe," McCloy wrote. "The extent . . . is unparalleled in history unless one goes back to the collapse of the Roman Empire, and even that may not have been as great an economic upheaval." The next day Truman met with Clayton and McCloy to review these findings. Although Truman did not order an explicit reversal of FDR's policy, it was clear that the Morgenthau plan was not going to form the core of his goals at Potsdam. "I had never been for that plan even when I was in the Senate," Truman wrote later, "and since reaching the White House I had come to feel even more strongly about it. I thought it was proper to disarm Germany. . . . But I did not approve reducing Germany to an agrarian state. That would have been an act of revenge, and too many peace treaties had been based on that spirit."[9] Clayton had persuaded his government to reject the punitive spirit of the Morgenthau plan. There was still the small matter of convincing the Russians to do the same.

Clayton arrived at Potsdam with Edwin Pauley, a personal adviser to Truman and U.S. representative on the Allied Commission on Reparations. The looting of Germany already under way shocked them. Early discussions with the Soviets had allowed for the removal of "war booty," which traditionally means guns, ammunition, and other supplies with direct military use. Instead, the Soviets were impounding knives, forks, rayon, optical instruments, paintings, carpets, chairs—anything movable of value—as fast as they could. International Telephone and Telegraph's plant in Berlin, Clayton and Pauley found, had been stripped of its machinery. In some cases the removal process was so frantic that the Russians stockpiled the booty in open fields; Soviet transportation could not keep pace with the plundering.

Clayton and Pauley were shown a point on the line between the Russian and American zones. Before the line had been fixed, Soviet troops had entered a plant that would end up in the U.S. area, stripped it clean, and moved its equipment onto the Soviet side. The booty lay out in the open and clearly visible at a point about 200 yards from the dividing line.[10]

On July 20, Clayton met his Soviet counterparts on the economic subcommittee. Andrei Vishinsky headed up the Soviet team. Vishinsky, who worked closely with Molotov, the foreign minister, was once called—with unintended irony—"one of the fathers of the Soviet judicial system." The *New York Sun* pronounced him "one of those just men by whom impartial laws are written," yet it was he who, as the leading state prosecutor throughout the 1930s, gave the purge its rallying cry: "Shoot them like the mad dogs they are."*

Ivan Maisky, who for eleven years had served as the Soviet ambassador to Britain, presented the Soviet proposal. Maisky was, in historian Charles Mee's words, "a cherubic fellow with a goatee," a fun-loving rake who had been a journalist on Fleet Street in London for several years. Was not the whole point of Potsdam, Maisky asked, to settle the German question? Well then, "the main task of the Control Council is the elimination of the German war potential." The general aim, therefore, "which will be carried out uniformly in all zones of occupation, will be in preventing recovery of those parts of the economy which are the basis of the heavy

---

*Clayton later recalled, "One day Vishinsky was late at a meeting where I was chairman. He always talked like a blue streak, and that day he came in talking and kept on talking as he sat down. I said, 'Mr. Vishinsky, before you came in we were discussing a suggestion by the British member. If you like, we can explain it to you.' He kept talking. I repeated. Then he said, 'We aren't children. We don't need so much talking to explain.' I said, 'Mr. Vishinsky, since you came in this room 10 minutes ago, no one's done any talking but you.' He was furious."

industry." How did one do this? seize the factories and send half of them as reparations to Russia![11]

Clayton said the Americans agreed with the desire to dismantle Germany's war-making potential and understood that after making heroic sacrifices, the Russian people were in need of the largest amount of reparations that could be extracted. The Americans, however, felt that a better way of maximizing reparations would be to tolerate and even encourage a resurgence of German production, not only of commodities but also of light industrial and consumer goods. To seize everything right at the start and leave Germany completely decapitalized would tend to reduce the reparations it could pay in the long run, Clayton observed.

To recover, Clayton reasoned, Germany would have to import food and capital equipment for permitted industries. The importers and the banks financing the imports would want to be paid for their goods or they would not deliver. Whatever was taken out of Germany should be applied first to paying for these shipments; otherwise there would be few reparations to divide after a few months. German reparations would have to come out of remaining production; the first thing was to pay for imports.

No, Maisky insisted; first comes reparations, then imports. Clayton tried to explain that the former would dry up without the latter.

> This is like the receivership of a big corporation. If a railroad company can't pay its debts, the receiver keeps that road going, issues receivers' certificates which take precedence over all creditors. Otherwise the creditors would get nothing.

The bankers, Clayton explained, would not finance it any other way.[12]

The analogy was not likely to reassure the Communists across the table. Bankers, corporations, receiverships? "We can never get the Russian people," Maisky said, "who have sacrificed so much, to understand why the Wall Street bankers have to be paid before they are!"[13]

Back and forth the panel went for several days and often well into the night. Clayton asked Pauley to devise an analogy that the Soviets could grasp and accept. In a letter to Maisky, Pauley wrote:

> When we say that essential imports are a prior charge on exports, this is not because we think imports are more important than reparations. Quite the contrary. All we are saying is that you must feed the cow to get the milk. The food is a "prior" charge, it comes first in time, but it is not more important.
>
> Without carrying this simile too far we could say that you want a plan which will give lots of milk. We both expect that the cow will lose both horns and get mighty thin. We want to be sure that the small amount of fodder required will be paid for with some of the milk.[14]

❏ ❏ ❏

Given the existence of such a gulf on general principles, Clayton and Vishinsky agreed that they could not agree, kicking the question up to the foreign ministers. On July 23, Byrnes brought the subject up with Molotov. American reports, Byrnes said, reveal that the Soviets were unilaterally removing a wide range of goods and supplies from their own zone. Maisky had admitted this in conversations with Pauley and Clayton, while striving to come up with a definition of war booty that would include such things as stuffed chairs, faucets, silverware, and bathtubs.

Were the Soviets proceeding on this unilateral basis? "Yes, that is the case," Molotov replied blandly. If the Americans were worried, they could deduct these items—he suggested $300 million would be a fair figure—from the Soviet reparations total of "$10 billion, agreed to at the Crimea conference." The Soviets thus were not budging, at least not at first.[15]

Byrnes, Pauley, and Clayton conferred that afternoon. Clayton's staff had compiled an economic profile of the different occupation zones. According to those studies, the Soviet zone contained 31 percent of Germany's movable manufacturing facilities, 35 to 39 percent of the total prewar manufacturing and mining, and 48 percent of the agricultural resources. The Soviets were likely to try to seize as much of this wealth as they could, regardless of what reparations might be paid to them out of the French, British, and American sectors.

Why not propose that each country satisfy its reparations claims out of its own zone? As a sweetener, the Western countries could offer to give the Russians a fixed percentage—say 12 percent—of whatever capital equipment they moved out of Germany. Some of this would be handed over to the Russians without charge; for some, they would have to exchange coal and agricultural produce. Taking reparations out of one's own zone, with a division of responsibility, might obviate endless paperwork over the valuation of assets.

Molotov realized that such a plan would end Stalin's hopes of obtaining riches on a large scale from western Germany. In gaining access to more of the riches from the East, the Soviets gained nothing, for they would shuffle about factories and goods within their zone as they saw fit. Molotov could not admit this, so he clung to the principle of a fixed figure but reduced the amount he would accept. Perhaps the Soviets could get by with $9 billion, he mused. Byrnes stuck with the new U.S. proposal. The issue remained unsettled, as the ministers continued to wrangle with the other great issue, the political future of Central and Eastern Europe.[16]

The talks on Eastern Europe had the same character as the reparations issue. Sweeping metaphors and frequent appeals to "the decisions reached at Yalta" pervaded the proceedings. Underneath the diplomatic politesse, however, the British and the Americans wanted a democratic Europe, and the Soviets did not.

Western diplomats in Hungary, Yugoslavia, Poland, Bulgaria, and Czechoslovakia reported heavy censorship of noncommunist political journals, arbitrary arrests, and close confinement of Allied control officials. The Soviets denied it flatly. "All fairy tales!" Stalin told Churchill, and later, "There must be some misunderstanding. . . . I assure you that the Government of Bulgaria is more democratic than the Government of Italy."

At a certain point, one either had to call the other party a liar and go home or accept the status quo and try to paper it over with promises of future conferences and fact-finding commissions. Truman had called the Soviet bluff months earlier in a clash with Molotov in the Oval Office. "I have never been talked to like that in my life," Molotov complained after a long, bitter exchange on Poland. "Carry out your agreements and you won't get talked to like that," Truman replied. Yet even the decision to confront the Soviets about the issue of political pluralism involved tacit U.S. acceptance of the status quo.

Clayton's recognition that his differences with the Soviets were not resolvable—producing the joint decision to refer the dispute to the Big Three leaders—paralleled and foreshadowed the political future of Central and Eastern Europe.

❏ ❏ ❏

The immediate point of contention at Potsdam concerned the recognition of the governments of Romania, Bulgaria, Hungary, Italy, and Finland. The Americans and the British, confident of the situation in Italy because they were in control, recognized an Italian government was to hold a referendum in 1946. The Western countries had not recognized the other Soviet-occupied republics. On paper, their governments were similar to Italy's, though they had behaved differently in cracking down on opposition groups. The only difference lay in whether the totalitarian countries were going to carry out promises of free elections at some later date.

A U.S. declaration that Central and Eastern Europe was lost, absent strong action, was not something anyone wanted to issue. So the discussion, as in the case of reparations, hinged on fine points of timing and nuance. Stalin wanted the governments recognized now. Truman refused. So Stalin pressed for a joint statement that their recognition would be considered "at an early date" or that the Allies "hope to conclude peace treaties" with their governments. (One can hardly conclude a peace treaty with a government, Stalin realized, without recognizing it in fact.) Truman demurred.

Stalin would not budge: the governments must be recognized. Truman also would not budge: they must first be reorganized. "The result was a complete impasse, and might be said to have been the beginning of the cold war," Admiral William D. Leahy (Truman's military chief of staff) later recalled.[17]

The thought that the Soviets might bring down an iron curtain across the middle of Europe caused Byrnes, after Churchill's departure, to propose a formulation to the new British delegation that proved acceptable to the Soviets as well. The countries would agree to "examine" the question of establishing diplomatic relations "to the extent possible." In return, the Soviets accepted the Clayton principle of reparations divided by zone. Years later, Clayton said of Potsdam, "On most of the big issues that I listened to around the conference table, it seemed to me that certainly in the answers that Marshal Stalin made and the decisions that he made . . . were pretty fair. I came away with the hope that we might be able to get along with the Russians."[18]

Were the Americans duped? Or, to put it more positively, was an opportunity missed? The answer is probably no on both counts. The United States and the Soviet Union wanted things that were mutually exclusive and contradictory. Potsdam was, in effect, an agreement to disagree about the future of Germany, about reparations, about the freedom of Central and Eastern Europe. If there was a delusion, it was an American one that a modus vivendi might yet be patched together.

❑ ❑ ❑

From Potsdam, Clayton flew to London, arriving on August 3 to take part in a meeting of UNRRA, the United Nations Relief and Rehabilitation Administration.[19] At its inception, UNRRA seemed poised to do the job we now generally credit to the Marshall Plan. Like the World Bank, the U.S. Export-Import Bank, and the British loan, UNRRA was created to bridge the gap between the end of the war and the postwar normalcy expected as Europe recovered. On recovery, it was hoped that such long-range institutions as the International Monetary Fund and the International Trade Organization (the General Agreement on Tariffs and Trade, or GATT) would begin to function successfully. UNRRA was, in fact, tailored to the purpose; congressional appropriations were conditioned on fervent promises from Acheson and Clayton that its job was temporary and that its operations, like those of lend-lease, would be completed within a few years.

In its three years, UNRRA distributed some $2.3 billion throughout Europe, mostly in vital food, clothing, fuel, and medical supplies. Seventy percent of the money came from the United States, another 4 percent from Canada, and, in an act of generosity and enlightened self-interest, about 20 percent from financially strapped Great Britain.*

Two-thirds of the aid went to countries in Eastern and Central Europe, including Yugoslavia, Poland, Czechoslovakia, and the Soviet Ukraine. "The hopes were placed too high, and the demands," British foreign minister Ernest Bevin said in a 1945 speech to the House of Commons urging continued UNRRA funding. UNRRA, however, helped keep Europe going until 1947, after which

---

*"This was at a time," as British historian Alan Bullock points out, "when the British government for the first time had to introduce bread rationing in their own country, something that had never been done during the war." (Bullock, *Ernest Bevin* [New York: Norton, 1983], p. 143.)

time the Marshall Plan and the concomitant General Agreement on Tariffs and Trade took over.

Historians Michael Balfour and John Mair credit UNRRA's timely assistance with saving many Austrians from starvation in 1946. Greece and Italy were hardly economic success stories, and under their weak governments much aid was mishandled; but their national income and foreign trade rose markedly in 1946 and 1947, UNRRA's assistance being a major factor. "It is no exaggeration to say," wrote historian Allen J. Matusow, "that American relief shipments in 1945–46 [made chiefly through UNRRA] were the salvation of Europe."[20]

Nevertheless, UNRRA was a troubled institution. "Clayton and I," Acheson recalls, "bore the burden of testimony for the Government before the House Foreign Affairs Committee . . . for such endeavors as UNRRA." The task was indeed a burden. Congressional suspicion had been present in 1943, when Acheson, then in charge of the program, crafted the document initiating UNRRA in the form of an executive agreement that would not require congressional approval. The manuver was silly because Congress would have to appropriate the funds for UNRRA anyway. Congress quickly reminded Acheson of that reality. Each annual appropriation was a battle with the usual allusions to Santa Claus and rat holes.[21]

Clayton, arriving in London in August 1945, was a man caught in the middle. The Soviets, Yugoslavs, and Lublin Poles (the Soviet puppet government) assailed the United States for being stingy, for dominating the operation, and for keeping a too-tight purse string. Australia, Brazil, and other would-be central committee members wanted to know why the United States was so weak; surely Clayton could arrange for them to be seated. Back home, Congress kept a suspicious eye on what seemed to be the latest New Deal giveaway scheme.

Clayton tried to navigate between those forces. He supported a resolution calling on the United States and other contributors to donate 1 percent of their 1942–1943 national income to UNRRA, thereby adding to his chores back home that of winning a congressional appropriation for that amount. At the same time, he warned his fellow delegates that if the U.S. share of UNRRA's funds exceeded 75 percent, Congress and Truman might balk.[22]

The administrative problems of UNRRA were another concern, as complaints poured over Clayton's desk all through the summer. The London-based Polish government in exile was incensed that UNRRA's director, Herbert A. Lehman, had declined to notify it of a forthcoming UNRRA council meeting. Acheson then cabled that Belgrade wanted assistance to Yugoslavian refugees in Italy stopped and the people shipped back. Harriman's information on Soviet diversion of supplies was "inadequate," but Kennan had his suspicions.

"Numerous indications point to following conclusions," Joseph Grew wired on July 30. "Machinery being shipped to Russia from Yugoslavia is perhaps expected to be replaced by UNRRA; wheat, livestock, sugar, and glass and other commodities are being hurried into Russia; strong suspicion that all UNRRA wool will go to [Tito's] Partisan Army; UNRRA food and medical supplies being used to foster Communist Party to disadvantage of bulk of population." In the midst of all the complaints, Moscow blithely informed the State Department that it would insist on provision to the Soviet Union of $700 million, or the bulk of UNRRA's forthcoming budget.[23]

One wonders why Clayton bothered to fight for UNRRA funding. He was certainly aware of the "difficulties and weaknesses in the UNRRA administration," as he later testified before Congress. Clayton, however, felt that as of the summer of 1945 it was the best if not the only relief agency in existence. Supplanting it, he argued, was for the time being "unthinkable and impractical." Instead, Clayton recalled, he tried to do "all in my power as this government's representative on the council to help overcome and correct" the problems, keeping the aid flowing until a better instrument could be devised.[24] He managed to deflect the Soviet demand for $700 million, noting that Moscow soon might have access to much larger sums under programs where its request would not be as outrageous—at once keeping the existing money from Moscow but blocking the Soviets from walking out of UNRRA altogether, as some feared would happen. He also managed, on a procedural point, to sidetrack Yugoslavia's request to cut off refugees in Italy.

It was not in Clayton's power to clean up UNRRA's operations within Central and Eastern Europe. Just as reparations reached a higher figure than the United States was willing to agree to, so too did monitoring UNRRA demands. What were we willing to do, for instance, when the Soviets lied, cheated, or broke their promises?

Clayton and Byrnes raised the matter of diversion of UNRRA supplies—at Potsdam, in London, and in the ongoing Soviet requests for credits and loans. Clayton also encouraged Lehman and the U.S. diplomatic missions to keep ferreting out and reporting on events. In August UNRRA finally got a mission into Yugoslavia, which reported that "observers free to move. . . . In all areas observers give no evidence of discrimination." Either the initial U.S. information had been wrong, or the continued diplomatic pressure from Clayton and Lehman had forced a correction.

In response to the changed situation in Yugoslavia, which Clayton attributed to Soviet influence, he supported UNRRA's shipment of $250 million in goods to the Soviet Ukraine. Harriman criticized this decision, but Clayton felt that $250 million was a small price to pay for preventing a Soviet walkout from UNRRA and the resulting uncertainty of congressional aid to Italy, Greece, Austria, and other countries. Besides, the Soviet Ukraine clearly qualified for the aid under UNRRA's rules.

The *Washington Post* and other newspapers editorialized in support of the Ukraine's request; the United States probably would have been defeated fighting it and appear hypocritical in doing so, as Acheson wrote Harriman in a memorandum defending Clayton's move. One could make a case in 1945 for all-out economic warfare against the Soviets; as that was not the U.S. government's policy at the time, Clayton did the best he could with the tools at hand.[25]

The end of UNRRA came a year later. As a device for winning congressional funding, Clayton had urged the London delegates to pass a resolution calling for the phased elimination of their own agency. The resolution passed, enabling Clayton to overcome congressional skepticism that UNRRA was going to become a perpetual drain on U.S. resources. Congress made it clear that no further money for UNRRA would be forthcoming.

Even so, as UNRRA prepared to meet at Geneva in August 1946, some countries entertained hopes that the United States had not really decided to terminate financial support for UNRRA. Anticipating trouble, Clayton scheduled a private conference with the British and Canadian delegates for July 23. The United States, Clayton told them, took his testimony to Congress seriously and would press for termination of UNRRA at Geneva. The British and Canadian delegates agreed that UNRRA had served its purpose and that the time had come to rely on the Bretton Woods institutions and to focus on commercial and trade talks to secure Europe's future.[26]

Clayton's final task in relation to UNRRA was to clarify his alleged remark that U.S. aid to UNRRA was a "gravy train" that soon would make its last trip. Like so many scoops in the Acheson-Clayton era, the gravy-train episode was first reported by James Reston, Acheson and Clayton's mutual friend at the *New York Times*. Someone had leaked the purpose of Clayton's July 23 meeting with the British and the Canadians; Reston used that leak as the basis for a story on July 28 that the United States and England would insist on terminating UNRRA at its forthcoming council meeting in Geneva. Reston reported that Clayton had told the assembled delegates that "the gravy train is going around for the last time." A *Times* editorial the next day took notice of Clayton's "unfortunate remark." The *Washington Post* called the statement "exceedingly inept."

Even though the remark caused remarkably little stir in Europe, it was a personal embarrassment for Clayton and later earned him the title of Lord High Executioner from UNRRA's historian.[27] On his return to Washington, Clayton wrote to the *Post* to set the record straight:

Your authority for asserting that I used the expression "gravy train" may derive from an article by James Reston. . . . The meeting to which Mr. Reston refers was a small meeting to discuss the future of UNRRA. Only six people were present besides myself. Three of the six are now abroad and cannot be consulted. I have conferred with the other three, two of whom categorically say that I made no such statement. . . . The third says that he has no recollection that I made any such statement. I myself do not recall making this statement; if I had made it, I think I would remember it.

On numerous occasions I have fought UNRRA's battles before congressional committees and elsewhere. Looking back on the original idea of the creation of a great international organization for emergency relief and rehabilitation, I have the highest admiration and praise for the men who first conceived it and whose leadership brought it into being. It was an act of real statesmanship . . . but UNRRA's job was of a temporary and emergency nature.[28]

Before Clayton left London in 1945, a different gravy train had ended, another one was about to begin, and, as with UNRRA, Clayton would find much of the pulling would be up to him.

11

The Battle of (Lending) Britain

On Sunday, August 19, 1945 (a few days after the surrender of Japan ended World War II), Dean Acheson was in Canada, taking a break before returning to Washington to become under secretary of state to James F. Byrnes.[1] Will Clayton, resting in London for the weekend, penned a few notes to a speech promising the UNRRA delegates that the United States had learned the interwar lessons of economic isolation and would commit another $1.3 billion to European relief and reconstruction.

Pete Collado remembers sitting at a Cambridge teashop, resting after a day of sight-seeing. Suddenly his attention was attracted by a bulletin coming over the radio. President Truman had announced the immediate end of America's lend-lease effort. (Truman later would call this the "worst decision" of his presidency.) Even goods in the pipeline, the terse White House announcement said, would be delivered only for payment. This dramatic change of policy applied not only to the Soviet Union but to Britain and other Allies.

At a cabinet meeting a few days earlier, Leo Crowley, director of the Foreign Economic Administration, reminded Truman that, according to the law that authorized monies for lend-lease, the program was supposed to end with the end of the war. Shortly after VE-day in May 1945, in fact, Crowley told the Soviets they would have to begin paying for lend-lease shipments for which they already owed $11 billion. The Soviets had refused to pay, so shipments stopped.

Byrnes, eager to stop aid to the Soviets, felt that the administration could not very well treat the British differently. Truman remembered the debates in Congress and the administration's repeated assurances that the end of the war would mean the end of lend-lease. After a short discussion, he gave Crowley approval and the release was issued.

But earlier, in London, Clayton (and the British) had been operating on a completely different assumption. Despite the legal requirement that lend-lease would stop once the war ended, it had long been assumed that some practical arrangement would be worked out to smooth the transition. Clayton and Treasury Secretary Fred M. Vinson had prepared memorandums on such an eventuality.

Whatever the testimony and legal niceties, the quick decision to end lend-lease was unexpected, witness the shocked reaction of Clayton, Collado, and the British. Once again, the swiftness with which war ended in the Pacific caught American and British planners unawares. Exacerbating Clayton's embarrassment was the fact that he was not informed of the coming announcement until after Keynes and the British learned of it.

The next morning, Clayton was on the transatlantic telephone "venting the vials of his wrath" against Byrnes and Truman, as Keynes's biographer, Roy Harrod, wrote. Harrod's account may be overstated. Clayton had a tendency to get icy cool, not hot, when he was especially mad. Still, Collado, who was in the room when Clayton talked to Byrnes, recalls that Clayton talked "more strongly than I've ever heard him," and Clayton recalls, "I was never so close to resigning."

Clayton managed to soften the terms, and the United States eventually wrote off most of Britain's existing lend-lease debt. It was not nearly enough of an adjustment to substantially ease the crunch on British finance. But neither would a few more months of lend-lease or UNRRA aid. In some respects, the "harsh and rough" announcement, as Winston Churchill called it, had a positive outcome in that it focused the minds of Keynes and Clayton on the larger problem of Britain's general economic plight. The situation was indeed serious, as Richard Gardner notes:

> About one-quarter (7.3 billion pounds) of Britain's pre-war national wealth (30 billion pounds) had been lost in the war. The main factors were physical destruction (1.5 billion); shipping losses (0.7 billion); internal disinvestment (0.9 billion); and external disinvestment (4.2 billion). . . . To make matters worse, exports by the end of 1944 had dropped to one-third their pre-war volume.
>
> The decline in exports was particularly alarming in light of the losses in shipping and investment earnings. . . . It would take at least three years before the [necessary] increase [in British exports] could be achieved; during this time, Britain would face a deficit in its balance of payments of an estimated 1.25 billion pounds ($5 billion.) Some form of transitional assistance was obviously required to avert a fall in British living standards to a point even below their war-time levels and to facilitate British participation in the ambitious projects for multilateral trade.[2]

Adding to these dislocations was the looming threat of nationalization for major industries under Britain's new Labour government. Nationalization was already chasing away urgently needed investment and talent, Clayton worried, just when England most required an economic boost.

For Clayton, Britain was more than a country in need. It was—along with France and whatever could be salvaged of Germany—a linchpin of the open political economy he hoped to build. Sterling had yielded its position at the center of the global banking system to the U.S. dollar, but it still ran second. In 1938, Britain accounted for 32 percent of Europe's trade. (France took up 10 percent, and the western zones of Germany, 19 percent.) In combination with the United States, Europe was the leader in world trade before

World War II, accounting for 65 percent of world exports and 68 percent of world imports.

Beyond these statistical realities, Clayton saw Britain as an appropriate partner for the United States, a bastion of political and economic liberalism. Clayton certainly thought some of Prime Minister Attlee's domestic spending and nationalization schemes ill-advised, and he had opposed Keynes's commodity cartel schemes in the Bretton Woods talks. Yet on matters of currency and trade, the British were sound and vital partners in the quest for economic liberalism.[3]

If the British were solvent, the new economic order could be built. Without them, Clayton pictured the world breaking up into a series of regional political fiefdoms and trading blocs: the Soviets, Latin America, Asia, continental Europe, and a tattered remnant of Britain's old empire. If a few billion more dollars had to be spent to secure economic recovery after a war effort that had cost hundreds of billions, it was, in Clayton's view, a bargain.[4]

Keynes and Clayton promptly sought to rescue a long-term victory from the short-term embarrassment of lend-lease's sudden end. Keynes prepared financial projections on Britain's plight for Clayton and the British cabinet, and the two men agreed to hold talks in Washington for a new U.S. loan of up to $6 billion. On the basis of his conversation with Clayton, Keynes felt certain that the money could be secured as a gift or, at worst, as an interest-free loan. In fact, he was overconfident; Clayton's sympathy and his reading of U.S. interest in the matter did not coincide with those of Congress, Treasury Secretary Fred M. Vinson, or public opinion. The British foreign minister, Ernest Bevin, also was skeptical. He might lack Keynes's urbane charm, but he had years as a labor organizer and negotiator. "When I listen to Lord Keynes talking," Bevin reportedly said, "I seem to hear the coins jingling in my pocket; but I cannot see that they are really there."[5]

Indeed, the political atmosphere on both sides of the Atlantic could hardly have been worse. Public opinion polls revealed that Americans feared an endless stream of demands for U.S. dollars and resented that their sacrifices in the war effort had not been sufficiently appreciated by the Russians or the British. They were also eager to get out of Europe and focus on domestic issues. A poll taken regularly from 1935 to 1949 asked if Americans felt foreign problems were the "most vital" facing the country. In October 1945 the percentage answering yes hit an all-time low at 7 percent.[6]

American reaction to England's response to the lend-lease decision indicates how cool public sentiment was likely to be to a proposed new loan to England. "I can't understand their [the British] attitude," Senator Robert F. Wagner exclaimed. "Unreasonable," chimed Sol Bloom, chairman of the House Foreign Affairs Committee. An unidentified Truman aide said that the British were putting on "a cry-baby act."[7] The *New York Daily News* likened the British reaction to "being mad at your rich uncle, who has been giving you handouts, because he died."[8]

Conversely, British public opinion bristled under its wartime sacrifices and the U.S. attitude that England was just another beggar asking for alms. "We require," said the *Manchester Guardian*, "an adequate acknowledgment . . . of the price we have paid." Fed by Keynes's projections, British leaders prepared the public for a $6 billion U.S. gift or a no-interest loan. "We have given in the common cause," Churchill had said that spring, "and may claim assistance to recover our normal economy from those we have helped to victory."[9]

Any assistance, Clayton warned Keynes in August, must have "a businesslike face" to it. Clayton recognized that there also would have to be a charitable element, but he could not ask Congress for any money unless there was a clearly perceived U.S. interest beyond helping an old ally. Keynes struck the same attitude on his arrival in Washington in September 1945: "The British Government had no reason to suppose that Lend-Lease would continue for a significant length of time after the end of the war," he said at a press conference. "We have received far too much liberality and consideration in the famous Lend-Lease act to make any complaint about the clean cut." In the same vein, Lord Halifax remarked, "We do not want to ask anything of you [the United States] which you are not satisfied is in the ultimate interest of your own country." That meant, Keynes explained, a faith "that the resulting general expansion of world trade will result in the final outcome in your and other countries as well as ourselves being much better off."[10] That linkage, connecting the loan to British action on multilateral trade and monetary policy, was precisely what Clayton sought as well.

In effect, the negotiation became an opportunity for both Clayton and Keynes to move the people in their countries to a position they believed to be in the national and international interest. The United States had to go outside the squeeze-the-debtor mentality that had wrecked the world order at Versailles. Britain had to follow through on its repeated promises—in the Atlantic Charter, at the Quebec talks, and at Bretton Woods—that it would cooperate in the new free-trade regime. The deadline for Bretton Woods ratification—December 31, 1945—was fast approaching. This meant that negotiations for a new British loan would have to be concluded by early December for Parliament to debate and act, thus increasing the pressure on the negotiators.

Treasury Secretary Fred M. Vinson chaired the American negotiating team with Clayton in charge of the "commercial policy" side of the loan, that is, the changes that the United States would demand in England's trade and monetary policies. Clayton certainly did not minimize the importance of the size of the loan or the interest rate; yet these were, to him, small issues. If 1 percent interest on a sufficient amount would save Britain and 2 percent on a smaller amount would not, why press for the 2 percent? Clayton's attitude was similar to that of General Robert E. Wood, chairman of Sears, Roebuck & Company, who wrote to Clayton, "If you succeed in doing away with the Empire preference and opening up the Empire to United States commerce, it may well be that we can afford to pay a couple of billion dollars for the privilege."

Accordingly, Clayton pressed for a generously low interest rate on a $5 billion loan; Vinson suggested $3.3 billion with higher interest; the president set the amount at $3.75 billion; and the British, while not reducing the 2 percent rate, negotiated a special distress clause that allowed them to skip the interest in years in which British trade failed to recover at a healthy rate. They also won a five-year grace period of no interest, making the effective rate on the loan closer to 1.6 percent.[11]*

Vinson, a cautious dealer, had only recently replaced Morgenthau at Treasury. A former congressman from Kentucky, then head of the Office of Economic Stabilization that was to cause Truman so much trouble in 1946, Vinson spoke with a mild drawl. He was "a reasonable man with a quick humor and even temper," author Allen Drury recalls, and "one of the six or eight most powerful men in the country. He wears the immense powers . . . as any other democratic citizen might—matter-of-factly, as though he were not very much impressed by them." Subsequent profiles have tended to portray Vinson as colorless; this he was not, with an easy wit with his friends on Capitol Hill.[12]

Vinson and Lord Keynes irritated one another, with Clayton and Harry White trying to bridge the culture gap. As the negotiations moved beyond the amount of the British loan to the British adjustment to free multilateral trade, Keynes often gave long, elegant discourses on the finer points of international finance. But Vinson's appreciation of these economic pearls was decidedly limited. His chief means of judging any idea seemed to center on how it would be greeted back in Louisville or Lexington, Kentucky. "Mebbe so, Lawd Keynes, mebbe so," Vinson would reply after a Keynesian peroration, "but down where I come from folks don't look at things that way." Clayton tried to warn Keynes that he was

---

*Gardner seldom errs but probably does not have it quite right when he says Clayton "recommended" $4 billion. That was the State Department figure, reached after some haggling. Clayton's own estimate of Britain's needs came to $5 billion, as his doodlings on a set of tables prepared for the October 11, 1945, session indicate. At the meeting, Clayton arrived at his first fallback position, suggesting that, with assistance from Canada, the agreed-on British needs might be met with a U.S. loan of $4.5 billion.

no longer dealing with Henry Morgenthau, which only made Keynes more pricklish and defiant. "Try to remember," a member of the British team pleaded, "that you are dealing with Kentucky." Keynes replied, "Well, Kentucky will have to like it."[13]

Keynes and Clayton largely agreed on the wisdom of the conditions being attached to the loan: British approval of Bretton Woods, the restoration of sterling convertibility, and the phasing out of preferential tariffs within the British Commonwealth. "It was quite clear" to Keynes, Roy Harrod later wrote, "that Britain, with her great dependence on invisible income, and her vulnerability on the side of international capital movements, would not flourish, whatever controls she might introduce, unless sterling was a currency that gave satisfaction. It could not do that if it was not convertible." Although Keynes was concerned about Britain's war debts, those negotiations "must not be allowed to stand in the way of convertibility. . . . In the last resort, it would be better to handle our creditors drastically, as, for instance, by freezing the balances, than to forego convertibility."[14]

The main focus of the negotiations between Clayton and Keynes thus lay on timing these steps. Keynes felt a longer adjustment period was necessary before Britain could submit to the rigors of trade competition, and he thus resisted Clayton's proposed deadline of December 1946 for convertible sterling. In place of Clayton's timetable, Keynes proposed a pledge to lift financial restrictions "at the earliest possible moment." But Clayton, who favored a soft stand on the size and interest terms of the loan, stood firm on the schedule for British policy reform.

Keynes finally got the Americans to push the timetable back to one year after the agreement took effect, which meant, if Congress acted in the spring of 1946, until the spring of 1947. Keynes also managed to insert an escape hatch allowing the postponement of convertibility in "exceptional cases" where other countries—who might not themselves have convertible currencies—were abusing the privileges of conversion.

Moreover, the Clayton-Keynes agreement's clauses on trade

policy did little more than reaffirm the Atlantic Charter. On this point, Keynes held firm. After all, he pointed out, the Americans had their own tariff system. Thus the loan emerged with a strong and immediate promise for Bretton Woods approval, a strong but delayed promise for convertibility, and a somewhat weak, but rhetorically important, repetition of existing British promises to negotiate a more open world trading order.[15]

Two points about the Clayton conditions should be noted. One is that although they could be considered a political quid pro quo—the British do something distasteful in return for a U.S. loan—that is not how Clayton viewed them. The concessions he pressed for were, in his view, actually in *England's* interest; they were also policies in which the United States had a special interest.

Clayton did not ask for a reversal of Britain's nationalization policy, even though Baruch and others criticized him for failing to attach this added condition to the loan. Nationalization for Clayton was a matter of British internal policy and thus not subject to U.S. dictates or pressure.[16] Yet Clayton saw the acceptance of the policies the Americans were urging as important not only to the United States and Britain's other trading partners but to Britain's recovery.

A second point—timing—should be also noted. Even such writers as Richard Gardner and Roy Harrod speak of convertibility and an easing of trade restrictions as desirable but having to be phased in owing to pressing financial difficulties. To Clayton, however, the press of financial difficulties made it all the more urgent that Britain adopt progrowth policies immediately.

Convertibility, if backed by England's central bank and the International Monetary Fund, would not drain resources. On the contrary, once convertibility was shown to be a stable policy, it would cause a surge of confidence in and demand for British currency and other financial instruments. In other words, said Clayton, sound money would attract investment and trade, not undermine it. Free trade was not some bitter pill to be swallowed only when the ailing patient, England, had recovered its health. It was a potent remedy for getting it well again and soon.

Clayton was pleased to write to Baruch during the negotiations that "we have loaded" the loan "with all the conditions the traffic will bear."[17] But Clayton did not view this achievement as an economic imposition on England. The more conditions that could be "loaded" on, provided they were good ones, the better. The only limiting factor—the ceiling on the amount of "traffic"—was political.

How generous would the Americans be, and how enlightened would the British policymakers be? In retrospect, even the delay allowed to the British on convertibility was probably too long a time, for it encouraged London to procrastinate. A bigger loan with even stricter conditions might have worked better. That was exactly the sort of loan Clayton would have preferred: $5 billion and at even lower interest but with airtight commercial and monetary guarantees. (In this, he favored much of what he later advocated in the Marshall Plan.)

As it was, the loan secured British compliance with the Bretton Woods agreement at a time when it could have wrecked it and kept open the issue of convertibility and a lowering of trade barriers. Like UNRRA it was not the way Clayton might have preferred, but it was the best tool available.

Signing the agreement on December 6, 1945, cleared the first hurdle. Now came Congress and Parliament. Clayton went to Arizona to rest and prepare for congressional hearings in January. Keynes dashed back to London to deal with Parliament before the December 31 Bretton Woods deadline. In a stirring address to the House of Lords, Keynes defended England's concessions both as necessary to secure aid and as generally wise in their own right. He spoke also of the dangers of a failure to ratify.

> How difficult it is for nations to understand one another, even when they have the advantage of a common language. . . . Everyone talks about international cooperation, but how little of pride, of temper, or of habit anyone is willing to contribute to it when it comes down to brass tacks.
> Has any country ever treated another country like this . . . for

the purpose of rebuilding another's strength and competitive position?[18]

Parliament approved the agreement, despite pervasive grumbling that it put British economic policy at the mercy of U.S. direction. A few days after his speech, Keynes wrote to Clayton in Arizona:

> My dear Will —
> Sorry to persecute you on your holiday with the old rag so thoroughly chewed out but you may perhaps glance through my speech in the House of Lords. . . . When I got back I found a good deal of misunderstanding. I think I may have done something to clear away a portion of it. I am sure that the general feeling of the country is one of intense relief and gratitude. . . .
>
> P.S.—Conversations here, now that the measure is through Parliament, convince me, to my very great satisfaction, that everyone here . . . is from now on going to work wholeheartedly to make a good job of policy along the lines which we have agreed.[19]

Clayton replied:

> Your remarks make good reading even on vacation. I only hope that I shall be able to make as able and effective a presentation before Congress.[20]

Clayton would need to be effective when he returned to Washington in January 1946 to lead the fight for the British loan. An early Gallup poll showed 60 percent of those interviewed opposed a loan to Britain; only 27 percent were in favor.

Clayton was never intimidated by initial poll numbers; they showed only what people think before an informed debate, not after. Still, influential leaders in Congress and business opposed the loan, including many who had supported Bretton Woods and Hull's reciprocal trade agreements. Jesse Jones led his Houston newspapers in a feverish editorial campaign against the Anglo-American financial agreement. Bernard Baruch wanted an inventory of America's ability to finance its own needs before it made any more loans abroad. "If we let England have billions," Baruch warned, "we will have to let Russia, China, France, Norway, Denmark, Belgium [Baruch listed six more potential recipients of U.S. largesse]."

This was no time to spend, warned the National Association of Manufacturers (NAM). "Unless the budget is balanced," a NAM release warned, "it may never be until America goes over the precipice." Senator Taft and other Republicans, who felt that they might at last have a winning issue, looked forward to victory in the fall elections and so girded for a fight. "Neither a borrower nor a lender be," admonished Senator Theodore G. Bilbo, a southern Democrat. "Keynes was the father of the New Deal," complained Senator Charles Brooks of Illinois, "and now want[s] a worldwide W. P. A."[21]

Clayton did his best to move Congress to an appreciation of the loan, starting with public opinion. He directed a State Department program that produced more than one hundred major speeches on behalf of the loan between February and April. James F. Byrnes, Henry Wallace, Dean Acheson, Secretary of Agriculture Clinton Anderson, and Marriner C. Eccles, the chairman of the Federal Reserve System, all joined in the effort, followed by business and labor leaders. Slowly, public opinion and elite, informed opinion began to shift. Of 147 major newspapers surveyed by the State Department, 87 supported the loan. Eleven of thirteen major magazines backed it as well.[22]

Despite potent opposition from Taft, the Senate Banking and Finance Committee voted fourteen to five for the loan, sending it to the floor on April 10. A long debate, lasting from April 17 to May 10, ensued, with Taft and the Republicans seeking to delay a vote until the press of other business forced the Senate to drop the measure. Clayton kept Senate leader Alben Barkley firmly behind the loan, and in late April, Clayton began a door-to-door canvass. He managed to switch Senator Kenneth McKellar of Tennessee from a doubter to a supporter and Senator Leverett Saltonstall of Massachusetts from a tepid supporter to an active one.

Late in April, Clayton was invited to debate the loan before a women's group in Washington. He declined until he learned that Taft would be appearing, along with Senator Bourke Hickenlooper, who still was listed as doubtful in the State Department's voting projections. The debate did not change Taft's thinking, but Clayton wrested a promise from Hickenlooper to let him finish making his case in person the next morning. "I know why you have come," Hickenlooper greeted him, "I have decided to go along." Clayton then went to Taft's office. His visit failed to win Taft's support but was a civil and wise gesture. The British loan was gaining new backing daily.[23]

Perhaps the most serious threat in the Senate came from Arizona's Ernest McFarland, who proposed that as an additional condition for the loan, the United States should be given permanent control of a number of British bases in the northern Atlantic that had been rented to the United States on a low-rate, long-term basis under lend-lease. Whatever its intent, it was a killer amendment. Keynes had worked hard to get the loan agreement approved by a skeptical Parliament that still was protective of the British empire and its preference system. On May 8, 1946, McFarland's amendment demanding control of the strategic bases was defeated by forty-five to forty.

On May 10, the Senate passed the Anglo-American Financial Agreement forty-six to twenty-four.[24] The measure now moved to the House where, because of the greater difficulties expected in that traditionally more parochial body, and because the Senate delays had pushed consideration of the loan into the summer, an important shift took place.

Clayton's early defense of the loan stressed the themes of peace, cooperation, and prosperity he had expressed in his Bretton Woods testimony. In a January letter to Senator Alben Barkley that set forth tactical ideas for winning passage of the deal, Clayton never mentioned the Soviets.[25]

In the spring of 1946, however, events began to reshape Clayton's perception both of how the United States should treat the Soviet Union economically and of how America's broader purposes should be articulated vis-à-vis the Soviet Union's own goals and behavior. It may help to review what had been going on as Clayton dashed about trying to keep the U.S.-British understanding intact.

On February 9, 1946, Stalin unleashed a tirade against the West in a statement accompanying the release of the newest Soviet five-year plan. Acheson marks Stalin's speech as the beginning of the cold war. Downgrading the hopes for peace, Stalin declared that "monopolists and militarists" were still in control in the capitalist countries and that Soviet policy would be appropriately ready.

Justice William O. Douglas told Secretary of the Navy James Forrestal that the speech was tantamount to "the declaration of World War III," while Walter Lippmann wrote, "Now that Stalin has [decided] to make military power his first objective, we are forced to make a corresponding decision." A few days later, George F. Kennan began writing a long memorandum calling for a policy of "patient and firm resistance" to Soviet advances—later, the containment doctrine, though it should be noted that Averell Harriman, the U.S. ambassador to Moscow, had been sending the same message for almost a year. Kennan's message found a ready audience. "I'm tired of babying the Soviets," Truman had just declared, and his closest advisers, including Forrestal, Vinson, Byrnes, and Acheson, seemed equally weary.

On March 4, 1946, Winston Churchill delivered his "Iron Curtain Speech" in Fulton, Missouri. But his proposal for a special Anglo-American alliance struck a discordant note with many Americans, forcing Truman to deny, falsely, that he had read or approved of the speech in advance. (Truman had in fact reviewed the speech enthusiastically on the train with Churchill.) Churchill's defiant anger at Soviet behavior in Central and Eastern

Europe matched America's own vexation. Meanwhile, Senator Arthur H. Vandenberg on February 27, and Secretary of State James F. Byrnes on February 28, frustrated with Moscow's hard line in talks over Soviet-occupied Europe, gave major speeches warning that there might have to be a wholesale rethinking of U.S. policy in light of Soviet belligerence around the world.

In short, Stalin's tirade added new impetus to the urgency Clayton felt toward shoring up democratic allies. On January 6 the Soviet puppet state in Poland nationalized the country's major industries, serving notice that any change in the status quo would require something stronger than Truman's scolding of Molotov. In February, Soviet forces in Germany stepped up their harassment of other Allied control officials, causing General Lucius D. Clay, military governor of the U.S. zone, to warn on February 24 that Moscow might be preparing to unify Germany under Soviet auspices. In March, pressing for advantageous terms in an oil barter with Iran, Stalin declined to pull out his troops as promised. Moscow eventually pulled back but only after a bitter televised debate gave Western audiences a firsthand view of the Soviet stonewalling that Clayton had witnessed at Potsdam. "Russia has served notice on the United Nations," the *New York Times* editorialized the next day, "that unless she gets her way she will paralyze it even at the risk of wrecking it."[26]

Here matters stood in May 1946 as Clayton prepared to brief members of the House of Representatives about the British loan. On May 3 he met with a group of New England congressmen led by Christian A. Herter. Herter was a Republican internationalist who would later serve as Eisenhower's secretary of state and, with Clayton, would draft the Herter-Clayton report, a key strategy document in the effort to pass the Kennedy Trade Expansion Act in 1962. The dinner, hosted by Herter, served its purposes, with Clayton explaining the benefits of free trade and growth in terms of the interest of each member's district.

Discussion turned, however, to the wider foreign policy problems of the day, particularly the Soviets. Although Clayton had not stressed the point in his testimony to the Senate, the British loan obviously could be viewed as a means of buttressing a vital ally against Stalin's imperialism.

Joseph P. Kennedy, the former ambassador to London and a man not noted for his friendship for England, advocated House passage of the loan on the grounds that "the British people and their way of life form the last barrier in Europe against Communism." Senator Vandenberg had made the same point in late April. Hence, the anti-Soviet argument for the British loan did not originate at the Herter dinner, but Clayton's sense of its persuasive power in Congress probably did.

A few days after the dinner, Herter wrote to Clayton, "I find the economic arguments in favor of the loan are much less convincing to this group than the feeling that the loan may serve us in good stead in holding up the hand of a nation we may need badly as a friend because of impending Russian troubles." Clayton replied, "I am sure you are right in your analysis of the reactions of our friends."[27]

Clayton took Herter's advice as the debate moved to the floor of the House in June. The cold war's rising intensity made the argument evermore attractive; new political difficulties, such as the defeat of Nebraska governor Dwight Griswold's bid for a Senate seat in the Democratic primary, made it seem unavoidable. (Griswold was an outspoken advocate of the loan; his defeat was interpreted as a grass-roots rejection of the measure in the critical political laboratory of the farm states.)

On June 12, Foreign Minister Ernest Bevin made an inflammatory speech attributing U.S. support for Israel to the fact that the country had "too many Jews in New York," stirring widespread anti-British sentiment not only among Jewish voters but among a broad cross-section of America as well. Clayton was able to persuade a number of leading rabbis to write or testify on behalf of the loan, despite Bevin's ill-considered speech, but they didn't help.

As the debate wore on into July, Clayton and his allies in Congress found the anti-Soviet rationale increasingly necessary and effective. On July 12, Representative James Wadsworth, an undecided Republican, indicated anticommunism as one of the reasons he would support the loan. House majority leader John McCormack cited the Russian menace repeatedly on the floor. Informal polls taken after the debate on July 12 showed the vote was still undecided: 188 tended to support the loan, 163 against, and 60 votes were too close to call.

One reason for the large number of undecided was that many southern Democrats were facing primary challenges at home. Clayton wired every absent southern congressman urging an immediate return to Washington for the crucial vote, while McCormack tried to win over undecided votes into the night. On July 13, matters brightened considerably when many Dixie Democrats returned to town. Early in the day, the Dirksen amendment, then regarded as the most serious threat to the loan, was beaten back on a 138 to 97 vote. Eleven other changes in the loan terms were defeated by close margins.[28] On the afternoon of July 13, 1946, after the truly Herculean efforts of Will Clayton, the British loan was approved, 219 to 155.

Looking back on the debate, it is clear that something significant had transpired. Soviet behavior and congressional concern had given the loan a new dimension not before present in the administration's appeals for UNRRA and other assistance programs. "Ever since Majority Leader McCormack spoke strongly on the urgency of Anglo-American solidarity in the face of the opposing [Soviet] ideology," the *New York Times* observed on July 15, "speaker after speaker asserted that it was the political importance of the Anglo-American solidarity, rather than any technical aspects of the Agreement, which compelled them to vote for the resolution."

The core idea of the Truman Doctrine and the Marshall Plan— U.S. aid as a lever both to win economic reforms and to thwart communist imperialism—had met its first test in Congress and the country. The loan did not immediately secure what to many had been its central purpose—the opening of the British Common-

wealth to liberal trade—but London did, grudgingly and ineffec-
tively, begin its long effort to abide by the monetary discipline of
the Bretton Woods pact. Appropriately enough, in a year of nondecisions, the British loan's most important effect was one largely
unintended and unforeseen by its negotiators.

Marshall's Team and the Greek Crisis

JANUARY 1947 BROUGHT A NEW SECRETARY TO HEAD UP THE STATE Department. In December 1946, Byrnes had completed the peace treaties he had been haggling over since Potsdam, and he now wanted Truman to accept the resignation he had submitted the previous April. It was then that Jesse Jones, Fred Vinson, and others close to Byrnes launched a fresh campaign to have Clayton named as Byrnes's successor.

In its December 8, 1946, issue, the *Kiplinger Newsletter*, an influential insider report on Washington, placed Clayton as "number one on the list" to succeed Byrnes. Associated Press put the story on its national wire the next day, with Jones's *Houston Post* (December 11) and assorted other papers editorializing on Clayton's behalf.[1] But the political equation had changed since the spring, when Truman had approached Clayton about taking Byrnes's place. The election had heightened the need for a bipartisan figure of stature, and although Clayton stood high on both counts, there was at least one man who ranked higher: General George C. Marshall.

Marshall was no match for Clayton, Acheson, or Kennan in a test of abstract intellectual brilliance, and he lacked Clayton's business know-how. He was, however, a consummate organizer and manager, with enough self-confidence to surround himself with outstanding men like Acheson, Clayton, Kennan, Charles F. Bohlen, and Benjamin Cohen and to heed their advice.*

With Acheson the fixer and Clayton the economist working for Marshall, a solid team was in place. Thus, despite worries about the frequent changeover at the State Department—from Hull to Stettinius to Byrnes to Marshall in just over two years—the prospects for an effective collaboration seemed bright.

Clayton's clout increased under Marshall, who, unlike Byrnes, was a delegator who made no effort to run all aspects of the department. Unlike Stettinius, Marshall was not knowledgeable about economic matters, so he relied heavily on Clayton's views.

"Clayton has outlined the Administration's foreign economic policy," James Reston wrote in the *New York Times* on January 23, 1947, "and this is now developing as the most important question in the foreign field." In a piece profiling the new Truman team, the *Times*'s Lester Markel named five men as the "inner council" to the president: Marshall, Clark Clifford, Charlie Ross, Francis Biddle, and Clayton. "Clayton is the person," Markel wrote, "to whom the president turns for advice on foreign economic matters to complement Marshall on foreign political matters."[3]

The administration's planning early in 1947 placed great emphasis on the Geneva trade negotiations set to take place in the spring. The year was expected to be decisive for trade in any case because it was the last full year of the Reciprocal Trade Act extension passed in 1945. Clayton and his staff—including Paul Nitze, Ben Moore,

---

*When he delivered one of his first speeches, Marshall asked Clayton and Acheson to observe as he spiced up his prepared remarks with extemporaneous comments. Afterward, bubbling over with the sense that his effort had been a brilliant success, he asked Acheson and Clayton what they thought. Gently, they suggested that in the future he should stick to his prepared text.[2]

Claire Wilcox, Norman Ness, Tyler Wood, and H. Van B. Cleveland—produced hundreds of pages of background documents for the eighteen-nation conference.

But events in Europe were moving even faster than Clayton and the State Department anticipated, and the news was all bad. The signs of distress in Europe in those early months of 1947 can be measured by Clayton's appointments calendar and paper flow:[4]

—Alarming reports on the deteriorating political economy of Greece from Franklin Mac Veagh, U.S. ambassador to Greece, and from the Porter commission, which Clayton had dispatched in 1946. (Greece had not experienced the minirecovery of 1946, and in 1947 production sagged again. Farmers throughout northern Greece were so certain of a communist invasion that many wouldn't even plant crops.)

—Frantic meetings at the State Department and the White House (January 7 and 14) with Alcide de Gasperi, Italy's prime minister, who was appealing for further U.S. aid, with an emergency loan approved on January 21. (Italian industrial production was still less than half its prewar level, while prices were 3,500 percent above the prewar level.)

—A worried memorandum from Norman Ness warning of England's depletion of the loan funds and its inability (or unwillingness) to stabilize sterling; from France, Jefferson Caffery sent jittery warnings of growing communist influence in the government; and from both France and Britain, embassy reports told of increasingly desperate food and coal shortages and communist-led strikes in key industries. (Both France and England experienced a fall of more than 15 percent in industrial production: England at the end of 1946 and first quarter of 1947, France in the second quarter of 1947. Food production in both countries plunged.)

Clayton met with Herbert Hoover on January 22 and with Truman on January 30 to discuss the mounting economic crisis in West Germany. Production in the U.S.-U.K. bizone area had dropped by a third from September 1946 to February 1947, falling as low as 28 percent of 1938 output. "Cigarettes, coffee, and chocolate," historian Charles Mee reports, "were better currencies than Deutsche marks."

Even as Clayton's desk piled up with news of these disasters, nature chipped in. During Christmastide 1946, a vast high-pressure area formed near the Arctic Circle. The front rolled across Norway and settled over Britain, bringing high winds, bitter cold, and one of the greatest blizzards in several centuries. Snow piled up as high as twenty feet. Machinery froze. Transportation and power stopped.

"For the first time in its history," Alan Bullock writes, "British industrial production was effectively halted for three weeks—something German bombing had never been able to do. Registered unemployment rose from 400,000 to 2.3 million." For twenty-two days, there was virtually no sunshine. Then a brief thaw was followed by a severe freeze that transformed the snow into treacherous ice. In all, it took four months and close to $1 billion—one third of the British loan, which was intended to last for five years—to dig Britain out from under the avalanche of January 1947.[5]

During the early months of 1947, Clayton asked his top staff and department heads to confer with him once a week about the deteriorating situation in Europe. He asked them to estimate Europe's needs and how the United States could meet them. (Ness, whom Clayton had selected to head the office of Finance and Development, later estimated that this effort originated as early as December 1946 and no later than February 1947.)

By March, the Clayton group agreed that without more free trade, even billions in U.S. aid would not save Europe. Yet they had also, as Joseph Jones writes, "influenced the [State Department's Foreign Aid Committee] to think in terms of aid to Europe as a whole, administered in such a way as to bring about economic unification, and were at that moment at work on further studies," among them the State-War-Navy Coordinating Committee Study. Thus well before the crises of 1947 were apparent to the public or even many in the government, Clayton had initiated efforts to deal with the rising tide of difficulties. Indeed, he and his aides had already discovered what was to be a key instrument of the Marshall

Plan's success: using U.S. aid as a wedge for economic reforms in Europe that many thought impossible during the troublesome spring of 1947.[6]

By February 1947, it was increasingly clear that domestic hardships would soon force England to make a major retrenchment in its overseas commitments. The cost of maintaining British forces—in Palestine, India, Ceylon, Burma, Egypt, Greece, Turkey, and elsewhere—could not be sustained. Walter Lippmann warned on February 12 that England's economic crisis would have far-reaching strategic and political consequences. British retrenchment, he wrote, "could shake the world and make our position highly vulnerable and precariously isolated." A few days later the British government released its annual economic survey presaging a radical, global retreat from the financial burdens of empire. *The London Times* called it "the most disturbing statement ever made by a British government."[7]

Official word from London came on Friday, February 21, after Marshall had left to deliver a speech at Princeton University's bicentennial celebration. Acheson was in his office when Lord Inverchapel, the British ambassador, called to say he had a "blue piece of paper," an important and formal message, with instructions to deliver it promptly and personally to Marshall. The message was that British aid to Greece and Turkey would end in six weeks, on March 31.[8] Acheson later recalled the reports he read:

> They were brief and all too clear. One described the state of the Greek economy and army, which we all knew. It estimated Greece's current foreign-exchange needs at from $240 million to $280 million. . . . The other reported Turkey as stronger but still unable to handle the financing of both the modernization and maintenance of the large army that Russian pressure demanded and the economic development of Turkey. . . . The British could no

longer be of substantial help in either. His Majesty's Government devoutly hoped that we could assume the burden.[9]

Marshall's team moved quickly to meet the March 31 deadline. In Marshall's absence, Acheson huddled with Loy Henderson and members of his and Clayton's staff over a long weekend preparing economic and military estimates, digesting on-the-spot reports from the U.S. missions, and creating the outlines of a proposed aid program. By Thursday, February 27, Acheson's basic design had been endorsed by the secretaries of state, war, and navy, approved by the president, and briefed to leading members of Congress. Joseph Jones of the State Department's public affairs office began drafting a message to Congress from the president requesting an emergency appropriation of funds.[10]

On March 12, President Truman delivered an historic plea before a joint session of Congress:

> I believe it must be the policy of the United States to support free peoples who are resisting attempted subjugation by armed minorities or by outside pressures.
>
> I believe that we must assist free peoples to work out their own destinies in their own way.
>
> I believe that our help should be primarily through economic and financial aid which is essential to economic stability and orderly political processes. . . .
>
> The free peoples of the world look to us for support in maintaining their freedoms.

But Congress was not going to rubber-stamp Truman's request no matter how urgent his tone. Senator Arthur H. Vandenberg, a leading Republican, submitted to Acheson and Clayton a list of more than a hundred questions that he wanted answered before he would consider supporting Truman's request. The answers were presented on March 26.

Clayton, who had gone to Arizona for a short rest on March 5, returned to Washington on March 10 to coordinate economic aspects of the aid proposal and oversee the drafting of congressional testimony on the economic aspects of the package. Important decisions were compressed into a matter of days. How would the aid be administered? Porter had surveyed the needs of the region after Clayton and Acheson began ordering advance assessments in the fall of 1946. Clayton advised that the Greek government was too weak to distribute assistance effectively, an assessment the Greeks themselves seemed to share when Vice-Premier Constantine Tsaldaris wrote a direct appeal to the United States for help on March 3. The Greek note stressed the need not only for economic aid but for "administrative" and "technical" assistance.

Clayton was strongly inclined to give it, although the degree of American involvement in Greece that this implied raised fears in Congress, as did the bypassing of the United Nations and an UNRRA-style scheme for distribution and the predominance, which could not be helped, of military over economic assistance in the package: about 62 percent of the total, as Clayton revealed in his March 24 testimony before the House Foreign Affairs Committee.

New tactical problems also arose. Congress moved quickly but not overnight; there was not time to act before the March 31 deadline for British withdrawal. Acheson convinced the British to delay their pullout until the United States could act, while Clayton suggested that the RFC might provide $100 million in assistance until the $400 million Greek program was passed.[11] The Greek-Turkish Aid Act passed the Senate by 67 to 23, the House by 287 to 107, and was signed by Truman on May 22. To coordinate the program in Washington, Truman chose George McGhee, one of Clayton's key staff members.

Secretary Marshall was absent during most of this period. He had left for Moscow during the first week of March to confer with Molotov and the other Big Four foreign ministers. During the many weeks Marshall was in Moscow, the Soviets never once mentioned the U.S. aid initiative. Perhaps they suspected it was merely a rhetorical weapon and placed their confidence in action, not words.[12]

❏ ❏ ❏

Clayton's role in the development of the Truman Doctrine helps put into perspective two chief criticisms of the policy. On the one hand, the Truman Doctrine has been attacked as being too universal, too sweeping. This attitude first surfaced during the drafting of Truman's speech to Congress. George Elsey, a Truman speechwriter, initially felt, and Kennan remained convinced, that the speech was too anticommunist and too sweeping in its commitments. Elsey wrote to Clark Clifford on March 7, "There has been no overt action in the immediate past by the USSR which serves as an adequate pretext for 'All-Out' speech."

Similarly, Kennan vigorously objected to Truman's statement that "it must be the policy of the United States to support free peoples who are resisting subjugation by armed minorities or by outside pressures." Twenty years later, Kennan wrote in his memoirs that the Truman Doctrine "implied that what we had decided to do in the case of Greece was something we would be prepared to do in the case of any other country, provided only that it was faced with the threat of 'subjugation by armed minorities or by outside pressures.'" Kennan attributed this sweeping pledge to the "congenital aversion of Americans to taking specific actions on specific problems, and by their persistent urge to seek universal formulae or doctrines in which to clothe and justify particular actions . . . [a] persistent American urge to the universalization or generalization of decision."

In March 1947, Congress and the press felt the same hesitation. "A seasoned diplomacy is very chary indeed of the grand pronouncements of policy," Walter Lippmann warned in a March 16 column. He continued:

> Instead of such a large promise . . . [it] would be better to say that in view of the pressure on Greece and Turkey, we are reinforcing them; that our object is to stop the invasion of Greece by bands armed and trained in Yugoslavia, Bulgaria, and Albania; to make

sure that the settlement between the Soviet Union and Turkey is
negotiated and is not imposed by force. . . . A vague global policy,
which sounds like the tocsin of an ideological crusade, has no
limits.[13]

Much of this critical commentary can be understood as a prej-
udice by many Western intellectuals against any statements that
articulate general principles. Yet the signers of the Declaration of
Independence did not flinch from saying that "all men" were en-
dowed with certain rights. This did not mean, however, that universal global warfare against undemocratic governments was justified; on the contrary, the Declaration assumed that a particular
revolutionary movement must enumerate the causes "which im-
pel" a change in the regime. Abraham Lincoln, in a speech in 1848,
once declared that "any people anywhere, being inclined and having the power, have the right to rise up and shake off the existing
government and form a new one that suits them." Yet Lincoln made
that speech in explaining his opposition to what he called the
"unjust" war against Mexico; in the same year, while cheering the
efforts of freedom fighters in Hungary, he opposed U.S. aid to
them. Lincoln, the founders, and Truman understood that the
enunciation of a general principle does not imply that we must
always make the same response in every situation. Prudence governs how a principle is applied to each case.

In testimony before Congress, Clayton and Acheson testified
that the United States would not embark on a similar program of
emergency aid to oppose communist gains in China because it was
not the same situation. Truman stressed that the chief instrument
for supporting democracy would be economic aid, not the use of
U.S. military forces; Kennan and Lippmann were guilty of over-
generalizing and failing to make proper distinctions. From a valid
universal statement of principle, "we will support free peoples everywhere," they wrongly concluded that U.S. support would always
take the same form that it took in Greece and Turkey.

One could argue that the program should be stated in the

broadest terms possible. One audience was in Greece, Turkey, and other countries faced with similar pressures, such as Italy. A speech that implied the widest application of the U.S. aid program would reassure such countries that the United States was prepared to act not just in Greece and Turkey but elsewhere too.

Another audience was in the Kremlin. Marshall understood that only the toughest possible statement would convince Stalin that the United States was serious in Turkey and Greece and provide support for the U.S. position on Germany, Austria, and Central and Eastern Europe. Shortly after arriving in Moscow, Marshall stressed several times that the basis of U.S. foreign policy was its belief that freedom and democracy were the only basis of a just government and that the Europeans must be free to choose democratic governments, as promised in the Atlantic Charter.

The most important audience for the Truman Doctrine was the American people. One purpose of the doctrine's strong statement of principles was to alert the public to the problems in Europe and around the world and to the need for vigorous U.S. leadership and the Truman administration's intent to provide it. The speech, as Clifford replied to Elsey's criticism, was "the opening gun in a campaign to bring people up to the realization that the war isn't over by any means."

"The United States must take world leadership and quickly, to avert world disaster," Clayton wrote in a memorandum of March 5 read by (or briefed to) Acheson and other members of the department (and probably briefed in some fashion to Truman). "But the United States will not take world leadership, effectively, unless the people of the United States are shocked into doing so. To shock them, it is only necessary for the President and the Secretary of State to tell them the truth and the whole truth."

The administration had been intentionally uncommunicative about the situation in the rest of Europe because it had not yet crafted a program to deal with the multifaceted situation. The administration also feared that if the full crisis were revealed before a program to deal with it were crafted, the results would be further distress in Europe and the United States. Even as Truman's speech to Congress was being written, efforts were under way to create a follow-up economic program, as well as to ensure a broad scope for presidential authority and congressional support for funding. On February 26, Joseph Jones noted:

> I think we must admit the conclusion that Congress and the people of this country are not sufficiently aware of the character and dimensions of the crisis that impends, and of the measures that must be taken in terms of relief, loans, gifts, constructive development programs, and liberal trade policies—all these on a scale hitherto unimagined—if disaster is to be avoided.[14]

Clayton made some of the strongest expressions of these arguments, not only in the March 5 memo but also, according to Clark Clifford and others, in his regular meetings with the president from January through April to discuss the growing European financial crises. For various reasons—Clayton's disinclination to puff his own achievements after retiring from public service, the lack of any personal memoirs by Clayton—much discussion of the Truman Doctrine takes place as though Clayton had not existed. One can disagree with the approach taken by Truman in his speech and in his policy toward the crisis; yet to understand the Truman speech and policy, and the logic that guided them, one must be aware of Clayton's role.

Kennan, a brilliant thinker who would soon play an important role at the State Department, was not yet part of the inner circle in March (and, arguably, not in June either). Thus to rely on Kennan for an understanding of the Truman Doctrine's logic is to fail to consider some of the critical arguments Clayton was making to Truman on a regular basis. Acheson, the consummate manager of day-to-day operations in Marshall's stead, had little time to sit back and think in broad, strategic terms. On the day Acheson received the British aide-memoire, a full two months before his speech in Mississippi, Clayton was in Arizona working on final drafts of a presidential speech for delivery at Baylor University in Waco, Texas. That speech was the first shot in a campaign to build public support for the reduction of trade barriers and aid to Europe—what became, in a few months, the Marshall Plan. Thus to leave Clayton out of the story is not simply to omit an important player; if one does not understand Clayton's role, his arguments, and the persistent drive of his years at the State Department, then an understanding of the Truman Doctrine and the Marshall Plan becomes almost impossible.

Another criticism of the Truman Doctrine, more prevalent at the time, was that it ignored the need for large, positive efforts to rebuild Greece, Turkey, and the rest of Europe economically. "I would like to have seen him indicate that you can fight communism in other ways—in economic ways—by a positive policy of lending, and so on," James Reston told James Forrestal in a March 13 telephone conversation. Reston, Lippmann, and Marquis Childs of the *Washington Post* all wrote pieces urging a broadening of the policy into something resembling the future Marshall Plan. Childs's column of March 13, along with the *Times* and *Post* editorials of that day, stressed that Greek-Turkish aid must be viewed as part of what Childs called a "larger picture" that would involve billions in aid.

On March 19 both Reston and another influential journalist, Joseph Alsop, saw hopeful moves toward the formation of just such a policy. Lippmann on March 20 said there was no longer any doubt that the United States would have to make a large outlay for reconstruction and peace. (Clayton's March 5 memorandum and his earlier discussions with Truman, Marshall, and Acheson in the wake of Nitze's December 1946 estimates were taking on a life of their own. In fact, according to Lippmann's biographer, Clayton briefed him on developments in U.S. policy, which would explain the presence in several of Lippmann's columns of economic estimates and developing diplomatic strategies that had taken their origin among Clayton's aides, including Nitze.)[15]

13

The Fifteen Weeks

Clayton's Memorandums

THE SUDDENNESS AND TOTALITY OF THE BRITISH PULLOUT FROM Greece and Turkey were a surprise, comparable to the sudden cessation of the U.S. lend-lease program in 1945. The speed with which the United States responded to this tactical crisis, however, was due to the fact that something like it had been foreseen by Clayton, Acheson, Henderson, and others in 1946 and that a program of strategic planning had already been launched.

Truman later stressed that the Truman Doctrine and the Marshall Plan had always been "two halves of the same walnut." Aid to Greece and Turkey acknowledged a military-strategic emergency in those countries, but propping up those most immediately threatened by Soviet and Soviet-backed forces did not remedy the broader economic decay of Europe. If anything, the Truman Doctrine emerged as a diversion from the larger program of economic reconstruction—a program already under consideration at the State Department in March 1947.[1] As Ness recalled later:

> In 1947 . . . I had a call from Acheson's office to come down at once. I was told that the British had said they would have to pull out of Greece and Turkey. We had feverish work; my wife asked

what this was. "Top secret," I said. . . . It was [Will Clayton's] audacity of imagination which saw this before anyone else.[2]

As a result of that planning, Truman had already asked, and would soon win congressional approval for, a separate package of $350 million in aid to Austria and Italy. The amount was inadequate for a general European recovery scheme but indicated that work on some sort of program beyond the Truman Doctrine was already in progress in February and March 1947.

Earlier, on February 10, 1947, Truman had asked the State Department to prepare a speech for him to deliver at Baylor University setting forth the administration's foreign economic policy. The first draft, written chiefly by Clair Wilcox, Acheson, and Clayton, was forwarded to the White House on February 20. Truman cites the Baylor speech at length in his memoirs as representing his early thoughts on the European recovery program.[3] Although the speech made no specific reference to a new recovery program as such, it was billed in advance as an important new statement and covered as such in news commentary and editorials. Speaking on March 6, Truman clearly hinted at things to come:

> Now, as in the year 1920, we have reached a turning point in history. National economies have been disrupted by the war. The future is uncertain everywhere. . . . In this atmosphere of doubt and hesitation, the decisive factor will be the type of leadership that the United States gives to the world.
> We are the giant of the economic world.
> Whether we like it or not, the future pattern of economic relations depends upon us.[4]

Equally significant as an indicator of U.S. planning is Clayton's suggested addition (made on February 26) to his draft of the speech. The proposed section reads:

The resources and productive capacity of the United States are so enormous in comparison with the wrecked and weakened productive resources of most of the other countries of the world that prodigious efforts on our part are going to be necessary if any equilibrium is [to be] achieved.

Last year exports from the United States amounted to ten billion dollars; and imports into the United States amounted to only five billion dollars. . . . It is up to us, if we are going to avoid economic disaster in the years to come, to see to it that the world does have through normal processes plenty of dollars to buy American goods. . . .

This is a time when American security and prosperity depend upon bold and imaginative economic thinking and acting. Getting our tariffs down and keeping them down to a low point is a beginning and a prerequisite to our own prosperity and security, but I doubt very much whether it is going to be enough. I think we are going to have to begin thinking in terms of bolder measures than have ever been seriously advanced before for getting American dollars abroad in sufficient volume to sustain a satisfactory level of economic activity.[5]

Clayton and Acheson did not include this section in the draft they sent to Truman, nor did Truman announce anything resembling it. It indicates, nonetheless, how far planning for a European recovery program had progressed even before the Truman Doctrine. In fact, Truman may have omitted the section only because, by the time the speech was given, the United States had been forced to focus on the immediate crisis in Greece and Turkey. (The administration feared criticism from Congress that a Greece-Turkey package would be only the tip of a funding iceberg.) Far from being an afterthought, much work on an economic recovery package preceded the Truman Doctrine. The designing of, and articulating the need for, such a program was held in abeyance because of the emergency in the Mediterranean.

In fact, during the drafting of the Greek-Turkish aid programs Eisenhower, Clayton, and Secretary of War Robert T. Patterson urged Acheson to move ahead with an overall program for European recovery. On March 5, 1947, Acheson asked Assistant Secretary of State John Hilldring, at that time chairman of the State-War-Navy Coordinating Committee (SWNCC), to study possible European requests that might be addressed to the United States for further aid. But the SWNCC, which had little experience in economics, after a few days largely farmed the work out to the Foreign Aid Committee and a series of ad hoc working groups. Joseph Jones names the key participants on economics as Ness, Cleveland, and Moore of Clayton's staff. Ty Wood, also a member of Clayton's team, began a series of Thursday luncheon meetings for office directors to discuss problems too broad or vague to be discussed by middle-level officials.

Thus was created a culture of discussion and free trade in ideas in which dozens of officials could swap facts, figures, and concepts. Joseph Jones, for example, sat in on the meetings of the Special Committee of the SWNCC, with the result that his speeches for Truman, Acheson, and Marshall were generally on the cutting edge of policy. Jones wrote prolifically to Acheson and others, pressing for European unity as part of a general recovery scheme and for greater efforts to inform the American people of the necessity for action.[6]

Another official who took an early and important interest in studying the economic gap Europe faced was Paul Nitze, whom Clayton had recruited for the warehouse war back when Nitze, then a registered Republican, had been blackballed by the rest of the administration. (Nitze was blackballed again in 1947 when Kennan proposed him as deputy of the Policy Planning Staff, but Acheson, angered by Nitze during the domestic battles of the warehouse wars, vetoed him.) In December 1946, Nitze hit on the idea that the U.S. surplus of payments to Europe—the rate at which the United States was absorbing gold and foreign exchange from other people, less their exports—was a reliable measure of the trouble they were in. The figure, it turned out, was in the neighborhood of $5 billion a year. Nitze, working with the Treasury Department, early in 1947 drafted a memorandum to Clayton suggesting a worldwide effort, stretched over four to five years, totaling $20 billion to $25 billion. (The figure is larger than later estimates for the Marshall Plan because Nitze's proposal was not limited to Europe.) "My suggestion was not unique," Nitze notes; Forrestal and Kennan were already suggesting a similar program. Nitze's approach to the estimation problem was original, however, and, as the planning for European recovery moved forward, the Nitze-Treasury figures were recycled again and again: in Clayton's March 5 memorandum, in the SWNCC study of April 21, in Acheson's Delta speech in Mississippi that followed, and in Reston's timely May 25 article just before the Harvard speech.

Nitze recalls that at the time—probably January or early February 1947—"Will had yet to be persuaded that the situation was as serious as I considered it to be." Within a few weeks, however, Clayton shared Nitze's view (if he had not shared it all along). As noted above, Clayton asked Ness, Cleveland, Moore, and others to begin studying the European problem in January or February.[7]

On March 5, 1947, Clayton flew to a favorite ranch near Tucson, Arizona. Removed from the daily pressures of Washington, D.C., he let his mind roam over the big problems confronting American decision makers: Soviet aggressiveness, British decline, and the potential U.S. role in restoring normalcy to the economy of Europe. The result was Clayton's March memorandum proposing a European recovery fund of $5 billion in the first year, Clayton's first clear call for a policy moving well beyond urging the Europeans to liberalize their own trade and adopt reforms of their currencies:

> I am deeply disturbed by the present world picture, and its implications for our country.
>   The reins of world leadership are fast slipping from Britain's competent but now very weak hands.
>   These reins will be picked up either by the United States or by

Russia. If by Russia, there will almost certainly be war in the next decade or so, with the odds against us. If by the United States, war can almost certainly be prevented.

The United States must take world leadership and quickly, to avert world disaster.

But the United States will not take world leadership, effectively, unless the people of the United States are shocked into doing so.

To shock them, it is only necessary for the President and the Secretary of State to tell them the truth and the whole truth.

The truth is to be found in the cables which daily arrive at the State Department from all over the world.

In every country in the Eastern Hemisphere and most of the countries in the Western Hemisphere, Russia is boring from within.

This is a new technique with which we have not yet learned how to cope.

We must cope with it and quickly or face the greatest peril of our history.

Several nations whose integrity and independence are vital to our interests and to our security are at the brink and may be pushed over at any time; others are gravely threatened.

If Greece and Turkey succumb, the whole Middle East will be lost.

France may then capitulate to the Communists.

As France goes, all Western Europe and Africa will go.

These things must not happen.

They need not happen.

The Secretary of State is leaving now for Moscow.

The odds are heavily against any constructive results there.

The Secretary will probably be back in Washington before May 1st.

Meantime, we have discussed with the Congressional leaders a program to help Greece maintain her independence. This only goes part of the way; it tells only part of the truth.

We must go all out in this world game or we'd better stay at home and devote our brains and energies to preparation for the third world war.

Assuming an unsatisfactory outcome of the Moscow conference, I think on return of the Secretary of State a joint statement should be made by the President and the Secretary to the Congress and to the American people.

Such a statement should say:

1. The United States is determined on the preservation of world peace by all honorable means.

2. The United States does not covet the lands or possessions of any other peoples.

3. The preservation of world peace depends first of all upon the preservation of the integrity and independence of sovereign nations.

4. Nations can lose their integrity and independence by attacks either from the outside or from the inside.

5. The United Nations is organized to deal with attacks from the outside but not from the inside.

6. The evidence is indisputable that a systematic campaign is now being waged to destroy from within the integrity and independence of many nations.

7. Feeding on hunger, economic misery and frustration, these attacks have already been successful in some of the liberated countries, and there is now grave danger that they may be successful in others.

8. The security and interests of the United States and of the world demand that the United States take prompt and effective action to assist certain of these gravely threatened countries.

9. This assistance should take the form not only of financial aid, but of technical and administrative assistance as well. The United States does not wish to interfere in the domestic affairs of any country, but countries to which it extends financial aid must put their internal affairs in proper order so that such aid may be permanently beneficial.

10. Congress is asked to create a Council of National Defense composed of the President, the Secretary of State, the Secretaries of War and Navy, and the Chairmen of the Foreign Affairs Committee of the House and the Foreign Relations Committee of the Senate.

11. The Congress is further asked to appropriate the sum of Five Billion Dollars, for use by the Council of National Defense, either as grants or as loans, for the purpose of assisting sovereign countries to preserve their integrity and independence, where such action is considered by said Council to be in the vital interests of the United States.

12. It had been expected that the International Bank for Re-

construction and Development would be able to furnish all requisite financial assistance to war devastated countries, but it is now clear that this institution is not organized to render the kind of assistance which is required in the circumstance herein described. The facilities of the Bank will nevertheless be needed for worthy projects of reconstruction and development.

13. Two objections will be made to the program here proposed: one political and the other economic.

14. It will be said that this will involve us in the affairs of foreign countries and lead us eventually to war. The answer to this is that if we do not actively interest ourselves in the affairs of foreign countries, we will find that such affairs will become so hopeless that the seeds of World War III will inevitably be sown.

15. It will be said that our national budget will not permit of this large expenditure. The war cost us over three hundred billion dollars and the blood of hundreds of thousands of our young men. We are now appropriating around ten billion dollars annually for the maintenance of our armed services. We are seriously talking of reducing taxes at a time when our people are enjoying the highest standard of living in their history, when our corporations and farmers enjoy the biggest earnings, after taxes, which they have ever known in peace time, and when our gross national product of goods and services has a greater dollar value than has ever been known in war or peace.

Just what use Clayton made of this memorandum is not clear. Coming as it did a full week before Truman's March 12 speech to Congress that announced the Truman Doctrine, it indicates that the chief architect of U.S. economic foreign policy had decided on the need for radical action and was actively pursuing the details of such a plan. The evidence strongly suggests that Clayton used the memorandum and the Nitze estimates in March meetings with Acheson, other members of the department, and probably Truman. Acheson, who in his writing was careful about such matters, quotes extensively from Clayton's March 5 memorandum in *Present at the Creation*.

❑ ❑ ❑

In April and May, Marshall, Acheson, and Clayton each set out to get a reading on the necessity and opportunity for a daring U.S. initiative. Marshall went to Moscow in a final effort to secure European recovery with Soviet cooperation rather than without it. Clayton went to Western Europe to assess the need for and proper scope of the massive program he had just recommended. Acheson went to Cleveland, Mississippi, to test and nurture public and congressional sentiment for spending roughly fifty times more money than Congress had been willing to commit to the Truman Doctrine.

"The odds," Clayton wrote on March 5, "are heavily against any constructive results" in Moscow. That was the consensus of opinion as Marshall set off for Moscow on the same date. Through four weeks of frustrating talks between Marshall, Bevin, Molotov, and Bidault, almost nothing was agreed on. For much of March, Marshall tried to produce a peace agreement on Germany and Austria, which he had promised members of Congress would be his first priority. But even minor discussions on reparations and management of the zones produced wrangling.[8] Marshall saw firsthand the Soviet attitude that Western Europe was about to fall into its hands and thus that Stalin saw no reason to make any agreements or grant any concessions to the Americans.

Marshall returned to Washington and reported on the Moscow conference in a national broadcast of April 28. Offering a detailed review of the negotiations over Germany and Austria, he left some hope, but not much, for future U.S.-Soviet cooperation. At the end, he warned that "we cannot ignore the factor of time involved. Disintegrating forces are becoming evident. The patient [Europe] is sinking while the doctors deliberate. So I believe that action can not await compromise through exhaustion."[9]

The next day, April 29, Marshall summoned George Kennan, asking him to head up a new policy planning staff to begin work immediately on a proposal for U.S. aid to European recovery. The State-War-Navy group submitted its initial report on April 21, drawing heavily on the contributions of Nitze, Wood, and Cleveland. Kennan began work on his own memo, drawing on the work of SWNCC and Clayton's other assistants; Jones specifically recalls that Kennan made use of these papers in preparing his study.[10]

Early in April, Dean Acheson began working on his May 8 speech to the Delta Council in Mississippi.[11] Truman had originally been the scheduled speaker, but when a local political feud erupted, he decided to send Acheson, promising that the under secretary of state would make a major foreign policy address. When he met with Truman on April 9 to discuss the subject, Acheson proposed to talk about European recovery. In his memoirs, Acheson recalls that he realized that any formal proposal would be premature. Still, the effort to build support for the program would have to be a long-range one. An early speech, setting forth the basic conditions in Europe and the urgency of some action, would help generate discussion. Truman warmed to the idea quickly. "The President had kept in touch with the increasingly gloomy prospects in Europe and in Moscow as seen by the Secretary of State," Acheson observes. "He knew Will Clayton's views and the work on which I had started the State, War, and Navy committee." Joseph Jones and Francis Russell began writing a draft using the "grisly facts," as Acheson put it, communicated in cables from Europe and the reports being churned out by the Special Committee.

The rush of events made it impossible to submit the speech at a full cabinet meeting, but when Acheson addressed the Delta Council on May 8, he spoke with the full authority of the president.[12] His speech, which Truman later called "the prologue to the Marshall Plan," did not say anything that would have been regarded as exceptional by those inside the State Department. In fact, in many passages it paralleled Clayton's March 5 memorandum and Clayton's April cables from Europe. The importance of Acheson's speech was that someone high in the administration was now saying publicly what was being thought privately.

Joseph Jones, who drafted much of Acheson's speech, notes that Clayton's emphatic cables from Europe had already alerted

Acheson and others to the urgent need for a program and, hence, the need to begin building support even before Clayton's return. Jones also notes that the statistical work of Ness, Cleveland, and Moore, three of the aides Clayton had instructed to begin surveys of the European plight in the months of January and February, was already gaining prominence in the State Department.

Acheson reviewed the ravaged condition of Europe, not just the "physical destruction" but the broader "economic dislocation" and disruption of "long-established business and trading connections." He reviewed the figures from the Nitze, Cleveland, and Clayton memorandums, concluding that to restore economic health in Europe—not mere relief but "full production" and a "self-supporting" Europe—about $5 billion for several years would be needed. The "facts of international life," and our own economic interest and national security imperatives, were such that "the United States is going to have to undertake further emergency financing." But the effort would have to involve Europe's economy "working together" as a "harmonious whole. . . . The achievement of a coordinated European economy remains a fundamental objective of our foreign policy."[13] Finally, time was running out:

> Not only do human beings and nations exist in narrow economic margins, but also human dignity, human freedom, and democratic institutions.
>
> It is one of the principal aims of our foreign policy today to use our economic and financial resources to widen these margins. It is necessary if we are to preserve our own freedoms and our own democratic institutions.[14]

Clayton left for Europe on April 10. His original assignment was to direct the U.S. delegation at the trade talks in Geneva—the session out of which flowed the 1947 General Agreement on Tariffs and Trade. By April, however, two developments altered his plans. The first was in the State Department, which viewed with growing interest the formation of the United Nations Economic Commission for Europe, or ECE, set to hold its first meeting in May. To Clayton, the ECE, which included the Soviet Union and its satellites, was vulnerable to the same obstructionism that had wrecked UNRRA. Many in the State Department, however, looked on it as a possible instrument for achieving European unity.

Clayton thought someone knowledgeable should give the ECE a closer look; either he was wrong and it would prove useful, or he was right and would be able to make a strong case against it. In addition, whatever its merits, the ECE's first conference would bring together many top central bankers, treasury officials, and economists of Europe and provide an ideal environment for collecting facts and proposals on Europe's economic plight. Clayton therefore accepted on April 24 when Truman asked him to represent the United States at the first ECE conference, scheduled for May 3.[15]

Clayton, convinced by this time that a European recovery plan would have to be, in large part, a European initiative, concluded that the ECE was not a working vehicle for the recovery plan. The U.S. goal was to spur European cooperation and economic union; the chief condition for dispensing U.S. aid was that Europe get its trade liberalization act together. Ivan White, a State Department aide working as economic counselor to the embassy in Paris, recalls a conversation in which Clayton read him a paper he had written on European recovery (probably Clayton's March 5 memorandum):

> Clayton came back to Geneva in the spring of 1947. . . . He asked me to come to Geneva to give him a report on the French situation. It was critical; I took along all the studies I'd made. . . .
> [Clayton] had put down on a piece of paper . . . the concept of European countries joining together to develop a program of self-help and mutual aid; it was a series of thoughts and he read it to me and asked my comments. . . . He set forth orally the thing he had in mind about European recovery . . . European countries gathering to help themselves, with the U.S. a partner to furnish

aid within a plan that Europe would work out, anticipating freer movements of goods between European countries. . . .

I went back to the Embassy in Paris and told Ambassador [Jefferson] Caffery about it; shortly after that, Dean Acheson made his Delta Council speech. It was apparent to Caffery and me that [Clayton's] thinking and planning really pioneered the Marshall Plan. We did not know what communications he had sent back—whether the communications were in the form of conversations or what—but he must have sent them. . . . Clayton may have sent just "eyes only" for Acheson on these cables.[16]

The second development to affect Clayton's plan took place in the now-Republican dominated Congress, eager to test its strength. In late April, the House Committee on Agriculture reported that it was considering favorable action on the Wool Act of 1947, establishing a 50 percent ad valorem fee on wool imports. The protectionists could not have picked a better item to wreck the trade talks. "There are at least five rates," aide Harry Hawkins advised Clayton as he prepared for the complex negotiations, "which are of critical importance, namely those on meat, butter, wool, cotton textiles, and woolen textiles. Commitments not to reduce the rate on any one of these products would wreck the whole plan."[17] Certain key countries (in the case of wool, Australia) were so dependent on their exports to U.S. markets that an increased rate on that item alone would cause them to drop out of the negotiations. Australia, in turn, was a member of the British Commonwealth. Its withdrawal would force England to withdraw as well. England, in turn, was still the key to European trade, and European trade was tantamount to world trade.

Clayton tried to patch matters together, but the House Agriculture Committee's action, as the *New York Times* correspondent in Geneva observed, cast "grave doubts on American sincerity." Early in May the Wool Act was reported out of committee, and Truman's veto of the measure was not certain because key members of the administration, including Agriculture Secretary Clinton Anderson, supported the tariff increase.

Hence there was no point in any further talks at Geneva until Clayton could return to Washington to block the measure. If it became law, Clayton's whole trade-liberalization effort was doomed. If the United States, the *Times* editorialized a few weeks later, "raised the barriers on wool imports, we would block the trade agreements we ourselves have been seeking. . . . This 'explosive issue,' as a Geneva dispatch to this newspaper called it, is preventing 'any real progress' in the trade negotiations. It is an ominous indication of a possible change in our whole trade policy."[18]*

After addressing the ECE conference on May 2, Clayton began touring the capitals of Western Europe, meeting with officials, compiling statistics, and gaining his own firsthand view of the shattered European economies. As America's top representative on the continent—"No. 1 envoy to Europe," the *New York Times* magazine called him—Clayton became a magnet for foreign officials pressing for assistance. What Clayton saw troubled him deeply. In France and Italy, the weakness of currencies and sagging industrial production had caused something akin to a breakdown of civilized society. Looting and hoarding were the rule, not the exception. At the same time, the United States seemed on the verge of another spasm of economic isolationism and a short-sighted creditor squeeze.

On April 23, Clayton cabled Marshall to present the French government's plea for fast shipment of a promised 553,000 tons of

---

*The *Times* editorial, "Beyond the Truman Doctrine," also perceptively and correctly linked Clayton's warnings about the wool tariff to Acheson's speech on foreign aid of May 8. If the Truman Doctrine and the Marshall Plan were two halves of the same walnut shell, a liberal world trading order was the nut inside, the immediate goal of U.S. foreign economic policy. It made no sense to lend and give away billions of dollars with one hand and then deny other countries the access to U.S. markets needed to repay their debts and deficits with the other.

grain. "France is in a rather desperate position," he advised. "Strongly recommend that you go to the President and ask him to request Agriculture to renew the procurement. . . . Grave social, economic, and political consequences will almost certainly flow from our failure to provide this aid." Marshall called Clayton that evening, blandly promising to do "everything possible." A few days later, after a cabinet meeting on the Clayton cable, Marshall cabled the administration's cold reply: "No commitment of 553,000 tons from U.S. ever made to French minister," adding that the United States had in any case already sent more than 400,000 tons. "Entire Cabinet and President are of opinion that any additional demands on grain market at this time will simply further inflate grain market and produce no additional grain for export." Suddenly everyone in the Truman administration understood what Clayton had tried to explain about global price mechanisms in the debate on controls, though they now failed to grasp that rising prices would call forth an increased quantity of supply. Marshall was particularly annoyed with press reports that had begun appearing on shortages and outright starvation in some sections of France: "French officials also should recognize that further pressure through the press will react adversely and perhaps reduce the quantity of grain available for shipment."[19]

On the very day he sent that telegram, Marshall called Kennan in to solicit his report on a European recovery program, so at least some thoughts were moving in the right direction. Still, the administration's reply to the French emergency illustrated to Clayton a large gap in thinking. On the basis of what he saw in Europe, Clayton felt that Europe's desperation had not yet hit home in Washington. How could it have? Marshall, Truman, and Acheson only drew their knowledge from terse cables and dry statistics. Late in May, Clayton returned to Washington to try to make clear what he had seen.

◻ ◻ ◻

The force of Clayton's reports is perhaps best captured by the
recollections of those to whom they were directed. One such official was Paul Nitze, who recalls:

> Will returned to town on May 19, 1947, and immediately assem-
> bled a group of us from his office for lunch at the Metropolitan
> Club to discuss not only the wool tariff but also the general
> situation in Europe. Will was genuinely alarmed that Europe was
> on the brink of disaster. The thing that had made perhaps the
> strongest impression on him was the unwillingness of the Euro-
> pean farmers to sell their produce to the cities, because the cities
> had nothing to sell in return. While the farmers were hoarding
> food in the country, people in the cities were starving. Something
> had to be done to break the impasse, to get industry and agricul-
> ture moving again, and to restore a sense of confidence in the
> economic and political system.[20]

That afternoon, Nitze says, Clayton returned to his office and
finished dictating a memo for Marshall on his findings and his
suggestions for a European aid program.

The various drafts of Clayton's second memo were circulated
between May 19 and May 27. It was discussed at several meetings,
including a session attended by Clayton, Kennan, Cohen, Thorp,
Bohlen, Henderson, and Acheson on May 28. It was also handed
to Marshall, on whom it had a major impact. Joseph Jones, who
wrote an excellent history of the Marshall Plan's genesis, calls
Clayton's second memo "one of the most direct and important
influences in the 'triggering' of the Secretary's speech at Harvard."[21]
The following, comparing passages from Marshall's speech with
the Clayton memo of May 27, buttresses Jones's assessment.

Clayton's May 27 Memo to Marshall (eight hundred words, ten main points)	Marshall's June 5 Speech at Harvard (twelve hundred words, eight main points)
(point number as indicated)	(paragraph number as indicated)

	1. General greeting
1. "It is now obvious that we grossly under-estimated the destruction to the European economy. . . . We understood the physical destruction but failed to take fully into account the effects of economic dislocation on production— the nationalization of industries, drastic land reform, severance of long-standing commercial ties, disappearance of commercial firms through death and loss of capital."	2. "In considering the requirements for the rehabilitation of Europe, the physical loss of life, visible destruction of factories, mines, and railroads [were] correctly estimated, but it has become obvious that this visible destruction was less serious than the dislocation of the entire fabric of the European economy. . . . Long-standing commercial ties, private institutions disappeared through loss of capital, absorption through nationalization, or simple destruction."
2. "Europe is steadily deteriorating. . . . Millions of people in the cities are starving. More consumers' goods and restored confidence in the currency are absolutely necessary if the peasant is again to supply food to the cities . . . . The modern system of division of labor has almost broken down in Europe."	3. "The farmer has always provided foodstuffs to exchange with the city. . . . This division of labor is the basis of modern civilization. At the present time it is threatened with breakdown. The farmer . . . has withdrawn many fields from cultivation . . . . Meanwhile people in the cities are short of food and fuel . . . . The modern system of division of labor upon which the exchange of products is based is in danger of breaking down."
5. "Without further prompt and substantial aid . . . economic, social, and political disintegration will overwhelm Europe."	4. "Europe's requirements . . . are so much greater than the ability to pay that she must have . . . help or face economic, social, and political deterioration."

Clayton's Memo (*continued*)	Marshall's Speech (*continued*)

5. (continued) "Aside from the awful implications which this political disintegration would have for the future peace and security of the world, the immediate effects on our domestic economy would be disastrous: markets for our surplus production gone, unemployment, depression, a heavily unbalanced budget on the background of a mountainous war debt."

6. "Aside from the demoralizing effect on the world at large and the possibilities of disturbances arising as a result of the desperation of the people concerned, the consequences to the economy of the United States should be apparent to all . . . . There can be no political stability and no assured peace . . . without the return to normal economic health in the world."

7. The policy is designed "in order to save Europe from starvation and chaos (*not* the Russians)."

6. "Our policy is directed not against any country or doctrine, but against hunger, poverty, desperation, and chaos."

8. Sets forth specific nation-by-nation needs.

9. "This three-year grant to Europe should be based on a European plan which the principal European nations, headed by the UK, France, and Italy, should work out."

7. "It is already evident that before the United States can proceed . . . there must be some agreement among the countries of Europe as to the requirements of the situation . . . . The initiative, I think, must come from Europe."

6. "This problem can be met only if the American people are taken into complete confidence . . . and told all the facts and only if a sound, workable plan is presented."

8. "An essential part of any successful action . . . is an understanding on the part of the people of America of the problem and remedies to be applied."

SOURCE: "May 27 and June 5: A Comparison of William Clayton's Memorandum and George Marshall's Speech," Alexis de Tocqueville Institution, December 20, 1989, adapted with grateful acknowledgment from Ross J. Pritchard, "William L. Clayton," Ph.D. thesis, Fletcher School of Law and Diplomacy, 1955, pp. 296–98.

Dean Acheson recalls Clayton's contribution at some length:

The memorandum came to me on May 27 and went on at once
to the General. Clayton began by stating . . . : "It is by now obvious
that we have grossly underestimated the destruction to the European economy by the war." We could see the physical destruction but the effect of vast economic disruption and political,
social, and psychological destruction from five years of Hitler's
remaking of Europe into a war machine completely escaped us.

Europe was steadily deteriorating, the memorandum continued. "The political situation reflects the economic. . . . Millions
of people in the cities are slowly starving." French grain acreage
was twenty-five percent under prewar and grain was fed to cattle.
The peasant had nothing to buy with the deteriorating currency.
The current annual balance-of-payments deficit of four areas
alone—the United Kingdom, France, Italy, and the U.S.-U.K.
zones of Germany—was five billion dollars for this subminimum
standard of living.

To survive, Clayton wrote, Europe must have two and a half
billion dollars annually of coal, bread grains, and shipping services
until her own shipping and production should be rebuilt. Further
study was unnecessary. The facts were well known. The problem
was to organize our fiscal services and our own vast consumption
so that enough could be made available out of our own vast
production. This should be paid for out of taxes and "not by
addition to debt."

According to the memorandum, Europe should have from us
a grant of "6 or 7 billion dollars worth of goods a year for three
years . . . principally of coal, food, cotton, tobacco, shipping
services," largely in surplus. . . .

The three-year grant should be "based on a European plan
which the principal European nations, headed by the UK, France
and Italy, should work out." (Clayton also recommended a European economic federation in which he was nearly a decade ahead
of the Treaty of Rome.)

Other nations might help with surplus food and raw materials,
Clayton concluded, "but we must avoid getting into another UN-
RRA. *The United States must run this show.*"

When Clayton sent this memorandum to me, he asked that a
meeting be arranged . . . with the General. This I did for the next

day, giving him the memorandum to read. Meanwhile Kennan's study, requested by General Marshall, had come in. It was more cautious than Clayton's, dwelling more on difficulties and dangers—which were certainly there—than on the imperative need for action. It agreed that European countries must produce a plan for recovery but pointed out how difficult a task this would be with the Soviet Union in its present mood. When we met on May 28 we had both papers before us.

Will Clayton was one of the most powerful and persuasive advocates to whom I have listened. Both qualities came from his command of the subject and the depth of his conviction. What he said at the meeting added to his paper principally corroborative detail to illustrate the headlong disintegration of the highly complex industrial society of Europe, through the breakdown of interrelations between the industrial cities and the food-producing countryside. Millions of people would soon die. . . . To organize the great effort needed to prevent this disaster would take time, but it had to begin here and now. . . .

On this main point there was no debate. It would be folly, the General said, "to sit back and do nothing." His principal concern was whether any proposal we might make should be addressed to all Europe or to Western Europe only. We were agreed—Clayton, Cohen, Kennan, Bohlen, and myself—that the United States should not assume the responsibility of dividing Europe. I pointed out that Russian obstruction in developing a European plan could be overcome by not requiring her agreement; what might be fatal to congressional support would be Russian support and demands. . . . Kennan suggested that we might blandly treat the Soviet Union as, like ourselves, a donor of raw materials. The matter was left inconclusive. The General cautioned sternly against leaks. . . . As one looks back on it, he left us with very little to leak. . . .

The next day . . . Bohlen was asked to draft something from the Kennan and Clayton memoranda. A few days later Clayton and I saw the draft, contributed our own suggestions, and heard no more. . . .

The speech was short, simple, and altogether brilliant in its statement of a purpose and a proposal adapted to the necessities of his position. A little more than half of the speech, just over a printed page, set forth the condition of Europe and the causes for it. This came straight from the two Clayton memoranda.[22]

On May 25, James Reston published an exclusive story in the *New York Times* on the emerging design of the Marshall Plan. It was all there: the careful estimates of trade flows and dollar shortage compiled by Nitze, Cleveland, and Clayton; the complex interdependency of Europe's national economies; the touchy problem of how to treat Moscow; the advanced stage of the work going on at the State Department; and the importance of both U.S. help on the one hand and European initiative on the other. Although careful not to name specific sources—only Acheson is mentioned, once, in a quotation from his public speech of May 8—it seemed clear that Reston had been briefed on everything SWNCC, Kennan, and Clayton had been writing and saying. There was little follow up to the Reston story in the press and no advance leaking of Marshall's plan to deliver the historic speech at Harvard. The secretary achieved both the careful inside planning and the outside surprise he had been hoping for.[23]

The influence of George Kennan's May 23 memorandum has been described in detail in many other works and need not be repeated here. A proper perspective of Clayton's role in the Harvard speech, however, demands that Kennan's major contribution be acknowledged. Although overemphasizing Kennan's role at the expense of Clayton is a common mistake, there are some who err in the opposite direction. Acheson's dismissal of the Kennan memorandum—"more cautious than Clayton's, dwelling more on difficulties and dangers . . . than on the imperative need for action"—is an example. Another is provided by Robert Ferrell, who seems to undervalue the Kennan memorandum when he writes:

> It appears as if this "memo" by the [Policy Planning] Staff had much less influence in the Department than the ideas of Will Clayton; the Marshall Plan took its inspiration and detail from Clayton rather than from the Kennan memorandum. . . . More-

over, on this question of the influence of the two memoranda, Kennan's paper was tentative and vague, whereas Clayton's set out the problems of Europe and their solution in clear detail. One of Clayton's assistants, Ambassador George C. McGhee, recalls carrying Clayton's memorandum of May 27 to the Department during Clayton's sickness, that is, before May 27 . . . and adds: "As you know, it is a controversial subject, but there is no question in my mind that Clayton should be recognized as the real father of the Marshall Plan."[24]

It is also true, as Nitze and Jones point out, that Kennan borrowed heavily from the work of many others. Marshall's emphasis on the need for European initiative, frequently described as emanating from the Policy Planning Staff, was hardly unique. Clayton had been preaching it for years, most notably in his talks with officials in the United States and Europe from March to May of 1947, and used it in his memoranda of late May to Marshall. Jones worked the concept into a speech Marshall had intended to deliver at the University of Wisconsin: "The Economic Commission for Europe can do all these things. What it actually does accomplish depends upon the initiative which the countries of Europe are willing to take. The United States . . . can only promise financial support for cooperative European ventures." Jones's draft, submitted May 20, was circulated widely in the department, probably made available to Kennan, and reportedly discussed by Clayton and Marshall on May 23. Similarly, a passage from Cleveland's memorandum of May 9 for SWNCC, which he generously shared with Kennan, reads: "Leadership—Morale—Ideological Goals . . . (1) The central idea—European Economic unity and a U.S.-backed European recovery program . . . not just words but material inducements to economic unity." The same memo stresses the "moral—political—psychological repercussions" of a European effort backed by U.S. aid, another insight commonly described as conceived, written, edited, and submitted to Marshall by George Kennan.[25] Kennan's admirers would do well to remember that most of the concepts, and nearly all of the figures and proposals, of the Policy

Planning Staff memorandum originated elsewhere. Yet the same could be said of most of the formation of the plan, whether by Acheson, Clayton, Lippmann, or Marshall himself. The Kennan memorandum was important not because of the originality of its parts—though Kennan's deft understanding of how to handle the Soviets was clearly his own—but because of the cogency of the whole.

Jones, Nitze, Cleveland, Clayton, Bohlen, Acheson, Reston, Truman, and Marshall himself all generated ideas toward what became the Marshall Plan. "What was still needed," as Charles L. Mee writes, "was someone who had the clarity of thought and the command of rhetoric to take all this jumble of potentially useful stuff and put it together in a single interoffice memo."[26] Kennan's function was to write an effective piece, collating and summarizing the indecipherable prose of the SWNCC group. Although the hard-hitting style of Clayton's memorandum was probably necessary to get Marshall's attention—reminiscent of the tone of Kennan's own February 1946 cable—the general generally preferred a cooler rhetorical approach.

Marshall, by the way, made his own substantial contribution to the Marshall Plan. Marshall sifted through the arguments and came up with just the right degree of vagueness to require European action, yet just the right degree of specificity to excite it. Marshall also blended together such substantial talents and egos as Kennan, Acheson, and Clayton into an effective team. "While I was in a position to get the information that would naturally make me the person to start the Marshall Plan," Clayton told his daughter, "still if the plan had been a failure Secretary Marshall would have had to take the blame. Since it was a success, Marshall should have the credit."[27] Perhaps, in the end, it really was the Marshall Plan.

14

Summer 1947

From Marshall's Speech to a Plan

MARSHALL'S SPEECH AT HARVARD WAS ONLY THE BEGINNING OF THE Marshall Plan story. Six weeks later, Kennan declared, "Marshall 'plan,' we have no plan." On July 28, Ben Moore wrote to Clair Wilcox, who was attending the Geneva trade talks, "The 'Marshall Plan' has been compared to a flying saucer—nobody knows what it looks like, how big it is, in what direction it is moving, or whether it really exists."[1]

Marshall never had a precise economic blueprint in mind when he spoke or in the weeks and months immediately following his speech. When Clayton requested more-detailed negotiating instructions for the Geneva trade talks, Marshall suggested he draw up his own. A few days later, when Clayton pressed Marshall to comment on his planned approach, Marshall responded with one of those terse, minimalist commands for which he was well known: "Go over there and interpret our situation to them and our proposal as best you can."[2]

Moreover, part of the plan had been to encourage the nations of Europe to craft a plan for themselves. Yet Clayton had already laid out the details for a plan in two memos completed on June 19, the eve of his departure for Europe. In his second preparatory

memorandum, Clayton offered arguments to justify excluding the
Soviets from Marshall Plan aid or, rather, of allowing the Soviets
to exclude themselves:

> The question of Russia and her satellites in any European reha-
> bilitation bothers me. Russia could use a large loan for reconstruc-
> tion and development but suffers no dollar shortage in respect to
> her ordinary requirements. . . . Russia is self-sufficient in food
> and fiber. She has exported both cotton and grain in modest
> quantities since the end of the war. . . . Over a year ago she
> contracted to sell conditionally 500,000 tons of wheat to France
> for dollars. . . . Russia is receiving about 5 million tons of coal
> annually from Poland as reparations. Before the war Russia ex-
> ported a little coal. . . .
>
> From the above it is difficult to see how Russia could expect
> any further financial assistance from the U.S. even if the Ameri-
> can people were willing to furnish it, which, I think, we would all
> agree, is not the case, unless accompanied by an overall settle-
> ment of our problems with Russia, particularly the Austrian, Ger-
> man, and Japanese peace treaties, and the question of Korea.[3]

Clayton's agenda for the summer of 1947 included persuading
the British to follow through on their repeated promises to begin
trade liberalization and monetary reform, cajoling the French government into approving German reindustrialization, and enticing
enough interim aid out of Congress to rescue several faltering
countries for 1947, yet not so much that it would wreck the incentive for European unity. The basic Marshall Plan design—U.S. aid
to countries willing to reduce trade barriers and create stable money—
had already been worked out, at least in Clayton's mind. There
were numerous other important players: Bevin and Cripps for the
British; Ramadier, Bidault, and Monnet for the French; Kennan,
Nitze, Douglas, and Caffery for the Americans; even the pope who,
when he urged Clayton to secure aid for the war-damaged countries, became the object of an equally urgent appeal to get the
Europeans to enact the monetary reforms promised at Bretton
Woods.

It is no overstatement, however, to place Clayton at the center. Certainly the Europeans placed him there, as did the *New York Times* in its coverage of the talks. "The long road," the *Times* reported the morning after Clayton's first talk, "toward economic cooperation began this morning, when William L. Clayton . . . went to 10 Downing Street."[4]

Reports of the imminent breakdown of French civilization led Clayton to conclude that the United States must announce its willingness to finance a plan well in advance of any final design. The advance of Communist parties in France and Italy made it likely that, without prompt action by the United States, there might be little of Europe left to save. The Marshall Plan, even without specific details, was already having a desirable effect;[5] by the end of June, within weeks of Marshall's speech, France and Italy had ousted Communists from important positions in their coalition governments.

Clayton was originally scheduled to depart for Europe shortly after the Harvard speech. But the wool bill delayed his departure. He felt that before he could do any good in Europe, he had to torpedo this major domestic threat to the world economy. On June 19, Truman summoned Clayton and Agriculture Secretary Clinton Anderson to his office to discuss the bill. He gave each fifteen minutes to make his case. Anderson, arguing for the bill, said that the optimism of the free traders was overdone and that the Geneva conference on removing trade restrictions was "a complete failure." If the administration did not support the higher tariff against Australian wool, Anderson warned, the Democratic party might lose support in up to seven wool-producing states in the 1948 election.

Clayton, in rebuttal, urged Truman to veto the measure, arguing that a veto was in the long-term national interest and pleading for a chance to work for success in the Geneva talks. Truman made no decision that day, but Clayton, encouraged by Truman's questions, immediately returned to his office and prepared a memo proposing to offer the Australians a 25 percent cut in the wool tariff.[6]

On June 20, the same day the Senate passed the wool act, Clayton saw Truman again, who said he was going to veto the bill. When Clayton presented his request for authority to offer a 25 percent tariff reduction in Geneva, Truman initialed his approval.[7] Truman's support gave Clayton the tool he needed to revive the stalemated Geneva talks. At about the same time, Truman also asked Clayton to become his roving ambassador in Europe to get the Marshall Plan started.

Meanwhile, the Europeans waited impatiently for Clayton's arrival to find out exactly what the Marshall Plan meant to them. Ernest Bevin, England's foreign secretary, was especially keen to talk with Clayton. Having been alerted by Acheson that Marshall's speech was not merely another ceremonial oration, Bevin responded to Marshall's appeal by urging the Europeans to take the initiative in their own recovery and salvation. With the aid of a vast team of economic experts, Bevin, who had already opened talks with the French, began immediately to produce a plan that fit Marshall's ambitious objectives. "It must," said Bevin, "appeal to businessmen, not only idealists, and convince the former that the proposals were not a request for charity, but a good investment."

But what was meant by cooperation? Was it trade liberalization and currency reform? Or did it mean a Keynes-style cartel for swapping coal, grain, and other commodities? Or did it mean—as the British feared—an effort to level European living standards? What was to be done about including the Russians in any Marshall Plan program? This last point seemed especially urgent because Marshall had stressed in his June 13 press conference that the Soviet Union was not to be excluded if it wanted to join. Some feared that the program would be harder to sell to Congress, which had to authorize the money, if Russia were included. But what if Russia excluded itself?

Remadier suggested that the French and the British invite Molotov to join their talks "because of the internal political situation in France," where the Communists were a strong minority. Bevin agreed if only for his own domestic reason; he felt it was as important to invite the Russians as it was to see to it that they did not disrupt the plan.[8]

Nonetheless, as Ambassador Jefferson Caffery cabled to Washington, "British feel that Russian participation would tend greatly to complicate things and that it might be best if Russians refused invitation. They tell me that French also [appear] to share this feeling." But was this what the Americans wanted? Bevin cabled the British embassy in Washington on June 16, asking for guidance. On June 20, Marshall cabled his reply to Clayton and Bevin. He answered that it would be fine for the Russians to be excluded but that the United States wanted Europe to do the job. In any case, "Mr. Clayton will discuss the whole matter with you in detail."[9]

Molotov accepted the French-British invitation on June 23, saying that he would come to Paris for discussions on June 27. "I feel sure," Ambassador Walter Bedell Smith wrote from Moscow, "that this [Soviet] participation will be for destructive rather than constructive purposes." Here matters stood when Clayton met with the British during June 24–26, "the first real exchange between the two governments since Marshall's speech," as Bullock writes.[10]

Clayton's instructions for the London talks stressed the need to leave the field open for European initiative. "Before the U.S. Government can take any effective action to be of help it must know from the European governments directly concerned what measures these Governments either jointly or separately have in mind in order to remove the causes of the present troubles."[11] Accordingly, the talks had a hedged, tentative quality: Bevin probing for information, Clayton trying to communicate answers indirectly.

In the first session, June 24, Bevin stressed what was to become a dominant theme among the Europeans: the need for emergency aid, "some temporary interim solution," even during coming months, to shore Europe up while talks on a plan proceeded. The weakness in Britain's economy, he noted, had deleterious effects on its strength as an American ally, Greece and Turkey being prime examples, though Bevin did not cite them, the effort to revive Germany's economy being another, which he did. "The rise in prices," he said, blaming prices for U.S. goods in part, "has thrown us a year out and the U.K. position compelled me at Moscow to draw in my horns."

What Britain wanted, Bevin disclosed, was "to establish a new financial partnership." Aid would put Britain in a position to "play its part," and the special partnership would in turn be a recognition that Britain's role was unique. Otherwise, he noted, Britain might feel itself in a position of weakness, standing in relation to the United States as Yugoslavia stood to Russia.[12] Clayton replied that the Americans could not consider creating any "special partner" in the Marshall Plan, for any such unique relationship would undercut the essence of Marshall's proposal: "the principle that no piecemeal approach to the European problem would be undertaken." He did not understand, Clayton said, how Britain's finances mandated a different approach than would be taken toward France or Italy.

Clayton also criticized the British management of the Ruhr coal (his May memorandum to Marshall had recommended that the United States assume control) and proposals for its socialization. He did not mention the Russians. In sum, Clayton's response was that the U.S. offer was already on the table: substantial aid if the Europeans came up with a workable plan. The United States was not interested in offering still further concessions in the form of interim aid.

Clayton and the British held their second round of meetings on June 25. Bevin tried again to develop the concept of a "special relationship" but this time on a more positive note. The Polish prime minister, Bevin said, seemed favorable to the Marshall Plan, and other Eastern European countries were interested. Bevin "was convinced that Yugoslavia would eventually come West"; Belgrade needed agricultural equipment, transportation, lumber mills, and other goods. These were things "which Russia could not supply." What could Britain offer Yugoslavia? Bevin asked Sir Stafford Cripps, the chancellor of the Exchequer. Alas, nothing right now, Cripps said, because of the steel shortage. Britain was spending its dollars on many U.S. goods and then turning them over to Europe. Bevin, turning back to Clayton, said that "if the U.S. took the line that the U.K. was the same as any other European country this would be unfortunate because the U.K. could contribute to economic revival."[13]

Clayton repeated that he did not understand Britain's uniqueness in this respect: every country in Europe could help by raising production. Clayton clarified, though, that the British need not think so much in terms of swapping commodities; if a country needed steel or rubber or grain, the U.S. program would help them to buy such supplies, but there would be no tied loan principle that would require recipients to "buy American."

Sir Edward Bridges, permanent secretary of the British Treasury, observed that perhaps everyone had been talking in circles. The United States had said, had it not, that the contemplated program would involve a unified scheme from Europe but that this was to be administered through a series of bilateral agreements with the recipient countries. Yes, Clayton responded, the United States had no intention of funneling supplies to a European superbureaucracy, as some had feared, because Britain would have low priority for supplies if other nations were worse off. Still less was it intended to lump Britain into a "European pool."

By that afternoon, the British had worked the handy formulation into an aide-memoire for review by Clayton:

It is understood that while it is hoped that the scheme [Marshall Plan] will cover Europe as a whole, the U.S. administration would be satisfied if it could be started with the Western countries of

Europe as a nucleus, on the understanding that the scheme would
be open to other countries if they so desired. . . .

It is understood that the United States Administration contemplate that, although the approach to the problem is essentially
European, the arrangements for giving help for immediate needs
would take the form of a series of agreements between the United
States government and each of the countries concerned.[14]

In other words, there would be a special relationship; if Bevin
found the Russians uncooperative, he was to go ahead with a plan
for Western Europe. To make sure everyone understood one another, the British pressed the point with Clayton again that afternoon. Bevin expected that at Paris Molotov would introduce the
usual demand for assistance to Russia as a condition for serious
negotiating. "Mr. Clayton said he could not give a categorical [re-
ply] . . . but stated as his opinion that there would have to be radical
changes in the Russian position regarding European recovery and
other related matters before the American people would approve
the extension of financial assistance."

But if the Russians were turned down, Bevin mused, they would
not participate in the Marshall Plan. If so, would the United States
support Britain in going ahead with France and the others? "Yes,"
Clayton answered. Bevin's prediction of Soviet behavior was accurate. No sooner did Molotov meet Bidault, on June 26, than he
asked what the French and the British had been doing behind his
back. The next day, when Bevin was present, Molotov resumed his
suspicious line of questioning but in a lower key. "What additional
information," he asked, had been "received from the United States
government?" Oh, nothing really, Bevin (falsely) said. "Really?"
Molotov asked. "You've just seen Clayton." Bevin repeated that
there had been no separate agreement or even any important information exchanged.[15]

Molotov then made known his proposals. In essence, they were
that, because none of the three governments knew any more than
was contained in Marshall's speech, they should ask the United
States how much money it was prepared to advance to Europe and

for assurances that it could win congressional approval of such a plan. Molotov's approach, according to one of the French participants, was "to put the United States in a position where it must either shell out the dollars before there is a real plan or refuse outright to advance any credits." Bevin responded with a minilecture to Molotov that "in a democracy" one cannot make promises that are binding on the legislative branch.

Bevin also observed that recipients of aid could hardly lay down conditions. He suggested that the British, Soviets, French, and others start exchanging information, draw up a plan for cooperation, and present it to the Americans. Bidault agreed, saying that this was what Marshall had asked for in his speech. Bevin and Bidault were prepared to do this with the Soviet Union or without it.[16] The meetings lasted for several more days, Bevin pressing matters by drawing up an invitation to the other European countries to join in preparing a plan. This put the issue—which the British had indicated they wanted resolved by July 5—squarely and immediately before the Soviets.

The next morning Molotov disclosed that the Soviet Union had no intention of joining such a scheme: "Inquiry into the resources of the European nations," he said, "would violate the sovereignty of the individual countries." Stalin recognized the dilemma: to receive any money, the participants would have to open up their economies, including information about their resources, assets, and current levels of output, which the Soviets construed as Western prying or spying. Disclosure of such information threatened not only the essence of internal Soviet rule but its empire in Central and Eastern Europe. (Molotov was only repeating the line taken in the official Soviet press as early as June 11. One writer in Pravda proclaimed Marshall's speech as "evidence of even wider plans of American reaction, of a new stage in Washington's campaign against forces of world democracy and progress.") In the last week of June 1947, the Soviets, forced to choose between disclosure and empire, chose empire. In the first week of July, Molotov flew home to Moscow. To Clayton's relief, the Soviet Union had exluded itself from the Marshall Plan.

Clayton's talks with the British had hardly been limited to the complicated Russian question. The British, who were just about to attempt the restoration of sterling convertibility (an effort that collapsed in August when the Bank of England failed to keep monetary expansion in line with the pegged rate), were already pleading for yet another extension of the pledges they had made at Bretton Woods and in the British loan agreement. Clayton listened sympathetically but would not budge. The British should immediately stabilize their money in their own interest, rather than waiting, as countries reluctant to accept monetary discipline invariably think they must wait, until other conditions somehow stabilize. Stable money, as Clayton had often stressed (from his 1930s stumping on behalf of Hull to the Bretton Woods negotiations to his May memorandum on the Marshall Plan), would be an important instrument for increasing output and efficiency, not just a by-product of them.

The British were in no mood, under American pressure, to make further promises that they felt they could not keep. At Clayton's insistence, however, Bevin agreed to insert a statement in the June 25 aide-memoire: "Public opinion in the United States attaches great importance to satisfactory assurances that the participating countries will take all reasonable action . . . toward the stability and convertibility of their currencies." The statement was hedged; on a formal level it simply acknowledged the state of public opinion in the United States, but it was something.[17]

The second pressing issue under discussion was restoring coal production in the Ruhr region. For Clayton, it was imperative that this production, which had been running at less than 50 percent of prewar levels under the British, be quickly increased. Ruhr coal would virtually eliminate one of Europe's two most pressing commodity shortages (the other was grain). Indirectly, increased coal would help solve the grain problem: if more coal were available, Europe could resume normal levels of steel production, at once decreasing its imports from the United States and generating foreign exchange for grain imports. Attlee bristled at the suggestion that Britain's socialization plan was the problem, and Bevin chimed in that in any case the French objected to the idea of increased production.

What were the Americans prepared to propose in the Ruhr coal mines? Should there be German management? Clayton turned the question away, repeating Marshall's instruction that the Europeans were to talk about these problems first. Instead, he answered with two questions of his own: why had recovery in Europe been so slow? and what could Europe do to help itself?[18] Clayton was thus not about to impose or even suggest an "American solution," at least not yet. Perhaps the British and the French could come up with a way to increase the coal output from the Ruhr; the United States was willing to step in only if they failed to do so. Clayton had already observed that nationalization of the coal mines was not the likely route to recovery but that that it was a decision for Europe to make.

On July 11, Bidault pressed Clayton that Germany not be reindustrialized to a position superior to France. No, Clayton said, no one wanted to see the continent dominated by Germany again. The United States wanted, however, to see a drastic increase in coal and steel production. Perhaps, Clayton suggested, the French and British could agree to increase production, while a moratorium on nationalization held the question of ultimate control of the mines in abeyance. Slowly, but deftly, one of the most explosive political bombs was being defused.

Clayton and Bevin next broached the sensitive subject of the relationship between the Marshall Plan and the Geneva trade talks. In Clayton's eyes, everything hinged on this trade relationship and on a policy of currency stability as opposed to more pledges. Clayton said that he was keenly aware of the U.S. need for export markets but that many of his fellow citizens "had other views." To put the Marshall Plan program across, the United States must know when Europe will get on its feet. "To supplement this," the United States would like "some proposals regarding a closer integration of European economy." Bevin, who knew Clayton's mind well by this time, understood the linkage that was now being suggested. This, Bevin said, "raises an interesting point" because whenever he took steps in this direction—for example, with France and Belgium—Sir Stafford Cripps and others said that he was violating the agreed principles of multilateralism. *

A related question was how Europe could negotiate for a special "European customs union" when one of the rules at Geneva was that there would be no special side deals, that all the participants would drop trade barriers jointly. Clayton was in fact convinced by Monnet later that summer that a pattern of interim bilateral trade agreements might be necessary and that it would not harm future prospects for broader international agreements. But Clayton, who was not about to concede Monnet's point immediately, mentioned that progress had been made in the Benelux customs union and that this certainly did not violate the spirit of the Geneva trade talks. But when Bevin raised the example of an exclusive French-British agreement for swapping tractors for musical instruments, Clayton responded that that certainly would be a violation. He indicated, however, that his thinking was flexible, adding that per-

---

*The parties at the trade talks had agreed not to advance discriminatory measures while the talks were taking place, a practice the United States had itself violated in passing the wool act, though Bevin did not say so. Separate agreements, even toward reduced trade barriers, might undermine the effort to win more sweeping, multinational reductions. As acting secretary of state in 1946, Clayton objected vigorously when Sweden signed a bilateral trade agreement with the Soviet Union, not because he objected to trade with the Soviets but because it undercut the principle of multilateralism.

haps a special exemption to the nondiscrimination pattern could be worked out at Geneva.[19]

That Clayton would give ground on an issue he had promoted for more than fifteen years indicates not only his open-mindedness and generosity but his concern for the ultimate condition of Europe. If Europe could not be put back on its feet, it would do little good to have its depressed markets open to American products. If Europe could get back on its feet by encouraging any measure of wider trade, the larger issue of unhampered free trade could be fought and won another day. Clayton left London satisfied that he had shown himself (and the United States) to be flexible, not dogmatic, compassionate, not intransigent.

Clayton next flew to Geneva to reassure the Australians about the U.S. tariff on Australian wool, then to Paris to confer with Bidault. The French, Clayton cabled to Marshall on July 9, wanted to know the same thing as the British. What would intra-European trade liberalization do to the Geneva talks, which aimed to eliminate all trade barriers between nations? What about an emergency appropriation for 1947?

The French also posed an important new question: Who spoke for the Americans? After all, Monnet explained, with a single channel of information, the Europeans would know whose "friendly aid" to listen to; without it, they would be sifting through possibly conflicting reports from different officials. Clayton tactfully suggested that Marshall and Truman spoke for the United States and that other officials spoke for the United States whenever they spoke for Marshall and Truman. Clayton also advised Bidault that a "European federation" of some sort would be looked on favorably, even at Geneva, and added that anything the Europeans could do to promote trade liberalization, as opposed to merely agreeing to it, would help persuade the U.S. Congress to appropriate money for Europe's recovery.[20]

While France and more than twenty other countries began crafting the European recovery plan in Paris on July 12, Clayton shuttled between Geneva and London trying to loosen the British attitude regarding imperial preferences. July and August were months of stalemate for nearly everyone. In a series of meetings with Sir Stafford Cripps, the chancellor of the Exchequer, in July and August, Clayton tried to make plain the increasingly explicit linkage between Geneva and Paris; direct U.S. cash assistance to individual countries, he argued, would do Europe little good without a more open trading system, and as for currency stability, the British would have to try again. The British, however, would not give in.

The conferees at Paris, meanwhile, seemed able to agree only that they did not agree. The Turks complained that the conference's Executive Committee included only Western Europeans. The Portuguese delegate noted that his country was not represented on the Food Committee. Bidault lectured everyone that his country "had been invaded" by Germany and of the need for Allied control of the Ruhr. H. M. Hirschfeld, representing the Netherlands, reminded him that "Holland, as well as France, had been invaded." The British lectured about avoiding shopping lists, while a half-dozen members of the British Board of Trade wrote shopping lists for food, transport, fuel, fertilizer, and equipment. Almost everyone concurred on the need for emergency financing; their needs were too pressing, the Europeans pleaded, to draw up four-year plans that would not begin for another six months.

Throughout the summer of 1947, Clayton was perpetually in motion between London, Paris, and Geneva. Everywhere he went, he cut a striking figure. His role as U.S. "ambassador to Europe," as the *New York Times* called him, attracted pleas from economic ministers and heads of state across the continent; they became so oppressive that he was forced to register at hotels under an assumed name, "Troutman," to get any peace. At the same time, Clayton doffed many of the trappings of power, showing a profile of businesslike simplicity. Day after day, he came striding briskly down the street to the scheduled meetings, while his European counterparts were dropped off in a train of limousines. Above all, the Europeans felt affection and respect for Clayton because they could tell he loved Europe.

During the talks in Geneva, he talked of the sheer social and physical breakdown he had witnessed elsewhere. One evening, a colleague later recalled, Clayton looked out over the balcony of his hotel down toward Lake Geneva at buildings and people largely unscarred because of Switzerland's wartime neutrality and at an economy and society where his old business contacts and personal friends, the comfortable relations of a lifetime, were intact and indeed thriving. "There," he remarked wistfully, "but for two wars, lies Europe."

Throughout July and August, Clayton pleaded the European case for interim assistance to Marshall, who grew impatient with Clayton's repeated messages. Did Clayton not understand that the whole key to the enterprise was for Europe to create a plan first and that only then could the administration address an appeal for funding to Congress? The Americans in Paris were equally miffed: Could private commitments for interim aid be made now, encouraging the Europeans to try a bit harder?

Thus, even as Clayton tried to move the British on trade and the French on Germany and the American officials on the need for German economic reform, Marshall dispatched a series of representatives to Europe. He sent Commerce Secretary Averell Harriman to talk to Jean Monnet about the need for German growth, "suitably controlled." In late July, he dispatched Nitze and Kennan to Paris—Nitze to question the Europeans about the huge estimates of their needs they kept cranking out and Kennan to give more vigor to the discussions.

Marshall concluded that Clayton was not pressing U.S. views with sufficient vigor and resolve even though it was Clayton who had written that "the U.S. must run this show." "It was the consensus" of a meeting of top officials with Lovett, the minutes of August 22 recorded, "that Mr. Clayton, while generally aware of departmental thinking with regard to the 'Plan,' holds fundamental divergent views on some aspects, notably the importance of a Customs Union for Europe, the overriding importance of financial and multilateral exchange arrangements, and his aversion to continuing [the present] European machinery to implement the European reconstruction plan." Lovett and Kennan impatiently demanded a detailed study of European negotiating strategies and how the United States should respond to them. Clayton, however, knew that he was bringing the Europeans ever closer to an agreement, for at Geneva, rapid progress was being made. The result would be reduced barriers not just between the European countries but between the Europeans and the United States, Australia, and other countries. By mid-August, most of the agreements, covering literally thousands of goods, had been completed. The sticking point was Britain, but British foot-dragging could not be solved, Clayton realized, by writing twenty-five-page reports to reassure Kennan, Lovett, and Bohlen. Cripps, backed by a substantial segment of British opinion, felt that this was no time to tamper with the empire's preference system. A British government hypnotized by the national trade balance was no more willing to join in a European customs union than it was the General Agreement on Tariffs and Trade (GATT).[21]

In Clayton's eyes, the most frustrating aspect of the British position was its lack of self-interest. On August 19, he tried again to reason with Cripps; if the British did not give ground in Geneva, Clayton said, the whole Marshall Plan would have to be rethought. Failure at the Geneva trade talks meant failure at the Paris talks on the European recovery plan. As a final compromise, Clayton revealed that the United States would agree to a phased reduction of imperial preferences, provided that there was a definite schedule for their eventual elimination and that an immediate lowering should take place. Cripps remained firm, saying his government could not accept any reductions in empire preferences.

Because Cripps was intransigent, Clayton went public, declaring on August 21 that the British position threatened to dash all the progress in the nearly completed Geneva GATT agreement. Perhaps public opinion in Britain would note the connection and impose a sanity that Cripps seemed to lack. Still no change. On September 10, Clayton made his message even more explicit. In a radio broadcast from Paris, he warned that the Marshall Plan would fail unless it could be accompanied by a substantial reduction in tariffs. Still the British held firm.

A few days later, Clayton made another appeal to Cripps. His aide-memoire on the September 19 meeting, entitled Final Offer to Cripps, was at least his third "final offer." The United States would not insist that the schedule for preference reductions begin immediately, Clayton said. There could be a waiting period, with preference reduction following over the next ten years.[22]

The decision to make such warnings, and make them public, represented the greatest gamble of Clayton's career. It could not have been reached lightly; everything Clayton had worked toward aimed at securing the breakthrough on free trade that Cordell Hull had not achieved. Yet Clayton realized that Britain's position had hardened to rock. If Britain could not be moved, the whole trade-liberalization enterprise would collapse. Only by indicating a willingness to walk away from his most cherished goals, Clayton realized, could the better part of those goals perhaps be salvaged.

While Cripps conferred with his government, and Clayton waited for a final reply, the delegates in Paris issued a preliminary report calling for nearly $29 billion in American assistance, an amount Marshall immediately dismissed as being far too large to present to Congress. Worse, the Europeans leaked the reports, hoping to put pressure on the Americans in Paris to capitulate. Meanwhile, Kennan and Lovett encouraged the Europeans to reconsider using a Keynes-style cartel to distribute scarce supplies. "The conclusions of the Conference," Clayton cabled to Marshall, "to us, are disappointing, and might, if formally advanced, prejudice the success of the entire Marshall program."[23] The Americans now seemed to face a choice as hard as the one Molotov had faced—giving aid for a program that would not work or admitting the effort a failure and packing up for the long flight home. Deadlock existed on all fronts.

❑ ❑ ❑

As he had on June 5, Marshall broke the logjam. First he met with his new deputy, Robert Lovett, approving a set of instructions to the U.S. negotiators drawing largely on a pair of memorandums from Clayton and Kennan. Lovett cabled the paper to Paris for the American negotiators on September 7. They were not to back down on the core economic essentials suggested by Clayton: currency stability, more free trade, definite schedules for increased production by Germany and by Europe generally. Yet, as Clayton had initially proposed in June, and Kennan now agreed, they were to "make efforts to have the report presented in such a way as to avoid the impression of finality."[24] This would end the haggling over amounts; the Paris report, asking for $29 billion in U.S. aid, would be presented in Washington in a few weeks, where the administration could doubtless find places to trim the totals. (The budgeting, as Vandenberg recognized early in the game, was not to be taken too seriously. There would probably have to be adjustments in the out years whatever the initial plan.) Thus the Europeans would score a partial success in issuing a report that stated their needs and demands in the starkest terms, whereas the United States would be afforded an opportunity to make modifications and cuts in a second draft. It was a face-saving arrangement for both sides.

At the same time, Marshall drafted a statement to give the Europeans the short-term reassurance of aid they so desperately craved. Approved by the president, Marshall's statement was released on September 10. It read in part:

> Bad droughts, following an unusually severe winter, increasing crop shortages and restrictive financial measures which certain European governments have already been obliged to take, have had serious repercussions and have accelerated the need of some European countries for assistance in reducing hunger and cold this winter.[25]

Marshall added that he could not commit Congress to any specific appropriations but, with several congressional delegations soon returning home from their fact-finding visits to Europe, that there would be working papers from the Europeans to consider. Soon, he hoped, Congress would have on hand all the information that it needed to act.

In less than forty-eight hours, Herve Alphand informed the Executive Committee that the French government had reconsidered its position and was prepared to "proceed along the lines suggested by the U.S." By September 22, the "initial" report of the Europeans had been redrafted to the liking of Clayton, Caffery, and Douglas. The new provisions, Caffery cabled, were entirely satisfactory and in some cases exceeded America's expectations.[26] Clayton lauded the revised report and dashed to London to remind Cripps and Harold Wilson (the British delegate to Geneva) that there still remained the matter of the GATT. This time it was the British who offered a concession. Rather than larger U.S. tariff reductions in return for preference elimination, the British would trade a reduction in preference margins for somewhat smaller U.S. concessions on tariffs on their exports to the United States.[27]

A few days later, the United States accepted the British offer and the GATT was born. Clayton defended the compromise to one skeptical friend as a "practical necessity," conceding that it was not everything that he had hoped for. However, in January 1948, a bill to approve the charter of the International Trade Organization (ITO), designed to grow further even than the GATT, would die a quiet death in a congressional subcommittee.*

---

*In December 1947, Clayton, who on his October 14th resignation promised Marshall to remain as special adviser, accepted our government's request to head the U.S. delegation to the U.N. Conference on Trade and Employment in Havana. As three previous such international trade conferences in Europe had been, in a way, his creation, Clayton was encouraged by the unusually large attendance of delegates from fifty-seven nations. In January 1948, there was still more encouragement when an ITO charter was agreed to by most of the delegates, the largest number for international free trade so far. But the charter had to be

Still, Clayton had no need to be defensive or apologetic. He had just successfully negotiated the most sweeping trade agreement—in terms of tariff reductions and the number of goods and countries involved—in the history of the industrial world. If the ITO did not survive, its spirit did, for, as scholar Robert Pastor notes, "the GATT, with U.S. support, serve[d] the same purposes as ITO meetings were originally intended to serve."[28] Under the GATT treaty, world exports would triple (in constant dollars) to $156 billion in 1965 from $53 billion in 1948. "Except for details, 106 agreements are ready for incorporation into the General Agreement on Tariffs and Trade," the *New York Times* reported on October 15, 1947:

> This vast project, which makes all previous international economic accords look puny, is the realization of Mr. Clayton's dream: that a group of like-minded democratic nations could deliberately reverse the historical trend toward the strangulation of world trade. It is the big step that nobody but Mr. Clayton and a few of his colleagues thought would ever be taken.[29]

---

approved by the respective governments' legislative bodies as well. And Clayton—no longer in the State Department—could not effectively argue before Congress for its adoption. The charter was pigeonholed in a subcommittee, where protectionist special interests had derailed it, though its spirit, as scholar Robert Pastor notes, guided international trade talks for over twenty years through GATT.

15

Final Challenges

By the autumn of 1947, Clayton had helped set in place the three pillars of postwar economic foreign policy. Stable international money, under the Bretton Woods agreement, had been accomplished. The International Monetary Fund and the World Bank were operational; most of the great trading nations of the world were observing their guidelines. The Marshall Plan—offering Europeans relief from the debt of World War I, as well as a tangible incentive to cooperate with one another—was now a true plan, and Congress overwhelmingly approved its funding in the spring of 1948.

Finally, with the negotiation of the General Agreement on Tariffs and Trade (GATT), Clayton's most cherished design had been accomplished. On October 11, 1947, Clayton aide Winthrop Brown cabled from Geneva: "Personal for Clayton and Wilcox only. . . . Now expect all negotiations be concluded October 15 with signature agreement just before end month. . . . Will stand by for messages all weekend." Soon the pact was signed, and the most sweeping multilateral reduction of trade barriers in the history of the world had become fact.[1] (The treaty was so voluminous that Truman had to wait several days to get his copy, as U.N. officials, unable to find a binding for the small mountain of paper, copied and collated.)

Clayton had done his job too well. He had completed the great challenges he had set for himself. The tantalizing offer to join the cabinet as Truman's secretary of state was now a remote memory. He knew, as one associate recalled, "that he had finished." There could be no more excuses to Sue. If the Claytons were ever going to get out of Washington, now was the time.

On October 7, Clayton drafted his sixth letter resigning from the State Department. He met with President Truman for the last time on October 13, reviewing the design of the Marshall Plan and the soon-to-be signed GATT agreements. Truman made one last effort to keep him on the job, but Clayton declined: "All my urgent and immediate Government tasks are now completed, and I must return to personal responsibilities."[2] Clayton walked out of the West Wing to his office in the old State Department building and finished packing boxes, dispatching paperwork, closing out files. He had already begun the most difficult task, saying good-bye to staff and colleagues who had become a central part of his life. One such friend, Paul Nitze, recalls Clayton's poignant ambivalence:

> Clayton called me to his office one Saturday morning [probably October 11] in 1947. He said, "Paul, I've decided to leave the department."
> I was shocked. I had heard the rumors, but still I was shocked.
> He described his concern over [Sue's] health.
> I asked, "What do you plan to do after you leave?"
> He said, "I guess I'll go back to Anderson, Clayton & Company."
> "That ought to be interesting," I said.
> "I'm not sure how interesting it will be," he answered. "Lamar Fleming has been running the firm with great success. . . . When I go back to Houston they'll give me a great big office and give me respect, but there won't be a thing for me to do."
> And tears came into his eyes.[3]

Clayton's resignation touched off concern in Washington and beyond. A few months earlier, when Marshall hinted to a group of leading businessmen that Clayton soon would be leaving the State Department, there was, David Lilienthal recorded in his diary, "a groan from the 40-odd men around the table." In their eyes, he was a voice for sanity and stability, a man with authentic business experience and thus a counterweight to radicals and visionaries who might tamper with the existing business system in America. Others, who did not share his business background or outlook, praised him too. Journalist I.F. Stone of *P.M.* magazine wrote: "Clayton, who was one of the architects of the Marshall Plan, seemed as much opposed to a dollar curtain as to an iron curtain. One felt in Clayton that he was not afraid of bogeymen."

Under Secretary of State Robert Lovett, Marshall, and other colleagues expressed personal tributes to Clayton well beyond the pro forma expressions that are common to such occasions. "Whole delegation [at the twenty-two-nation Geneva GATT talks] has asked me express our deep regret," Winthrop Brown cabled. "We will greatly miss your magnificent leadership."

On the Senate floor, Alben W. Barkley, Arthur H. Vandenburg, and others praised Clayton's achievements. "American and foreign officials," the *New York Times* reported,

> are unanimous in holding that during these critical months Mr. Clayton has been the greatest single force operating in the direction of bringing order out of the European chaos. . . . Europeans regard Mr. Clayton . . . as both the symbol and the dynamic force behind the most constructive aspects of American international economic policy. . . . All the estimates of United States ability and determination to lead the world in economic reconstruction will be revised downward by substantial percentages.[4]

Newsweek called him "the principal architect of American postwar foreign policy." Leading European publications echoed the same tributes, lamenting the retirement of the man that Britain's *Everybody's Weekly* had called "General Marshall's guide and mentor" on economic matters. The *London Observer* compared Clayton with Adam Smith and John Stuart Mill, while even *The Econ-*

omist, a Tory advocate of British protectionism, praised Clayton as a capable exponent of the economic growth credo.

From Paris, *L'Aurore* described Clayton's resignation as "a bombshell," the retirement of "the first economist of the United States. . . . He was the first who took cognizance of the famous agreement of the Sixteen Marshall Plan participants and it was on his recommendations that the final version, now being studied in Washington before being sent to Congress, was drawn up. . . . It is, then, a little the 'Clayton Plan' that is found to be up for consideration."

Clayton, the "champion of liberalism," echoed *Le Monde,* "played a chief role in the labors of the committee of Sixteen for the preparation of the Marshall Plan. Our diplomats . . . will deplore the absence of one of the Americans who knew best European affairs."

An editorial in the *New York Times* declared:

> Mr. Clayton had more to do than anyone else with shaping postwar economic policy for the rest of the world as well as for the United States. He was the driving force in a score of efforts to bring order out of chaos . . . a symbol of American constructive energy and faith in the future.

(Within a few weeks, James Reston and other reporters were noting troubled complaints from Europe and Capitol Hill that America's diplomatic representation in Europe might now be "too weak" to carry out the program without Clayton.)[5]

Harry Truman's reaction was more personal and more blunt: "I'd like to spank Sue," he told Clark Clifford, who was delivering the small mountain of documents to Truman's office that embodied Clayton's GATT agreement. Clayton, Truman observed, had been "pulled out by the hair" by a loving but jealous wife.[6]

The polite, official reason for Clayton's departure from Washington was that his wife was sick. "Mrs. Clayton isn't seriously ill," Clayton wrote confidentially to a few close friends, "but it was evident that sixteen hours a day for seven years in Washington had begun to get on her nerves." Clayton never complained that Sue's "illness" was simply a frantic longing to pry her husband out of government or that she probably cost him an opportunity to serve as secretary of state. "If I have any talent, any usefulness left in me, it is for this kind of work," Clayton said to his friend Clair Wilcox. "This is where I belong."[7] But he also belonged with his wife. Forced to choose between public service and her intense need for his time and attention, Will Clayton chose Sue.

One danger in writing about any public figure is that the person under study may seem to lack balance. But Clayton was a rounded man, and his sphere of interests and activities extended well beyond tariffs and monetary policy. He relished his long walks to work each morning, two to three miles for most of the time the Claytons lived in Washington, a trip to the theater to see *Oklahoma* or *My Fair Lady*, two of his favorite musicals, and the quiet games of bridge that occupied many evenings in the Clayton home.

For the Claytons, though, the return to a life of retirement was not all easy. Will remained on call at the State Department through the fall of 1948, negotiating the charter for the International Trade Organization at Havana and teaming up with Acheson, who was also out of government, to encourage passage of the European Recovery Act.

"He's with me but his mind still isn't," Sue complained to their daughter Julia during this period. He was still sitting on the board meetings of the International Monetary Fund in the summer of 1949 when Sue finally insisted that Clayton sever his last formal tie with the government. Sue also demanded that he resign from a number of other organizations related to his government activities that he had been pressured to join by former colleagues and by the president. Clayton had thought Sue would not mind his attendance at meetings of these groups as much as she objected to his more time-consuming government positions and felt her objections were unreasonable.

Clayton, however, remembering Sue's lifetime of sacrifice for his career, resigned from all committees to devote himself to caring for her. Sue could now accompany him on his less hectic trips, and together they could entertain old friends at their home in Houston. She continued to bristle, however, even under his reduced attention to work and his increased attention to home life. She had long wanted him to buy a farm in her home state of Kentucky where they could live during the hot Texas summer months and become still closer together. So far, Will had not made the purchase.

In April 1949, Sue—ironically having finally won her wish to get Will out of Washington—filed for a divorce. The petition for dissolution cited "neglect" as the cause, though the period claimed was for the years 1947 to 1949. Will did not want the divorce but acquiesced in Sue's wishes. In their court appearance Clayton's attorney, Dan W. Jackson, and Mrs. Clayton's advocate, Dillon Anderson, asked if she would consider a reconciliation. Sue remained firm, however, and the divorce was granted on May 24, though with considerably less looting of Will Clayton's fortune than she had predicted.[8]

If nothing else, the divorce provided Clayton with an occasion to prove his love to Sue. During the divorce proceedings, Clayton went to South America to visit some of Anderson-Clayton's subsidiaries. He had not been gone more than a day or two when Sue called, asking him to come back to see to it that her attorney obtained everything for her that she had asked—practically Will's entire fortune. This demonstration of Sue's trust in Will and her need for him brought them together again. Within a few weeks he proposed, she accepted, and, on August 6, 1949, they were remarried in Jasper, Canada, where they were visiting their daughter Susan.[9]

For the first time in nearly half a century, Will devoted himself to Sue with the same attention and vitality he had poured into business and politics. Finally complying with one of Sue's longtime wishes, they bought a former plantation in Kentucky, and Will spared little effort or expense in converting their new summer home back into the beautiful house it had once been. The Claytons spent much of the next ten summers at Cave Hill, where Will tended the garden and where they walked together through the estate's rolling hills; in the evenings they read to each other or entertained their neighbors.

But seclusion and the quiet life did not suit Sue's temperament. With her husband retired, she wanted them to work together on local causes and charities. At Sue's urging, Will Clayton helped lead the fight to create low-cost housing for the poor in Houston. His reputation as a businessman made him able to defend charges that the plan was socialistic, as its opponents claimed. He argued that "in order to protect free enterprise, it is sometimes necessary to depart from it a little." In what the *Houston Chronicle* called a "suave dig" at the Council for Free Enterprise, which opposed the program, Clayton noted that "one other departure from free enterprise has been the government's guaranteeing of loans by the [Federal Housing Administration], to which these gentlemen do not object." Among others who were supporting public housing at the time, Clayton observed, were such noted "socialists" as Senator Robert Taft.[10]

One reason Clayton supported the proposal, however, which took the form of a local ballot initiative, was precisely that it involved a large degree of free-market cooperation. Unlike many federal housing units that sprang up in the 1960s and 1970s, the Houston Housing Authority (HHA) was a local entity with private board members. Although it received funds from the federal government, they came with no micromanaging controls, and the HHA also depended on private gifts, such as Will and Sue Clayton's donation of Schrimpf Alley, a notorious Houston slum, for one $20 million project.[11]

In 1952, when the HHA's director misused some of the funds associated with the Clayton property, the city prosecuted and removed him.[12] Today, the quasi-public, quasi-private Susan Clayton Homes still stands, providing safe, affordable housing to Houston's poor. Although others saw the poor as a drain on the economy, using up resources and capital without making any contribution, Will and Sue saw their potential as citizens, parents, workers, and consumers. If the poor were afforded opportunities to transcend their poverty, if they were given the right incentives for self-improvement and a bit of help, their productive capabilities could be liberated. "They all become potential consumers," Clayton wrote in pressing for the Houston slum-clearance program.[13]

During the 1950s, the Claytons donated their Houston home as an addition to the city's library, gave a 184-acre tract of land to create a park in northeastern Houston, and provided the bulk of the $300,000 used to establish a hospital in Clinton, Kentucky.[14]

Clayton was part of the national fund-raising drive for Planned Parenthood, helped set up Clayton Chairs in International Economics at the Fletcher School of Law and Diplomacy and Johns Hopkins University, and helped his former aide Paul Nitze establish the Foreign Service Educational Foundation in Washington.[15]

Clayton did not limit his gifts to institutions that were rich or prestigious. He sat on the Board of Regents for Texas State University to improve education for blacks, and he and Sue were both early and large sponsors of the United Negro College Fund. Earlier, the Claytons had been the first white family in Houston to entertain black guests at their home.

With Joseph Grew, a State Department colleague, Clayton helped establish a Christian university in Japan, contributing $11,000 to the $10 million fund drive. "A new generation of teachers with freedom of thought and intellect," he explained, "is the most urgent need in Japan."[16]

In 1952, Clayton enthusiastically endorsed and contributed to Adlai Stevenson's presidential campaign. In part, his active role reflected his deepening disgust with the Republicans led by Senator Taft and bullied by Senator Joseph R. McCarthy. Clayton was outraged and appalled at McCarthy's vitriolic attack on the loyalty and patriotism of General George C. Marshall, whom McCarthy called "the man who lost China." Clayton also wrote and placed a full-page advertisement in the *Houston Post* and other Texas newspapers in which he condemned the opportunism of General Dwight D. Eisenhower, the Republican nominee:

> Lifted to eminence by his friend, General Marshall, Eisenhower has now joined hands with men who called Marshall a front for traitors and has asked the voters to return those men to the United States Senate. To win votes, he has surrendered to the greatest reactionaries of our times.

Undaunted by Eisenhower's victory in 1952, Clayton served as cochairman of Stevenson's fifty-member National Business Council in 1956.[17] He thus renewed his friendship with Joseph P. Kennedy, former ambassador to Great Britain and father of John F. Kennedy. Four years later, Clayton, after initially joining a group of third-try-for-Adlai supporters, fell in with JFK and backed him with vigor.*

Kennedy's confident global outlook probably came closer to expressing Clayton's own positive ethos than any other American president in his lifetime. JFK at once articulated and personified the feeling that it was time for the United States and the West to get moving again, to pay less attention to fighting communism (even though it was the greatest enemy in the struggle) and more

---

*Clayton also helped catapult Lyndon Johnson to the U.S. Senate—endorsing LBJ, the underdog in the Democratic primary, early in 1948—but by 1960 he had grown weary of the Texan's wheeling and dealing. He thought Johnson "too unprincipled" to be a good president. In 1964, the last time he would ever have the opportunity to vote, Clayton headed for the polling place intending to vote for LBJ. "But I couldn't do it," he told one of his daughters. He turned around and went home without casting his ballot.

attention to building freedom and democracy. Clayton expressed this view in a 1955 article:

> In this vast struggle which is raging throughout the world for the minds and loyalties of men, the weakness of the foreign policies of the democracies lies in the fact that such policy is mostly negative—it is against something. The communist policy, on the other hand, is positive. They have a program to cure all the ills of all people everywhere. It is a false program, of course, but anyway it is something positive. . . .
>
> Communism is but an outward manifestation of the world revolution now in progress—a revolution of the "have nots," not so much against the "haves," as against their own lot in life. . . . There are just too many people in the world who go to bed cold and hungry every night to expect that victory in the fight to contain communism will bring peace to the world.
>
> The free world must shift from the negative to the positive if it is to win this struggle.[18]

Indeed, Kennedy's election provided Clayton with an opportunity to strike his last major blow for worldwide free trade. To understand Clayton's brief but important contribution to the Kennedy Round of trade liberalization, the most successful since the Clayton Round of 1947, we must understand Clayton's strategic view of world events from the time of the GATT and Marshall Plan initiatives in 1947 until Kennedy's inauguration in 1961.

Throughout the 1950s, Clayton's writings and speeches suggest a thwarted and impatient man. He viewed the West as being passive, smug, and reactive, failing to promote democratic ideals or free market institutions in any serious or systematic way. In a 1958 letter, written after the Russians had successfully launched their Sputnik satellite, Clayton wrote:

The sputniks may be in time to save the world. Let us hope they
will do for us what should have been done by our President: slap
us in the face with the facts and wake us up before it is too late.
. . .

In the end we will make more and better sputniks than the
Russians—that is, if we have time. . . . Many of our individual
luxuries must give way. . . . But military power alone won't qualify
us for leadership. . . .

We must also adjust our thinking and acting in the political and
economic fields to the needs and interests of the free world rather
than selfish interests.[19]

During his years of retirement, Clayton was sometimes not the
cool, analytic man he had been through eight years of government
service. "Stalin is winning the cold war," he told the House Foreign
Affairs Committee in 1950. "The Communists are awakening the
masses, and make no mistake about it, the masses are listening." In
1951, he worried that "the oil dispute in Iran might explode into a
crisis leading to a third world war." Again in 1955: "The West is
losing the cold war." In 1958:

If we don't stop the prostitution of national policy to serve selfish
ends . . . we will lose the feeble hold we now have on the leadership of the free world, lose the cold war, and lose our own freedom. This can happen without a shot being fired.[20]

Clayton was hardly alone in feeling a nagging doubt about
America's vitality during the Eisenhower years. Unlike many others, however, his fears were balanced by the belief that communism, particularly its imperialist endeavors, was not the core enemy. Nor, accordingly, were military intervention or military buildup
necessarily the critical instruments for its dismantling; indeed, in
Clayton's eyes, they might be part of the problem. "National defense and aid to other countries cost us half our present budget,"
he warned in one speech. "We can't stand those expenses." One of

the gravest dangers was that fear might prompt an overreaction toward militarization and regimentation.

> Stalin knows that his most destructive weapon is the fear which causes democratic governments to spend excessively for armaments and sends private capital, on which free enterprise depends, into hiding. The economic burden of fighting the cold war is getting too heavy for the democracies, and is straining even our strong back.

Although he favored a strong Western defense program, Clayton felt it could only be carried out as part of a broader, cooperative merging of the free countries. In a 1951 debate he rejected the idea that the West could win an arms race, in the sense of breaking the back of the admittedly weaker Soviet economy, because the misery and poverty that accompany huge defense expenditures weaken freedom more than they do communism.

"There can never be peace as long as most of the world is stricken with poverty," he argued, echoing the message of his second Marshall Plan memorandum that "starvation and chaos (not the Russians)" were the key threat to Europe. "As vicious and repugnant as communism is, permanent world peace will never be secured by simply fighting communism."[21]*

In 1958, Clayton worked with Sam Rayburn to promulgate a resolution, passed by Congress, proclaiming the Middle East as a "vital interest" to the United States and promising to use armed force "if necessary" to preserve the independence and integrity of Israel and the other states of the region. (Clayton's main interest in strengthening the resolution was procedural; he favored giving the

---

*Clayton retained this reserved attitude toward military involvement, especially outside of Europe, even after Kennedy's election and the consequent revival of the interventionist spirit. Sensing an overcommitment in Vietnam, he wrote to one friend in 1965, "We just can't defend our way of life all over the world, and I doubt very much, even if we should have the power to do this, that it would succeed."

president the widest possible discretion to respond to a crisis if, by implication, one had already developed.)[22]

During his retirement years, Clayton's main sources of concern were not so much the advance of communism but the lack of positive initiative on the part of the democracies. He recommended two parallel and complementary policies as key elements in a broader foreign policy aimed at promoting prosperity and democracy. For the industrialized West, he urged an Atlantic union, a merging of the United States and the Western European nations to create a common currency, a free-trade zone, and a coordinated diplomacy. This visionary proposal had first been conceived by former *New York Times* correspondent Clarence Streit, who published a magazine and wrote a book on the subject. The idea attracted support from former Secretary of War Robert Patterson, former Supreme Court justice Owen Roberts, and former Under Secretaries of State Joseph Grew and William Phillips.

With Justice Roberts as president, Clayton amd Patterson became the two vice presidents of the Atlantic Union Committee, plugging the idea in speeches, articles, and congressional testimony from 1949 to 1959. Like the International Trade Organization, the idea was perhaps too visionary and ambitious to capture the serious attention Clayton hoped for. The leaders of the West faced so many immediate crises that there seemed little time to work on such a massive political restructuring.

Yet the world was, albeit in a slow-motion, piecemeal fashion, evolving toward the very vision Clayton had in mind. The Marshall Plan was implemented, and Western Europe was rebuilt; the North Atlantic Treaty Organization (NATO) was formed; West Germany and Japan were brought into the democratic family of nations; and the GATT agreement was extended to a broader group of nations, culminating in the formation of the European Economic Community and the Common Market. Clayton cited these steps as demonstrating the plausibility of his Atlantic union blueprint.

With bold leadership, the West could, as *Life* magazine editorialized, take "a giant step." The idea lost considerable steam during the long Eisenhower hibernation, but even at the end of Ike's second term was still under serious discussion.[23] The general expansionary effects of such a union, Clayton argued, would be of great benefit to the developing nations and help integrate them into the wider league of democracies. Clayton recognized, though, that the West's approach to promoting growth in the nonindustrial countries would have to change. In occasional spasms of generosity, the United States dispensed subsidies and handouts. Yet these spurts of emergency relief did little to improve the fundamental structural imbalances in the Third World.

"Now and then we give some millions of bushels to the needy," he noted, "but people want to earn their way by trade, not aid."[24] Access to Western markets would promote solid and substantial growth. Instead of opening its markets to their goods, the United States in the 1950s preserved and in many cases expanded the array of quotas, tariffs, and export subsidies on those goods that were major exports for most Latin American and African nations. In Eisenhower's second term, a severe limitation on oil imports was imposed, striking at a third major developing region, the Middle East. The United States, Clayton warned, was setting a bad example for the world:

> They see the richest country in the world fixing prices above the world market, using its wealth to create artificial scarcities, diverting food and fiber from the channels of trade into government warehouses, paying farmers not to produce and in the past paying them to destroy what they had produced.[25]

Elaborating on the same theme, he told an interviewer in 1961:

> We have quotas on lead, zinc, petroleum, sugar. We have an export subsidy, and a big one, on the export of raw cotton, and to some extent on wheat. All of these commodities are produced in Latin America. They [also] produce a great deal of sugar. . . .
> When we put on the import quota on petroleum, Venezuela was hurt and hurt badly. When we put on the import quota on

lead and zinc, Mexico and Peru particularly were hurt and hurt badly. . . .

The first way [to help] will be for the developed countries—the Western countries, the U.S., Canada, Western Europe—to take off the impediments that they now have on the receipt of imports from these underdeveloped countries. For example, Germany still has a big tariff on the importation of coffee from Brazil or Latin America. It is done to favor African coffee. Other European countries have devices of that kind. . . .

All the African countries—all of these underdeveloped countries, as a matter of fact—depend for eventual industrialization on free trade.

For example, take a country like the Central American countries: Guatemala, Nicaragua, Honduras, and so on. A few million people in each one. How can they industrialize? They can't, with the present world system of international trade, with our tariffs and with the Western European tariffs. They simply are unable to build mass production in industries that can compete with the big industries in the United States and Western Europe. . . . Today, you can only get a giant industry built in a great industrial country like the United States with 185 million people. . . . Because of that sure market, at home, they can build giant industries which have a very low unit cost of production of any item. But when you take a little country that can only figure 5 or 10 or 15 or 20 million people as a home market, they have great difficulty.[26]

In the immediate aftermath of World War II, Clayton had placed greater emphasis on European reconstruction than on Third World development. By 1960, with Europe shored up economically, politically, and militarily, the Third World might be the more vital area of U.S. concern. "Khrushchev has declared war on us in this field," Clayton noted, in the form of aggressive efforts to Sovietize the Third World with both guns and butter. Cuba, Egypt, Congo, and Vietnam were increasingly viewed by Clayton as the turbulent frontiers where communism and democracy would wage a critical struggle.[27]

Clayton also favored extending Western economic influence inside the communist world. Thus in 1958 he supported Acheson's critique of U.S.-China policy and called for U.S. recognition of the People's Republic of China (PRC) and the end of most trading restrictions, with the exception of armaments. He wrote to the press:

> It is said that if we fail to help Chiang Kai-shek keep Formosa, Quemoy, and Matsu, it would mean not only the loss to communism of all Southeast Asia, but probably in time the Philippines and Japan as well. The risk that this will happen is less likely and, if it did happen, the consequences much less terrible than the risk of a devastating war if we continue our present illogical position.

He urged the United Nations to mediate the dispute between Taiwan and the PRC. He repeated his proposal in a 1959 letter to Senator William Fulbright, adding that the United States should open up most trade "unilaterally and immediately" to China and the Soviet Union. In 1960 Clayton joined a friendship group promoting short-term travel programs as a further instrument for nurturing fragile forces for private enterprise that might exist in the totalitarian countries.

The Voice of America, Radio Free Europe and Radio Liberty, *Deutsche Welle*, *Kol Israel*, and other efforts provided a potential new instrument for U.S. policy.[28] Although Clayton did not devote the same time or energy to this third prong of foreign policy—penetrating the iron curtain with information—that he did to the proposal for Atlantic union and Third World development through trade, it was, nevertheless, an important component of his overall design and puts the design's more traditional anti-Soviet elements in perspective.

The election of 1960 afforded Clayton and his free-trade enthusiasts a new opportunity to put their proposals on the national agenda, as did events in Europe. In 1959, the Group of Six of the Common

Market—West Germany, France, Italy, Holland, Belgium, and Luxembourg—enacted a modest tariff cut and quota increase. Trade surged; the following year German exports rose by 12 percent, Italian, by 27 percent, and French, by 33 percent. These minifederations demonstrated the possibility and benefits of union. "Under the leadership of the United States," Clayton argued, "the 20 [including the United States and Canada] cooperating Atlantic countries could become one free trade area open to any country of the free world willing to subscribe to the conditions."[29]

In April 1960, Clayton and a group of U.S. leaders, including U.S. ambassador to NATO Ralph Burgess, submitted a petition to the Atlantic governments calling for an Atlantic Economic Community to reduce trade restrictions "and to increase the flow of capital, public as well as private, from the industrial countries to Asia, Africa, and Latin America."[30] Neither presidential candidate, Kennedy or Nixon, explicitly endorsed the design, but there was movement by both parties in that direction. As Arthur Krock noted in the *New York Times*:

> "New ideas" to deal with the great and growing problems of these times have been conspicuous by their absence from the 1960 presidential campaign.
> But from Will L. Clayton of Houston, who served the government with distinction in high offices concerned with the international economy, has come a new and bold idea—"an economic federation of the free world" as the strongest force to dispel the threat of international communism.
> "Under a free world market," he submits, "the standard of living would rise, sound industrialization of the poorer countries would occur, the economic gap between them and the richer would be narrowed progressively, and the whole world would become a more healthful and peaceful place in which to live."
> The Los Angeles and Chicago platforms proclaim their support of this objective. But Clayton offers specifications.[31]

Kennedy's election coincided with growing interest in trade liberalization on the part of U.S. business and labor. Some preferred to fight for protection or subsidies for their own industries; others, though, noted that the Common Market was a success. Economic growth rates in the European countries had been running at twice the U.S. levels since the Common Market's formation.

Kennedy's first few months in office were devoted to a package of domestic legislation aimed at fighting the recession through traditional New Deal methods. In the spring of 1961, however, Clayton joined with Christian Herter, Eisenhower's second secretary of state, to press for trade expansion as the key to long-run growth.

Their instrument was the Citizens Commission on NATO, created by an act of Congress in 1960 to study and propose ways to achieve a greater merging of political and economic policies in the NATO alliance. Speaker of the House Sam Rayburn and Vice President Lyndon Johnson chose Herter and Clayton to cochair the bipartisan panel in April 1961.

By the fall, the administration and its allies on Capitol Hill were preparing for the coming debate on the Reciprocal Trade Act, due to expire in 1962. George Ball, the under secretary of state for economic affairs, began working with Herter, Clayton, Acheson, and other proponents outside the administration to refine and improve the design for trade expansion. "The 1962 trade bill," as Kennedy's aide Theodore Sorenson wrote in his memoirs, "became the centerpiece of all that year's efforts—the subject of extra emphasis in the State of the Union Message, the subject of the year's first special legislative message, several presidential speeches, and the subject of an intense White House lobbying effort with priority over almost all other bills."[32]

In the fall of 1961, Hale Boggs, chairman of the Joint Economic Committee, traveled to Europe and came back convinced that Kennedy, Rayburn, and the other free traders had their priorities right about trade expansion. A mere extension of the old trade act, he told the press on October 6, would be "grossly insufficient" to meet the European challenge. He invited Clayton, Herter, and a dozen other prominent thinkers on international economics to

submit their proposals and analysis to the committee.[33] The resulting manifesto reads in many ways like a broadened, updated version
of Clayton's May 1947 memorandum on the Marshall Plan. In a
few months, the Herter-Clayton report begins, the Trade Agreements Act (as it was now called) would come up for renewal.[34]

> But "renewal" is a deceptive word if it suggests that what has been
> done eleven times in the past quarter century will suffice another
> time. It will not. Instead, the United States must "take a giant
> step," unifying the Atlantic community both for its own sake, and
> as a magnet for eventual integration of all democracies into a free
> world trade union.
>
> Here is the situation: There are 3 billion people in the world.
> About one-third live under communist rule. One-sixth live in the
> major free industrial lands. The rest, who are one-half of the
> total, live in the poorer, less developed countries—the uncom-
> mitted or, as we prefer to call them, the "contested."
>
> The one-half billion in the major industrial countries—the
> West plus Japan and Australia—live under stable, popular govern-
> ments. They possess preponderant economic power in the world
> community. This is a point of critical importance for the purpose
> we have under consideration. Eighteen percent of the world's
> population commands two-thirds of its industrial capacity.
>
> It is our firm conviction that the way in which this power is
> used will be a major factor determining the issues and outcome
> of the cold war.[35]

Meanwhile, the report continues, the Soviets were boring from
within, "concentrating their subversive efforts" principally on poor,
underdeveloped countries. Khrushchev, they note, in his declaration to the Twentieth Party Congress in 1956, called for "a contin-
uous attack on the bourgeois ideology . . . and against the remnants
of capitalism." The Soviet economic offensive, they note, was not
without success. "Hunger and political instability go hand in hand.
And who can say that people who have always been slaves to hunger
will not put food before freedom?"[36] None of these developments
took place in a vacuum:

In forming policies to meet the situation described, . . . significant facts of current life must be kept in mind.

1. The increasing interdependence of nations. Domestic economic policy can no longer be made without regard to possible external effects. . . . This country has known for years that it is not an isolated political system. It must realize now that that is no less true of the body economic. . . .

It is ironical that the United States should continue to erect barriers against the nations whose raw materials it, in fact, must have. . . . The Automobile Manufacturers Association lists 38 imports necessary to the production of motor vehicles. The telephone companies list 20 imports from many lands—in Asia, Africa, and South America—which are essential. . . .

2. The new role of technology. We are impressed by a statement of Dr. Guy Suits, of the General Electric Laboratories: "Growth in science and technology is so rapid that 90 percent of all the scientists who ever lived must be alive today. . . . Lord Keynes didn't recognize technological innovation as a factor in the economy 20 years ago, yet today it assumes major proportions."

Technological change has been a determining factor in the conflicts of the past two decades. It would be folly to suppose that it will be a smaller force in the future. . . .

3. The population eruption. Our main concern in the population explosion is with the contested countries. These populations are growing at a rate double that of the Western community, but they possess only a negligible fraction of the economic resources of the West. . . . The daily struggle for food and space among populations already undernourished cannot fail to become more bitter. This is our concern.[37]

The gap between the poor and the affluent, Clayton and Herter warned, "must . . . and can be narrowed, while raising the living standards of both groups." The danger is that U.S. economic policy continues to operate "at the behest of politically powerful groups in this country" for whose benefit the government erects import quotas on a wide array of goods. Furthermore, the narrow formulas imposed on the Reciprocal Trade Act by Congress—as Herter learned during the extensions of the trade act in 1953 and 1958—had given insufficient flexibility to U.S. trade negotiators.

Despite the long term of both extensions, the authority to negotiate trade liberalization they granted had been small and the strong voice of protectionist interests had been revived. "The Trade Agreements Act is as it stands today hopelessly inadequate to meet conditions as they are and we can see them developing." Kennedy and Congress could reverse the slide.

The Europeans had gone well beyond the item-by-item approach of even the successful Clayton GATT Round of 1947:

> But time is running out.
>
> We believe that the United States must form a trade partnership with the European Common Market and take the leadership in further expanding a free world economic community.
>
> As a minimum in that direction, the Trade Agreement Act must give the president authority to negotiate tariff reductions across the board in place of his present authority to negotiate item by item. . . .
>
> The United States was formed into a common market when the Thirteen Colonies were welded into one by adoption of the Constitution. . . . If the United States is to continue to meet its responsibilities of Western leadership in preserving the freedom of the Western World, it must again, as in 1947, put the national and international interest ahead of the short-term, special interest of its politically powerful . . . groups.
>
> The longer the United States waits, the more difficult it will be to align its trade policies to match the Common Market's own actions. By the end of this very year, the "Six" will have reduced their tariffs to each other by 40 to 50 percent. . . . Official reports show that, since 1958, trade among the "Six" has risen by approximately 50 percent—a growth far greater than shown by any other industrial nation.[38]

The growth that would accompany the creation of an Atlantic common market, Clayton and Herter averred, would set off "the greatest expansion in productive facilities, including those of the United States, that the world has ever known." The initiative, however, must not focus wholly on the West. The U.S. proposal for an Atlantic common market must, at the same time, "stress the absolute necessity of enlarging the [trading] area."[39]

> One way to ease the adjustment for the contested countries, and to meet our principal objective of raising their living standards, would be to grant unilaterally to groups of contested countries, as distinguished from industrial countries, the right to free trade on their exports of raw materials to industrial countries. Another way would be by reduction in import tariffs by the contested countries at the rate of 5 percent per annum in consideration of the industrial countries reducing their duties at the rate of 10 percent per annum. . . .
>
> In this way, sound development of the contested countries would take place. Their standards of living would rise. The economic gap between the richer and the poorer would be narrowed. Communism as a threat to world peace would recede.[40]

The impact on both Congress and the administration was instantaneous and immense. Boggs personally delivered a copy to Kennedy, recommending that it be released and highlighted by administration spokesmen to kick off the trade bill effort. (The *New Leader* later reported that Kennedy viewed the Herter-Clayton report as providing the core ideas that made the 1962 trade act possible.) On November 1, the Herter-Clayton paper was published by the Joint Economic Committee (JEC) and released to coincide with a speech the same day by George Ball before the National Foreign Trade Council asking for new negotiating authority "sufficiently broad in scope to meet the opportunity and challenge of the European Economic Community."

The *New York Times* ran the trade story as its front-page lead on November 2, 1961, and published extensive excerpts from the Herter-Clayton report and Ball's speech. The JEC opened hearings immediately, with Clayton and Acheson making the front page of the *Times* again on December 4.

Clayton presciently warned that, without a drastic change in monetary and trade policy, the United States would eventually be forced to devalue the dollar. By this time, Kennedy had already approved a general outline for the Trade Expansion Act, as he labeled the legislation in submitting it to Congress in January 1962. The *Times* reported:

> The Herter-Clayton views on forming ties with the European Common Market are stronger than anything that Administration officials have said publicly. But some officials are thinking along the same lines, and, in fact, some important ties are already in effect.[41]

Perhaps the most important effect of the Herter-Clayton report was that it provided an adroit ideological and political defense of the Kennedy administration's trade program and gave a blue-ribbon imprimatur to radical trade liberalization. In addition, two of its recommendations proved particularly important to the passage of Kennedy's Trade Expansion Act. First, the report proposed a small program of domestic subsidies to help industries and workers damaged by tariff or quota reductions convert their capital to more competitive uses. Herter and Clayton made this concession reluctantly: "We believe that the dislocation of labor or capital as a result of increased imports can be adjusted better by the affected parties than by the Government. But we would support a public program for extreme cases." As realists they recognized that their proposal for trade was sufficiently sweeping to alarm many industries and unions. The subsidy program for displaced firms and workers might provide a safety valve and thus preclude an all-out assault against the trade act. As he had in the Bretton Woods, Marshall Plan, and British loan negotiations, Clayton cheerfully embraced a small step backward, or even several, if it generated a large, principled step forward to a free market.

Kennedy, also a political realist, granted relief to the powerful textile lobby congressmen in exchange for their promise not to oppose the Trade Expansion Act. President Kennedy, as Congressman Tom Curtis later said, "caught the spirit" of the proposal by appointing Herter, a former secretary of state and a Republican, as the first U.S. special trade representative.[42]

The second and more important feature of the Herter-Clayton proposal was its promotion of linear or across-the-board tariff reductions, thereby moving beyond the item-by-item approach of the earlier GATT trade talks. Coming at a time when the administration was keen to liberalize trade but uncertain how to achieve that end, the Herter-Clayton report was vital and timely—"contributing greatly," as Kennedy later wrote to Clayton, both to "public awareness" and the "development of new directions in international policy."

The result, as Robert Pastor writes, was, "in a sense, the first 'modern' trade bill. . . . For the first time, the Administration requested authority to negotiate on the basis of linear reduction rather than an item-by-item basis; and for the first time, the president requested an adjustment assistance package which would presumably help industries and workers who were substantially injured."[43]

The Trade Expansion Act of 1962 passed the House by 298 to 125 in late June. Kennedy expected trouble in the traditionally protectionist Senate, but the bill passed by 78 to 8, one of the largest margins for any trade bill, let alone one so generous in its provisions. In winning congressional approval of the ambitious design of the Trade Expansion Act, President Kennedy had secured the key achievement of what is rightly called the Kennedy Round of talks. As Pastor writes:

> On June 30, 1967, the expiration date for U.S. negotiating authority, the United States joined with forty-five other nations in signing the General Agreement of 1967, concluding the Kennedy Round. Prior to 1967, the most successful trade negotiations for the U.S. in terms of the scope of tariff reductions occurred twenty years earlier in the first MTN [the Clayton Round]—when tariffs were reduced on products constituting about 54 percent of the U.S. total dutiable imports. In the Kennedy Round, with many more governments participating and tariffs much lower than in 1947, the tariffs on 64 percent of all dutiable imports were reduced. John Evans thinks that "the decisive reason" for the exten-

sive commodity coverage was the linear method of tariff reduction adopted in 1963.

Not only were the reductions wide, but they were also quite deep. The average tariff cut for all industrial products was about 35 percent, and although this represented only about one-quarter of world trade, it represented 80 percent of the trade of those products which still had tariffs. On agricultural products (excluding grains) the average reduction by the major industrial countries amounted to about 20 percent and affected almost half of the dutiable imports of the four majors—the United States, U.K., EEC, and Japan. . . . President Kennedy called the Trade Expansion Act "the most important international piece of legislation . . . affecting economics since the passage of the Marshall Plan," and his emphasis on the international dimension was . . . correct.[44]

One of Will Clayton's favorite verses, which he liked to quote in speeches and articles on the Marshall Plan, was James Russell Lowell's, "The gift without the giver is bare,"[45] and Clayton certainly gave both. For several years he arose early to prepare a tray with Sue's favorite breakfast and carry it up to her bed with a flower. During the final years of her life, Sue Clayton suffered the progressive consequences of hardening of the arteries, including memory lapses and extreme emotional volatility. As a means of protecting her, the family decided to keep her heavily sedated, which meant that she was largely confined to a sickbed.

"For two years now, I haven't been away from her more than two hours at a time," Clayton wrote to Dean Acheson, who had invited the Claytons to dinner on the night Acheson was scheduled to begin a lecture series at the Fletcher School's Clayton Center. "I would come myself except for the fact that she needs me now, and it isn't right for me to leave her."

As her illness worsened, Sue lapsed into comas that often lasted for days. Nevertheless, Will spent long hours sitting by her bed to be present in the evermore-rare moments when she briefly regained consciousness. He sent almost daily letters to his youngest daughter, Julia, during these years, reports about how her mother was doing interspersed with his optimism or pessimism about world events. One morning, as Sue appeared to be sleeping, Will took her hand and said softly, "Sue, you know, I've always loved you." Suddenly, her eyes opened, she raised up a bit, and demanded, "Give me a demonstration!"[46] Susan Vaughan Clayton died in 1960 in Houston, her long ordeal of physical illness and emotional torment finally at an end. Always unconventional, she left half of her estate—two million dollars—to the United States of America, to be used to pay off a fraction of the national debt.

After Sue's death, Will immersed himself in politics again. When he celebrated his eighty-fifth birthday in February 1965, he showed no signs of decline except a slight trace of angina and having to give up horseback riding. Otherwise, he was remarkably fit, still lean and a vigorous walker. In January 1966, he traveled to Europe in an effort to help the GATT negotiations pick up speed. The talks in Europe had stalled, and reports of bickering among the delegates made him fear that the whole enterprise of trade liberalization might be derailed.

A few days after his return, he attended a birthday party given in his honor by the employees of Anderson-Clayton. The next afternoon, February 8, he went for a walk with his daughter Burdine. When they returned home, he seemed unusually tired and lay down on the sofa. She was worried and wanted to call a doctor. Typically, he didn't want to be helped and said, "Don't go to all that trouble." But she insisted and he was taken to the hospital. As the doctors probed and tested, Clayton joked with his daughter Susan and the nurses. "Now, you don't need to do all that," he smiled. "I'm going to live to be a hundred." A moment later he doubled over in pain from a severe heart attack and was dead at the age of eighty-six. Even in his last moments, Will Clayton did not want anyone to make a fuss over him.

16

Will Clayton's Legacy

CLAYTON'S LIFE SPEAKS FOR ITSELF, AND HE WOULD BE THE LAST TO desire an overelaboration of its merits. It may be useful to review his accomplishments, however, all the more so because Clayton himself was not given to talking or writing about them.

From the day he left home at fifteen to work as an apprentice in a Saint Louis cotton firm until his final years struggling to make the Atlantic common market a reality, his eyes always seemed to focus on the next horizon. The thing to do when one great task was finished was to take a brief rest, summon up one's strength, and begin the next. In one sense, the resulting design, like a series of widening circles, seems spiritual and visionary. In another, it is merely practical, almost homespun in its simplicity.

From an early age, Clayton developed a deep faith in the possibility for human action—individual action but also collective action, in which one found the highest satisfaction. He drew this belief in progress first and foremost from his mother, from whom he also drew his strong moral code—a code that was part of Fletcher Burdine's ancestral background. Likewise, he also drew from her a native resourcefulness, a positive confidence that troubles could be overcome with enough application of creative intelligence and intense effort.

Clayton had a keen eye for the potential. Where others might see his early jobs as a discouraging grind, he saw them as an opportunity to help his family while expanding his own skills and understanding. Where the American Cotton Company eroded the value of their physical assets through bad management, he saw that if the web of human relationships that caused that impersonal machine to run could be improved, there would be a new order of vastly greater worth to the company and to the society around it. Alter the incentives, unleash creativity, and imbue the people in the system with a spirit of enterprise, and a novus ordo would emerge.

Clayton saw possibilities for action that others missed. With his fortune made by the 1920s, he turned to a much wider field, first as an activist and agitator for improved U.S. policies and then as an economic statesman seeking to alter nothing less than the political economy of the world. To many, his designs seemed impractical; it is the curse of the visionary to see what others miss. Clayton recognized, with patience and sympathy for the occasional blind spots of others, that someone who feels he can see must explain the pattern, draw out and inculcate the principle of animation that to him seems so stark and self-evident in its operation.

Keynes worried that the Bretton Woods order would chain the world to a monetary system of insufficient liquidity; Clayton responded that, with expanding trade and production, the demand for currency would surge, and there could be a vast expansion of gold-backed currencies without artificial injections. Others worried that a surge in the "money supply" would bring a vast inflation or that a mountain of debt would come crashing back on the United States and the West. Clayton, who had borrowed and spent millions, knew that debts could be serviced and reduced gradually and painlessly, if only the leaders of the world would focus their energies on expanding the amount from which debts are repaid.

Some New Dealers pined for a forced redistribution of goods and a wide array of controls to smooth the violent dislocations of the market; Clayton saw the market as a magnificent redistributor and stabilizer. The Republicans resisted with equal fervor almost any device to promote even the adjustment of those displaced by the process of creative capital destruction; Clayton saw that if governments, in economic unity, would speed up adjustments efficiently, they would be aiding, not retarding, the workings of the capitalist superstructure.

Will Clayton was not blind to the reality of human conflict. No one who reads his scornful appraisals of special interests in the fight for southern delivery or against Smoot-Hawley or his concerned pleas for action to turn the tide of communist advance in the 1940s and 1950s could think that he was. But for a democratic statesman such rivalries must be transcended; they are the temptations that one must plan for but not be hypnotized by. For Clayton, it was the quintessential task of leadership to craft a new order from which not only the general interest would benefit but most of the particular interests as well and even then to ameliorate the loss suffered by others.

This insight applied with even more force to the broadest political field of Clayton's life, foreign affairs. To the unsophisticated analyst, as Henry Kissinger has observed, the success of any negotiation can be measured by a weighing of the relative concessions of each side. A treaty—whether on trade or arms control—can be measured like a stack of poker chips, and a good one is one in which our leaders amass a large stack of chips from the pile of the loser. It is precisely such an agreement, however, that will likely be of little use. As long as nations create barriers out of their sovereignties, they will be free to leave the game or, worse, to grow frustrated and kick over the table. The trick in a negotiation, then, is to construct an order *that will benefit both sides.* This is more difficult when the bargainers are nations that may not only lack the common cultural and civic bonds of two businesspeople but actually share a mutual hostility. Yet it is the only sound foundation on which democratic diplomacy can be built.

Clayton's vision was not limited to matters of commerce and

politics; it served him with people, too. His personal qualities were most obvious at the beginning and the end of his life—periods of relatively less involvement with matters of commerce and state. In evidence, however, throughout his life, they stand in even greater relief in those situations where many of us fall back on the hardened, antiseptic etiquette of professionalism. Although Clayton's friends and colleagues often describe him as brilliant, hard-working, honest, and direct, the adjectives that seem to come through in almost every interview about him are more personal in nature. "Courteous" is one of the most common. "Fair" and "concerned" are two others. "The staff adored him," says one of Clayton's aides. Another described him as "a kind of saint." Aides who came in to hand Clayton important dispatches often found him on the phone making travel plans for his wife or one of the Clayton girls. One aide, Arthur Stevens, reported that it was a chore simply to get Clayton to accept a new piece of furniture for the office; he insisted that a couch provided for him to nap on be put out in the lounge where the secretaries could use it. "I can sleep in my chair," he argued.

Clayton's advice to his friends and subordinates seemed always to draw them outward into new endeavors that would leave a more rounded whole. For a young man swamped by day-to-day work in New York, Clayton urged a program of reading and study, of intellectual development. Writing to his friends in business, Clayton encouraged them to become more involved in public affairs. Pete Collado, who had spent many years in government, was advised by Clayton to get into business for a while, that the experience would make him a better public servant someday. Paul Nitze had worked as an aide in both government and big business; Clayton encouraged his efforts to found a new institute devoted to the study of foreign service. There is a vast difference, Clayton realized, between operating in a large corporation and creating new wealth, new ideas, new institutions.

It has been said that neither Abraham Lincoln nor Winston Churchill could be elected today. One certainly doubts that they would be appointed, much less confirmed, by the Senate. Neither, perhaps, could Clayton, Acheson, or many of the great architects of the postwar order, architects of a series of creative and successful political initiatives and of the greatest economic expansion in history.

Clayton would say that at such times, as in the 1920s and 1950s, the leader of vision plugs away waiting for the next opening. He would also, though, be one of the first to chafe under such an interlude. Generally one speaks of vision as a gift, but vision tormented Winston Churchill; lacking the power to affect events in the early 1930s, he could only watch as Hitler carried out his conquests over an unbelieving world. Events were a similar vexation for Clayton; he was, like Keynes and Hull, an economic equivalent to Churchill.

Early in his life, that gap between his own sight and the more limited sight of others often proved too much for Clayton to bear with equanimity. He disciplined his oldest daughter, Ellen, sternly at times, sometimes spanking her night after night and ignoring or overlooking her efforts to gain his attention. Soon, though, he learned to control his active temper and later in life grew closer to Ellen. As his love of Washington grew, he sometimes devoted too little time to Sue, and when her desperation to have his full attention made her frantic and obsessive, Clayton tuned her out still further. Yet he eventually left Washington and during the last years of Sue's life cared for her with a devotion that more than made up for any slights during his years of intense devotion to public service.

Everyone has flaws. Perhaps the best that can be said of anyone is that they strive to overcome them. Clayton learned the art of forbearance in business, and, as the multiple testimonies to his unusual patience demonstrate, he carried the lesson with him throughout his life. His painfully cool treatment of Sue gave way to a warm, reactivated love that made the end of their life as tender and innocent as their courtship and even richer for more than fifty years of love.

For Clayton, if new data did not fit with his ideas about the world, then his ideas about the world must change. "Never wrestle with the facts," Clayton told his aide Winthrop Brown. "Wrestle with what you can do about them." But if some principles had to be adjusted and some discarded, Clayton never ceased looking for more solid and functional principles to replace them.

Many people, of course, profess a faith in free markets, in democracy. Clayton's faith, however, conformed with his life; it was not something he kept on a shelf. Faith was a guide to positive action. If people behaved according to certain principles, one could use those principles to create new products, improve services, or bring about a more economic line of transit. In the struggle to bring about "a new way of doing things," there were bound to be frictions. Faith, though, supported by repeated experience, told him that human ingenuity could nearly always master the challenge.

Clayton not only believed this; he lived it. In business he sought consistently not to make a profit at the expense of someone else but to bring about situations where all would gain. He carried that same approach to government service and diplomacy.

His drive, then, was for the common purpose. Harry Truman, who benefited so greatly from that drive, delivered perhaps the definitive tribute to Clayton, writing to his family in 1966:

> Will Clayton was one of those rare public servants who was not only dedicated to the public's interest but had a world outlook in which he saw the position of the United States in relation and harmony to all nations. His work for world cooperation in peace constitutes an enduring monument for which history will inscribe his name in bold letters.[1]

Notes

Notes to Chapter 1

1. This apocryphal account and the discussion that follows are based on a number of sources, most of which have only recently come to light. The most important, and the source of the quotations from the meeting between Truman and Clayton, was the late Senator and Representative Claude Pepper's interview with the author, September 17, 1988. Pepper said he heard Truman's account of the meeting with Clayton when he expressed concern to Truman about press reports, in the fall of 1946, that Clayton was in line to succeed James L. Byrnes. Pepper respected Clayton, he told Truman, but did not feel that Clayton's views were appropriate for a high position in a Democratic administration. (Indeed, Pepper and a group of New Deal colleagues in the Senate fought against Clayton's appointment as assistant secretary of state when Franklin Roosevelt nominated him in December 1944.) "You're wrong about Clayton," Truman told Pepper, "but you don't have to worry about him because I've already tried to offer him the position and he wouldn't even discuss it." Truman went on to recount the conversation he had had in the Oval Office with Clayton "in the spring of 1946," as Pepper recalled, and thus we have the few scraps of the conversation, as reported by Truman to Pepper.

Pepper also said he joked with Truman about Truman's ability to keep the matter out of the press for such a long time, and Truman laughed, saying the meeting with Clayton proved he could have at least one confidential meeting, having provided some ostensible purpose for the meeting other than a discussion of replacing Byrnes. Truman told Pepper that he had taken Clayton aside after a meeting with the cabinet or some cabinet officer—Pepper's memory was unclear—again providing an opportunity to defuse any press leaks that might result.

Truman made a number of cabinet appointments in this fashion. He approached Marshall, after the meeting with Clayton, using Dwight Eisenhower as an intermediary to obviate the necessity of sending cables or letters. When Truman approached Dean Acheson about the position in November 1948, Acheson had thought originally that he was meeting the president to talk about a blue-ribbon commission Acheson had been serving on. Like many presidents, Truman seemed to relish his achievement on those rare occasions when he could say and do things, even momentous things, without reading about them days later in the newspapers.

Representative Pepper, of course, was not an eyewitness to the Truman-Clayton meeting. Supporting his account, however, is evidence that Truman approached Clayton about appointing him secretary of state and, improbable as it may seem, that the most serious approach took place in the spring of 1946, some weeks before George C. Marshall accepted a general offer to serve in that post and some eight months before Marshall ultimately took office. (Many scholars find credible the notion that Truman approached Clayton about replacing Marshall in the fall of 1948. But to suggest Marshall was a second choice seems almost a sacrilege.)

After my talk with Representative Pepper, Hoover Institution researchers Jim Christie and Frank Miele helped me check several key details in his account. Not only do they fit closely with what evidence remains of the offer made to Clayton, but they lend credence to the story. None of the collaborating sources we found has appeared in any of the fifty or more standard memoirs and histories of the period. It is unlikely, then, that Pepper's memory was based on reading anyone else's account of the matter. The historical record supports his memory, but his memory could not reasonably be supposed to be based on these records and materials.

For example, the White House meeting and telephone logs show that Truman met with Clayton several times in March and April 1946 before the meeting with Eisenhower. Yet these meetings are recorded only in the "black book" listings kept by Truman's personal aide, James Steelman. That is, they were listed privately after the fact, not in either of the two visible and available daily sheets commonly given out to the press. The ostensible purpose of one meeting, attended by Clayton, Truman, and the treasury secretary, was to discuss appointments to the International Bank. But this was hardly something that would be kept secret; the vacancy at the just-established bank was a public fact, and it would be standard practice for Truman to talk to two of his ranking advisers on international economic affairs about the appointment. Notably, there is at least one other meeting in the March to April period that shows up only in the black log: Truman's meeting with Ike, evidently to offer the position to Marshall or, at least, establish Marshall's willingness to serve, after Clayton's polite declination.

A second interesting point of collaboration: There was press speculation that

Clayton was to replace Byrnes in the fall of 1946, when Pepper remembers having a concerned conversation with the president. Yet again, the clips we found are not mentioned or cited in any of the standard histories. When we wrote to the Truman Library to ask if their files showed any evidence of such speculation, the answer was negative—not a single clip (Benedick K. Zobrist, letter to the author). The *Kiplinger Newsletter* of December 8, 1946, reported that Clayton was expected to be named secretary of state. The Associated Press put the story on its national wire the next afternoon, with the *Houston Post* editorializing on behalf of the idea on December 11.

(The *Post* was an especially influential paper in Washington at the time. Its publisher, Jesse Jones, a wealthy banker from Houston, had served with distinction under Franklin Roosevelt from 1932 to 1945 and was widely credited with saving much of the U.S. banking system as head of the Reconstruction Finance Corporation. Jones remained in Washington after being forced out as secretary of commerce by the New Dealers, writing editorials and manifesting his considerable influence on the administration of Harry Truman, whose views were more in line with those of the free-enterprising Jones and his friend Will Clayton. Jones was one of the first people Truman called on for advice after the death of FDR placed him behind the desk in the Oval Office. [Harry S. Truman, *Year of Decisions* (New York: Doubleday, 1955) p. 29]. Hence, a *Post* editorial had a quasi-official status and would certainly have been noticed on Capitol Hill—with enthusiasm by Clayton's friends and concern by Pepper and others.)

2. Benjamin Cohen, Byrnes's deputy, attended the meeting with Truman and took notes, though they apparently do not survive in his collected papers. Cohen also discussed the meeting with journalist Robert J. Donovan, a *New York Times* correspondent for many years and author of a respected two-volume set on Truman's presidency. Donovan spoke to me on October 25, 1989, commenting that "Clayton was definitely being considered as secretary of state. . . . Clayton was mentioned almost deferentially when Truman would speak of him, though I think it is clear he wanted Marshall for secretary of state."

3. Interview with the author, October 16, 1989. Clifford felt that the most serious consideration of Clayton would have been in the fall of 1948, after Truman's reelection and the concomitant reclaiming of the Democratic majority in Congress. "At the time he appointed George Marshall," Clifford said, "Truman needed a man with General Marshall's prestige, and acceptance, and with his nonpolitical background. So I would be quite surprised to think that he had offered the position to Clayton at that time, although I know of his respect, almost adulation, of Clayton."

That had been my feeling, too, during initial research on the question. Two caveats, however, must be entered. First, Clifford's memory, or at least his analysis, is faulty on a critical matter of timing; for at the time Clayton and Marshall were actually approached—spring 1946—the Democrats were in the congressional majority. Marshall agreed, in a meeting with Ike on May 9, to take over as secretary as soon as Byrnes had concluded negotiations on some of the Eastern European and Balkan states. Those negotiations were expected to last until roughly July, but talks dragged on through most of the year. Hence, the arragements to replace Byrnes were consummated in January 1947, when bipartisanship was an urgent imperative.

Second, Clayton was a man of stature and bipartisan appeal. He was widely respected on Capitol Hill. Unlike Marshall, he was in Washington in 1946 (Marshall was in the midst of his sensitive mission to China) and had hands-on knowledge of the State Department. His credentials as an anticommunist were unassailable, while his reputation as an economic statesman had helped secure approval of the Bretton Woods monetary pact, the massive 1945–1946 relief program, and a controversial $3.5 billion loan to Britain—with not only Democrats but a majority of the budget-minded Republicans voting in favor. It would be hard to name a man who enjoyed greater veneration than George C. Marshall in the Congress. Clayton, however, might have run a close second. (See, for example, Allen Drury, *A Senate Journal, 1943–1945* [New York: McGraw-Hill, 1963], pp. 247–49, 310–16.)

4. For fall 1946 see the *Kiplinger Newletter*, December 8, 1946, and the *Houston Post*, editorial, December 11, 1946. The *Post* observed that under the rules of succession then in force, "should Mr. Truman die or resign . . . the Secretary of State could automatically become President." The utility of naming a man from Texas—a state without which few Democrats have been elected president—could hardly have been lost on Truman. For 1948: just after the election, the Associated Press carried a dispatch by Francis M. Le May naming Clayton and Dean Acheson as "likely choices" for secretary of state. Clayton's old friend Jesse Jones (see note 1) immediately went back to work promoting the choice, running a front-page banner—"Ickes, Clayton Mentioned for Cabinet Posts . . . Houston Man Talked of for State Secretary"—in his *Houston Chronicle* on November 5. Clayton issued a statement saying he intended to return to Houston but hinted at some interest in the position. "I am just one of those who has been named in press reports as a possible successor," he said. (*Houston Chronicle*, November 11, 1948.)

5. Ellen Clayton Garwood, interview with the author, October 23, 1989; Dean Acheson, *Present at the Creation* (New York: W. W. Norton, 1969), pp. 249–50; Dean Acheson, seminar at Princeton University, July 2, 1953, transcript on file in the Papers of Dean Acheson, Box 74, pp. 7–9, Harry S. Truman Library.

In his memoirs, Truman makes no mention of discussing the position with Clayton and writes that "I knew all that time [from his April 1946 meeting with Byrnes onward] whom I wanted for the job. It was General Marshall" (Truman, *Year of Decisions*, p. 552). Truman describes the arrangement as hinging chiefly on his own discretion—the major delaying factor being Marshall's own mission. "The general was on a vital assignment in China that had to run its course before the change in the State Department could be carried out."

This recollection of Truman's must be placed in context, particularly given his repeated affirmations of interest in Clayton at the time (see notes below). For one thing, Truman differs with the accounts of Byrnes, Eisenhower, Acheson, and the historians as to the details of his understanding with Marshall and Byrnes. Any of their versions might be consistent with an approach having been made to Clayton before the appointment of Marshall or with the idea having been discussed while Eisenhower was in transit and Truman uncertain if Marshall would even serve. The diversity of accounts, however, suggests that the arrangement with Byrnes and Marshall was hardly as firm, as of Eisenhower's return in late May, as Truman seemed to believe in writing his memoirs.

Byrnes, for example, describes his April 16, 1946, meeting with Truman in terms suggesting there was no pressure to name a replacement. "I agreed that regardless of the July 1 date I had set, I would remain until whatever date the treaties were completed." Note that this formulation leaves the arrangement not only vague but contingent on Byrnes's actions rather than Truman's decision. (James Byrnes, *All in One Lifetime* [New York: Harper and Brothers, 1958], p. 355.)

According to Byrnes—who by this writing knew of the accounts that his successor had been designated as early as April 1946—the matter was still an open question as of December 1946, and it was January 1947 "when my resignation had finally been accepted" (Byrnes, *All in One Lifetime*, p. 355). Truman's account appeared in 1955; Byrnes's, in 1958. Byrnes continues: "A few days after my return to Washington [now December 1946], I called on President Truman to remind him that my letter of resignation, given him in April, was to take effect upon the completion of the treaties. As this was now accomplished, I hoped that he could release me. He said he hoped I had forgotten it. In a very friendly talk he gave me several reasons why he felt I should remain. . . . But I was sincere in wishing to leave. . . . We talked long and freely. He asked what I thought of General Marshall as a successor, and my answer was that it would be a splendid appointment and would be well received. Some days later, the President told me he was going to appoint General Marshall, but that the General wished to take a short rest and could not take office until about the middle of January. He said he hoped I could remain until then, and of course I readily agreed."

Byrnes's account is the most amenable to the possibility that Truman approached Clayton about the same position and fits better with subsequent events in 1946. For example, Byrnes's pique at Henry Wallace's Madison Square Garden speech that fall—a speech advocating greater comity toward the Soviets that ultimately got Wallace fired—was hardly the reaction of a man who knew he was a lame duck. Byrnes's cable raises the matter of his April letter for what appears to be the first time since his meeting with Truman that spring. (Truman, *Speaking Frankly* [New York: Harper and Row, 1947], p. 240, and *Year of Decisions*, p. 559.) It makes no direct reference to an existing arrangement for a successor, and its tone suggests a man threatening to resign, and seeking to heighten Truman's dilemma, rather than a man who regards himself as on the way out of office. "If it is not possible," Byrnes wired, for Wallace to be fired for contradicting Truman's foreign policy, "it would be a grave mistake from every point of view for me to continue in office, even temporarily." The wording implies that to Byrnes, it was possible he would "continue in office" more than temporarily. (See Byrnes, *All in One Lifetime*, pp. 370–77.)

The Byrnes cable goes on to say that if Wallace could not be fired or muzzled, "I would *then* have to insist on being relieved" (my emphasis). Again, this can be read either way, but the tone in which Byrnes wrote it, the lack of even an allusion to a designated successor, and Byrnes's evident encouragement of statements by Senators Vandenberg and Connally that increased the pressure on Truman point toward the conclusion that Byrnes, at least, did not feel he would necessarily be stepping down, even with the completion of the agreements. Byrnes, Marshall, and Truman knew that a resignation that sits unexecuted for five months is in some sense beyond the statute of political limitations.

Analysts commenting on the affair years later often speak as if Byrnes's resignation had not, in fact, been sealed months before. "The situation had simply gone too far for Truman to tolerate," Donovan writes. "He could not risk a resignation by Byrnes in the circumstances. It doubtless would have cost the administration the backing of Vandenburg. Republican support of foreign policy would have been jeopardized." (Robert J. Donovan, *Conflict and Crisis: The Presidency of Harry S. Truman, 1945–1948* [New York: W. W. Norton, 1977], p. 228.) But why so, if Marshall were waiting in the wings?

Whatever Byrnes's understanding or version of his own replacement, of course, Truman may have had a different one. Yet Truman's timetable is not inconsistent with the possibility of an approach to Clayton. Eisenhower did not meet with Truman until April 26 and returned from Shanghai only in the second half of May. A prudent and honorable politician might have approached Clayton about the possibility at any point during those two months without violating an understanding that did not yet exist with Marshall. It is also possible that Truman was considering whom to have replace Byrnes before Byrnes's formal letter of April 16. The *Washington Star* of March 4 speculated about a Byrnes successor, naming General Marshall as Truman's choice. John Snyder, perhaps Truman's closest personal adviser at the time, later commented that the rift with Byrnes really was decisive from the time of the Williamsburg incident (December 1945) on. Note that it was Snyder who shuttled Clayton into the Oval Office for the secret meeting with Truman some months later.

One rule of politics is not to decide something you don't have to decide; a related rule of thumb is to make a deal that neutralizes any major potential opponent, especially if it doesn't cost you anything. If Harry Truman was anything, he was a solid and efficient politician. There was real genius in his handling of the Byrnes resignation, stringing things along for almost a year. With an accord from Marshall to become secretary at Truman's will, Truman had Marshall and Byrnes on hold, with an option on either one. With Eisenhower as the messenger, Truman roped a third potential foe into the bargain. (We know that Truman was sufficiently afraid of Eisenhower to twice offer to back him for the Democratic nomination in 1948 if he wanted it. [See Peter Lyon, *Eisenhower: Portrait of the Hero* (New York: Little, Brown, 1974), and Donovan, *Conflict and Crisis*, pp. 86–

87, 142, 338.] It seems likely that Truman's offer was aimed more at neutralizing and befuddling the as-yet politically naive general than at actually convincing Eisenhower to run.) Any of the three men might have opposed Truman in 1948 and beaten him for the Democratic party nomination.

Where did all this leave Clayton? He had deflected Truman's first feeler in the spring of 1946. But that summer, he was moved up to under secretary and was acting secretary of state for much of the fall. Acheson was already making noises about leaving the department and ultimately would in the middle of 1947. As under secretary Clayton was becoming the real number-two man in the department, being brought more into the management of its general affairs than would an assistant secretary with a specific sphere of interest. Acheson (*Present at the Creation*, p. 185) explains Clayton's promotion as a maneuver designed to win Sue Clayton's approval for Will to remain in Washington. But the last thing Sue wanted for her husband was a promotion. She wanted to leave town and had evidently gone so far as to ask Truman aide John Steelman to block any promotion for Clayton. (Diary of Eban A. Ayers, on deposit at the Harry S. Truman Library, entry for April 19, 1948.) A better explanation was that the promotion to under secretary tested the waters for a final promotion to secretary of state, appealed politically to Clayton's backers, and salved Mrs. Clayton's guilty conscience. The Clayton's daughter Ellen Garwood reports that Sue Clayton can best be described as ambivalent and mercurial about Clayton's rise—angry one minute, proud the next, undercutting Clayton, then feeling compuction for harming him, making a gesture to fix the damage, then regretting it, and so on in a vicious circle. (Ellen Garwood, interview with the author, October 23, 1989.) In effect, Truman kept a Clayton option in his portfolio, too.

Once it became apparent to Snyder, Jones, and Clayton's other advocates in the Truman circle that Byrnes was indeed leaving, they drummed up a bit of press speculation, possibly reflecting interest on Truman's part, possibly the phenomenon of leaking a story you hope will become fact. (Marshall's intimates evidently did some competitive leaking of their own shortly after the Williamsburg incident. The *Washington Star* story on Marshall of March was written by a close friend of Admiral William D. Leahy's.) Although press speculation about Clayton at this point does not tell us anything about Truman's mind, it tells us a great deal about the minds of those who knew his mind. Jones and Snyder were not political naifs; they valued economy of effort. Their minicampaign for Clayton in the fall of 1946 suggests that they thought that his appointment was a live possibility—that Truman took the idea seriously.

It is likely, then, that the accounts of Pepper, Truman, Eisenhower, Ayers (see following notes), and Byrnes are all, when read carefully, generally correct; where there are seeming inconsistencies, it is because the arrangements themselves were more vague than any of the accounts tends to indicate if taken alone. Truman is "prone to exaggeration," as James Donovan has written. His account of the Wallace affair, for example, significantly embellishes his own acumen in firing Wallace. (Truman writes of a polite telephone conversation; Wallace and Truman's own press secretary includes the important detail that on the night before the conversation, Truman fired off a strongly worded letter, with some profanity, and had the letter expressed to Wallace's office. Wallace graciously destroyed the letter and phoned Ross the next morning to suggest that the matter be handled differently.) George Marshall proved brilliant in the job, and his selection and the eighteen months that followed may be regarded as the turning point of Truman's presidency. As time wore on, Truman began to think of the decision as having been ordained in his mind, in his general feelings of respect and admiration for Marshall, long before it actually took shape and form. As Clark Clifford noted when we discussed various accounts and discrepancies regarding the slow-motion replacment of Byrnes: "This relates to the whole question of how presidents generally make decisions, and certainly President Truman specifically. There may be some people who say today, 'Well, Marshall was appointed—and therefore it was Marshall all the time, and the whole thing was predestinated, or could only have happened one way.' But of course that isn't the way presidents make decisions. They have options and alternatives and it may be that they consider one option or man for a job and eventually go with another. They may even put out a feeler, or make an offer, and after it doesn't come about, they approach someone else. The president felt very strongly about Clayton and something like an offer to be secretary of state may well have happened. I do not know, though, that it did happen." (Clifford interview, June 16, 1989.)

There may even have been an element of discretion in Truman's omission of the Clayton approach from his memoirs. The revelation that Clayton had been discussed and declined becoming secretary of state might have served some small purpose, but the explanation that he did so because of his wife's almost frantic behavior would have embarrassed an old friend. Truman did discuss his offer to Clayton with aides (see notes 7 and 8 below) when news of the Claytons' marital difficulties became public.

6. See Diary of Eban A. Ayers, on deposit at the Harry S. Truman Library, entries for April 19 and June 1, 1949. My special thanks to Charles Palm and Jim Christie of the Hoover Institution, to Dennis Bilger and others at the Truman Library, and to Danielle Bujnak of the Alexis de Tocqueville Institution for their assistance in ferreting out these passages. After both I and the aforementioned had failed to locate the suspected Clayton entries, it was Bujnak, a high school sophmore doing research and office work for de Tocqueville, who succeeded where several scholars and professional archivists had failed.

7. Ayers diary, entry for April 19, 1949. On June 1, 1949, Ayers wrote," Several other subjects came in for discussion and one of them was a column this morning by Marquis Childs, the newspaper columnist [for the *Washington Post*]. Childs is usually fairly accurate and friendly. Today's column dealt with what he termed the waste of public men. The men whose government service, he said, was interrupted in mid-career and he complained that their services were wasted. He enumerated several—Wilson Wyatt, the former mayor of Louisville who served for a time as administrator of the National Housing Agency; Robert P. Patterson,

former under secretary of war; Will Clayton, former assistant secretary of state; [and others]. . . .

The President pointed out that Wyatt quit in something of a huff but that he has continued friendly and comes to see the President; Patterson, the President said, could have stayed as long as he wanted to and Clayton was 'pulled out by the hair.' The truth was that Clayton might have been secretary of state but for the fact that his wife raised so much rumpus about his staying in Washington."

8. Ellen Clayton Garwood has written *Will Clayton: A Short Biography* (Austin: University of Texas Press, 1958; republished by Regnery-Gateway). Mrs. Garwood would be the first to say, however, that it does not completely fill the void left by the historians. Mrs. Garwood was denied access to many of Clayton's materials at the State Department, and a number of his most important memorandums were made available to the general public only years later. She also wrote at a time when the fact that Clayton was a major catalyst of such policies as the Marshall Plan had not been called into question by the revisionist histories of the last twenty years. The same limitation applies to a Ph.D. dissertation written by Ross J. Pritchard ("Will Clayton: A Study of Business-Statesmanship in the Formulation of United States Economic Foreign Policy" [Fletcher School of Law and Diplomacy, 1955]). Pritchard aptly describes the building of Anderson-Clayton, the cotton brokerage firm Clayton made into a multimillion-dollar conglomerate, and Clayton's handling of a series of congressional inquiries into his business in the 1920s and 1930s. My thanks to the Fletcher School for making available a copy of Professor Pritchard's thesis.

9. Acheson, *Present at the Creation*, pp. 217–25. Ever scrupulous, Acheson does record (p. 217) at least some of the initiatives and reports launched throughout 1946, largely by Clayton during his period as acting secretary from August to October, that by January 1947 were producing repeated warnings of Greek and Turkish collapse and even regular British hints that their commitment would soon end. Acheson's two-paragraph scan of those efforts, however, fails to capture the flavor of the effort's breadth and scope. Those citing Acheson, or those basing their works on the atmosphere of excited activity that followed the decision to launch a major aid program, are not always as careful as Acheson himself. The same can be said of the brisk and widely praised memoir of another principal, *The Fifteen Weeks*, by State Department aide Joseph Jones (New York: Viking, 1955).

10. See George F. Kennan, *Memoirs: 1925–1950* (Boston: Atlantic Monthly Press, 1967), pp. 320–22.

11. *Foreign Relations of the United States* (hereafter, FRUS), 1946, vol. 7 (Washington, D.C.: U.S. Government Printing Office, 1969), pp. 209–13, 857–58.

12. Alan Bullock, *Ernest Bevin: Foreign Secretary, 1945–1951* (New York: W. W. Norton, 1983), p. 315.

13. See FRUS, 1946, vol. 7, pp. 209–13, 857–58.

14. Walter Millis, ed., *The Forrestal Diaries* (New York: Viking, 1951), entry for September 25, 1946, and editor's comments, p. 210.

15. Bullock, *Ernest Bevin*, p. 316.

16. *FRUS*, 1946, vol. 7, p. 213.

17. There is a legitimate debate as to whether and if so, how broadly, Clayton circulated this memorandum. That question will be taken up later in the book. It did, however, represent Clayton's considered reflections on the subject and, presumably, includes many of the salient points he would have made at meetings to review the president's speech, prepare congressional testimony on the aid program for himself, Acheson, and others, and so on.

18. See Kennan, *Memoirs*, pp. 320–22.

19. William Clayton, memorandum of March 5, 1947.

20. Kennan, *Memoirs*, pp. 320–22.

21. Ibid., p. 314; Jones, *Fifteen Weeks*, pp. 246–47, 255.

22. Acheson, *Present at the Creation*, pp. 226–33.

23. Cabell Phillips, *The Truman Presidency* (New York: Macmillan, 1966), p. 178.

24. For further affirmation, see Mark A. Stoler, *George C. Marshall: Soldier-Statesman of the American Century* (Boston: Twayne, 1989), pp. 166–67: "Kennan and Clayton were primarily responsible for the specific proposals enunciated by Marshall in 1947, and Bohlen drafted the Harvard speech from their memoranda." Charles L. Mee, *The Marshall Plan* (New York: Simon and Schuster, 1984) p. 97: "Clayton's memo got to Marshall on May 27. . . . [On May 29], Marshall called Charles Bohlen into his office and asked him to work up a speech, using Kennan's material and . . . Clayton's recent memorandum." John W. Snyder, Oral History Interview, Harry S. Truman Library, November 1982, pp. 174–75: "The man who's most responsible for the Marshall Plan was William Clayton. . . . The report he came back with was so shocking. . . . That's how it really got started." Robert H. Ferrell, ed., *The American Secretaries of State and Their Diplomacy*, vol. 15, *George Marshall* (New York: Cooper Square, 1966), p. 280: "It appears as if this [Kennan] 'memo' by the Staff had much less influence in the Department than the ideas of Will Clayton; the Marshall Plan took its inspiration and detail from Clayton rather than the Kennan memorandum." Ferrell also offers evidence that information contained only in Clayton's March 5 memorandum did pop up throughout the department; it simply did not go to George Marshall, who was leaving for Moscow.

25. John Gimbel, *The Origins of the Marshall Plan* (Stanford: Stanford University Press, 1976), pp. 13–14. Gimbel suggests that even the May 27 memo may not actually have been written until May 31, meaning it could not have been discussed at the critical meetings with Marshall of May 28–29 and perhaps not even in Bohlen's speech draft. But readers should compare this hint with the numerous and very specific statements by the principals, in the text and in note 24, that they had seen the memo on May 27. The explanation, as with the March 5 memorandum widely briefed but probably never circulated, is simple. Clayton's memorandum, like many he wrote, was retyped and updated—becoming in effect several

versions of the same memo with different dates. It is possible that Marshall and the president read one version of Clayton's memo as early as May 21. Nitze recalls: "Clayton went to the office that afternoon [May 19] and dictated a memo along those lines and I thought then that this was circulated. He had just gotten off the plane. I further remembered he'd sent back cables about these conditions while he was over there—April, May, 1947." (Interview, on deposit at Columbia University Library, Oral History Project.) George McGhee, another aide to Clayton, recalls taking a draft of the memo from Clayton's sickbed for typing and circulation several days before his return to the department on May 27. Charles P. Kindleberger, chief of the State Department's Division of German and Austrian Economic Affairs, wrote that in any case "it was common knowledge in the Department that Mr. Clayton was deeply exercised by what he had seen in Europe. . . . He was depressed by what he had seen and heard of black markets, hoarding, etc. He was worked up about the state of the economy of Europe and felt strongly that something should be done. . . . I have understood for some time that the speech is a merger of paragraphs from separate memos on the problem of European recovery written by Mr. Clayton and Mr. Kennan. The part laying out the analysis of what is wrong in Europe seems to be very much the product of Mr. Clayton's mind. The emphasis on trade and exchange is striking." (FRUS, 1947, vol. 3, p. 243.) Charles Bohlen, who drafted the June 4 speech, confirms that Clayton's memorandum "prompted one part of the speech—that dealing with the consequences of the war on the European economy. I submitted the first draft to General Marshall based on these two documents" [i.e., the Kennan and Clayton memorandums], and added some ideas of my own, the chief being 'our policy is not directed,' etc." (Letter to Mrs. Ellen Clayton Garwood, October 29, 1969, on deposit at the Hoover Institution Archives.) Note that this theme is also in Clayton's May 27 memo, which says that the plan must be, and must be explained to be, one directed at saving Europe from hunger and poverty "(not from the Russians)."

Although one can doubt the precise weight or merit of Mr. Clayton's contribution, there can be no doubt that his contribution was timely and substantial. See also Hadley Arkes, *Bureaucracy, the Marshall Plan, and the National Interest* (Princeton, N.J.: Princeton University Press, 1972), pp. 51–52. Kennan himself writes, "Once again, the background and conception of the Marshall Plan has been so well and accurately set forth by Mr. [Joseph] Jones, in his book already referred to, that there could be no useful purpose served by going over the same ground here. I can do no more than relate in somewhat greater detail the circumstances of my own participation." (Kennan, *Memoirs, 1925–1950*, p. 326.) Here is Jones's assessment: "In talking with the Secretary, [Clayton] urged, as he had in his memorandum, that the Secretary and the President take the case for aid to the people and initiate a program. His was probably one of the most direct and important influences in the 'triggering' of the Secretary's speech at Harvard." (Jones, *Fifteen Weeks*, pp. 248–49.)

26. I. F. Stone, *P.M.* magazine, October 17, 1947.

27. Interviews with Winthrop Brown, Emilio Collado, and Paul Nitze, on deposit at Columbia University Library, Oral History Project.

28. William L. Clayton, "Atlantic Union—The Road to Peace," *International Yearbook* of the *Cotton Trade Journal* for 1955–1956.

Notes to Chapter 2

1. The story that follows and most of the material from Clayton's early life are taken from Ellen Clayton Garwood, *Will Clayton: A Short Biography* (Austin: University of Texas Press, 1958), pp. 43–93. The less-than-romantic view of the South is based on sources other than Mrs. Garwood's fine book. See, for example, Wilbur J. Cash, *The Mind of the South* (New York: Doubleday, 1954).

2. Ellen Garwood, *Will Clayton*, p. 49; "Cotton's Clayton," cover story (no byline), *Time* magazine, August 17, 1936.

3. Ellen Garwood, *Will Clayton*, p. 47.

4. Ellen Garwood, interview with the author, October 23, 1989; Ellen Garwood, *Will Clayton*, pp. 45–52.

5. Ibid.

6. Ellen Garwood, *Will Clayton*, p. 54.

7. Ellen Garwood, interview with the author, October 23, 1989.

8. William L. Clayton, private correspondence, on deposit at the Hoover Institution Library, Stanford, California.

9. Ibid.

10. Ibid.

11. Ernest Jones, excerpted from Ellen Garwood, *Will Clayton*, pp. 69–70.

12. Ibid.

Notes to Chapter 3

1. The quotation is excerpted from pages 57–62. A reproduction of the cover appears in the photograph section of this book. Copyright, *Time*, Inc., reprinted by permission.

2. Ellen Clayton Garwood, *Will Clayton: A Short Biography* (Austin: University of Texas Press, 1958), p. 78.

3. Arthur Baum, "They Say He Is a Dangerous Man," *Saturday Evening Post*, May 1935, p. 15.

4. The overview that follows in this paragraph relies chiefly on Wilbur J. Cash, *The Mind of the South* (New York: Doubleday, 1954).

5. See *Time*, August 17, 1936, p. 57.

6. Cash, *Mind of the South*; Ross Pritchard, "Will Clayton: A Study of Business-Statesmanship in the Formulation of United States Economic Foreign Policy" (Ph.D. diss., Fletcher School of Law and Diplomacy, 1955); Ellen Garwood, *Will Clayton*.

7. William L. Clayton, personal correspondence, especially from the 1902–1908 period, on deposit at the Hoover Institution, Stanford University (hereafter, Clayton correspondence); Pritchard, "Will Clayton."

8. *Time*, August 17, 1936, p. 60.

9. Ellen Clayton Garwood, interview with the author, October 23, 1989 (hereafter, Ellen Garwood interview); Ellen Garwood, *Will Clayton*, pp. 77–79; Beverly Smith, *American Magazine*, April 1938; *Time*, August 17, 1936.

10. Clayton correspondence; Pritchard, "Will Clayton"; Ellen Garwood interview.

11. George Champion, interview with the author, April 1989.

12. Ellen Garwood, *Will Clayton*, excerpted from pp. 79–81.

13. Pritchard, "Will Clayton," pp. 9–23; Ellen Garwood interview.

14. Harlan S. Byrne, "The Anderson, Clayton Story," *Wall Street Journal*, December 4, 1953, p. 12; Ellen Garwood, *Will Clayton*, p. 79.

15. Smith, *American Magazine*, April 1938.

16. Pritchard, "Will Clayton," p. 23.

17. Ellen Garwood interview.

18. Ellen Garwood, *Will Clayton*, excerpted from pp. 82–83.

19. Ibid., p. 96.

20. Excerpted from Ellen Garwood interview; Ellen Garwood, *Will Clayton*, p. 85.

21. Ellen Garwood, *Will Clayton*, pp. 90–91.

22. Ibid., pp. 91–92.

23. Pritchard, "Will Clayton," pp. 27–28.

24. Ibid., pp. 29–30.

25. Ibid., pp. 31–32.

26. Baum, "They Say He is a Dangerous Man," p. 15.

27. William L. Clayton to Sam Williams, October 15, 1932, Clayton correspondence.

28. William L. Clayton to Michael O'Shaughnessy, June 4, 1932, Clayton correspondence.

29. William L. Clayton, address in Augusta, Georgia, April 1928, Clayton correspondence.

30. William L. Clayton, letter to Michael O'Shaughnessy, May 23, 1932, Clayton correspondence.

31. William L. Clayton, memorandum of December 13, 1933, Clayton correspondence.

32. William L. Clayton, letter to John Robbins, December 1, 1934, Clayton correspondence.

33. Editorial, *New York Times*, September 20, 1936.

34. William L. Clayton, "A Business-Man Looks at Capitalism," speech at Harvard University, Cambridge, Massachusetts, September 16, 1936, transcript on file with the Clayton correspondence.

35. Ibid.

36. Ibid.

37. These recollections are based on more than two dozen conversations with two of Clayton's daughters, Ellen Garwood and Julia Baker, from 1988 to 1991.

Notes to Chapter 4

1. Committee on Southern Delivery, New York Cotton Exchange, reports of 1904 and 1907, cited in William L. Clayton, "Manipulation of the Cotton Futures Market," address to the American Cotton Shippers Association, Atlanta, Georgia, April 1926.

2. Arthur Baum, "They Say He Is a Dangerous Man," *Saturday Evening Post*, May 1935, p. 42; Ross J. Pritchard, "Will Clayton: A Study of Business-Statesmanship in the Formulation of United States Economic Foreign Policy" (Ph.D. diss., Fletcher School of Law and Diplomacy, 1955), p. 40; Ellen Clayton Garwood, interview with the author, February 8 and October 23, 1989.

3. Ellen Garwood, interview with the author, February 8, 1989.

4. Federal Trade Commission, *Report on the Cotton Trade*, submitted to the U.S. Senate, Washington, D.C., 1924.

5. The account that follows is based primarily on Clayton's testimony at a subsequent congressional hearing. See U.S. Senate, "Cotton Prices," Hearings before a subcommittee of the Senate Committee on Agriculture and Forestry, Washington, D.C., 1929, 1,514 pages.

6. William L. Clayton, correspondence with W. M. Jardine, December 1925 through January 1926, on deposit with the William L. Clayton Papers, Hoover Institution Library, Stanford University (hereafter, Clayton Papers, Hoover Library). See also Ellen Clayton Garwood, *Will Clayton: A Short Biography* (Austin: University of Texas Press, 1958), pp. 97–99.

7. A text of Clayton's address was printed in the May 1926 edition of *ACCO Press*, on deposit with the Clayton Papers, Hoover Library.

8. R. H. Claggett, *Memphis Commercial Appeal*, February 19, 1928.

9. Arthur Marsh, quoted in the *New York Times*, February 7, 1928.

10. See the *New York Times*, February 8, 9, 1928, and the *Houston Press*, February 13, 1928.

11. U.S. Senate, "Cotton Prices," excerpted from pages 410–11.

12. Ibid.; see also Pritchard, "Will Clayton," p. 57.

13. U.S. Senate, "Cotton Prices," p. 836.

14. William L. Clayton to Carl Vinson, January 22, 1929, Clayton Papers, Hoover Library.

15. William L. Clayton, address to the Knife and Fork Club in Houston, Texas, May 1, 1928; the text appeared in the *Houston Post* May 2, 1928.

16. William L. Clayton, letter to Jerome Fentress, April 25, 1928, Clayton Papers, Hoover Library.

17. Republican and Democratic party platforms of 1928, cited in Donald Bruce Johnson and Kirk H. Porter, eds., *National Party Platforms, 1840–1972* (Chicago: University of Illinois Press, 1973), pp. 282, 272. One 1928 statement that did not mince words about protectionism was the platform of the Communist party, which proclaimed, "The interests of the working class are against high tariff" and pledged to abolish it for all consumer goods and agricultural equipment (page 315).

18. For a blow-by-blow acount, the best source remains Jude Wanniski's *The Way the World Works* (New York: Simon and Schuster, 1978: revised editions published in 1983 and 1988).

19. Pritchard, "Will Clayton," pp. 65–160.

20. William L. Clayton, letter to Leon O. Wolcott, October 26, 1929, Clayton Papers, Hoover Library; William L. Clayton, "Notes on My European Trip, Arriving Liverpool, May 4, 1920, Sailing for New York, June 19, 1920," 18–page log, Clayton Papers, Hoover Library.

21. Cordell Hull, *Congressional Digest*, July 1929, pp. 175–76.

22. U.S. Tariff Commission, *Trade Barriers: An Overview*, part 1, *Report to the Subcommittee on International Trade of the Senate Committee on Finance*, TC Publication 665 (Washington, D.C.: April 1974), p. 80, cited in Robert Pastor, *Congress and the Politics of U.S. Foreign Economic Policy, 1929–1976* (Berkeley: University of California Press, 1980), p. 78.

23. Pastor, *Congress and Politics of U.S. Foreign Economic Policy*, p. 76; William L. Clayton, correspondence files for 1920–1930, Clayton Papers, Hoover Library; Arthur M. Schlesinger, *The Crisis of the Old Order* (Boston: Houghton Mifflin, 1957), p. 164; President Hoover, quoted in his economic message of March 1930, *New York Times*, March 8, 1930; see also Joseph Jones, *Tariff Retaliation: Repercussions of the Hawley-Smoot Bill* (Philadelphia: University of Pennsylvania Press, 1934). Note that Jones felt, years before my friend Jude Wanniski helpfully resurrected the idea (see note 18 above), that Smoot-Hawley (as it is called today) was a chief catalyst for the crash, writing, "As a score of writers have pointed out, the world depression and the Hawley-Smoot tariff are inextricably bound up one with

the other, the latter being not only the first manifestation of but a principal cause of the deepening and aggravating of the former."

24. Pritchard, "Will Clayton," pp. 127–45; William L. Clayton, quoted in Pritchard, "Will Clayton," p. 138.

25. Pritchard, "Will Clayton"; William L. Clayton, letters to E. F. Duggan, September 20, 1928, to Henry Wallace, October 24, 1934, and to Eugene Thomas, August 15, 1934, Clayton Papers, Hoover Library; William L. Clayton, Papers of Will Clayton, Harry S. Truman Library (hereafter, Clayton Papers, Truman Library), files on Allied war debts (32–33). See also Pritchard, "Will Clayton," especially pp. 65–121.

26. William L. Clayton, letter to Jack Johnson, July 8, 1934, Clayton Papers, Truman Library, American Liberty League folders.

27. Arthur M. Schlesinger, *The Coming of the New Deal* (Boston: Houghton Mifflin, 1959), quotation excerpted from pp. 484–86. See also J. F. Essary, "Liberty League Found Taking Role of Chief New Deal Foe," *Sun*, July 16, 1935; editorial, "Unsound Policy," *Evening Star*, April 16, 1935; editorial, "Dear Roast Pig," *Sun*, September 17, 1935; "Bar Group Studies Constitutionality of New Deal Acts," *New York Times*, August 22, 1935; Franklin Roosevelt, quoted in Schlesinger, *Coming of the New Deal*, p. 487.

28. Ellen Garwood, *Will Clayton*, p. 103.

29. William L. Clayton's voluminous files of clips and correspondence on the Liberty League, Clayton Papers, Truman Library, Liberty League boxes; see especially files 4–12; "Houston Cotton King's Wife for New Deal; Says Husband Has Quit Liberty League," *Houston Chronicle*, June 25, 1936.

30. William L. Clayton, letters to Brian Mooney, December 23, 1935, and to Franklin Roosevelt, February 28, 1935, Clayton Papers, Hoover Library; Pritchard, "Will Clayton," p. 144; Alfred Landon, quoted in the *New York Times*, September 27, 1936; William L. Clayton, press statement of October 11, 1936, and letter to George Sealy, November 7, 1936, Clayton Papers, Hoover Library; Arthur M. Schlesinger, *The Politics of Upheaval* (Boston: Houghton Mifflin, 1960), pp. 634–35.

Notes to Chapter 5

1. James MacGregor Burns, *Roosevelt: The Lion and the Fox* (New York: Harcourt, Brace, 1956), pp. 437–40. Willkie supported American aid after FDR's announcement but declined to support a bill to provide it in advance; after the deal was a fact, he said that he supported the idea of aid but that Roosevelt should have gone through Congress—precisely the idea he had declined to support when his word would have been timely. Key Republican senators, such as Walsh, declined to support and even opposed the aid idea. Bear in mind that respected

observers—including Winston Churchill—were arguing and have since argued that U.S. aid, without prolonged delays, was the hinge of fate on which Britain's survival depended. As Churchill cabled FDR in July: "Mr. President, with great respect, I must tell you that in the long history of the world this is a thing to do now (Winston Churchill, *The Second World War*, vol. 2, *Their Finest Hour* [Boston: Houghton Mifflin, 1949], chap. 18).

2. Ellen Clayton Garwood, interview with the author, October 23, 1989; William L. Clayton, interview with Ellen Garwood, 1957, on deposit at Columbia University Library, Oral History Project.

3. See, for example, White's memorandums to Morgenthau and Roosevelt, "Preliminary Report on the Possibility of Depriving the Aggressor Countries of Needed Strategic War Materials," on deposit with the Papers of Harry Dexter White, Box 6, File 15–B, Harvey Mudd Library, Princeton University. Memorandums of March 31, October 17, June 6, 1939, and March 27, 1940, also in Box 6, are also of interest. An excellent published account is provided by John Morton Blum, *Roosevelt and Morgenthau* (Boston: Houghton Mifflin, 1970), for example, pp. 210–11, 220–23, 225–31, 240–49, and 268–70.

4. Henry Luce, editorial, "The American Century," *Life* magazine, February 17, 1941.

5. Burns, *Roosevelt*, pp. 438–39.

6. Dean Acheson et al., letter, *New York Times*, August 11, 1940. Clayton passed on his recollections of the meeting with Pershing to his daughter Julia (later Mrs. Julia Baker) during the war. Interview with the author, October 1990.

7. Burns, *Roosevelt*, pp. 438–40, quotation taken from p. 440.

8. For background, see William L. Clayton, speech to the Business and Professional Women's Club of Houston, as cited in "Budget Must Be Balanced, Says Clayton," *Houston Chronicle*, May 27, 1937.

9. William L. Clayton, speech to the U.S. Chamber of Commerce, cited in "Tariff Rates Are Hit by Houstonian," *Houston Chronicle*, May 6, 1938.

10. Ibid.

11. See U.S. Office of Inter-American Affairs, "History of the Office of the Coordinator of Inter-American Affairs" (Washington, D.C.: Superintendent of Documents, 1947); William Pirsein, "The Voice of America: A History of the International Broadcasting Activities of the United States Government, 1940–1962" (Ph.D. diss., Northwestern University, June 1970). The Voice of America and a number of other U.S. public diplomacy efforts evolved out of the coordinator's office, as Pirsein notes.

12. Arnold A. Rogow, *James Forrestal: A Study of Personality, Politics, and Policy* (New York: Macmillan, 1963), pp. 89–91.

13. Paul Nitze, interview with Ellen Clayton Garwood, November 4, 1958, on deposit at Columbia University Library, Oral History Project. See also Paul H.

Nitze, *From Hiroshima to Glasnost* (New York: Weidenfeld and Nicholson, 1989) p. 10.

14. Staff correspondent, "Clayton and 13 Others Put on U.S. Board," *Houston Chronicle*, September 6, 1939. In 1924, Jesse Jones asked Clayton to serve as fundraising chairman for John W. Davis, the Democratic nominee for president. He took Clayton to visit Davis at his home in Locust Valley, West Virginia. Clayton, however, after promising to contribute substantially, joined with Davis in suggesting that Jones take the position, a combined effort that proved as successful as the Davis compaign was not. (Bascom N. Timmons, *Jesse H. Jones* [New York: Henry Holt, 1956], p.136.) In 1931, Herbert Hoover, grasping at straws, tried to get Clayton to handle the cotton operations of his ill-starred Federal Farm Board. Clayton, at odds with the entire policy of the board, declined. (*New York Times*, September 9, 1931.) In 1938, Henry Morgenthau approached Clayton about the possibility of assisting in negotiations with the French to stabilize the dollar against the franc, a miniature Bretton Woods. Clayton evidently was interested in this idea, but FDR was not. He told Morgenthau to have nothing to do with Clayton, terming him "thoroughly reactionary." (Morgenthau discussed the incident with Henry Wallace, who recorded it in his diary on December 11, 1944. See Henry A. Wallace, in John Morton Blum, ed., *The Price of Vision: The Diary of Henry A. Wallace, 1942–1946* [Boston: Houghton Mifflin, 1973], pp. 400–401. On the monetary negotiations, see Blum, *Roosevelt and Morgenthau*, pp. 65–66, 72–84, 231–32.)

15. No byline, "Clayton Shocked by Political Objections to President's Ball," *Houston Chronicle*, January 14, 1939. See also Timmons, *Jesse H. Jones*, pp. 351–61.

16. William L. Clayton, "The World Cotton Situation," address to the Cotton Research Congress, Waco, Texas, June 27, 1940 (ACCO Press, July 1940); William L. Clayton, "A Program of Action," in U.S. Office of Inter-American Affairs, "History of the Office Coordinator of Inter-American Affairs," p. 11.

17. William L. Clayton, correspondence with friends, October 1, 1941, to October 11, 1941, on deposit with the William L. Clayton Papers, Hoover Library, Stanford University (hereafter, Clayton Papers, Hoover Library); U.S. Office of Inter-American Affairs, "History of the Office of the Coordinator of Inter-American Affairs," p. 11; no byline, "Retirement of W. L. Clayton Is Announced," *Houston Chronicle*, October 29, 1940. The account of Clayton's discussion with FDR is taken in part from Ross J. Pritchard, "Will Clayton: A Study of Business-Statesmanship in the Formulation of United States Economic Foreign Policy" (Ph.D. diss., Fletcher School of Law and Diplomacy, 1955), p. 167. Pritchard lists no prior source but had extensive conversations with Clayton; presumably the account emerged from one of these. Pritchard seems to feel there was a personal meeting, and no doubt there was at some point; Clayton's daughter recalls the exchange of phone calls that probably preceded such a meeting. Ellen Clayton Garwood, *Will Clayton: A Short Biography* (Austin: University of Texas Press,

1958), pp. 109–10. In an interview with his daughter, Clayton recalls returning to Houston, but his memory may be faulty: Clayton also told Mrs. Garwood that he resigned in August of 1940, when in fact his resignation took effect October 21 and was made public October 15. See also William L. Clayton, letter to Lamar Fleming, Junior, April 30, 1941, Clayton Papers, Hoover Library.

18. Nitze, *From Hiroshima to Glasnost*, quotation from p. 5.

19. Paul Johnson, *Modern Times* (New York: Harper and Row, 1983), p. 320; Suzanne Garment, "U.S. Sanctions Just a Sideshow in African Drama," *Wall Street Journal*, August 16, 1985; editorial, "They Shoot Airplanes, Don't They?" *New Republic*, October 3, 1983; Jack Kemp, interview with the author, July 23, 1982; Eugene Rostow, in symposium, "Beyond Containment?" *Policy Review*, Winter 1985, p. 27.

20. Dean Acheson, *Present at the Creation* (New York: W. W. Norton, 1969), p. 53; see also Commerce Department statistics, cited in Dwight Eisenhower, *Economic Report of the President* (Washington, D.C.: Superintendent of Documents, January 1955), p. 137.

21. Timmons, *Jesse H. Jones*, pp. 289–93; Acheson, *Present at the Creation*, pp. 48–62.

22. Acheson, *Present at the Creation*, pp. 48–62. See also Omar Bradley, A *General's Life* (New York: Simon and Schuster, 1983), p. 130; Nitze, *From Hiroshima to Glasnost*, p. 18.

23. Timmons, *Jesse H. Jones*, pp. 301–11.

24. Ibid., pp. 285–94; William L. Clayton, Columbia University Library, cited above, pp. 4–12; Livingston Merchant, interview, October 28, 1958, Columbia University Library, Oral History Project; Ellen Garwood, interviews with the author, October 23 and February 8, 1989; William L. Clayton, correspondence, 1942–1943, Clayton Papers, Hoover Library; see also Nitze, *From Hiroshima to Glasnost*, p. 19; Acheson, *Present at the Creation*, pp. 49–64.

25. Acheson, *Present at the Creation*, pp. 49–64.

26. William L. Clayton, Columbia University Library, Oral History Project.

27. See Nobutaka Ike, ed., *Japan's Decision for War: Records of the 1941 Policy Conferences* (Stanford: Stanford University Press, 1967), p. 188, for example; W. N. Medlicott, *The Economic Blockade*, vol. 2 (London: Longmans, Green, 1952), quotation from p. 647.

28. Acheson, *Present at the Creation*, p. 62. See also Medlicott, *Economic Blockade*, vol. 2, p. 647; Gary Clyde Hufbauer et al., *Economic Sanctions Reconsidered* (Washington, D.C.: Institute for International Economics, 1985), p. 161; Margaret Doxey, *Economic Sanctions and International Enforcement* (London: Oxford University Press, 1971), pp. 20–21.

Notes to Chapter 6

1. The sketch of Henry Wallace that follows is based chiefly on the following sources: Arthur M. Schlesinger, *The Coming of the New Deal* (Boston: Houghton Mifflin, 1959), pp. 28–34; John Morton Blum, ed., *The Price of Vision: The Diary of Henry A. Wallace, 1942–1946* (Boston: Houghton Mifflin, 1973), esp. pp. 3–54, 363, 420–22; Bascom N. Timmons, *Jesse H. Jones* (New York: Henry Holt, 1956), esp. pp. 312–61; Richard Walton, *Henry Wallace, Harry Truman, and the Cold War* (New York: Viking, 1976), pp. 1–32; Livingston Merchant, interview, October 28, 1958, Emilio Collado, interview, November 6, 1958, and James Stillwell, interview, November 9, 1958, Columbia University Library, Oral History Project; William L. Clayton, interview with Ellen Clayton Garwood, April 5, 1955, p. 2 of transcript in author's personal files; William L. Clayton, interview, Columbia University Library, Oral History Project.

2. The sketch of Jesse Jones that follows is based primarily on Timmons, *Jesse H. Jones*, in particular, pp. 13–46, 75–91, 101–5, 134–41, 155–61, 165–77, 186–96, 249–57, 266–81. It is supplemented by information from Clayton's interview, Columbia University Library, Oral History Project, and the William L. Clayton Papers at the Hoover Institution Library, Stanford, California (hereafter, Clayton Papers, Hoover Library).

3. See note 1.

4. See note 1.

5. See Dean Acheson, *Present at the Creation* (New York: W. W. Norton, 1969), pp. 39–47; Paul H. Nitze, *From Hiroshima to Glasnost* (New York: Weidenfeld and Nicholson, 1989), pp. 13–23.

6. Blum, ed., *Price of Vision*, pp. 363.

7. Timmons, *Jesse H. Jones*, pp. 266–67; Ellen Garwood, interview with the author, April 5, 1955.

8. See Collado interview, November 6, 1958, Columbia University Library, Oral History Project; Allen Drury, *A Senate Journal: 1943–1945* (New York: McGraw-Hill, 1963), pp. 246–49.

9. Timmons, *Jesse H. Jones*, pp. 286.

10. Ibid., pp. 280–86, 280–81.

11. Acheson, *Present at the Creation*, pp. 40–41.

12. Ibid.; Ellen Garwood, interview with the author, April 5, 1955; Bernard Baruch, *Baruch: The Public Years* (New York: Holt, Rinehart and Winston, 1960), pp. 301–7; Henry Wallace diary, entries of April 23, May 19, May 26, May 28, 1942, in Blum, ed., *Price of Vision*.

13. Wallace, in Blum, ed., *Price of Vision*, p. 85.

14. Ibid.; see also William L. Clayton interview, Columbia University Library, Oral History Project; Nitze, *From Hiroshima to Glasnost*, pp. 13–17; and Timmons, *Jesse H. Jones*, pp. 321–24. Timmons's account seems somewhat tendentious and out of character; at a meeting with RFC officials, for example, he pictures the vice president turning purple, shouting at subordinates, blurting out non sequiturs. My wording strives to be neutral, but the Timmons account is more lively and probably accurate in some of its particulars, albeit exaggerated in spots.

15. Timmons, *Jesse H. Jones*, pp. 321–24.

16. Ibid.

17. Ibid.

18. Ibid.

19. Cited in Timmons, *Jesse H. Jones*, pp. 320–21.

20. Ibid., pp. 321, 324–25, on narrative that follows; Henry Wallace diaries, entry of April 23, 1942, in Blum, ed., *Price of Vision*, pp. 70–71, 166n.

21. Henry Wallace diaries, Blum, ed., *Price of Vision*, pp. 203–34; Timmons, *Jesse H. Jones*, pp. 325–30.

22. Timmons, *Jesse H. Jones*, pp. 325–30.

23. Ibid., pp. 326–27.

24. Ibid.; Henry Wallace diaries in Blum, ed., *Price of Vision*, pp. 220–21.

25. Blum, ed., *Price of Vision*, pp. 326–27; William L. Clayton interview, Columbia University Library, Oral History Project; Ellen Garwood, interview with the author.

26. Ellen Garwood, interview with author.

27. Blum, *Price of Vision*, pp. 221–27.

28. Timmons, *Jesse H. Jones*, pp. 328, 330; Blum, ed., *Price of Vision*, p. 233.

29. Ellen Garwood, interviews with the author, February and October 1989.

30. Ibid.; Baruch, *Baruch*, pp. 330–33.

31. Ellen Garwood, *Will Clayton: A Short Biography* (Austin: University of Texas, 1958), p. 19; Bascom N. Timmons, "W. L. Clayton Due for New Federal Job," *Houston Chronicle*, February 20, 1944; Henry Wallace diaries, entries for May 26, June 3, 1942, and June 28, 1943, in Blum, ed., *Price of Vision*, pp. 82, 85, 218; David Lilienthal, *The Journals of David E. Lilienthal*, vol. 1, *The TVA Years, 1939–1945* (New York: Harper and Row, 1964), pp. 632–33, 660–61. Lilienthal also felt that Clayton's appointment in January was a deal worked out in advance from the inside by Baruch and Byrnes. Perhaps it was the sense that Baruch and Byrnes knew who they wanted, Clayton, and lobbied for their choice. Perhaps Clayton was playing hard to get. The fact that it took them weeks to close a deal with Clayton—whose appointment was not announced until mid-February 1944—and that FDR himself had to join the campaign suggests otherwise. (Note the date of Timmons's report in the *Houston Chronicle* in this note.)

32. See the House floor debate on the legislation in *Congressional Record—*

House, vol. 90, pt. 5, August 15, 1944, pp. 6951–78, and pt. 6, September 18, 1944, pp. 7856–60.

33. Drury, *Senate Journal*, pp. 244–71; William L. Clayton, interview with Ellen Garwood, Columbia University Library, Oral History Project; Ellen Garwood, interviews with the author; James G. Patton, press release reprinted in *Congressional Record—Senate*, December 19, 1944, p. 9699; editorial, "Surplus Property— Must a Great Chance to Broaden Economic Freedom Go by Political Default," *Life*, December 1944. This account attempts to spare the reader the details of the battle over surplus property. A more complete account is contained in Ross J. Pritchard, "Will Clayton: A Study of Business-Statesmanship in the Formulation of United States Economic Foreign Policy" (Ph.D. diss., Fletcher School of Law and Diplomacy, 1955), pp. 175–84.

34. Drury, *Senate Journal*, quotations from pp. 248–49.

35. Timmons, *Jesse H. Jones*, pp. 345–50; Henry Wallace diaries, entry from December 20, 1944, in Blum, ed., *Price of Vision*, p. 412; "W. L. Clayton to Take New Federal Post," *Houston Chronicle*, December 1, 1944.

36. William L. Clayton, "Democracy and Cotton," address to the National Cotton Council, Augusta, Georgia, 1941, Clayton Papers, Hoover Library.

37. William L. Clayton, speech to the National Foreign Trade Convention, New York, October 25, 1943, cited in Associated Press report, "America Must Choose Path, Clayton Says, Alternatives Are Proper Place in World Trade or Becoming Armed Camp, Convention Told," *Houston Chronicle*, October 26, 1943.

38. Franklin D. Roosevelt, telegram to Clayton, November 29, 1944, Clayton Papers, Hoover Library.

Notes to Chapter 7

1. Richard N. Gardner, *Sterling-Dollar Diplomacy* (New York: McGraw-Hill, 1969), pp. 18, 40–52. The account that follows relies heavily on Gardner's scholarly narrative of the period. See also Roy F. Harrod, *The Life of John Maynard Keynes* (New York: Harcourt, Brace, 1951); Dean Acheson, *Present at the Creation* (New York: W. W. Norton, 1969), p. 81.

2. Sumner Welles, quoted in the *New York Times*, October 8, 1941; Harrod, *The Life of John Maynard Keynes*, p. 513; Gardner, *Sterling-Dollar Diplomacy*, p. 42.

3. Agreement cited in *Department of State Bulletin*, vol. 6, 1942, p. 192; Gardner, *Sterling-Dollar Diplomacy*, pp. 81–82; Henry Morgenthau, memorandum to Franklin D. Roosevelt of May 16, 1942, on deposit with the Harry Dexter White Papers, Mudd Library, Princeton University: "It seems to me that the time is ripe to dramatize our international economic objectives in terms of action which

people everywhere will recognize as practical, powerful, and inspiring." Gardner writes that indeed, "agreement on the plans *might only be possible* in the midst of the close working war-time alliance. . . . All projects for post-war organization were interdependent—a beginning had to be made somewhere" (my emphasis).

4. See Harry Dexter White Papers, in particular "Suggested Plan for a United Nations Stabilization Fund and a Bank for Reconstruction of the United and Associated Nations," undated but presumably from January or February 1942, and the two versions that follow, dated March 1942 and April 1942; U.K. Treasury, "Proposals for an International Clearing Union," London, 1943; and John Maynard Keynes, in Harrod, *Life of John Maynard Keynes*, pp. 526–32. Keynes's November 1942 draft was published in *Foreign Relations of the United States* (hereafter, *FRUS*) 1942, vol. 7 (Washington, D.C.: U.S. Department of State), pp. 203–21. FDR's own attitude is described in Sumner Welles, *Seven Decisions That Shaped History* (New York: Harper, 1951), pp. 8–14. Sketches of the participants are drawn from Harrod, *Life of John Maynard Keynes*, various pages; Gardner, *Sterling-Dollar Diplomacy*, pp. 41–121; Ellen Clayton Garwood, *Will Clayton: A Short Biography* (Austin: University of Texas, 1958), pp. 7, 28; and Robert Heilbroner, *The Worldly Philosophers* (New York: Simon and Schuster, 1972), pp. 240–55.

5. The portrait of White is based largely on David Reese, *Harry Dexter White: A Study in Paradox* (New York: Coward, McCann, & Geoghegan, 1973); Acheson, *Present at the Creation*, pp. 81–82; and John Morton Blum, *Roosevelt and Morgenthau* (Boston: Houghton Mifflin, 1970), pp. 430, 460–61, 517. Elizabeth Bently, a self-confessed communist spy, said that White had helped her obtain printing plates used in the production of marks printed by the United States for use during the occupation of Germany. The Soviets were planning to counterfeit the marks but had been unable to master the complicated ink process. On the charges against White, see also speech of U.S. attorney general Herbert Brownell, cited in the *New York Times*, November 7, 1953.

6. See the preceding chapter in this book; Acheson, *Present at the Creation*, pp. 55, 81–88; Emilio Collado, interview, November 6, 1958, on deposit at Columbia University Library, Oral History Project.

7. William L. Clayton, speech to the Business and Professional Women's Club of Houston, May 26, 1937, cited in news story, "Budget Must Be Balanced, Says Clayton," *Houston Chronicle*, May 27, 1937. See also John Maynard Keynes, *The Means to Prosperity* (London: Macmillan, 1933); William L. Clayton, interview with Ellen Clayton Garwood, 1957, transcript on deposit in the author's files.

8. William L. Clayton, address of March 24, 1945, over the Columbia Broadcasting Service (CBS) radio network. A transcript appears in the *Congressional Record*, 1945, vol. 91, pt. 2, Appendix, pp. A1591–A1592.

9. Ibid.

10. John Maynard Keynes, in Harrod, *Life of John Maynard Keynes*; William L. Clayton, 1957 interview; Emilio Collado, interview of November 6, 1958; William L. Clayton, marginalia on minutes from Harry Dexter White, October 1942, on

deposit with the Papers of William L. Clayton, Hoover Institution Library, Stanford University.

11. Henry Wallace, "The Road to an Expanding World Trade," interview with Sterling Fisher, National Broadcasting Company (NBC) radio network, July 1946, cited in State Department press release number 477, December 12, 1946, p. 4 of transcript. See also Gardner, *Sterling-Dollar Diplomacy*, pp. 78–80. On Morgenthau's reaction, see Henry Morgenthau, cited in Blum, *Roosevelt and Morgenthau*, p. 432.

12. William L. Clayton, interview with CBS radio.

13. William L. Clayton, quoted by Ellen Clayton Garwood, interviews with the author, October 1989. For more on Morgenthau's approach, see Henry Morgenthau, letter to Harry S. Truman, quoted in the *New York Herald-Tribune*, March 31, 1946.

14. William L. Clayton, correspondence with Cordell Hull, 1942 and 1943, on deposit with the papers of William L. Clayton, Hoover Institution Library, Stanford University; Ellen Garwood, interviews with the author, October 1989.

15. Ibid.

16. Ibid.

17. Acheson, *Present at the Creation*, pp. 73–76.

18. The exchange of letters and cables is reprinted in *FRUS*, 1943, vol. 1, pp. 820–50.

19. Following paragraphs see William L. Clayton, interview with Ellen Garwood, transcript in the author's files; Acheson, *Present at the Creation*, pp. 33–34, 73–76.

20. See note 17.

21. Gardner, *Sterling-Dollar Diplomacy*, p. 199.

22. "Meeting with British Experts on Proposal for a United Nations Bank for Reconstruction and Development, at the Treasury, October 11, 1943," minutes published in *FRUS*, 1943, vol. 1, pp. 1092–96.

23. Ibid.

24. Collado interview.

25. *FRUS*, 1943, vol. 1, memo of October 11, 1943, p. 1095.

26. *Joint Statement by Experts on the Establishment of an International Monetary Fund*, cmd. 6519 (London, 1944); see also U.S. Treasury, *The Bretton Woods Proposals*, 1945; Louis Rasminsky, "International Credit and Currency Plans," *Foreign Affairs* 22 (1944): 589–603; Gardner, *Sterling-Dollar Diplomacy*, pp. 114–21; Henry Morgenthau, "Bretton Woods and International Co-operation," *Foreign Affairs* 23 (1945); Walter R. Gardner, "The Future International Position of the United States as Affected by the Fund and the Bank," *American Economic Review* 25 (supplement) (1945): 272–88.

27. Ibid.; *FRUS*, 1943, pp. 1092–96.

28. Harry Hawkins interview with Ellen C. Garwood, April 18, 1959, on deposit at Columbia University Library, Oral History Project.

29. Harrod, *Life of John Maynard Keynes*; Gardner, *Sterling-Dollar Diplomacy*, p. 112.

30. Emilio Collado, interview, November 6, 1958; Leory Stinebower, November 6, 1958; Harry Hawkins, April 18, 1959.

31. William L. Clayton, interview on file at Columbia University Library, Oral History Project, 1958.

32. Wallace diaries, in Special Collections, University of Iowa, Iowa City, October 15, 1943, excerpt from pp. 261–63.

33. Author's interview with Chamberlain, April 1983.

34. Gardner, *Sterling-Dollar Diplomacy*, pp. 114–21;

35. William L. Clayton CBS speech.

36. Clayton to Cordell Hull, December 31, 1944.

Notes to Chapter 8

1. Profile based on Allen Drury, *A Senate Journal: 1943–1945* (New York: McGraw-Hill, 1963); John F. Kennedy, *Profiles in Courage* (New York: Harper and Row, 1956), chap. 9; Dean Acheson, *Present at the Creation* (New York: W. W. Norton, 1969), pp. 219, 224.

2. See *Congressional Record—Senate*, vol. 91, pt. 6, July 2, 1945, to September 10, 1945, especially July 16–19, pp. 7597–7626, 7666–91, 7747–80; Drury, *Senate Journal*; for Clayton and Acheson's intelligent but at times sparse-on-detail testimony, see *Bretton Woods Agreements Act*, Committee on Banking and Currency, House of Representatives, Hearings on H.R. 2211, 79th Congress, First Session, vol. 1 (Washington, D.C.: Government Printing Office, 1945), pp. 249–85.

3. Robert Taft, *Congressional Record*, cited above, July 16, 1945, p. 7573; American Bankers Association, February 1, 1945, *Practical International Financial Organization*; Lord Keynes, cited by Taft in *Congressional Record*, July 16, 1945, p. 7572.

4. Editorial, *New York Times*, July 1, 1944. See also U.S. Senate, *Bretton Woods Agreement Act*, Committee on Banking and Currency, Hearings on H.R. 3314, 79th Congress, First Session (Washington, D.C.: Government Printing Office, 1945), pp. 377–78, and Senators Wherry and Taft, from *Congressional Record*, pp. 7762–63.

5. Richard N. Gardner, *Sterling-Dollar Diplomacy* (New York: McGraw-Hill, 1969), pp. 133–34; Emilio Collado, interview, on deposit at Columbia University Library, Oral History Project.

6. William L. Clayton, speech to the Economic Club of Detroit, May 21, 1945, reprinted in the *Department of State Bulletin*, May 27, 1945, pp. 979–82; U.S. Treasury Department estimate, cited in the *New York Herald-Tribune*, February 7, 1945.

7. William L. Clayton, with Dean Acheson and Archibald MacLeish, "World Trade and World Peace," NBC interview broadcast on February 10, 1945, reprinted in the *Department of State Bulletin*, March 11, 1945, vol. 12, no. 298, pp. 401–8; William L. Clayton, speech of March 17, 1945, cited above; see also William L. Clayton, speech to the Women's National Press Club, Washington, D.C., March 13, 1945, transcript in the Papers of William L. Clayton, Hoover Institution Library, Stanford University (hereafter, Clayton Papers); CIO pamphlet, "5 Million New Jobs!" 1945, on deposit at Green Library, Stanford University, and cited in the *New York Times*, February 4, 1945.

8. U.S. Treasury Department, *Questions and Answers on the Fund and Bank* (Washington, D.C.: 1945), p. 8; Dean Acheson, subcommittee testimony reprinted in the *Department of State Bulletin*, 1944, vol. 11, p. 1127; William L. Clayton, letter to Bernard Baruch, March 26, 1945, Clayton Papers; William L. Clayton, House committee testimony, cited above in note 2: *Bretton Woods Agreement Act*.

9. Harry Dexter White and Robert Taft, Senate committee hearings, cited above, p. 170; William L. Clayton and Representative Wolcott, excerpted from House committee hearings, cited above, pp. 259–61.

10. This exchange was heavily edited for the general reader, excluding such exchanges as the chairman's interruption of "Dr. Clayton" (as he called the eighth-grade graduate) to warn him to leave for a conference at the State Department that was fast approaching. The amended version, in my opinion, captures the flavor of the session, but this writer's "flavor" may be another man's "butchered distortion." Scholars should refer to the full transcript, pp. 277–83 of the House committee hearings, cited above.

11. William L. Clayton, House committee hearings, cited above, p. 265.

12. William L. Clayton and Representative Wolcott, in House committee hearings, cited above, p. 262; John Maynard Keynes, House of Lords, debate of May 23, 1946, p. 841.

13. Senators Ball and Wagner, Senate debate, cited above, pp. 7771–72.

Notes to Chapter 9

1. Emilio Colladao, interview with Ellen Clayton Garwood, November 6, 1958, Columbia University Library, Oral History Project; Ellen Clayton Garwood, interview with the author, October 23, 1989; Robert J. Donovan, *Conflict and Crisis: The Presidency of Harry S. Truman, 1945–1948* (New York: W. W. Norton, 1977), p. 17.

2. Harry S. Truman, *Year of Decisions* (New York: Doubleday, 1955).

3. Harriman dispatch quoted in Walter Millis, ed., *The Forrestal Diaries* (New York: Viking, 1951), pp. 39–40.

4. James Byrnes, *All in One Lifetime* (New York: Harper and Brothers, 1958), p. 282; Richard G. Hewlett and Oscar E. Anderson, Jr., *A History of the United States Atomic Energy Commission* (hereafter, *History of the U.S. AEC*), vol. 1, *The New World 1939/1946* (University Park: Pennsylvania State University, 1962), pp. 342–43; Cabell Phillips, *The Truman Presidency* (New York: Macmillan, 1966), pp. 53–54; Truman, *Year of Decisions*, pp. 10–11; Donovan, *Conflict and Crisis*, pp. 45–49.

5. See sources listed in note 4; see also U.S. Department of State, *Foreign Relations of the United States* (hereafter, *FRUS*), 1945, vol. 1 (Washington, D.C.: U.S. Government Printing Office).

6. The following discussion is taken, in addition to the sources listed in notes 4 and 5, from the log and minutes for the committee: R. Gordon Arneson, "Notes on Meeting of Interim Committee of Manhattan Project (Atomic Bomb), May–July 1945," on deposit at the Harry S. Truman Library, File MHDC #671. In addition, see Herbert Feis, *Japan Subdued* (Princeton, N.J.: Princeton University Press, 1966), esp. pp. 1–65. My understanding of the positions taken by different participants also benefited from extensive discussions with a source close to the committee who was not present at its meetings but who later had access to records and to several of its members, including Clayton and Conant. The source requested anonymity; that request is respected here.

7. See sources in note 6; quotation of Feis, *Japan Subdued*, p. 39.

8. Truman, *Year of Decisions*, p. 419.

9. Elting E. Morison, *Turmoil and Tradition* (Boston: Houghton Mifflin, 1960), esp. pp. 622–33.

10. Hewlett and Anderson, *History of the U.S. AEC*, vol. 1; Truman, *Year of Decisions*, pp. 419–22.

11. Arneson, "Notes on Manhattan Project," minutes for May 31, 1945, pp. 13–14.

12. Arthur Compton, *Atomic Quest* (New York: Oxford University Press, 1956), quoted from pp. 220, 238.

13. Arneson, "Notes on Manhattan Project," minutes for June 1, 1945, quoted from p. 10.

14. Ibid., minutes for May 9, 14, 31 and June 1, 1945; Hewlett and Anderson, *History of the U.S. AEC*, p. 354.

15. Ibid., pages 2–3 of the running log, covering the meeting of May 18, 1945.

16. Morison, *Turmoil and Tradition*, pp. 629–30.

17. Arneson, "Notes on Manhattan Project," minutes for May 31 and June 1,

1945. Hewlett and Anderson, *History of the U.S. AEC*, pp. 354–58; see also notes 4 and 6 above.

    18. Ibid.

    19. Ibid.

    20. Ibid.

Notes to Chapter 10

    1. John Kenneth Galbraith, quoted on the back jacket of Charles L. Mee, Jr., *Meeting at Potsdam* (New York: M. Evans and Company, 1975).

    2. Cordell Hull and Henry Morgenthau, quoted in John Morton Blum, *Roosevelt and Morgenthau* (Boston: Houghton Mifflin, 1970), pp. 582, 588; for a general discussion of the German issue from Morgenthau's perspective, see pp. 573–631.

    3. Ibid., pp. 574, 584–86.

    4. Ibid.

    5. Ibid.

    6. Ibid., Stimson memorandum quoted from pp. 589–90.

    7. Blum, *Roosevelt and Morgenthau*, pp. 614–30; James F. Byrnes, *Speaking Frankly* (New York: Harper and Brothers, 1947), pp. 183–87.

    8. Ibid.

    9. See Harry S. Truman, *Year of Decisions* (New York: Doubleday, 1955), pp. 101–2, 235.

    10. William L. Clayton, interview with Ellen Clayton Garwood, Columbia University Library, Oral History Project; Byrnes, *Speaking Frankly*, pp. 82–83.

    11. Ibid.; see also Mee, *Meeting at Potsdam*, pp. 44–45, 100–102.

    12. Mee, *Meeting at Potsdam*, p. 127

    13. Ibid.

    14. Edwin Pauley, letter to Maisky, quoted in Mee, *Meeting at Potsdam*, p. 151.

    15. Byrnes, *Speaking Frankly*, pp. 82–83; William L. Clayton interview, Columbia University Library, Oral History Project.

    16. Byrnes, *Speaking Frankly*, pp. 83–85.

    17. Admiral Leahy, quoted in Mee, *Meeting at Potsdam*, p. 175.

    18. Harry Truman and Clement Attlee, quoted in Mee, *Meeting at Potsdam*, p. 235; William L. Clayton, interview with John T. Mason, Jr., Columbia University Library, Oral History Project, pp. 154–56.

    19. Many aspects of UNRRA described here and in the following paragraphs are taken from the official history of the project, prepared by a special staff under the direction of UNRRA chief historian George Woodbridge in *UNRAA: The History*

of the United Nations Relief and Rehabilitation Administration (New York: Columbia University Press, 1950), 3 vols.

20. Ernest Bevin, quoted in Alan Bullock, *Ernest Bevin: Foreign Secretary, 1945–1951* (New York: W. W. Norton, 1983), p. 143; Michael Balfour and John Mair, *Four Power Control in Germany and Austria 1945–46* (New York: Oxford University Press, 1956), pp. 327–28; Allen J. Matusow, *Farm Policies and Politics in the Truman Years* (Cambridge, Mass.: Harvard University Press, 1967), pp. 28–32. Related statistics were compiled by Margaret Garvey for the Alexis de Tocqueville Institution from United Nations and national figures, chiefly the *Monthly Bulletin of Statistics* (Statistical Office of the United Nations, 1949–1950). Interestingly, countries under the firmest Soviet control did not experience so sharp a drop. See, for example, Bulgaria and Romania. See also Dean Acheson, *Present at the Creation* (New York: W. W. Norton, 1969), pp. 68–70; Associated Press dispatch, "Clayton Elected UNRRA Finance Committee Head," *Houston Chronicle*, August 13, 1945. On the assorted problems with UNRRA, see U.S. Department of State, *Foreign Relations of the United States* (hereafter, *FRUS*), 1944, vol. 2, pp. 331–54, and 1945, vol. 2, pp. 958–1116 (Washington, D.C.: U.S. Government Printing Office). The Grew cable of May 30, 1945, is reprinted in *FRUS*, 1945, vol. 2, pp. 983–84.

21. Acheson, *Present at the Creation*, pp. 71–72, 132. Just once it would be wonderful to hear a politician accused of playing "Santa Claus" plead guilty: "Very well then, I am Santa Claus, and all members of Congress who are opposed to Santa Claus should vote against this bill."

22. Associated Press dispatch, "UNRRA Asks 1 Per Cent of Incomes," *Houston Chronicle*, August 24, 1945.

23. *FRUS*, 1945, vol. 2, cables cited are on pp. 984–1005.

24. William L. Clayton, cited in Associated Press dispatch, "Clayton Urges Solons to Add to UNRRA Fund," *Houston Chronicle*, November 14, 1945.

25. *FRUS*, 1945, vol. 2, pp. 1014–42.

26. Ross J. Pritchard, "Will Clayton: A Study of Business-Statesmanship in the Formulation of United States Economic Foreign Policy" (Ph.D diss., Fletcher School of Law and Diplomacy, 1955), p. 257.

27. Woodbridge, *UNRRA*.

28. Excerpted from William L. Clayton, letter to the editor, *Washington Post*, August 16, 1946.

Notes to Chapter 11

1. The following narrative is based on Roy F. Harrod, *The Life of John Maynard Keynes* (New York: Harcourt, Brace, 1951), p. 595; Emilio Collado and William L. Clayton, interviews with Ellen Clayton Garwood, Columbia University Library,

Oral History Project; James Byrnes, *All in One Lifetime* (New York: Harper and Brothers, 1958), pp. 309–10; Dean Acheson, *Present at the Creation* (New York: W. W. Norton, 1969), pp. 119–20.

2. Richard N. Gardner, *Sterling-Dollar Diplomacy* (New York: McGraw-Hill, 1969), pp. 189–79.

3. W. S. Woytinsky and E. S. Woytinsky, *World Commerce and Governments: Trends and Outlook* (New York: Twentieth Century Fund, 1955), pp. 54–55.

4. See, for example, Associated Press, "Clayton Sees 'Bloc' Danger if Loan Fails," *Houston Chronicle*, January 6, 1946.

5. Harrod, *Life of Keynes*, p. 596.

6. Gabriel A. Almond, *The American People and Foreign Policy* (New York: Harcourt, Brace, 1950), p. 73.

7. Various reactions quoted in the *New York Herald-Tribune*, August 26, 1945; various reactions quoted in Gregory A. Fossedal, *The Democratic Imperative* (New York: New Republic Books, 1989), p. 187.

8. Editorial, *Manchester Guardian*, September 9, 1945; Winston Churchill, 410 House of Commons Debate 711, April 24, 1945.

10. Lords Keynes and Halifax, quoted in Gardner, *Sterling-Dollar Diplomacy*, pp. 190–91.

11. General R. E. Wood, letter to William L. Clayton, November 26, 1945, William L. Clayton Papers, Hoover Institution Library, Stanford University (hereafter, Clayton Papers, Hoover Library); the 1.6 figure is from Clayton's doodling on a sheet of statistics prepared for the talks on October 11, 1945, Clayton Papers, Hoover Library; see also "Suggested Terms of British Credit" for State Department estimates.

12. On Clayton, Keynes, and Vinson, see Allen Drury, *A Senate Journal: 1943–1945* (New York: McGraw-Hill, 1963), pp. 148–51; Gardner, *Sterling-Dollar Diplomacy*, pp. 199–201; William L. Clayton interviews, Columbia University Library, Oral History Project.

13. Ibid.

14. Ibid.

15. Harrod, *Life of Keynes*, pp. 593–94; Gardner, *Sterling-Dollar Diplomacy*, pp. 204–5; Lord Keynes, quoted in the *New York Times*, October 15, 1945. The text of the Anglo-American Financial Agreement is contained in U.S. Department of State, *Anglo-American Financial and Commercial Agreements*, Commercial Policy series, no. 80 (Washington, D.C.: 1945).

16. See Bernard Baruch, quoted in Walter Lippman, "Mr. Baruch Writes a Letter," *New York Herald-Tribune*, November 6, 1945.

17. William L. Clayton, letter.

18. John Maynard Keynes, quoted in "Parliamentary Debates," House of Lords, 5th series, London, 1945, no. 138, December 18, 1945, pp. 778–79.

19. John Maynard Keynes, letter to William Clayton, December 21, 1945, Clayton Papers, Hoover Library.

20. William L. Clayton, letter to John Maynard Keynes, December 29, 1945, Clayton Papers, Hoover Library.

21. Gallup poll cited in the *Chicago Daily News*, October 10, 1945; Bernard Baruch, quoted in Gardner, *Sterling-Dollar Diplomacy*, pp. 193–94; NAM release quoted in Fossedal, *Democratic Imperative*, p. 187; Senator Bilbo, cited in "Summary of U.S. Opinion on Anglo-American Commercial and Financial Agreements," Public Attitudes Survey conducted by the State Department's Public Affairs Office, Clayton Papers, Hoover Library; see especially surveys of January 31, February 7–14, 15–20, 1946.

22. "Summary of U.S. Opinion."

23. Clayton's lobbying effort is captured in Ross J. Pritchard, "Will Clayton: A Study of Business-Statesmanship in the Formulation of United States Economic Foreign Policy" (Ph.D. diss, Fletcher School of Law and Diplomacy, 1955), pp. 233–53.

24. See the *Congressional Record—Senate*, 1946, 79th Congress, Second Session, vol. 92, pt. 4, pp. 4269–74, 4601, 4687–90, 4806–7.

25. William L. Clayton to Alben Barkley, January 28, 1946, Clayton Papers, Hoover Library. See also William L. Clayton, speech on the British loan, reprinted in the *Department of State Bulletin* 12 (1945): 37; see also Robert J. Donovan, *Conflict and Crisis: The Presidency of Harry S. Truman, 1945–1948* (New York: W. W. Norton, 1977), pp. 195–97; Acheson, *Present at the Creation*, pp. 194–96. Truman was briefed on the Churchill speech before its drafting, Byrnes read a copy well in advance, and Truman saw a copy on the train out to Missouri, commenting that "it was admirable and would do nothing but could though it would cause a stir." The next day Truman told the press, "I didn't know what would be in Mr. Churchill's speech." (Donovan, *Conflict and Crisis*, pp. 190–92.)

26. See sources in note 25; also editorial, *The Economist*, September 26, 1945.

27. Joseph P. Kennedy, cited in the *New York Times*, March 4, 1946; Arthur Vandenburg, in the *Congressional Record—Senate*, 79th Congress, Second Session, vol. 92, April 22, 1946, p. 4080; William L. Clayton to Christian Herter, April 18, 1946, Herter to Clayton, May 8, 1946, Clayton to Herter, May 10, 1946, all on deposit with the Clayton Papers, Hoover Library.

28. "U.S. Opinion on Anglo-American Economic Relations," June 13–20, 1946, Clayton Papers, Hoover Library; for floor debate comments, see the *Congressional Record—House*, 79th Congress, Second Session, vol. 92, pt. 7, pp. 8669–73, 8823–26; see also Pritchard, "Will Clayton," pp. 244–53.

Notes to Chapter 12

1. Truman almost certainly did talk to Clayton about serving as secretary of state in the spring of 1946. He probably did not that fall for reasons explained in the text. The leaks probably represent the Washington phenomenon of putting

out the word that what one wants to happen is what is going to happen. For a more complete discussion of this matter, see chapter 1.

2. Dean Acheson, *Present at the Creation* (New York: W. W. Norton, 1969), p. 215.

3. James Reston, "State Department's Growth Sets Problem for Marshall," *New York Times*, January 9, 1947; James Reston, "Acheson Will Stay as Aide at the Request of Marshall, Observers Believe General Will Also Urge Under-Secretary Clayton to Keep His Post," *New York Times*, January 23, 1947; Lester Markel, *New York Times*, March 16, 1947.

4. For the chronology and related figures that follow, see Charles L. Mee, *The Marshall Plan* (New York: Simon and Schuster, 1984), pp. 17–18; William L. Clayton, interviews in 1958 and 1962, on deposit at Columbia University Library, Oral History Project; Hadley Arkes, *Bureaucracy, the Marshall Plan, and the National Interest* (Princeton, N.J.: Princeton University Press, 1972), pp. 238–44; Ross J. Pritchard, "Will Clayton: A Study of Business-Statesmanship in the Formulation of United States Economic Foreign Policy" (Ph.D. diss., Fletcher School of Law and Diplomacy, 1955), pp. 266–73; U.S. Department of State, *Foreign Relations of the United States* (hereafter, *FRUS*), 1947, vol. 3 (Washington, D.C.: U.S. Government Printing Office), pp. 1–4, 688–701, 709–13, 864, 859–60, 837–65; *New York Times*, January 31, 1947.

5. Pritchard, "Will Clayton"; Alan Bullock, *Ernest Bevin: Foreign Secretary, 1945–1951* (New York: W. W. Norton, 1983), p. 361.

6. Norman Ness, interview, November 7, 1958, Columbia University Library, Oral History Project.

7. Walter Lippman, *New York Herald-Tribune*, February 12, 1947; *The Times* (London), February 22, 1947.

8. Acheson, *Present at the Creation*, p. 217.

9. Ibid.

10. Ibid., pp. 217–25; Joseph M. Jones, *The Fifteen Weeks* (New York: Viking, 1955), pp. 121–97.

11. Ibid.; see also C.P. Trussell, "Bid to Help Korea Forecast Because Russia Bars Unity, 3 Cabinet Aides Defend Help to Mid-East," *New York Times*, March 25, 1947.

12. See notes 8–11.

13. George Elsey, memorandum to Clark Clifford, March 7, 1947, Papers of Clark M. Clifford, Greek speech folder, Harry S. Truman Library; George F. Kennan, *Memoirs: 1925–1950* (Boston: Atlantic Monthly Press, 1967), pp. 320–23; Walter Lippman, "Policy or Crusade?" *Washington Post*, March 16, 1947. See also "Great Debate over 'Truman Doctrine,'" *New York Times*, News of the Week in Review section, March 23, 1947. See also C. L. Sulzberger, *New York Times*, March 21, 1947; Clark Clifford, notation to George Elsey of March 9, Papers of George M. Elsey, Truman Doctrine speech folder, Harry S. Truman Library;

William L. Clayton, memorandum of March 5, 1947, original with the Papers of William L. Clayton, Harry S. Truman Library (copy at Hoover Institution Library).

14. Joseph Jones to Mr. Benton, memorandum of February 26, 1947, Papers of Joseph M. Jones, Box 2, Harry S. Truman Library.

15. Reston's comments to Forrestal evidently were taped and transcribed in "Excerpts from Telephone Conversation," Papers of Joseph M. Jones, Harry S. Truman Library; the newspaper dates cited are from Jones, *Fifteen Weeks*, pp. 226–28.

Notes to Chapter 13

1. See Constantine Tsaldaris, interview with Philip C. Brooks, May 4, 1964, Harry S. Truman Library (hereafter, HSTL), pp. 1–4; Lyle C. Wilson, United Press dispatch, printed in the *Washington Daily News*, March 12, 1947; William Martin, letter to Harry S. Truman, December 20, 1946, and William L. Clayton and Truman aide William D. Hassett, exchange of notes, January 28, 1947, Papers of Harry S. Truman—Official File 27-B, "Export-Import Bank of Washington" folder, HSTL; Loy Henderson, interview with Richard D. McKinzie, June 14, December 5, 1973, HSTL, pp. 80–82. Henderson: "I was not surprised when Mr. Acheson had approved our memorandum of action. He and I had been discussing the problems of Greece and Turkey for some time, and both of us felt that a crisis with regard to them was imminent."

2. Norman Ness, interview, November 7, 1958, Columbia University Library, Oral History Project. See also Ness's letter to Ellen Clayton Garwood, May 6, 1959: Clayton's "request that we undertake to inquire into the state of Western Europe came much before March or May, 1947. It was certainly as early as February of that year, and may very well have been in the last months of 1946."

3. Dean Acheson, *Present at the Creation* (New York: W. W. Norton, 1969); Joseph Jones, *The Fifteen Weeks* (New York: Viking, 1955); Herbert Hoover reports to Harry S. Truman on "The President's Economic Mission to Germany and Austria," February and March 1947, Papers of Harry S. Truman, "Economic Mission as to Food," File 950-B, HSTL; the drafts and memorandums regarding Truman's Baylor speech are contained in the Papers of Harry S. Truman, Files of Clark M. Clifford, HSTL; Truman's assessment in Harry S. Truman, *Memoirs: Years of Trial and Hope* (New York: Doubleday, 1955), pp. 111–12.

4. Text of Baylor speech is with Truman Papers, Files of Clark Clifford, HSTL.

5. Memorandum from F. H. Russell to Claire Wilcox, February 20, 1947, and attached proposal for addition to Truman's speech drafted by Jones, Papers of Joseph M. Jones, HSTL. Press reaction was swift and substantial: "Mr. Truman's address . . . justified its advance billing as one of importance," observed the *Baltimore Sun*, March 7, 1947. "This was no perfunctory speech on the part of

the President," the *New York Times* agreed: "Announced in advance as a major address, it measured fully up to that standard," March 4, 1947. "President Truman's address at Baylor University was a forceful and persuasive appeal for support of the Administration's foreign trade policy," the *Washington Post* wrote: "It was well timed, to stimulate a waning enthusiasm . . . for the forthcoming trade negotiations." Although Clayton was already thinking in terms of a U.S. grant-and-loan program to back that interest up—as his March 5, 1947, memorandum makes clear—he felt, and Acheson and Truman agreed, that Truman's statement on policy should focus on firming up interest in the trade-liberalization package that was a key to the Marshall Plan's success. Had Truman's speech included the section suggested by Jones, it would have let the larger cat out of the bag in a week when the administration was about to appeal for aid to Greece and Turkey. Republicans in Congress were sensitive, as testimony revealed, about the costs of a broader commitment than that asked for in the Truman Doctrine speech. Again, the interest in a European recovery program, far from being hastily thrown together after the March 12 Greece-Turkey initiative, had to be artificially stalled owing to the exigency of the Mediterranean situation.

6. Acheson, *Present at the Creation*; Jones Papers, HSTL; Forrest C. Pogue, *George Marshall: Statesman* (New York: Viking, 1987), pp. 200–201; Robert J. Donovan, *Conflict and Crisis: The Presidency of Harry S. Truman, 1945–1948* (New York: W. W. Norton, 1977), pp. 281–91; Jones, *Fifteen Weeks*, pp. 200–204, 211n; Charles P. Kindleberger, "Memorandum for the Files: Origins of the Marshall Plan," July 22, 1948, published in U.S. Department of State, *Foreign Relations of the United States* (hereafter, *FRUS*), 1947, vol. 3 (Washington, D.C.: U.S. Government Printing Office), pp. 241–47.

7. Cabell Phillips, *The Truman Presidency* (New York: Macmillan, 1966), pp. 177–78; Paul Nitze, *From Hiroshima to Glasnost* (New York: Weidenfeld and Nicolson, 1989), pp. 47–52; James Reston, "U.S. Studies Shift of Help to Europe as a Unit in Crisis," *New York Times*, May 25, 1947. Nitze does not give the exact date or further details of his memo, which was not published in *FRUS*, and the State Department archives was unable to locate it.

8. Pogue, *George Marshall*, pp. 186–91.

9. Ibid.

10. Charles Bohlen, *Witness to History* (New York: W. W. Norton, 1973), p. 263.

11. Pogue, *George Marshall*, pp. 197–200; the SWNCC report is reprinted in *FRUS*, 1947, vol. 3, pp. 204–20; Acheson, *Present at the Creation*, pp. 226–30; Jones, *Fifteen Weeks*, pp. 231–32.

12. Acheson, *Present at the Creation*, pp. 226–30; Jones, *Fifteen Weeks*, pp. 206–13.

13. Dean Acheson, speech to the Delta Club, May 8, 1947, transcript reprinted in Jones, *Fifteen Weeks*, pp. 274–81, 231n. Ness's estimate of the date Clayton asked his assistants to begin studying Europe's situation, in preparation for what

became the Marshall Plan, was made in an interview November 7, 1958, Columbia University Library, Oral History Project.

14. See sources in note 13. See also Frank L. Dennis, "Acheson Asserts U.S. Must Start Rebuilding Germany and Japan," *Washington Post*, May 9, 1947; James Reston, "Administration Now Shifts Its Emphasis on Foreign Aid," *New York Times*, May 9, 1947. For follow-up commentary on Acheson as an improvement on or alternative to the Truman Doctrine, see Walter Lippman, *New York Herald-Tribune*, May 10, 1947; Martin Agronsky, ABC, May 9, 1947, commentary, transcribed in the State Department's Surveys of Public Opinion, Papers of Joseph M. Jones, HSTL; Jennings Perry, *P.M.*, May 13, 1947. For Acheson speech as a complement to or extension of the Truman Doctrine, which is how Jones regarded it, see Marquis Childs, *Washington Post*, May 13, 1947; Reston "Administration Shifts Emphasis"; Arthur Krock, *New York Times*, May 19, 1947; editorial, "Beyond the Truman Doctrine," *New York Times*, May 25, 1947; Ronald Steel, *Walter Lippman and the American Century* (Boston: Little-Brown, 1980), pp. 440–42; Ellen Garwood, interviews with the author, February 8 and October 23, 1989; Walter Lippman, "Cassandra Speaking," *Washington Post*, April 5 and May 1, 1947; Pogue, *George Marshall*, p. 203; Jones, *Fifteen Weeks*, pp. 228–32. "Two of these young economists," Jones writes—Clayton aides Ben Moore and H. Van B. Cleveland—"had already influenced the Department's Foreign Aid Committee to think in terms of aid to Europe as a whole administered in such a way as to bring about economic unification, and were at that moment at work on further studies that Kennan was to use in carrying out the assignment given him by Secretary Marshall. But Lippman, timing his suggestion for the psychological movement following the Moscow conference, had a powerful impact on policy thinking. . . . One immediate result of his suggestion was that State Department advocates of European union began to be listened to with greater attention, and their memoranda read, by their superiors." (Pp. 231–32.)

15. Ross Pritchard, "Will Clayton: A Study of Business-Statesmanship in the Formulation of United States Economic Foreign Policy" (Ph.D. diss., Fletcher School of Law and Diplomacy, 1955), pp. 280–81.

16. Ivan White, interview, October 31, 1958, Columbia University Library, Oral History Project.

17. Harry Hawkins, memorandum to William L. Clayton, March 6, 1946, William L. Clayton Papers, Hoover Institution Library, Stanford University.

18. Geneva dispatch, *New York Times*, May 2, 1947; editorial, "Beyond the Truman Doctrine," *New York Times*, May 25, 1947.

19. William L. Clayton, telegram to the acting secretary of state, April 23, 1947, *FRUS*, 1947, vol. 3, pp. 701–2, and George Marshall, reply of April 29, 1947, pp. 706–7.

20. Nitze, *From Hiroshima to Glasnost*, pp. 51–52. See also John Gimbel, *The Origins of the Marshall Plan* (Stanford: Stanford University Press, 1976), pp. 13–14. See also the discussion in chapter 1. It is not my intention to raise this cavil

with Gimbel's work, which is a valuable source of both information and perspective. Nor do I want to single him out for dismissing Clayton, or at least failing to understand his role, that can be seen in many other books, among them Mee's and Donovan's. Gimbel's statements are often the most quotable because he has confronted these issues and made clear statements about them.

21. Jones, *Fifteen Weeks*, pp. 248–49.

22. Acheson, *Present at the Creation*, excerpted from pp. 230–33.

23. James Reston, "U.S. Studies Shift of Help to Europe as a Unit in Crisis," *New York Times*, May 25, 1947, p. 1.

24. Robert H. Ferrell, ed., *The American Secretaries of State and Their Diplomacy*, vol. 15, *George Marshall* (New York: Cooper Square, 1966), p. 280.

25. See the Clayton May 27 memorandum. "Proposed Address for Secretary Marshall," May 16, 1947, draft with additions of May 20, 1947, Papers of Joseph M. Jones, Box 1, File on "Correspondence re Transfer of Material," HSTL; Joseph M. Jones, "Memorandum for the Files, Re: The Secretary's Harvard Speech of June 5, 1947," July 2, 1947, Papers of Joseph M. Jones, Box 2, File on "Truman Doctrine* . . . 15 Weeks," Folder 1, HSTL; H. Van B. Cleveland, "Outline of Memorandum on a U.S. Program for Europe," May 9, 1947, Papers of Joseph M. Jones, Box 2, same folder as July 2, 1947, memo HSTL.

26. Charles L. Mee, *The Marshall Plan* (New York: Simon and Schuster, 1984), p. 80.

27. Clayton interview, Columbia University Library, Oral History Project.

Notes to Chapter 14

1. George F. Kennan, "Memorandum Prepared by the Policy Planning Staff," date estimated as July 21, 1947, in U.S. Department of State, *Foreign Relations of the United States* (hereafter, FRUS), 1947, vol. 3 (Washington, D.C.: U.S. Government Printing Office), p. 335.

2. William Clayton, quoted in Ellen Clayton Garwood, interviews with the author, February 8 and October 23, 1989. See also Charles Burton Marshall, "Creating the Marshall Plan Was a Complex Process," report to the U.S. Information Agency, June 22, 1987.

3. Ben T. Moore, memorandum to Claire Wilcox, July 28, 1947, in FRUS, 1947, pp. 239–41. (In his note, Moore also states flatly that Kennan had one of Clayton's May 19–27 memorandums on hand when writing the PPS report.)

4. *New York Times*, June 25, 1947. The extent to which there was a plan is a controversial matter. "When Clayton went to Europe for consultations in June," John Gimbel (*The Origins of the Marshall Plan* [Stanford: Stanford University Press, 1976]) writes, "he had only very general vague conceptions of what was to become the European recovery program." This is not true, as Gimbel's next few

sentences suggest: "What he did in the capitals of Europe with respect to the latter eventually caused much concern in the State Department. The minutes of a round of discussions in the State Department show a 'consensus that Mr. Clayton, while generally aware of department thinking with regard to the "Plan" holds fundamental divergent views on some aspects.'" Clayton had a clear idea of the economic policies he wanted to accomplish. Marshall and Kennan, who were not economists, had a series of political imperatives, such as a desire to rebuild Germany, that had to be promoted subtly lest they arouse suspicion at home and in Europe, particularly France. They also sensed that Americans felt that the scheme had to be as European as possible, not so much because this was economically desirable—though Clayton felt this—but because an aid package was more likely to be approved if it could follow some sign of Euro-seriousness. But it was Clayton who had written in May that "we must avoid getting into another UNRRA."

Gimbel also picks on Clayton's next sentence—"the United States must run this show"—as indicating that he did not appreciate the importance of European cooperation and initiative. But this ignores the earlier sentences in the memo promoting a "European federation." Virtually everyone describing the talks of May 28 and 29, including Acheson and Kennan, agrees that Clayton was in favor of European initiative and cooperation, as he had been for some forty years. The memorandum of conversation for May 29—Clayton, Acheson, Bohlen, Cohen, Kennan, and others—records that Clayton stressed that "some system for closed European economic cooperation must be devised to break down existing economic barriers." This point, the memo notes, "parallels the recommendation in the Policy Planning Staff paper." (*FRUS*, 1947, vol. 3, pp. 234–35.)

Clayton meant that the United States must "run the show" in several senses. First, the United States must summon forth the minimal confidence needed to get the Europeans moving. This Marshall did well and subtly at Harvard. Second, the United States must avoid another UNRRA, in which the problem was not European initiative but lack of initiative owing to Soviet-bloc disruption. Thus the administration of the plan must leave the United States a free hand. This was achieved by excluding countries that declined to join in the cooperation scheme; by Europe turning its plan over to the Americans for finance; and by the joint instruments of bilateral aid packages from the United States being overseen by a cooperative self-policing European effort with a U.S. director (Hoffman). As Charles Kindleberger, another economic specialist at the State Department, put it, any clash of views "was ultimately resolved through the device of multilateral *and* bilateral agreements, with Europe operating the program under a series of mutual pledges, but each country being responsible for its performance under the program to the U.S. if it received assistance." (Memorandum for the files, July 22, 1947, in *FRUS*, 1947, vol. 3, pp. 241–47.)

Finally, the program must be an effective one: the Europeans must cooperate in something useful, namely, more open trade and currency stabilization and not merely cooperate in drawing up lists of needs. This was necessary both for the plan to work and for it to be sold at home. Cohen, Thorp, and Bohlen all stressed this point. Again, Marshall settled on a brilliant device. Merely vaguely announcing that the United States was prepared to help drew the Europeans together. Once together, one of their most pressing questions was, "What do you have it in mind for us to do?" That was Clayton's department.

Thus, to show, as Gimbel claims, that the Marshall Plan was "actually a series of pragmatic bureaucratic decisions" having little to do with economic planning is possible if you ignore the credo of Hull and Clayton enunciated over their combined fifteen years in the State Department as the core of U.S. foreign economic policy. (Gimbel, like Mee—see next note—virtually never mentions Bretton Woods or the GATT, and unlike Mee, virtually never mentions the British loan, either.) Gimbel is only one of the more clear-cut examples of what is a general trend among historians. To write as if the details of the plan—read "economic substance of the plan"—were of little import is to assume that which is to be proved. Gimbel advances a thesis that is almost impossible to disprove, in that any government policy is likely to involve bureaucratic maneuver and ad hoc compromise and that there can be no government intention or plan because the government is at best a collection of individual human plans, motives, intentions. But this only italicizes the fact that the Marshall Plan was the product of at least twenty or thirty minds in the United States and Europe.

5. Charles L. Mee, *The Marshall Plan* (New York: Simon and Schuster, 1984), pp. 159–60. Mee places great emphasis on the negotiations that took place after June 5. He relies heavily on a reading of Kennan's work, which makes it hard to give a full account of events. Mee, for example, overlooks many substantive details in Clayton's talks with the British of late June. Mee (pp. 125–29) describes the talks as an isolated, confused interlude on whether Britain would have a special role in the plan. This was part of the discussions but only a small part. In a book on the Marshall Plan, Mee hardly mentions the Bretton Woods agreement or the GATT. He takes the view that economic policy was not the key—that the important business was all psychological. (Why, then, didn't UNRRA or the World Bank or the British loan et al. have similar psychological effects?) Believing economic policy to be a game of smoke and mirrors, he has little ability to decide what information about economic policy is important and what is not. This book is in many ways better written than most and certainly more interesting for the general reader. Mee concentrates on the narrative details and writes a fast-paced accout. Hence his book is a useful contribution to the literature, though it is not to be relied on as an overall guide to the development of the Marshall Plan as a substantive policy.

6. Ross J. Pritchard, "Will Clayton: A Study of Business-Statesmanship in the Formulation of United States Economic Foreign Policy" (Ph.D. diss., Fletcher School of Law and Diplomacy, 1955), pp. 336–37. Pritchard does not list a specific source for his account of the session, but it presumably derives from his long and frequent talks with Clayton in the mid-1950s. See also Clayton's letters to Clinton Anderson, June 19 and 20, 1947. Papers of William L. Clayton, Hoover Institution Library, Stanford University (hereafter, Clayton Papers, Hoover Library).

7. Pritchard, "Will Clayton." See also Inverchapel to Marshall, June 14 and 17, 1947, in *FRUS, 1947*, vol. 3, pp. 253–57. Harry B. Price, interview with Denny Marris, Harry S. Truman Library; Mee, *Marshall Plan*, pp. 99, 116–20; Cafferey telegram to George Marshall, June 16, 1947, in *FRUS, 1947*, vol. 3, pp. 255–56; Alan Bullock, *Ernest Bevin: Foreign Secretary, 1945–1951* (New York: W. W. Norton, 1983), pp. 405–9.

8. Cafferey cable to George Marshall, June 18, 1947, in *FRUS, 1947*, vol. 3, p. 258; Bullock, *Ernest Bevin*, p. 405; Marshall cable to U.S. embassy in London, June 20, 1947, *FRUS, 1947*, vol. 3, pp. 263–64.

9. Bullock, *Ernest Bevin*, p. 409; Beedel Smith, telegram to George Marshall, June 23, 1947, *FRUS, 1947*, vol. 3, p. 266.

10. Instruction memorandum, in *FRUS, 1947*, vol. 3, pp. 247–49.

11. This paragraph and the account that follows are based on "Memorandum of Conversation," June 24, 1947, in *FRUS, 1947*, vol. 3, pp. 268–73; Bullock, *Ernest Bevin*, pp. 405–17.

12. See Mee, *Marshall Plan*, pp. 124–25. This paragraph and the account of the meeting that follows are based on "Memorandum of Conversation," June 25, 1947, in *FRUS, 1947*, vol. 3, pp. 276–83.

13. *FRUS, 1947*, vol. 3, pp. 284–88.

14. Bullock, *Ernest Bevin*, pp. 409–21; Ellen Garwood, interviews with the author, February 8 and October 23, 1989.

15. Ibid.; see also Forrest C. Pogue, *George Marshall: Statesman* (New York: Viking, 1987), pp. 223–24. A useful *Pravda* editorial was cabled back by the U.S. embassy. See Beedel Smith cable to Marshall, June 26, 1947, in *FRUS, 1947*, vol. 3, p. 294. See also *The Spectator*, quoted in Mee, *Marshall Plan*, p. 137.

16. Cited in *FRUS, 1947*, vol. 3, p. 287.

17. Ibid., pp. 269–73.

18. Ibid., pp. 276–83.

19. See, variously, Cafferey's cable to George Marshall, July 4, 1947, in *FRUS, 1947*, vol. 3, pp. 310–12. "I reminded him of our reluctance to act in a piecemeal way," Caffery reported; Pritchard, "Will Clayton," p. 339; William L. Clayton, telegrams to George Marshall, July 9 and 10, 1947, in *FRUS, 1947*, vol. 3, pp. 315–18.

20. "Minutes of Meeting on Marshall 'Plan,' 3:00 p.m.," August 22, 1947, *FRUS, 1947*, vol. 3, pp. 369–72.

21. William L. Clayton, "Memorandum on Conversations," August 20, 1947, Clayton Papers, Hoover Library; *New York Times*, August 22, 1947.

22. Clayton cable to George Marshall, August 31, 1947, *FRUS, 1947*, vol. 3, pp. 391–96.

23. Ibid.; George F. Kennan, "Report, Situation with Respect to European Recovery Program," September 4, 1947, in *FRUS, 1947*, vol. 3, pp. 397–403.

24. George Marshall, statement of September 10, 1947, cited in Pogue, *George Marshall*, pp. 231–32.

25. Mee, *Marshall Plan*, pp. 200–201.

26. Harold Wilson, House of Commons debate, October 29, 1947, later printed in a British White Paper, cmd. paper 7285.

27. Robert Pastor, *Congress and the Politics of U.S. Foreign Economic Policy, 1929–1976* (Berkeley: University of California Press, 1980), p. 98.

28. Ibid., p. 99; "U.N. Tariff, Trade Pact Too Thick for Bindery," *New York Times,* October 16, 1947.

29. Michael G. Hoffman, "Europe Will Feel Loss," sidebar to Felix Belair, Jr., "Clayton Resigns U.S. Economic Post," *New York Times*, October 15, 1947, p. 1.

Notes to Chapter 15

1. Winthrop Brown, cable of October 11, 1947, printed in *Foreign Relations of the United States 1947*, vol. 1 (Washington, D.C.: U.S. Government Printing Office, 1973), pp. 1010–11.

2. William L. Clayton, letter to Harry S. Truman, quoted in the *New York Times*, October 16, 1947; Eben Ayers diary, entry of October 13, 1947, on deposit at the Harry S. Truman Library (hereafter, HSTL).

3. Paul Nitze, interview with Ellen Clayton Garwood, on deposit at Columbia University Library, Oral History Project.

4. David Lilienthal, *The Journals of David E. Lilienthal*, vol. 2, *The Atomic Energy Years: 1945–1950* (New York: Harper and Row, 1964); Felix Belair, "Clayton Resigns U.S. Economic Post," *New York Times*, October 15, 1947, and Bertram D. Hulen, "Clayton Agrees to Stay on Call," *New York Times*, October 16, 1947; Winthrop Brown cable of October 16, 1947, the Papers of William L. Clayton, HSTL, Box 62, Folder 1; Michael G. Hoffman, "Europe Will Feel Loss," *New York Times*, October 15, 1947.

5. John Dalgleish, "Man behind Marshall," *Everybody's Weekly*, August 30, 1947; following articles cited in Michael Hoffman, "Number One Envoy to Europe," *New York Times* magazine, September 21, 1947; editorial, *Le Monde*, October 17, 1947; editorial, "Economic Ambassador," *New York Times*, October 16, 1947; and James Reston, "Prestige of State Department Seen Tested by ERP Set-Up," *New York Times*, January 29, 1948. "Clayton," Reston wrote, along with Lewis Douglas, ambassador to Britain, was at this point "still in line for the job as roving ambassador to the sixteen Marshall Plan countries, and if either of them is appointed, the problem of divided authority in the sixteen capitals and Berlin may be minimized." Dalgleish continues, "When the full story of the genesis of the Marshall Plan is told, it will become evident that the inspiration was Clayton's."

6. Harry S. Truman, quoted in the diary of Eben Ayers, entries for October 28, 1947, and June 1, 1949. The latter entry is quoted at greater length in chapter 1 of this book.

7. See, for example, Clayton's letter to William V. Griffin, November 1, 1947, on deposit with the Papers of William L. Clayton, HSTL. Clayton sent a virtually identical letter to about fifteen similarly close friends; Ellen Clayton Garwood, interview with the author, October 23, 1989; and Claire Wilcox, interview on deposit at Columbia University Library, Oral History Project.

8. Ellen Clayton Garwood, interview with the author, October 23, 1989; see also, "Suit for Divorce Is Filed against W. L. Clayton Here," *Houston Chronicle*, April 21, 1949; "Mrs. W. L. Clayton Granted Divorce by Judge Jackson," *Houston Chronicle*, May 24, 1949.

9. "Will L. Clayton Is Remarried to His Former Wife," *Houston Chronicle*, September 5, 1949.

10. "Will Clayton Defends Public Housing Plans," *Houston Chronicle*, June 11, 1950; "Others Will Seek Public Projects, Citizens Warned," *Houston Chronicle*, June 15, 1950.

11. "Clayton Buys Site for Low-Cost Housing," *Houston Chronicle*, 1950. There was no further date on the clip, but it can be obtained from the author's files or from the Houston Public Library.

12. "Rent Fund Agreement Is Denied," *Houston Chronicle*, August 13, 1952; "Clayton Called in Blum Trial," *Houston Chronicle*, January 5, 1953.

13. William L. Clayton, signed opinion column, "Benefits of Slum Clearance to Houston of Future Cited," *Houston Chronicle*, June 25, 1950.

14. Ellen Clayton Garwood, *Will Clayton: A Short Biography* (Austin: University of Texas, 1958), p. 185; "Park Development Asked by Schools," *Houston Chronicle*, 1959 (see note 11 on dating of some *Chronicle* articles); "Clayton Credited with Providing Kentucky Hospital," *Houston Chronicle*, December 29, 1950.

15. "Clayton Urges Better Control of Parenthood," *Houston Chronicle*, February 9, 1949; "Fletcher School to Get Clayton Chair of Finance," *Houston Chronicle*, May 16, 1950.

16. "Clayton Named to Negro School Board of Regents," *Houston Chronicle*, December 23, 1949; "Clayton Joins Fund Campaign For Jap University," *Houston Chronicle*, November 17, 1949; "Clayton Urges Support of Jap Christian School," *Houston Chronicle*, April 26, 1950; "Clayton Donates $11, 500 in Drive for Jap University," *Houston Chronicle*, May 28, 1950; on the donation and the beginning of the exchange with Cardinal Francis Spellman, see the correspondence on file with the Papers of William L. Clayton, HSTL, Box 89, Folder "Ca-Ch"; further letters are on file with the Clayton Papers, Hoover Institution Library, Stanford University; "William L. Clayton Named Director of Goethe Foundation," *Houston Chronicle*, March 4, 1949.

17. "W. L. Clayton Joins Adlai," *Houston Chronicle*, October 11, 1952.

18. William L. Clayton, "Atlantic Union—The Road to Peace," *International Yearbook* of the *Cotton Trade Journal* for 1955–1956.

19. William L. Clayton, "Removing Trade Barriers," *New York Times*, January 5, 1958.

20. Associated Press dispatch, "Clayton Says Stalin Is Winning Cold War," *Houston Chronicle*, January 24, 1950; "W. L. Clayton Fears Iran May Explode into War," *Houston Chronicle*, May 17, 1951; William L. Clayton, *Cotton Trade Journal*; William L. Clayton, "Removing Trade Barriers," *New York Times*, January 5, 1958.

21. "Russia Winning in 'Cold War,' Clayton Says," *Houston Chronicle*, April 27, 1950; "Pressure in Cold War to Increase, Clayton Declares," *Houston Chronicle*, December 17, 1949; "William L. Clayton, Urging Free World to United, Disagrees with Herbert Hoover," *Houston Chronicle*, December 25, 1950; "Will Clayton Wants to Abolish U.S., Odessa Man Charges," *Houston Chronicle*, March 9, 1951; "Reduce Poverty to Avoid Wars, Clayton Urges," *Houston Chronicle*, March 7, 1951.

22. William L. Clayton, letter to R. F. Moody, February 15, 1965; William L. Clayton, cited in the *New York Times*, January 8, 1957, on deposit with the Papers of William L. Clayton, Hoover Institution Library, Stanford University.

23. "Atlantic Union Committee to Seek Aim Formed," *Houston Chronicle*, March 15, 1945; "Clayton and Others Urge N.A.T.O. Aid," *Houston Chronicle*, November 24, 1949; for one of the most cogent and comprehensive arguments for Atlantic union, see William L. Clayton, "We Must Trade Sovereignty for Freedom," *New York Times* magazine, October 29, 1950; for the exchange of letters between Clayton, Acheson, and Truman on the subject, see their collected correspondence, 1948 to 1952, on deposit at HSTL, in the files for Clayton, Acheson, and Truman.

24. William L. Clayton, quoted in Arthur Krock column, *New York Times*, July 8, 1960.

25. Ibid.

26. William L. Clayton, interview with John T. Mason, Jr., August 21, 1961, Columbia University Library, Oral History Project, excerpted from pp. 198–201.

27. Ibid., p. 198; Maryrice Brogan, "Clayton Urges Forming Free World Market," *Houston Chronicle*, April 24, 1960.

28. William L. Clayton, quoted in "Clayton Says Policy on China 'Tragically Wrong,'" *Houston Post*, p. 1, September 14, 1958; William L. Clayton, letter to William Fulbright, dated February 29, 1959 (presumably February 28 or March 1); "Friendship Group Names Houstonian," *Houston Chronicle*, December 6, 1960; William L. Clayton, interview with John T. Mason, Jr., p. 202.

29. Committee on Foreign Affairs, Report Number Two, "Winning the Cold

War: The U.S. Ideological Offensive," 88th Congress, House Report number 1352, April 27, 1964, pp. 6–7.

30. Clayton, quoted in Brogan, "Clayton Urges Forming Free World Market"; Krock, cited above.

31. Krock column.

32. See John W. Evans, *The Kennedy Round in American Trade Policy* (Cambridge, Mass.: Harvard University Press, 1971), pp. 139–59; Theodore Sorenson, *Kennedy* (New York: Harper and Row, 1965), p. 460.

33. Evans, *Kennedy Round*, pp. 139–59.

34. William L. Clayton and Christian A. Herter, "A New Look at Foreign Economic Policy," report to the Joint Economic Committee, Subcommittee on Foreign Economic Policy, October 23, 1961, on deposit with the Papers of William L. Clayton, Hoover Institution Library. A large portion of the document, reprinted in the record of the JEC hearings, appeared in "Excerpts from Report Urging U.S. Link to Common Market," *New York Times*, November 2, 1961.

35. Clayton and Herter, "A New Look at Foreign Economic Policy," p. 1

36. Ibid., p. 2.

37. Ibid., pp. 2–4.

38. Ibid., pp. 6–7.

39. Ibid., p. 8.

40. Ibid., p. 8.

41. Evans, *Kennedy Round*; Ellen Clayton Garwood, interview with the author, October 23, 1989; former Congressmen Thomas Curtis and Wilbur Mills, interviews with the author, February 10, 1990; "Freer U.S. Policy on Trade Asked by Kennedy Aide," twin stories by Richard E. Mooney and Brendan M. Jones, *New York Times*, November 2, 1961, and accompanying excerpts, cited above; Felix Belair, Jr., "Acheson Warns of Soviet Gains if U.S. Rejects Common Market," *New York Times*, December 6, 1961; John F. Kennedy, speeches cited, reprinted in Allan Nevins, ed., *The Burden and the Glory* (New York: Harper and Row, 1964), pp. 18–19, 103–8. For brief but insightful summaries of the Trade Expansion Act and the Kennedy GATT Round, see also Robert Pastor, *Congress and the Politics of U.S. Foreign Economic Policy, 1929–1976* (Berkeley: University of California Press, 1980), pp. 105–23; Ernest H. Preeg, *Traders and Diplomats* (Washington, D.C.: Brookings Institution, 1973), pp. 44–56.

42. Herter-Clayton report, p. 5; Evans, *Kennedy Round*; Pastor, *Congress and Politics*; Curtis interview, February 10, 1990.

43. Curtis interview, February 10, 1990; John F. Kennedy, letter to William L. Clayton, January 25, 1962, copy provided to the author by the Houston Public Library; Pastor, *Congress and Politics*, p. 190.

44. Pastor, *Congress and Politics*, pp. 117–19.

45. See William L. Clayton, "Is the Marshall Plan Operation Rathole?" *Saturday Evening Post*, November 29, 1947.

46. William L. Clayton, letter to Dean Acheson of October 6, 1957, on deposit with the Dean Gooderham Acheson papers, Yale University, Sterling Memorial Library, Manuscripts and Archives, Manuscript Group Number 1087, Series I, Box 6, Folder 77; see also Ellen Clayton Garwood, interview with the author, October 23, 1989.

Note to Chapter 16

1. Harry S. Truman, letter to Ellen Clayton Garwood, February 15, 1966, from the back jacket of Ellen Garwood, *Will Clayton: A Short Biography* (Austin: University of Texas Press, 1958).

Bibliography

Acheson, Dean. *Present at the Creation*. New York: W. W. Norton, 1969.

———. Seminar at Princeton University, July 2, 1953. Papers of Dean Acheson, Box 74, Harry S. Truman Library.

———. Papers. Yale University, Sterling Memorial Library, Manuscripts and Archives.

Arkes, Hadley. *Bureaucracy, the Marshall Plan, and the National Interest*. Princeton, N.J.: Princeton University Press, 1972.

Ayers, Eban A. Diary. Harry S. Truman Library.

Baruch, Bernard. *Baruch: The Public Years*. New York: Holt, Rinehart and Winston, 1960.

Blum, John Morton. *Roosevelt and Morgenthau*. Boston: Houghton Mifflin, 1970.

Bohlen, Charles. *Witness to History*. New York: W. W. Norton, 1973.

Bradley, Omar. *A General's Life*. New York: Simon and Schuster, 1983.

Brown, Winthrop. Interview. Columbia University Library, Oral History Project.

Bullock, Alan. *Ernest Bevin: Foreign Secretary, 1945–1951*. New York: W. W. Norton, 1983.

Burns, James MacGregor. *Roosevelt: The Lion and the Fox*. New York: Harcourt, Brace, 1956.

Byrnes, James. *All in One Lifetime*. New York: Harper and Brothers, 1958.

———. *Speaking Frankly*. New York: Harper and Brothers, 1947.

Cash, Wilbur J. *The Mind of the South*. New York: Doubleday, 1954.

Churchill, Winston. *The Second World War*, vol. 2, *Their Finest Hour*. Boston: Houghton Mifflin, 1949.

Clark M. Clifford. Papers. Harry S. Truman Library.

Clayton, Benjamin. *Some Notes on Cotton Operations 1905–1929*. 1973.

Clayton, William L. "Atlantic Union—The Road to Peace." *International Yearbook of the Cotton Trade Journal* for 1955–1956.

———. "GATT, The Marshall Plan and OECD." *Political Science Quarterly* 78 (December 4, 1963):493–503.

———. Interviews. Columbia University Library, Oral History Project.

———. "Is the Marshall Plan Operation Rathole?" *Saturday Evening Post*. November 29, 1947.

———. "Manipulation of the Cotton Futures Market." Address to the American Cotton Shippers Association. Atlanta, Georgia, April 1926. Hoover Institution Library, Stanford University.

———. "Removing Trade Barriers." *New York Times*. January 5, 1958.

———. Speech to the Business and Professional Women's Club of Houston. May 26, 1937. News story, "Budget Must Be Balanced, Says Clayton." *Houston Chronicle*. May 27, 1937.

———. Speech to the Economic Club of Detroit. May 21, 1945. Reprinted in *Department of State Bulletin*. May 27, 1945.

———. Speech at Harvard University, Cambridge, Massachusetts. September 16, 1936. "A Business-Man Looks at Capitalism." Clayton correspondence, Hoover Institution Library, Stanford University.

———. Speech to the U.S. Chamber of Commerce. "Tariff Rates Are Hit by Houstonian." *Houston Chronicle*. May 6, 1938.

———. "The World Cotton Situation." Address to the Cotton Research Congress, Waco, Texas, June 27, 1940. Published in ACCO Press, July 1940.

Collado, Emilio. Inteview. Columbia University Library, Oral History Project.

Committee on Foreign Affairs, Report Number Two. "Winning the Cold War: The U.S. Ideological Offensive." 88th Congress, House report number 1352. April 27, 1964.

Department of State Bulletin. Vol. 6, 1942.

Dobney, Frederick J. *Selected Papers of Will Clayton*. Baltimore, Md.: Johns Hopkins University Press, 1971.

Donovan, Robert J. *Conflict and Crisis: The Presidency of Harry S. Truman, 1945–1948*. New York: W. W. Norton, 1977.

Doxey, Margaret. *Economic Sanctions and International Enforcement*. London: Oxford University Press, 1971.

Drury, Allen. *A Senate Journal: 1943–1945*. New York: McGraw-Hill, 1963.

Eisenhower, Dwight. *Economic Report of the President*. Washington, D.C.: Superindenent of Documents, January 1955.

Elsey, George M. Papers. Harry S. Truman Library.

Evans, John W. *The Kennedy Round in American Trade Policy.* Cambridge, Mass.: Harvard University Press, 1971.

Federal Trade Commission. *Report on the Cotton Trade.* Submitted to the U.S. Senate, Washington, D.C., 1924.

Ferrell, Robert H., ed. *The American Seretaries of State and Their Diplomacy.* New York: Cooper Square, 1966.

Foreign Relations of the United States, 1946. Vol. 7. Washington, D.C.: U.S. Government Printing Office, 1969.

Gardner, Richard N. *Sterling-Dollar Diplomacy.* New York: McGraw-Hill, 1969.

Garwood, Ellen Clayton. *Will Clayton: A Short Biography.* Austin: University of Texas Press, 1958; Lake Bluff, Ill.: Regnery-Gateway, 1985.

Garwood, Will, Jr. *Will Clayton: Economic Statesman.* Princeton thesis 1979. Published with a foreword by John Chamberlain by the American Studies Center, 1981.

Gimbel, John. *The Origins of the Marshall Plan.* Stanford: Stanford University Press, 1976.

Harrod, Roy F. *The Life of John Maynard Keynes.* New York: Harcourt, Brace, 1951.

Hawkins, Harry. Interview, April 18, 1959. Columbia University Library, Oral History Project.

Heilbroner, Robert. *The Worldly Philosophers.* New York: Simon and Schuster, 1972.

Henderson, Loy. Interviews with Richard D. McKinzie. Harry S. Truman Library.

Hufbauer, Gary Clyde, et al. *Economic Sanctions Reconsidered.* Washington, D.C.: Institute for International Economics, 1985.

Hull, Cordell. *Congressional Digest.* July 1929.

Ike, Nobutaka, ed. *Japan's Decision for War: Records of the 1941 Policy Conferences.* Stanford: Stanford University Press, 1967.

Johnson, Donald Bruce, and Porter, Kirk H., eds. *National Party Platforms, 1840–1972.* Chicago: University of Illinois Press, 1973.

Johnson, Paul. *Modern Times.* New York: Harper and Row, 1983.

Jones, Joseph. Papers. Harry S. Truman Library.

Jones, Joseph M. *The Fifteen Weeks.* New York: Viking, 1955.

Kennan, George F. *Memoirs: 1925–1950.* Boston: Atlantic Monthly Press, 1967.

Kennedy, John F. *Profiles in Courage.* New York: Harper and Row, 1956.

———. In Allan Nevins, ed. *The Burden and the Glory.* New York: Harper and Row, 1964.

Keynes, John Maynard. *The Means to Prosperity.* London: Macmillan, 1933.

Lilienthal, David. *The Journals of David E. Lilienthal.* 2 vols. New York: Harper and Row, 1964.

Lyon, Peter. *Eisenhower: Portrait of the Hero*. New York: Little, Brown, 1974.

McCloy, John J. *Introduction to the Testament of Will Clayton*. April 29, 1968. Published by the Declaration of Atlantic Unity, February 28, 1968.

McGhee, George. Interview with Richard D. McKinzie. June 11, 1975. Harry S. Truman Library, Oral History Interview.

Marshall, Charles Burton. "Creating the Marshall Plan Was a Complex Process." June 22, 1987. An article for which USIA has full publication rights.

Medlicott, W. N. *The Economic Blockade*. London: Longmans, Green, 1952.

Mee, Charles L. *The Marshall Plan*. New York: Simon and Schuster, 1984.

Merchant, Livingston. Interview, October 28, 1958. Columbia University Library, Oral History Project.

Millis, Walter, ed. *The Forrestal Diaries*. New York: Viking, 1951.

Ness, Norman. Interview, November 7, 1958. Columbia University Library, Oral History Project.

Nitze, Paul H. *From Hiroshima to Glasnost*. New York: Weidenfeld and Nicholson, 1989.

———. Interviews. Columbia University Library, Oral History Project.

Pastor, Robert. *Congress and the Politics of U.S. Foreign Economic Policy, 1929–1976*. Berkeley: University of California Press, 1980.

Phillips, Cabell. *The Truman Presidency*. New York: Macmillan, 1966.

Pirsein, William. "The Voice of America: A History of the International Broadcasting Activities of the United States Government, 1940–1962." Ph.D. dissertation, Northwestern University, June 1970.

Pogue, Forrest C. *George Marshall: Statesman*. New York: Viking, 1987.

Preeg, Ernest H. *Traders and Diplomats*. Washington, D.C.: Brookings Institution, 1973.

Price, Harry B. Interview with Denny Marris. Harry S. Truman Library.

Pritchard, Ross J. "Will Clayton: A Study of Business-Statesmanship in the Formulation of United States Economic Foreign Policy." Ph.D. dissertation, Fletcher School of Law and Diplomacy, 1955.

Reese, David. *Harry Dexter White: A Study in Paradox*. New York: Coward, McCann, & Geoghegan, 1973.

Rogow, Arnold A. *James Forrestal: A Study of Personality, Politics, and Policy*. New York: Macmillan, 1963.

Rostow, Eugene. Symposium, "Beyond Containment?" *Policy Review*. Winter 1985.

Schlesinger, Arthur M. *The Coming of the New Deal*. Boston: Houghton Mifflin, 1959.

———. *The Crisis of the Old Order*. Boston: Houghton Mifflin, 1957.

———. *The Politics of Upheaval*. Boston: Houghton Mifflin, 1960.

Snyder, John W. Oral History Interview, November 1982. Harry S. Truman Library.

Sorenson, Theodore. *Kennedy.* New York: Harper and Row, 1965.

Stillwell, Henry. Interview, September 9, 1958. Columbia University Library, Oral History Project.

Stinebower, Leory. Interview, November 6, 1958. Columbia University Library, Oral History Project.

Stoler, Mark A. *George C. Marshall: Soldier-Statesman of the American Century.* Boston: Twayne, 1989.

Timmons, Bascom N. *Jesse H. Jones.* New York: Henry Holt, 1956.

Truman, Harry S. Papers. Harry S. Truman Library.

———. *Memoirs. Years of Trial and Hope.* New York: Doubleday, 1955.

———. *Year of Decisions.* New York: Doubleday, 1955.

Tsaldaris, Constantine. Interview with Philip C. Brooks, May 4, 1964. Harry S. Truman Library.

U.K. Treasury. "Proposals for an International Clearing Union." London: 1943

U.S. House of Representatives. *Bretton Woods Agreements Act.* Hearings before the Committee on Banking and Currency on H.R. 2211, 79th Congress, First Session, vol. 1. Washington, D.C.: Government Printing Office, 1945.

U.S. Office of Inter-American Affairs. "History of the Office of the Coordinator of Inter-American Affairs." Washington, D.C.: Superintendent of Documents, 1947.

U.S. Senate. "Cotton Prices." Hearings before a Senate Committee on Agriculture and Forestry Subcommittee. Washington, D.C., 1929.

U.S. Senate. *Bretton Woods Agreements Act.* Committee on Banking and Currency, Hearings on H.R. 3314, 79th Congress, First Session, Washington, D.C.: Government Printing Office, 1945.

U.S. Treasury Department. *Questions and Answers on the Fund and Bank.* Washington, D.C., 1945.

Wallace, Henry A. In Blum, John Morton, ed. *The Price of Vision: The Diary of Henry A. Wallace, 1942–1946.* Boston: Houghton Mifflin, 1973.

Walton, Richard. *Henry Wallace, Harry Truman, and the Cold War.* New York: Viking, 1976.

Wanniski, Jude. *The Way the World Works.* New York: Simon and Schuster, 1978; revised editions, 1983 and 1988.

Welles, Sumner. *Seven Decisions That Shaped History.* New York: Harper, 1951.

White, Harry Dexter. Papers. Box 6, File 15-B, Harvey Mudd Library, Princeton University.

White, Ivan. Interview, October 31, 1958. On deposit at Columbia University Library, Oral History Project.

Wilcox, Claire. Interview. On deposit at Columbia University Library, Oral History Project.

Index

About the Author

Gregory A. Fossedal is a research fellow at the Hoover Institution and author of the widely praised book *The Democratic Imperative*. He is a former editorial writer for the *Wall Street Journal* and has also written for the *New York Times*, the *New Republic*, *Commentary*, *Reader's Digest*, and the *American Spectator*.